T0187914

The Routledge Dictionary of Nonverbal Communication

Every day, the human awakes to a new world, a new dawn and a new cascade of nonverbal communication. It may be the pleasant scent of a rose, the soft touch of a loved one, the sight of sun rays on a bedroom floor or the excited chatter of a child. Whatever form it takes, your environment and all who inhabit it send nonverbal signals all day long – even while they sleep.

The Routledge Dictionary of Nonverbal Communication celebrates this communication, examining a very wide selection of nonverbal behaviors, actions and signals to provide the reader with an informed insight on the world around them and its messages. Compiled in the form of a dictionary, the book is presented as a series of chapters with alphabetical entries, ranging from attractiveness to zeitgeist. The book aims to provide the reader with a clear understanding of some of the relevant discourse on particular topics while also making it practical and easy to read. It draws on a wide selection of discourse from fields such as neuroscience, psychology, anthropology and psychiatry.

The dictionary will be an essential companion for anyone wishing to understand nonverbal communication. It will also be especially useful for those working in the field of nonverbal communication.

David B. Givens teaches in the School of Professional Studies at Gonzaga University, USA, and is the Director of the Center for Nonverbal Studies. He began studying "body language" for his Ph.D. in anthropology at the University of Washington in Seattle, USA. He served as Anthropologist in Residence at the American Anthropological Association in Washington, D.C., from 1985–97 and has previously taught anthropology at the University of Washington. His expertise is in nonverbal communication, anthropology and the brain.

John White is Assistant Professor of Education in Dublin City University, Ireland. He has worked as a primary teacher, primary-school principal and primary-school inspector. His doctoral research examined nonverbal communication within the context of education. His research interests include human communication (with a specific focus on nonverbal communication), classroom communication, arts-based research, mathematics education, narrative inquiry, embodied cognition and primary-school leadership. He is the co-author of The Classroom X-Factor: The Power of Body Language and Nonverbal Communication in Teaching.

The Routledge Dictionary of Nonverbal Communication

Prof. David B. Givens and
Dr. John White

Routledge
Taylor & Francis Group

LONDON AND NEW YORK

First published 2021
by Routledge
2 Park Square, Milton Park, Abingdon, Oxon OX14 4RN

and by Routledge
605 Third Avenue, New York, NY 10158

Routledge is an imprint of the Taylor & Francis Group, an informa business

© 2021 David Givens and John White

British Library Cataloguing-in-Publication Data
A catalogue record for this book is available from the British Library

Library of Congress Cataloging-in-Publication Data
Names: Givens, David B., author. | White, John, 1968– author.
Title: The Routledge dictionary of nonverbal communication / Prof David
   Givens and Dr John White.
Description: Abingdon, Oxon ; New York : Routledge, 2021. | Includes
   bibliographical references and index.
Identifiers: LCCN 2020053537 (print) | LCCN 2020053538 (ebook) |
   ISBN 9780367265304 (paperback) | ISBN 9780367265298 (hardback) |
   ISBN 9780429293665 (ebook)
Subjects: LCSH: Nonverbal communication—Dictionaries.
Classification: LCC P99.5 .G58 2021 (print) | LCC P99.5 (ebook) |
   DDC 302.2/2203—dc23
LC record available at https://lccn.loc.gov/2020053537
LC ebook record available at https://lccn.loc.gov/2020053538

ISBN: 978-0-367-26529-8 (hbk)
ISBN: 978-0-367-26530-4 (pbk)
ISBN: 978-0-429-29366-5 (ebk)

Typeset in Bembo
by Apex CoVantage, LLC

Contents

Abbreviations and key

3D	Three dimensional
A.D.	Anno Domini
B.C.	Before Christ
Bold	Bolded words and phrases serve as textual cross-references
BP	Before present
bya	billion years ago
ca.	circa (about)
cap.	capital
cf.	compare
CO.	county
DNA	Deoxyribonucleic Acid
e.g.	exemplii gratia (for example)
esp.	especially
et al.	et alii (and others)
FACS	Facial Action Coding System
FAQ	frequently asked question(s)
FBI	U.S. Federal Bureau of Investigation
fMRI	functional magnetic resonance imaging
I.D.	identity
i.e.	id est (that is)
lbs	pounds
mph	miles per hour
mya	million years ago
NA	Nucleus Ambiguus
N.B.	nota bene (note well, notice)
NBA	National Basketball Association
n.d.	no date
neuro-notes	neurological notes added to dictionary entries
PC	personal computer
RNA	Ribonucleic Acid
®	registered trademark
ret.	retired
rpm	revolutions per minute
U.K.	United Kingdom
U.S.	United States
viz.	videlicet (that is, namely)
vs.	versus

Acknowledgements

David and John:

We wish to sincerely thank the team at Routledge for their unerring interest, support and professionalism during the various stages of creating this book. We would also like to acknowledge Alan Crawley (Universidad del Salvador) for the many insightful suggestions and ideas he offered, as we wrote our way through the various entries – gracias! We are also deeply indebted to our illustrator, Shane McCann (initialled SM throughout the book) for his very artistic and skilful work in producing pictures which 'speak a thousand words'!

David:

I lovingly dedicate our nonverbal Routledge Dictionary to my sisters, Chris (Givens) Shea and Susie (Givens) Wong. In childhood, we read each other like open books – and this book could not have been written without them.

John:

I would like to dedicate this book to my parents, Jack and Nellie and also my darling wife, Sineád. Mum and Dad gave so much care and love, typically speaking through actions not words. Since the first time I met her, until this minute, I do believe that Sineád has the most magical smile I've ever seen. Thanks for all your support and pleasantness Ms Magic!

A

Accent

Voice quality

Nonverbally, accent is a voice quality and form of paralanguage (see *Tone of voice*). It is a manner of pronunciation that pertains to a particular group of speakers.

Usage

Accent can be used to infer personal attributes, such as a person's national origin, regional roots and social status. Communication accommodation theory argues that humans bring their accent into either a convergent or divergent manner with the person to whom they are speaking. Convergence occurs when the accommodated accent is similar to the speaker's accent, and divergence occurs when the accommodated accent is different. In contexts where the speaker's accent is similar to the listener's, the listener is more likely to view the speaker as similar, friendly and a member of their co-culture (see *Isopraxism*).

Actions

Darwinian third principle

The idea, proposed by Charles Darwin (1872), that the nervous system can produce reflexive body movements, such as coughing, sneezing and trembling, which are neither habitual (as in Darwin's principle of associated habits) nor antithetical (as in his principle of antithesis).

Usage

Darwin used his third principle to account for the meaning of nonverbal signs, such as, sweating (see *Sweaty palms*) and trembling in fear (see *Fear*). Additionally, these behaviors are difficult to fake and inhibit (as in crying or blushing)

See also *Associated habits, Antithesis*.

Action units

Muscle contractions

In the Facial Action Coding System (see *FACS*), action units (AUs) are specific muscular contractions involved in a given movement or expression of the face or body.

Usage I

Action units are serially numbered, beginning with "0" (for "neutral face"; see *Blank face*) and continuing upward, for example, to "4" ("Brow lower"; see

Brow-lower), "19" ("Tongue show"; see *Tongue-show*), "26" ("Jaw drop"; see *Jaw-droop*) and so on.

Usage II

Expressed in AUs, the emotion of anger, for example, is $4+5+7+23$, disgust is $9+15+16$ and happiness $6+12$. To cope with the complexity of FACS and AUs – and with the incredible mobility of faces themselves – researchers may use computers to work with the FACS's alphanumeric scheme.

See also *Artificial intelligence*.

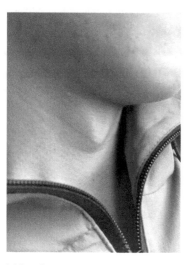

Adam's-apple jump

Body movement

A conspicuous up-and-down motion of the Adam's apple. A movement of the throat visible while gulping or swallowing, as in nervousness.

Usage

The Adam's-apple jump is an unconscious sign of emotional anxiety, embarrassment or stress. At a business meeting, a listener's Adam's apple may inadvertently "jump" should he or she dislike or strongly disagree with a speaker's suggestions, perspective or point of view. Unconscious and uncontrollable, the movement gives a look into the sympathetic – fight-or-flight – division of the autonomic nervous system.

Neuro-notes

Acting through the vagus nerve (cranial X), emotional tension from the brain's limbic system causes unconscious muscular contractions of the sternothyroid, thyrohyoid and associated inferior pharyngeal constrictor muscles of the Adam's apple. Movement is evident as the muscles contract to swallow, to throat-clear or to vocalize an unspoken objection. The Adam's apple is emotionally responsive and reflects visceral or "gut" feelings because its muscles are mediated by the vagus nerve, one of five cranial special visceral nerves.

Affect

Emotion

In nonverbal studies, emotion is often referred to as "affect." The English word, affect, is "a feeling or emotion as distinguished from cognition, thought, or action" (Soukhanov, 1992, 29). Across all cultures, there are a very limited number of common facial displays of affect. For example, research has found that across literate and non-literate cultures around the globe, people can translate the six facial expressions of emotion (Ekman et al., 1969; Ekman, 2003). These emotions are: anger, disgust, fear, happiness, sadness and surprise.

Typically, expressions of affection are characterized within verbal and nonverbal domains. Within nonverbal parameters, examples include holding hands, patting (e.g., a pat on the back), kissing, hugging, cuddling, smiling and sitting on another's lap. Verbal statements could include expressions of love, praise and friendship (see also Twardosz et al., 1987). Floyd (2006b) proposes a third category which argues that "within particular relationships, individuals may express affection through the provision of social and instrumental support, such as doing favors for each other, helping with projects, or loaning the use of resources" (Floyd, 2006b, 29).

Nonverbal affectionate behaviors which are aimed at forming and maintaining relationships can have specific physiological benefits. Such behaviors can include hugging, kissing, caressing and holding hands. It is argued that such nonverbal behaviors raise levels of the hormone oxytocin, which is associated with stress alleviation. In particular, it lowers blood pressure and heart rate, suppresses pain and promotes a feeling of calmness (Altemus et al., 1995). One of the most common nonverbal expressions of affection is kissing. There is significant research to contend that kissing can strengthen the immune system and can also have stress-alleviating effects (Burgoon et al., 2010b).

Neuro-notes

From an evolutionary brain perspective, affect and emotions are based on generic vertebrate arousal patterns (see *Emotion*). Some researchers argue that many non-verbal affectionate behaviors have evolved from the protective behaviors of mothers (Floyd, 2006b).

See also *Emotion, Love*.

Affect blend

A blending of two or more emotions (see *Emotion*), feelings or moods visible in simultaneous facial expressions, body movements or postures. Ekman (1977) used affect blend as a label for two simultaneous facial signs expressive of primary emotion. Researchers today may restrict affect blends only to facial expressions.

Affective blindness

In cases where the amygdala is severed from the rest of the brain, the resultant effect on the human is a pronounced inability to gauge the emotional significance of events. This condition is sometimes termed "affective blindness" (Goleman, 1996, 15).

Affective Communication Test (ACT)

Test design

This test contained a range of self-reporting items designed to measure nonverbal expressiveness. In validating the test, the authors H. Friedman, L. Prince, R. Riggio and M. DiMatteo found the test was a "likely element of social influence in face-to-face interaction" (Friedman et al., 1980, 333).

Afferent cue

Neuro term

A nonverbal sign received, as opposed to one sent. An incoming sign received by receptors in the eyes, ears, nose, mouth, skin, hair follicles, muscles, tendons, joints, vestibular apparatus or viscera, relayed to centers in the spinal cord and brain for processing. Bones and teeth conduct incoming signs of vibration and temperature; otolith organs and semicircular canals process signs of motion, balance and gravitation. Additionally, pleasure areas of the brain may respond to afferent cues of sex, drugs and rock-and-roll.

Usage

As concepts, afferent and efferent reflect the two sides of every nonverbal cue: (1) ingress (as an in-bound sign to be processed) and (2) egress (as an out-bound sign to be produced).

Affiliative cue

Friendly cue

An emotionally positive nonverbal sign.

Usage

Affiliative cues – such as palm-up gestures and the smile – suggest that one is willing to interact and form a social bond (see *Palm-up, Zygomatic smile*).

Antonym: see *Aversive cue*.

Agnosia

Neuro term

The inability to recognize a coin, key or other object merely by its feel when held in the hand. The inability to recognize a door by the sound of its slamming or from a photograph of it alone. In agnosia, while perception itself, such as feeling a coin's shape or hearing a door slam, is normal, recognition of objects themselves is not.

Neuro-notes

Inability to recognize a coin by the sound of its dropping suggests problems with auditory association areas of the temporal lobe. Inability to recognize a coin held in the hand suggests problems with tactile association areas of the parietal lobe. Inability to recognize a coin by its photograph suggests problems with visual association areas of the occipital lobe. These nonverbal brain modules exist independently of the cortical modules used to recognize and produce speech sounds.

See also *Apraxia*.

Akinesia

Difficulty *beginning* or *maintaining* a body motion.

Symptoms include (1) slowed voluntary movements; (2) difficulty reaching for objects; (3) inability to perform repetitive, simultaneous or sequential body movements; (4) immobile, expressionless or masked face; (5) loss of normal "restless" body movements while sitting; (6) loss of arm swinging while walking; (7) shuffling gait and (8) diminished finger dexterity.

Usage

Akinesia points to a variety of neurological problems (including Parkinson's disease and brain damage associated with strokes). Akinesic behaviors affect an individual's normal nonverbal response and may be, especially in older people, misconstrued as signs expressive of emotions, feelings and moods.

See also *Apraxia*.

Alexithymia

Alexithymia is the inability of individuals to describe their emotions in words. Some recent studies indicate that among children, it can predict poor spontaneous emotional facial expressions (Trevisan et al., 2016). Alexithymia can present as mild, moderate and severe. Ongoing research on the condition links it to autistic spectrum disorder.

See also *Autism*.

Alley

Unscenic route

A usually narrow, undecorated, sometimes uncared-for urban passageway between buildings or homes, often associated with darkness, garbage and crime.

Usage

While the front of a structure may be tastefully decorated for display, regularly maintained and sited on a paved, tree-lined avenue, its back side often opens to an unpaved alleyway designed for trash storage and parking off the street. As "out of sight, out of mind" spaces, alleys may become venues for criminal activities, drug dealing, gambling, prostitution and theft.

Darkness

Recognizing the dangers darkness portends, many of the world's cities have launched efforts to illuminate alley spaces with electric lights. In the U.S., the Chicago Smart Lighting Project is a case in point. As diurnal primates, humans have difficulty coping with nocturnal conditions and may find darkness fearful (see *Fear*).

Garbage

With its collection of dumpsters, rolling containers and trash cans, an alleyway may be sensed as an unhealthy, unsanitary and otherwise unsavory place of pollution. Anthropologists have recognized pollution and purity as universal conceptual opposites. The former may confuse, emotionally upset and disturb wellbeing and interfere with rational thought.

Amphibian brain

Evolution

Many of our most basic nonverbal behaviors are rooted in the amphibian brain. Collectively, it includes those older parts of the human brain that developed during the amphibian transition from water to land in the Devonian period of the Paleozoic Era. Specifically included are those modules of the amphibian midbrain and forebrain that evolved to further life above the waterlines of ancient seas. Amphibian-inspired paleocircuits for hearing and seeing in a higher, drier world, and for postural stance in terra firma's gravitational pull, continue to be operative in the human brain today.

Usage

Several common human gestures and body postures, for example, those derived from the auditory startle and the high-stand display, originated ca. 380 bya in modules of the amphibian brain. The latter itself evolved from modules and paleocircuits of the aquatic brain. Today these play key roles in the expression of dominance and submission.

Neuro-notes I: midbrain

As amphibian ancestors emerged from primeval lakes and seas to live part of their lives on land, seeing and hearing sharpened. Two paired centers of the amphibian midbrain – the inferior and superior colliculi – evolved as processing centers for audio-visual cues. The former's hearing centers (the auditory lobes) unconsciously prompt us to crouch from loud noises. The latter's vision centers (the optic lobes) reflexively focus our attention on body motions, gestures and objects that move.

Neuro-notes II: forebrain

Unlike water's buoyancy, land presents an incredibly heavy environment in which antigravity signs (e.g., the reptilian press-up to a high stand) evolved. The forebrain module in charge of the earliest aggressive "push up" was a motor area presently called the striatal complex (see *Basal ganglia*).

See also *Reptilian brain*.

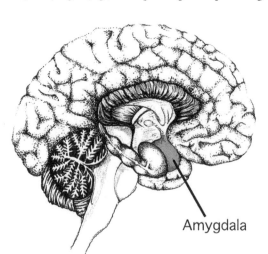

Amygdala

Amygdala

Nonverbal brain

An almond-shaped neuro structure involved in producing and responding to nonverbal signs of anger, avoidance, defensiveness, fear and sexuality. A small mass of grey matter that inspires and mobilizes the fight-or-flight response. Such responses may include aversive cues, such as the freeze reaction, sweaty palms and the tense-mouth display. A primeval arousal centre, originating in early fishes and central to the expression of often negative human emotion today.

Usage

Many nonverbal gestures reflect the amygdala's turmoil. During an anxious business meeting, for example, we may unconsciously flex our arms and lean or angle away from colleagues who upset us. Lip, neck and shoulder muscles may tense as the amygdala activates brain-stem circuits designed to produce protective facial expressions, such as the tense-mouth, and postures such as the human bow and mammalian crouch. The amygdala prompts releases of adrenaline and other hormones into the bloodstream, thus stepping up an avoider's response and disrupting the control of rational thought.

Neuro-notes

In addition to its other duties, the amygdala's grey matter evolved to mediate the evolutionary ancient chemical nervous system, represented today by the bloodstream. Working through the brain's hypothalamus, the amygdala releases excitatory hormones into circulating blood. After surgical removal of the amygdala, growls, screams, angry voices and other negative signs may lose their meaning and become incomprehensible as afferent cues.

See also *Cingulate gyrus*.

Anatomical position

Nonverbal standard

An arbitrary position of the body used to define movements as deviations from the standard it defines. An unusual posture, suggestive of humility or supplication, in which the body stands upright with arms extended by its sides, palms rotated forward and feet resting flat upon the floor.

Usage

Myriad joints in human hands, arms, feet, legs, shoulders, pelvis and spine make the possible number of body movements and gestures incalculably immense. Thus, in recording an observation, anatomical position is useful as a schematic, standardized device for description. Movements away from its standard may carry information as signs.

Media

Few of us ever use or see this unnatural posture. However, in the classic 1951 film 'An American in Paris', Gene Kelly waited in anatomical position below a fountain for dance partner, Leslie Caron, to return to his side. With hands in the supinated, palm-up position, Kelly's humble, beseechingly "open" posture invited approach.

See also *Baseline demeanor, Trunk*.

Anger

Emotion

A sudden, usually unpleasant feeling of annoyance, resentment or rage.

Usage

Nonverbally, anger shows in (1) jaws tensed to a biting position; (2) postures of the broadside display (e.g., hands-on-hips); (3) cut-off and head-jerk cues; (4) fist, hand-behind-head and palm-down beating gestures; (5) frowning and tense-mouth expressions; (6) growling voice tones and (7) staring. Anger is responsive to and reflects visceral or "gut" feelings because its muscles are mediated by the vagus nerve, one of five cranial special visceral nerves (see *Special visceral nerve*).

Anatomy

In the human face, motion energy maps reveal that anger shows most prominently in contortions around the eyebrows for frowning. Corrugator supercilii muscles, blended with occipitofrontalis and orbicularis oculi, draw eyebrows down, as if to shield the eyes, producing vertical furrows above the nose. At the same time procerus, blended with occipitofrontalis, produces horizontal wrinkles over the nasal bridge. Anger shows in contracted obicularis oris and masseter muscles of the tense-mouth, as well.

Research reports

Signs of anger include body held erect; contracted brows; compressed mouth, flared nostrils and "flashing eyes" (Darwin, 1872, 242–243). Anger shows most clearly in the lower face and brow area (Ekman et al., 1971). Facial expressions of anger emerge in human infants between 3 and 4 months of age (Burgoon et al., 1989).

See also *Emotion cue*.

Angular distance

Posture

The spatial orientation, measured in radial degrees, of an individual's shoulders relative to those of another. The position of a speaker's upper body in relation

to that of a listener (e.g., facing or angled away). The degree of body alignment between a speaker and listener, as measured in the coronal plane, which divides the body into front and back.

Usage

Angular distance reveals how we relate to and feel about people sitting, standing or waiting nearby. Our upper body unwittingly squares up, addresses and "aims" at those we like, admire and agree with but angles away from disliked persons and people with whom we may disagree. In a friendly conversation, formal interview or staff meeting, a greater angular distance (turning away) substitutes for greater linear distance. Angular distance may range from 0 degrees (directly facing) to 180 degrees (turning one's back).

See also *Body wall, Cut-off.*

Animal sign

Primatology

Many primatologists have experienced a profound change in their attitude towards anthropoid apes after making eye-contact with one for the first time. The spark across the species barrier is never forgotten (De Waal and Lanting, 1997, 1).

Signal

A message emitted by the nonverbal behavior, cries, markings, body movements or shapes of a multicellular organism of the kingdom Animalia.

Usage

Animals provide an endless nonverbal source of inspiration for artists, philosophers, photographers and cinematographers. They are a major source of companionship, entertainment, symbolism and food for human beings.

Anthropology I

There is a curious ambivalence between *Homo sapiens* and all other species. On the one hand, we find compelling similarities between ourselves and beasts. Yet on the other, a cultural universal of human thought is the postulate that people and animals are fundamentally un-alike. Between the human and the animal lies an immense chasm.

Anthropology II

The earliest animal art, naturalistic renderings of deer, horses and bulls, appear in the archaeological record by ca. 30,000 years ago in western Europe. The Upper Paleolithic cave paintings of Cro Magnon reveal that hunter-gatherers incorporated animals in thought processes and rituals at least 30 millennia ago.

Dogs. A dog's lateral tail-wag (through contractions of the sacrococcygeus ventralis muscle) is mediated by limbic-system fiber links to the pelvic floor (Holstege, 2016). Street photography: "Prévert at a Cafe Table," taken by Robert Doisneau, shows the companionship of French poet Jacques Prévert and his pet canine at a cafe in France in 1955. Prévert's lone drinking glass resonates with a solitary, upright human figure in the distance. Without his dog, the photo would feel quite sad and lonely. With the dog's close proxemic physical presence, however, the classic photograph is both animated and humanized.

Gorillas. Human beings are fascinated by "humanlike" gestures and mannerisms of the African gorilla. Some gorilla watchers sit for hours patiently watching lowland gorillas at the National Zoo in Washington, D.C. As one gorilla groupie remarked, watching them "is the happiest thing I've done with my spare time" (Mundy, 1992). The peak experience of a gorilla watcher is sharing direct eye contact with the apes.

Space

A world without animal signs would be a lonely world, indeed. Nearing completion of her 5-month mission in orbit from March to August 2001, international-space-station resident Susan Helms said she "misses animals almost more than anything" (Anonymous, 2001, A7). "It's really strange not to see animals for such a long period of time, [I] hadn't realized what an important part of our lives animals are," she said in an interview (Anonymous, 2001, A7).

Neuro-notes 1

According to PET imaging studies, animal picture identification activates both the right and left occipital region (specifically, the right and left lingual gyrus and left fusiform gyrus) (Perani et al., 1999). Artifact picture identification, on the other hand, activates only the left brain hemisphere (Perani et al., 1999).

Neuro-notes 2

Mirror neurons. Cells in the human brain's superior temporal sulcus (STS) respond selectively to biological motion and specifically to distinctive body movements of animals such as walking, running, throwing and leaping. Point-light research reveals that we may decode such actions from a very small number of cues. Our ability to decode animate actions from minimal cues is likely due to mirror neurons (Ulloa and Pineda, 2007).

Antigravity sign

Evolution

One of several nonverbal cues derived from body movements designed to counter-act the pull of gravity. An assertive gesture or posture utilizing antigravity extensor and pronator muscles. Specifically, palm–down speaking gestures (see *Palm-down*) and dominant postures of the high-stand display.

Usage

One may accent a spoken word or phrase with authority and show serious intentionality by squaring the shoulders, lifting the face and chin and visibly standing tall. Around the world, antigravity signs are prominently featured in military uniforms and business suits (see *Business suit*).

Paleontology

Fossils of the oldest known North American amphibian, *Hynerpeton bassetti* (ca. 365 mya), suggest that its forelimbs were strong enough to do a "pushup" akin to the aggressive press-up posture of today's lizards, basilisks and iguanas. *Hynerpeton*'s jointed elbows would have permitted the animal to extend its forelegs in what may have been among the first high-stand displays. A mobile shoulder girdle and muscular forelimbs would have enabled *Hynerpeton* to lift its body higher above the earthly plain, to dominate and command respect by looming larger (see *Loom*).

See also *Broadside display*.

Antithesis

Darwinian principle

The idea, proposed by Charles Darwin (1872), that opposite emotions such as certainty and uncertainty evoke precisely opposite bodily responses.

Usage

Darwin used his principle as a device to account for the meaning of certain non-verbal signs, such as the shoulder-shrug gesture (see *Shoulder-shrug display*). As an emotional sign of uncertainty, lifted shoulders contrast with squared-shoulder postures that convey a mental state of certitude (see *Certainty*).

"Useless" behaviors

Darwin's antithesis principle was a creative yet flawed hypothesis. Regarding the shrug, for example, Darwin did not explain why lifted shoulders – rather than, say, palm-down hands – should signal uncertainty. By casting shoulder-shrugs as functionally "useless," he is left to suggest that they are inherited as acquired characteristics, a most un-evolutionary and un-Darwin-like point of view.

See also *Associated habits*.

Apocrine odor

Aroma cue

A pungent, musky scent produced by dense concentrations of apocrine glands in the underarms, and by lesser concentrations in the face, scalp, ears, eyelids, genital area and navel. A natural, animal-like aroma which can be emotionally stimulating and sexually attractive. A urinous odor, from glandular secretions that increase after puberty, thought to have been – and may still be – used as messages of personal identity, territoriality and courtship (see *Courtship*).

Usage

Many consider apocrine scent offensive (e.g., as a sign of poor grooming), and use deodorants to mask its smell. Ironically, some deodorants, colognes and perfumes contain scents designed, like apocrine odor itself, to mimic the musky, urinous odor of human sexual steroids.

Neuro-notes

Controlled by sympathetic nerves of the fight-or-flight response, apocrine glands are highly responsive to emotional stimuli (see *Fight or flight*). About two dozen chemical compounds contribute to apocrine underarm scent. Odorless until digested by bacteria, millions of possible smell combinations suggest that apocrine odor may be used to announce one's personal identity, presence and sexual moods.

See also *Arpege®*, *New car smell*.

Apraxia

Neuro term

A total or partial loss of the ability to carry out learned body movements (e.g., whistling, clapping hands, tying a shoelace), despite the presence of an otherwise healthy sensory-motor nervous system. Apraxia is the inability to plan a body movement, rather than a problem carrying it out.

Usage

In a conversation, higher-level gestures (e.g., mime cues) mark the presence of conceptual thought. Seeing a listener's steeple gesture, for example, indicates a thoughtful, rather than an emotional, disagreeing or uncertain response to spoken remarks. Studies of apraxia suggest the neurological reason for this point of view. Mime cues, such as imitating the act of threading a needle (unlike lower-level emotional gestures such as expressing anger with a table-slap) are controlled by neocortical brain areas of the parietal and left frontal lobes – areas also used in the thoughtful expression of speech.

Neuro-notes

A common nonverbal sign of ideomotor apraxia (IMA) is using the hand itself as a tool, for example, as a screwdriver, rather than using the hand to gesturally "grip" the tool.

Aquatic brain and spinal cord

Evolution

The original design of humankind's central nervous system was established ca. 500 mya in the sea. Collectively, those primeval parts of the brain and spinal cord that arose in the jawless fishes. Specifically, those circuits, nuclei and modules of the spinal cord, hindbrain, midbrain and forebrain that evolved in ancient oceans.

Usage

Many of our most basic human gestures, postures and bodily responses originated in paleocircuits of the aquatic brain and spinal cord. Though our nervous system has greatly evolved since 500 mya, circuits for smell-related cues, such as disgust; for touch, such as tactile withdrawal; for locomotion, such as the rhythmic, alternating movements of walking and for chemical arousal, as evident in the fight-or-flight response, remain functionally the same today.

Spinal cord

The oldest proto-gestures can be traced to tactile-withdrawal spinal reflexes of the earliest known vertebrates. Based on studies of newly hatched fishes, for example, it is likely that touching the skin of the earliest, now extinct animals would have elicited the same alternating, side-to-side flexion movements designed to remove swimmers from predators and to deliver them from harm's way.

Hindbrain

A chemical storage area (comparable to our brain's locus ceruleus or "blue spot") was a primary source of the neurotransmitter norepinephrine. Fiber-linked to the spinal cord below and to the forebrain above, this chemical was, and still is, important in regulating arousal. Today in humans, highly aroused spinal reflexes may show in faster and stronger gestures and body movements.

Serotonin

Another early chemical reservoir, comparable to our brain's raphe nuclei, was for serotonin. As old as vertebrates themselves (possibly older), serotonin has been found in living crabs and lobsters. Injected into the bloodstream of a lobster, serotonin leads to an elevated body posture expressive of dominance. In our own nervous system, serotonin promotes the expression of confident body signs such as squaring-up with and facing a partner, returning eye contact and smiling.

Midbrain

The aquatic midbrain had a chemical storage area for the neurotransmitter dopamine. Comparable to our own midbrain's substantia nigra ("black spot"), it supplied dopamine to primitive motor centers of the striatal complex (see *Basal ganglia*), which influenced body movements for locomotion and for keeping upright in gravity's downward pull (see *Antigravity sign*). Lowered dopamine levels in humans caused, for example, by Parkinson's disease, may show in an awkward shuffling gait, an expressionless face and rotary trembling movements of the arms and hands.

Forebrain

Incoming (afferent) taste and aroma cues dominated the aquatic forebrain via fiber-links from the amygdala to chemical-control areas of the hypothalamus. On the former's command, nuclei of the latter released neurohormones into the bloodstream, arousing body movements and postures of the fight-or-flight response.

See also *Amphibian brain*.

Arm-cross

Posture

Folding the arms over the lower chest or upper abdomen, with one or both hands touching the biceps muscles. A common resting position of the arms upon and across the torso. An often self-comforting, self-stimulating posture, unconsciously used to alleviate anxiety and social stress.

Usage

Frequently decoded as a defensive or "barrier" sign, the arm-cross may also be used as a comfortable position for relaxing the arms. When the forearms and elbows are pulled tightly into the upper body (i.e., are noticeably adducted), the gesture may reveal acute nervousness or chronic anxiety. Held less tightly against the chest, with elbows elevated and projecting outward away from the body (i.e., abducted), the arm-cross may project a guard-like stance suggestive of arrogance, disliking or disagreement.

See also *Self-touch*.

Arm-show

Display

1   To bare the arm, from the roundness of the shoulder to the bony wrist.
2   To display the femininity of often slender (gracile) arms or the masculinity of often thicker (robust) arms (1) for sexual appeal and (2) for competition (among males) in courtship.

Usage

1   Because they reflect differences between the female and male body (i.e., are sexually dimorphic) people may display their arms on behalf of sex appeal.
2   Thicker, often more muscular male arms may be displayed to challenge rival men in courtship, much as bull moose display their antler size.
3   As men may have broader shoulders, their arms tend to swing farther from their torso's sides. Additionally, the forearm bend angle is 6° wider in females, so the posture of the forearm itself may be a strong gender sign (Morris, 1985).

See also *Armwear*.

Arm-swing

Body movement

To move the upper limbs back and forth rhythmically with the legs while walking.

Usage

As a counterweight, the arm-swing helps balance our upright body while walking, jogging and running. In dance moves such as the Locomotion, Swim and Twist, vigorous arm-swing gyrations express inner feelings and moods in time to music's rock-'n-roll beat.

Walk-away sign

Restless back-and-forth motions of the arms above a conference table may reveal an unspoken wish to "walk away" from the meeting.

Evolution

Spinal-cord paleocircuits that govern the rhythmic, alternating movements of arm-swinging evolved in tandem with those of the legs for locomotion. The act of swinging arms while walking, and pumping them while running, is an evolutionary holdover from earlier days when the arms used as forelimbs participated with legs in quadrupedal locomotion.

See also *Walk*.

Arm wear

Fashion statement

Clothing worn to cover and modify the color, thickness, length, shape and texture of the arms. Ornaments such as bracelets and wristbands worn to attract notice and accent an arm's masculine or feminine traits.

Usage

What we place upon our arms accents their thickness or taper. Flannel shirts, for example, add bulk, while short sleeves may reveal the slimness and accent the length of thin arms. In business settings, wrist watches and starched shirt cuffs add visibility and authority to hand gestures delivered above a table (see *Conference table*).

Antonym – *Arm-show*. See also *Attire, Leg wear, Neck dimple*.

Arousal-labeling theory

Advanced by Patterson (1976), this theory proposes that expressed intimacy (see *Immediacy*) may cause a positive or negative state of arousal. This cognitive interpretation then determines either a compensatory or reciprocal response. If, for example, a partner's change in nonverbal behavior, such as a high level of gaze, prompted an arousal which was labeled positive, then the recipient would reciprocate this high involvement with a positive reciprocation, for example, with a smile. On the other hand, if a high level of gaze came unexpectedly from a stranger, this might result in negative arousal with a cognitive label of discomfort. In this case, the recipient might compensate by avoiding the gaze.

Aroma cue

Scent sign

1   Incoming: A chemical sign received through the nose or mouth.
2   Outgoing: A chemical sign emanating from various natural sources, including scent glands (see *Apocrine odor*), flowers, resins, herbs and cooked foods, as well as from synthetic substances found in deodorants, room fresheners and vinyl.

Usage

Aroma cues are powerful triggers of emotion and memory. Though our sense of smell is weaker than that of most other animals, we still recognize some 10,000 scents (Axel, 1995, 154), many of which can subtly alter moods. Manufactured aromas (see, for example, *New car smell*) can influence decisions to buy consumer products.

Evolution I

Smell is our oldest nonverbal channel, and aroma cues can be traced far back in time to the first chemical messages sent and received by single-celled organisms.

The earliest communicating creatures date to ca. 3.7 mya, with the oldest known life forms, called blue-green algae (cyanobacteria), living in shallow-water communities known as stromatolites.

Evolution II

The olfactory sense evolved as an "early warning" system to detect food, mates and predators from a distance. As eating, mating and warning signs, aroma cues are therefore taken quite seriously by the brain. Smell is a volatile, "thin-skinned" sense because scent receptors lie on the bodily surface itself (on the nasal cavity's olfactory epithelium) rather than beneath layers of skin as in the case of touch. Few changes have been made in aroma receptors since the time of the jawless fishes (ca. 500 mya), making smell a conservative, compelling and most trustworthy sense.

Primary odor qualities

At least six primary odors have been identified: floral (e.g., rose), ethereal (pear), musky (musk), camphor (eucalyptus), putrid (rotten eggs) and pungent (vinegar). Mint is a common seventh candidate, and smoke is an eighth.

Sexuality

"I am convinced," says Ann Gottlieb [the fragrance designer who created Calvin Klein scents], "that men find fruitiness, especially in combination with something sweet and warm (for example, musk, vanilla, or amber, or a combination thereof) very, very sexy indeed" (Dyett, 1992, 95).

Research reports

1   The olfactory sense is self-absorbing and narcissistic, while the visual sense is futuristic (MacLean, 1973).
2   More than any other sense, smell evokes strong emotional tendencies to approach or avoid.
3   In fish, for example, the most primitive reaction to a waterborne aroma cue is a reflexive contraction of muscles, leading the animal toward or away from the source of the scent (Kent, 1969). Potent colognes may have a similar effect in buses and elevators today.

Arpege®

Aroma cue

A commercial perfume for women created in 1927 by Jeanne Lanvin.

Usage

Like other scented signs, Arpege bypasses thinking centers of the brain and "speaks" directly to emotions through the limbic system. Combining rose, jasmine, orange blossom and (3) 60 natural oils and extracts, Arpege is a classic consumer product for the nose. The name, derived from the Italian word arpeggio (a musical term for playing the tones of a chord in quick succession rather than simultaneously), reflects the perfume's stratigraphic layers of smell.

Message

Like other successful fragrances, Arpege has three layered odor groups or notes. The top note (rose) registers first, the middle (jasmine) provides body and the base note (musk) gives warmth, texture and staying power. Initially, our nose detects the floral aromas of the top and middle notes, which smell sweet. Then the sexually stimulating erogenic aroma of animal musk registers, creating an "unforgettable" mood.

See also *Emotion*.

Art cue

Aesthetic sign

An aromatic, auditory, tactile, taste, vestibular or visual sign designed by human beings to affect the sense of beauty. Arrangements, combinations, contrasts, rhythms or sequences of signs, designed as an emotional language bespeaking elegance, grace, intensity, refinement and truth.

Artistic emotion

Before neuroscience, sculptor Auguste Rodin (through his artistic eye) knew that an important link between muscle movement and emotion existed in the human nervous system. Rodin expressed emotion through the mobility of the muscles.

Sfumato

Italian artist Leonardo da Vinci's Mona Lisa suggests a smile on the woman's face. That her smile seems both alive and elusive, according to Harvard visual physiologist, Margaret Livingstone, is due to the way our brain's visual system perceives it. Viewed directly, neurons for sharp vision see less of a smile than when viewed indirectly by peripheral-vision neurons (i.e., as when we focus on her eyes), which are more responsive to blurry details. Da Vinci intentionally blurred Mona Lisa's lips through the Italian sfumato ("smoky") brush-stroke technique. When we look directly at her lips, after having looked at her eyes, the smile seems to disappear.

See also *Color cue*.

Artifact

Durable sign

A material object, such as a consumer product, deliberately fabricated by humankind.

Usage

Like gestures, artifacts have a great deal to "say." The simplest message transmitted by an artifact is, "Something human made is here." "Human made," that is, intelligently fabricated by humans, is evident in the deliberately patterned shape, the grammatical syntax (i.e., the structured arrangement of parts) and the negative entropy encoded in artifacts as material signs, signals and cues.

Word origin

The word artifact comes from the Latin arte ("by skill") factum ("made"; via the ancient Indo-European root dhe-, "to set," "to put," derivatives of which include deed, did and do; skill "by hand" is implied).

Anthropology

"At dozens of archaeological sites in Africa, razor-sharp stone flakes and round hammer-stones mark the handiwork of anonymous craftspeople who forged tools as early as 2.6 million years ago" (Gibbons, 1997, 32).

Prehistory

Oldest sign artifacts. The oldest human sign artifacts, consisting of engraved animal bones such as the Bordes ox-rib, date to ca. 300,000 BP from the pre-Neanderthal period in France (Marshack, 1971). The symbolism is as yet unexplained; however, the V-shaped engravings appear to be constructed, distinctively patterned, rather than natural, so a quite general message of "human made" reaches the contemporary viewer.

Monumental

The Great Wall of China, Egyptian pyramids, the U.S. interstate highway system and Manhattan skyscrapers are immoveable human artifacts that carry diverse non-verbal messages, meanings and signs. Monumental artifacts were constructed after humans had transitioned from hunter-gatherer wandering ca. 10,000 years ago to settle down as farmers.

Classic

A classic U.S. 20th-century monument is the looming 1,046'-high, 77-floor, brick-and-steel Chrysler Building in East Side Manhattan, New York, completed in 1930. Readable signs include hubcaps, fenders, radiator caps and hood ornaments attached to the exterior as iconic suggestions of automobiles; eagle-gargoyle figures suggestive of flight and upward-pointing triangles crowned with a vertical, stainless-steel needle to suggest otherworldly height.

See also *Object fancy*, *Emblem*.

Artificial intelligence

Digital information

In nonverbal communication, artificial intelligence (AI) researchers are designing robotic devices that can mimic and understand human movements, gestures, postures and facial cues. In the U.S., robotic facial expressions have been designed by the MIT Humanoid Robotics Group, whose robot, Kismet, can produce facial signs for basic human emotions, including anger, surprise, disgust, happiness, sadness, calmness and interest. Human posture has been researched at MIT's Computer Science and Artificial Intelligence Laboratory. Using AI, the lab has learned how to sense human body movements and postures through walls.

Askance

Sideward glance

An English word, of unknown origin, for turning the eyeballs in their sockets fully to the left or right side, in a look suggesting disapproval, doubt, mistrust, skepticism or suspicion. The askance position may be accompanied by frowning (see *Eyebrow-lower*) or squinting and may be aimed toward or away from the eyes of another.

Usage I

Askance looks often convey negative feelings and moods (see *Aversive cue*). The face angles away from a partner's face (see *Angular distance*), marking an intention to move away physically in space (see *Intention cue*).

Usage II

British zoologist Desmond Morris has identified "eyes side-glance," used world-wide as a flirtatious version of the askance gaze (Morris, 1994). Eyes side-glance is performed with a slight forward head-tilt suggestive of submissiveness (see *Gaze down*).

See also *CLEM*, *Eye contact*, *Eye-roll*.

Associated habits

Darwinian first principle

The idea proposed by Charles Darwin (1872) that certain emotional states of mind (disliking), whether feeble or strong, are associated with characteristic, habitual body movements. The idea is the first of three often-confusing "general principles of expression" that Darwin himself concluded "remain inexplicable" (p. 87).

Usage

Darwin's first "principle of serviceable associated habits" was used to explain the meaning of nonverbal signs. Darwin alluded to a "push-away" gesture, for example, given while yelling (see *Shout*) to make something, or someone, "go away." Though push-away is a pantomimed gesture reflecting the physical act of pushing away (see *Mime cue*), Darwin regarded it as an arbitrary and "useless" body movement without function (see *Antithesis*, *Shrug*).

See also *Antithesis*.

Asymmetrical tonic neck reflex

1   A gross motor reflex that provides neural programming for basic postures of the torso and limbs (e.g., in crawling and reaching).
2   The anatomical "fencing posture," produced by turning an infant's head to one side (e.g., leftward), showing (1) arm extension and upward palm-rotation of the "face" or "jaw hand" (i.e., baby's right hand in this case), and (2) arm flexion and palm pronation of the "head" or "skull hand" (Peiper, 1963, 156).

3   Reflexive in infancy, fragments of asymmetrical tonic neck reflex (ATNR) emerge as nonverbal signs in stressful, emotional or physically demanding situations and in sleep.

Usage

ATNR provides the basic wiring for one of our tell-tale mood signs, the hand-behind-head. ATNR's reflexive, brain-stem circuitry makes this unconscious gesture an often trustworthy indicator, variously, of disagreement, uncertainty, frustration and anger.

Art

Michelangelo's The Three Labours of Hercules (ca. 1530) and Rodin's The Age of Bronze (1875–76) are classic examples of how artists may depict strong emotion through tense limb postures released by the ATNR (see *Nonverbal release*). One arm stretched fully forward, for example, with the other flexed and curled behind the head, shows feelings powerful enough to have triggered the reflexive fencing posture.

See also *Hand-behind-head*.

Attire

Psychology and clothing

Positive first impressions are established when the style of clothes you wear is similar to those who are judging you (Reid et al., 1997). Both females and males look first at clothes in same-sex encounters. However, females look at clothes first when they meet a male, but when a male meets a female, he looks at clothes third, with figure and face apparently taking precedence over glances at her clothes (Knapp and Hall, 2006).

In some situations, we judge the person's intelligence based on the appropriateness of their clothes for the particular social situation they find themselves in (Rees et al., 1974). Lennon and Miller (1984) suggest that if you are a female and wear conservative clothes which consist of a skirted suit or a blazer, then there is a stronger possibility that you will be perceived as more intelligent. In contrast, Paek (1986) argues that very dressy styles are less likely to convey an image of intelligence.

There are a number of findings which identify the wearing of clothing in terms of being "cool" or being "warm" (Gorham et al., 1999). When we make cool perceptions of clothes, we are making judgments about the wearer's knowledge, educational background, preparation, level of sophistication and competence (Harris et al., 1983; Miller and Rowold, 1980). On the other hand, warm judgments of clothes have to do with perceptions of the wearer as trustworthy, sociable, likable, enthusiastic and interpersonally attractive (Leathers, 1992). If the clothes you wear prompt the observer to perceive you as being competent and well educated, they may be less likely to make judgments about you in warm terms, that is, in terms of being sociable, likeable or enthusiastic. Females tend to be more receptive to these kinds of clothing cues than males (Kuehne and Creekmore, 1971; Solomon and Schopler, 1982).

There is evidence to suggest that while dressing provocatively can enhance one's chances of attracting a sexual partner, such dress may in fact be counterproductive in attracting a long-term partner (Hill et al., 1987).

Other research evidence suggests that the clothes you wear can have an effect on how you behave. Work by Tharin (1981), by Roach (1997) and by Gorham et al. (1999) would indicate that in certain contexts, the clothes you wear can affect how you feel and, accordingly, how you behave.

Clothing in the workplace

First impressions often have a base in appearance cues. The clothes people wear can provide information about their preferences and also are often associated with certain professions. For example, uniforms can provide immediate information about someone's occupation (Kuster et al., 2019). Moreover, this information can have a persuasive value (Lawrence and Watson, 1991).

Research on clothing in the workplace shows that conservative attire is connected with impressions of effectiveness and dominance. For women, a skirted suit makes a professional impression. Women wearing skirted suits are rated as more assertive and decisive (Kaiser, 1997).

See also *Attractiveness, Artefact, Business suit, Emblem*.

Attractiveness

Nonverbal markers

Human physical attractiveness is largely determined by nonverbal markers. Burgoon et al. (2016) provide a very useful summary of the five key factors typically associated with attractiveness:

1 Koinophilia. This is the tendency to perceive faces which have average features as being attractive.
2 Waist-to-Hip Ratio. While there may be some cultural variations, across the globe, there is very considerable agreement that men prefer women with waist-to-hip ratios of about .70. The hour-glass figure. This ratio suggests health and fertility. For men, the waist to hip ratio is 0.9. With men, this can be represented in the shape of a "V."
3 Symmetry: The more symmetrical a face is, the more it will be judged as attractive.
4 The Golden Ratio or Phi. Phi is the ratio of 1:1.618. Pythagoras, the Greek mathematician and philosopher, made a case for an association between human beauty and Phi. For the perfectly beautiful body, the distance from your belly button to the bottom of your feet would be 1.618 times the distance from the top of your head to your belly button. Likewise, the distance from the top of your head to your elbow would be 1.618 times the distance from your elbow to the end of your middle finger. Beautiful faces are also marked by Phi. For instance, in especially beautiful faces, the mouth is 1.618 times as wide as the nose.
5 Facial Neoteny and Sexual Maturity. The degree to which a face displays sexual maturity and baby-like features (facial neoteny) has a bearing on

perceptions of attractiveness (Berry and McArthur, 1985; Cunningham, 1986). Facial neoteny for a woman would include attributes such as fuller lips, wider eyes, small chin and shorter distances between the eyes and nose, and larger distances between the eyes and hairline. For men, facial neoteny can be signaled by large eyes (Cunningham et al., 1990). Indeed, Cunningham et al. note that men who possess "the neotenous features of large eyes, the mature features of prominent cheekbones and a large chin, the expressive feature of a big smile, and high-status clothing were seen as more attractive than other men" (Cunningham et al., 1990, 61). Within the sphere of sexual maturity for women, high cheekbones are viewed as attractive. For men, sexual maturity is signaled by a strong jaw line and a large chin, combined with the less mature features of large eyes and a wide smile (Cunningham et al., 1990).

Perception of attractiveness

Humans tend to associate all sorts of positive internal characteristics, such as friendliness, popularity, confidence, ambition, likeability and intelligence, with an outwardly attractive appearance (Dion, 1986; Dion et al., 1972; Hatfield and Sprecher, 1986). Indeed, Hargie and Dickson (2004) point out that in day-to-day evaluative decisions about the quality of people's work or their suitability for selection, bias may favor the attractive, especially in situations of limited protracted contact.

While there is evidence that physically attractive people are generally more self-confident and more socially skilled than average-looking or unattractive people, there is no evidence to indicate that being physically attractive means you are actually nicer or more trustworthy than other people (Feingold, 1992). See *Halo effect*.

Nonetheless, being attractive does seem to confer benefits. In a meta-analysis of 11 studies, Langlois et al. (2000) found that:

1   raters agree about who is and is not attractive, both within and across cultures;
2   attractive children and adults are judged more positively than unattractive children and adults, even by those who know them;
3   attractive children and adults exhibit more positive behaviors and traits than unattractive children and adults (Langlois, 2000, 390).

Attractiveness and culture

There is significant research to show that there are a number of physical attributes within and across cultures which are remarkably similar. For example, Cunningham et al. (1995) examined how people across different races judged the attractiveness of Caucasian, Asian, Hispanic and black women. Their work points to the fact that "beauty is not in the eye of the beholder." Rather, many signals of attractiveness are judged consistently both within a culture and across various cultures (Floyd, 2006a). This is particularly true for judgments of the face. There may be some differences across cultures in terms of judgments of the body. In parts of the world which are prone to famine or disease, fleshiness can be an indicator of health, whereas in others, slender physiques are an indicator of access to high protein and low-fat foods (Anderson et al., 1992).

Evolution

The human develops a sense of the importance of physical appearance early in life. In preschool, children are able to identify the better-looking children (Berscheid and Walster, 1974). Indeed, there are some who argue that the value of attractiveness has an evolutionary and biological basis, with the human being very conscious of the need to attract a mate (Buss, 1994). This beauty bias, which is sometimes called the halo effect, begins in childhood, the inference being that beauty connotes goodness (Larose and Standing, 1998).

Attractiveness and health

Attractive people have been shown to be somewhat happier; more self-confident, assertive and socially skilled and in better psychological health, especially in the case of women (Mathes and Kahn, 1975). But there are a number of exceptions to this, of course. The relationship between personal appearance and self-esteem is surprisingly small. For example, in the workplace, Major et al. (1984) argue that attractive people discount praise more quickly, as they fear it may be more a product of their personal appearance than the actual quality of their work.

See also *Attire*.

Autism

Communication disorder

A related family of conditions, from producing repetitive body movements to showing a special gift for drawing, music or mathematics, marked by a lack of empathy and inability to send and receive nonverbal cues. An autistic person may fail to use socially normal patterns of eye contact, facial expression and gestures and may be unable to use normal speech. An autistic individual may also display an intense interest in arranging, organizing or hoarding a restricted range of physical objects.

Usage

When kept from handling a favored object, an autistic person may yell, become aggressive or engage in property destruction.

Asperger's syndrome

Like autism, Asperger's syndrome (AS) includes problems in social behavior, along with abnormal responses to the environment. Unlike autism, however, cognitive and communicative skills may be relatively normal, and verbal skills are strong. AS individuals may show an unusually strong interest in specific objects and life forms, including bus schedules, videotape cassettes and frogs.

Eye contact

Avoidance of looking at other people's eyes is a commonly cited behavioral sign used to diagnose whether a child is likely to be autistic.

See also *Nonverbal learning disorder*.

Aversive cue

Unfriendly sign

An emotionally negative nonverbal signal.

Usage

Aversive cues; such as eyebrow-lower, palm-down and frown, suggest that one is unwilling to interact or form a social bond.

Antonym: see *Affiliative cue*.

B

Backchannel responses

Response signals

Back-channel responses are forms of verbal (e.g., "Yes"), vocal ("mmm-hmmm") and nonverbal (head-nodding) communication performed by a listener that act as reinforcement for the speaker, indicating that the listener is being attentive (see *Head-nod*). Argyle (1988, 111) notes that backchannel responses have a "powerful effect" on speakers. They afford an opportunity to communicate messages to the speaker without disrupting the flow of the latter's speech. Indeed, the speaker does not perceive them as interruptions (Duncan, 1975). A speaker will carefully monitor the listener's backchannel responses in order to modify his/her talk (Clark and Krych, 2004). Work by Bavelas et al. (2000) shows that backchannel responses actively shape spontaneous storytelling, with poor backchannel responses deleteriously affecting a story's quality.

Forms of response

Backchannel signals include head-tilts, head-shakes, short vocalizations (e.g., "Right"), glances, posture changes (leaning forward to indicate interest), smiles, postural congruency (mimicking the speaker's posture), facial expressions (raised eyebrows) and verbal statements ("I see"). Such responses typically occur at the end of rhythmic units of speech or at junctures between speech clauses. The speed and manner of the backchannel response may carry meaning as well. Where head-nodding is fast, for example, it can communicate engaged attentiveness with the speaker (Clark, 1996).

Absence of backchannel responses

Absence of back-channel responses can prove disconcerting. Indeed, in some instances, the listener may deliberately withhold backchannel responses in order to signal disinterest or disapproval with what the speaker is saying. Gender differences have been noted with regard to backchannel responses. Male strangers may display fewer backchannel responses than interacting pairs of female strangers (Ickes et al., 1988).

Balance cue

Vestibular sign

While most nonverbal cues travel through visual, auditory, touch, taste and smell channels, some move through the vestibular sense of balance. Balance sensations include generally pleasant incoming signs received as the body's head is suddenly accelerated, decelerated or tilted.

Usage

Though we tend to keep our head stabilized in equilibrium, we enjoy accelerating, dropping and spinning it in such sports as auto racing, skiing, sky diving, skate boarding, cliff diving and surfing. Stimulation of motion sensors in the inner ear is not only pleasurable but diverts cognitive attention from anxiety regarding future concerns. This is because, as accelerometers of the inner ear are stimulated, older centers of the brain's basal ganglia and cerebellum are engaged. In these brain areas, there is no sense of a future "tomorrow." There is only "today" – now – here in the present moment of time.

Anatomy

The inner ear's utricle and saccule are sensitive to both linear acceleration and gravity. Its three semicircular canals are sensitive to angular and rotational acceleration. Since rotation upsets the normal circulation of fluid in the ear's balance loops, it may produce an unpleasant sensation of dizziness.

Pleasure

University of Rochester geriatric researchers found that after an hour in rocking chairs, nursing home patients diagnosed with dementia showed up to a one-third reduction in signs of anxiety and depression (Watson et al., 1998). Facial expressions provided evidence in support of this finding. According to lead researcher, Nancy Watson, "You could see immediately by their faces that they were enjoying themselves" (Watson et al., 1998, 299).

Barbie doll®

Product speak

Nonverbally, consumer products – such as cars (see *Vehicular grille*), jackets (see *Business suit*) and toy dolls like Barbie – have a great deal to "say." Barbie is a sexual icon, a hand-held product displaying exaggerated signs of feminine beauty (see *Facial beauty*). She is a portable, 11-inch plastic symbol of Americana whose messaging features – high heels, hourglass figure and youthful face – appeal to millions of consumers in over 140 countries throughout the world. Barbie's permanently pointed feet assume a high-heel stance (see *High heel*). The plumper, rounder Upper Paleolithic Venus of Willendorf figurine has pronged legs, as well (see *Reproductive imagery*).

Statues

In his book Falling in Love with Statues: Artificial Humans from Pygmalion to the Present (2009), art historian George Hersey includes Barbie along with statues, Venus dolls, robotic forms and computer-imaged avatars as artificial humans capable of inspiring romantic interest in real human beings (see *Statue signs*). "One of the odder things that our culture has derived from antiquity," Hersey writes, "is the love – moral, theological, poetical, physical – of statues by humans" (Hersey, 2009, 5).

Neuro-notes

The primate brain dedicates distinct modules of visual cortex to the recognition of faces and facial expressions. The same dedicated nerve cells of the lower temporal lobe which respond to human faces respond – with perhaps equal feeling – to Barbie doll faces, rendering them psychologically "real."

See also *Consumer product*.

Baseline demeanor

Standard

1 The inventory of gestures and postures observed in relaxed settings free of social anxiety or stress.
2 Nonverbal behaviors observed in solitary subjects who may be reading, snacking or watching TV.
3 Those nonverbal cues presented during the initial "friendly" phase of an interview or interrogation, as opposed to those in the subsequent "stress" phase.

Usage

Before assigning significance to a body movement (e.g., as a sign of deception), it is necessary to make preliminary and follow-up observations of the subject's baseline demeanor. Tense individuals, for example, may chronically touch themselves (see *Self-touch*), which makes the latter cues less likely to be signs of situational stress (in response, for example, to a *Probing point*).

Noteworthy cues

Body-motion behaviors not recorded in the baseline phase may carry special weight as signs expressive of hidden attitudes, unvoiced moods, deceit, disagreement and uncertainty.

See also *Anatomical position*, *Probing point*.

Basic emotion theory

What is basic emotion theory?

Basic emotion theory (BET) works on the premise that emotions are discrete and short-lived states which have physiological, subjective and expressive components. It is also grounded in the assumption that facial expressions signal interior emotional states (Ekman, 1999). The theory propounds that emotions "enable humans to respond in ways that are typically adaptive in relation to evolutionarily significant problems, from negotiating status hierarchies, to avoiding peril, to taking care of vulnerable offspring" (Keltner, 2019b, 133).

Basic emotion theory and nonverbal communication

In terms of the nonverbal expression of emotion, the theory posits that these expressions have the following common properties: First, the expressions are culturally congruent. They have degrees of cross-cultural similarity both in the manner in which they are created and also the manner in which the emotional expression is recognized. Second, they signal the current emotional state of the situation in which the human finds themselves. Third, they "covary" with emotion-related physiological responses (Hess and Fischer, 2013; Keltner and Lerner, 2010; Keltner et al., 2019a).

Basic emotion theory in this decade

Some say that basic emotion theory has been "the central narrative in the science of emotion" (Keltner et al., 2019a, 195), while others would argue that it is grounded in "a simplistic and antiquated view of biology – culture interactions" (Crivelli and Fridlund, 2019, 187).

Questions about the "robustness" of basic emotion theory have been raised in the past few decades. For example, some of the early research on BET made over-use of "exaggerated" and "stereotypical" expressions (Russell, 1994; Matsumoto and Hwang, 2017; Nelson and Russell, 2013). Recent work by Duran et al. (2017) questions whether individuals from remote cultures can actually identify emotion in static photographs (which was the basis of some of the BET research), while others such as Fridlund (1991) argue that human facial displays do not signal interior feelings but rather express social intentions and motives in line with behavioral ecological theory.

Baton-twirl

Movement

Just as the human body may communicate nonverbally by moving its parts (see *Gesture*), human artifacts may be moved to send messages as well. A popular case in point is the baton-twirl.

Spin sign

Baton-twirling is the often contagious act of manually rotating a baton – or pencil, pen, club, knife, torch or other oblong artifact – at accelerated rpm to visually project a pleasing kinetic blur. Often set to drumbeats or melody (see *Music*), a twirled baton attracts notice and may lead viewers to whirl an object themselves (see *Isopraxism*).

Usage

Baton-twirling may be used in band performances (e.g., twirled drumsticks), dances (Tahitian torch-twirling), parades (drum major baton-twirling) and school-rooms (informal pencil-twirling and pen-spinning) to attract attention, entertain and display manual skill. Twirling is featured in widespread competitions, for example, as sanctioned by the U.S. Twirling Association and the World Baton Twirling Federation.

Neuro-notes

Twirled batons please the eyes and may release serotonin into the central nervous system. Serotonin, a pleasure hormone, has been linked to Kluver's "form constants," as visual flickers, rotations and spirals are mediated by serotonergic brain receptors and are thus aesthetically pleasing (Haberstadt, 2015)

See *Art cue, Form constants*.

Bat-Signal®

Danger sign

A nonverbal appeal for help from Batman, the caped, cinematic, comic-book superhero of the late 1930s to current times. A circular-enclosed visual image of paired, prickly bat wings projected overhead into the night sky from an illuminated searchlight.

Usage

The Bat-Signal was used to summon law-enforcement help in fictional "Gotham City," USA. Instead of a verbal cry for "Help!," the Bat-Signal was projected instead.

Iconic symbol

The Bat-Signal combines iconicity with symbolism. Iconically, its curvilinear, rhythmically repeated, projecting-pointed lines resemble the signature silhouetted shape of outstretched bat wings (order Chiroptera). Symbolically, its warning message is learned through reading or watching the Batman narrative in comic books, motion pictures or TV.

Warning coloration

The Bat-Signal evolved from an original bat-shaped Batman logo designed in 1939 for Detective Comics. In 1966, the black bat figure was set upon a yellow background, giving it an aposematic suggestion of "danger" not unlike the warning coloration of a stinging yellow jacket, also known as a wasp (Vespula sp.).

See also *Color cue, Symbol*.

Bauhaus

Design sign

That diverse nonverbal messages are encoded in architectural design is clearly evident in Bauhaus. Bauhaus (German "building house") is the name of an influential school of design and architecture founded in 1919 by Walter Gropius. Distinctive nonverbal signs encoded in Bauhaus designs rest upon a unified set of messaging features – such as function over form, rhythmic repetition and unembellished information – which reshaped architecture, graphic symbolism and typography in the 20th century. Bauhaus seeks to maximize design function while minimizing artistic flourishes and details of aesthetic form (see *Isotype*).

Usage

Bauhaus includes work by dozens of men and women who collaborated from 1919 to 1933 and beyond to the present day to design consumer-product signs, signals and cues from a rationally functional point of view. Key examples include Berlin's

Bauhaus-Archiv, Helsinki's Glass House, La Jolla's Geisel Library, Helvetica type-faces, and the Italian Bauhaus Desk & Chair.

Messaging features

Bauhaus' nonverbal communication includes the following messaging features:

1   Rhythmic repetition, in which repeated design elements, such as an office building's stacked linear terraces, suggest a unified composition, harmony and movement.
2   Unembellished information, in which the main message is not distorted by artistic flourish. In the Bauhaus-inspired typeface, Helvetica, for example, umlauts, ligatures, serifs and other flourishes of early Fraktur and Gothic type-faces were omitted to achieve a "clean" typography. Helvetica's usage by BMW, GM, Jeep, Lufthansa, Panasonic and Toyota bespeaks its expressive power.
3   Curvature, a "friendly" shape, was introduced to Bauhaus by the Russian painter Wassily Kandinsky, whose interest in gestalt and form psychology led to curves being encoded in Bauhaus architecture.

Antonym: *Art cue.*

Figure B.1 Beats

Beats

Usage

Resembling a musical beat, gestural beats primarily involve the use of the hands to demarcate a speaker's linguistic clauses. They are typically short and quick, in the form of a simple flick of the hand or movement of fingers up and down or back and forth (McNeill, 1992).

Beats and semantics

Beats mark those parts of discourse which the speaker considers most significant and "give a clue as to the inner workings of the mind of the speaker" (Beattie, 2004, 75). In so doing, these hand movements are not actually used to convey semantic information but rather have a rhythmic relationship to the accompanying speech (Suppes et al., 2015).

Bend-away

Posture

To contract muscles of the primitive body wall, causing the spinal column to curve or rotate sideward, away from standard anatomical position (see *Anatomical position*).

Usage

Psychiatrists and anthropologists have long known that the postures of our upper body reflect social attitudes and key emotional states (e.g., Bateson and Mead,

1942; Richmond et al., 1991). Bending away and other gross postural shifts often reveal negative feelings (Mehrabian, 1972).

Anatomy

Lateral flexion (bending) and rotation (twisting) movements of the spine are made by contracting deep muscles of the back (e.g., erector spinae and transversospinalis) – the muscles that influence our most basic bodily postures.

Evolution

Among the oldest body movements were those for locomotion. Muscles of the body wall contracted to produce rhythmic sideward bending motions. The earliest, oscillatory swimming movements – which took animals toward food and mates and away from harm – were wired into paleocircuits of the aquatic brain and spinal cord. Thus, bending away from a disliked person at a table is not unlike swimming away in the sea.

See also *Angular distance, Body-shift*.

Beep

Auditory cue

Any of several short-lived, single-tone, high-pitched electronic sounds emitted by a consumer product such as a computer, smoke alarm or microwave oven to attract the attention of users.

Usage

Beeps are often used as warning signs, for example, in motor vehicles to warn of backing and in smoke detectors to warn of failing batteries. Beeps may also signal lapsed time intervals, as in electric-oven timers. In radio and TV broadcasts, beeps may mask obscene vocalization on the air.

Meaning

In a consumer product, a beep or series of beeps is an auditory bid for attention, that is, "I am here – pay attention to me." The sudden onset and abrupt ending of a beep, like that of a bird-call's tweet, set it apart from ambient environmental sounds, which have both gradual onsets and endings. Abruptness adds psychological urgency to a beeped or avian-tweeted sign.

Word origin

English "beep" is an imitative or onomatopoeic word that sounds like the sound it labels. B-ee-p has a high-pitched vowel sound in the middle, which can be short or elongated, enclosed on both ends by plosive, bilabial-stop consonants.

Evolution

Electronic beeping messages evolved, in part, from mechanical horns used in motor vehicles to warn against collision. After World War II, many horn signals were replaced by sounds emitted via piezoelectric technology and later by digital means.

Neuro-note

Beeps address subcortical auditory lobes of the primitive amphibian midbrain in charge of the startle reflex (see *Amphibian brain*). Thus, we take the beep's nonverbal imperative seriously and promptly respond to its call.

See also *Gavel*.

Big Mac®

Edible sign

1   A hand-held consumer product with chemical emanations that appeal to the senses of smell and taste.
2   A portable, fast-food symbol of the American way of life.
3   A mass-produced beef sandwich whose stratified layers mark an incredibly long prehistory in time.

Usage

The Big Mac "speaks" with a simple eloquence millions appreciate but few understand. Its meaty taste is enhanced by the rush of primary salty, sour and sweet ingredients which address tongue receptors directly but have little effect on more discerning nerves of the nose.

Prehistory

The Big Mac encodes a potpourri of flavor messages from the distant past. Because many of the sandwich's aroma and taste cues precede written history, *The Routledge Dictionary of Nonverbal Communication* excavated a Big Mac to decipher its chemical signs:

Layer I: top bun

Harmonious flavor molecules released in cooking have made bread and meat an age-old combination. Invented by the Greeks, the first oven-cooked bread was eaten with opson (i.e., "non-bread" vegetables and meats) on top; the open-faced sandwich later evolved as pizza. From the Dark Ages to the Renaissance, thick bread slices (or trenchers) were prepared with meat and sauce on top, paving the way for double-decker sandwiches, such as the Big Mac.

Layer I: seeds

Sesame seeds on top had earlier spread from the Nile to the Orient, where they were mixed with wheat flour by pastry chefs for centuries. Roasted seeds add a nutty flavor, which appeals to the primate palate. Seeds provide tactile enjoyment for the tongue, as well (in reptiles, the tongue evolved as a sensory organ for touch; see *Existential taste*).

Layers II and VIII: meat

The Maillard or browning reaction of cooked beef releases furans; pyrones and other carbon, hydrogen and oxygen molecules which provide the complex oniony, chocolaty, nutty, fruity and caramel-like tastes we prefer to the bland taste of uncooked flesh (McGee, 1990). At the heart of a Big Mac are two ground-beef patties, whose cooked flavor compounds would have been familiar to *Homo erectus* in Africa 1.6 mya.

Layer III: pickle horizon

Gherkins, eaten in India with salt or lemon juice for 3,000 years, came to Europe during the Renaissance. Along with their crunchy texture, pickles add a primary sour taste which has been enjoyed with lettuce since the Roman era.

Layers IV and X: lettuce

A Big Mac contains 1/4 cup of chopped head-lettuce (*Lactuca sativa*), a plant preferred by the ancient Greeks above all other greens. Wild lettuce was prized for the soothing properties of its magnesium content as an aid to digestion. Because of a burger's high fat content, our enteric nervous system considers lettuce a welcome ingredient today.

Layers V and XI: onions

One-half teaspoon of finely diced onion, a root bulb, appears in each of two strata. An onion's volatile sulfur compounds evolved as warning messages to deter hungry grubs and insects (see *Secondary products*). Wild onions were used 4,000 years ago by Egyptian peasants to season bland meals, and Egyptian mummies sometimes included onions, wrapped in separate bandages, as carry-out for the afterlife.

Layers VI and XII: sauce

Sauce adds moisture, required for the tongue to taste chemicals in solution. Taste cues in sweet and sour sauces have flavored meats for thousands of years, and the Big Mac uses a variant of thousand-island dressing (made from salad oil, orange and lemon juice, minced onion, paprika, Worcestershire sauce [a spicy Indian recipe], dry mustard, parsley and salt). The nonverbal secret of a Big Mac is the riddle of its sauce.

Layer IX: cheese

A layer of American cheese lies above the lettuce horizon. Cuneiform tablets place cheese in the Near East by ca. 6,000 years ago. Researchers trace the origin of cheese to 7,000 years ago in northern Europe. Cheese sends salty signals to the tongue tip, and its smoothness blends well with the coarser texture of beef. Flavorful fatty acids and esters of glycerol in cheese satisfy a natural human craving for fat.

Neuro-notes

While the subtlety of Cabernet, truffles and haute cuisine is processed by higher brain centers capable of culinary learning, the primary tastes of fast food are handled subcortically in the thalamus and in a buried part of the cerebral cortex called the insula, which is emotionally linked to the amygdala and limbic system. Like primary colors, the basic bitter, salty, sour and sweet tastes of fast-food coffee, fries, pickles and soda make brash rather than subtle statements.

See also *Coca-Cola®*.

Bite

Body movement

The act of closing one's jaws tightly to cut, grip, grasp or tear with the teeth, as in (1) eating a Big Mac sandwich, (2) clenching the jaws in anger or (3) inflicting pain.

Usage

Our animal nature shows clearly in the eagerness with which we may bite our enemies. In New York City, for example, ca. 1,500 human beings report having been bitten by other humans each year (Conn and Silverman, 1991, 86). (N.B.: This is five times greater than the reported figure for rat bites [Wurman, 1989, 177].)

Anatomy

The muscles of mastication are masseter and temporalis (which close the mouth) and the lateral and medial pterygoids and anterior belly of the digastric (which open the mouth).

Evolution

Along with their role in chewing and eating, our remote ancestors' jaws, jaw muscles and teeth played a defensive role: the face was used as a weapon (as is dramatically the case today, for example, in crocodiles, grizzly bears and tigers).

Media

In their televised June 28, 1997, boxing rematch, challenger Mike Tyson committed a major foul by biting off a one-inch piece of Evander Holyfield's ear and spitting it onto the floor of the ring. Two points were deducted from his score, but in the third round, Tyson tried to bite Holyfield's other ear and was disqualified from the competition.

Neuro-notes

Biting muscles are innervated by mandibular branches of the emotionally sensitive trigeminal nerve (cranial V; see *Special visceral nerve*). Acting through the trigeminal's motor nucleus, emotional stimuli associated, for example, with anger, may cause the jaw muscles to contract in uncontrollable biting movements.

Antonym: *Jaw-droop.*

Blank face

Facial sign

1   A neutral, relaxed, seemingly "expressionless" face.
2   The face in repose, with the eyes open and the lips closed.
3   A condition in which the neck, jaw and facial muscles are neither stretched nor contracted.
4   A baseline "emotionless" face, the muscle tone of which reflects a mood of calmness.
5   The deadpan face we adopt at home alone while resting, reading or watching TV.

Usage

Though "expressionless," the blank face may send a strong emotional message: "Do Not Disturb." In shopping malls, elevators and subways, for example, we adopt neutral faces to distance ourselves from strangers. The blank face is a subtle sign used to keep others a polite distance away. (N.B.: A blank face with naturally downturned lips and creased frown lines may appear "angry" as well.)

Research reports

1   Infants 7 to 12 weeks old interacting with mothers whose faces were voluntarily immobilized became unhappy and puzzled, grimaced, stared at their own fisted hands, avoided mother's eyes and made quick glances at the mother (Trevarthen, 1997, 267).
2   A review of research on the neutral face shows that, even though faces at rest emote no clear emotions, people respond as if they did. Neutral faces "seem to have a perceptual status comparable to a prototypical expression of basic emotion" (Carrera-Levillain and Fernandez-Dols, 1994, 282).

Neuro-notes

The unconscious background level of muscle tone in our face is set by the brain stem's reticular activating system. In the blank face, muscle tone is neither aroused nor sedated, but "normal." Studies show that, as in monkeys, for whom the face sends important emotional signs, neurons in our forebrain's amygdala "respond briskly" to the sight of another person's blank face (LeDoux, 1996). Imaging studies suggest that while encoding pictures of neutral and expressive faces, three brain areas – the temporal cortex, hippocampus and left prefrontal cortex – show high levels of activity.

See also *Facial expression*.

Blackface

Racist sign

The practice of applying dark pigment to the face to demean and ridicule the physical appearance of African Americans. According to The American Heritage Dictionary, "blackface" is "Makeup for a conventionalized comic travesty of Black people, especially in a minstrel show" (Soukhanov, 1992, 196). Blackface performers deride the speech, mannerisms, clothing, culture and intelligence of Blacks comically burlesqued on stage. Blackface signaling was popularized in 1930 by the American minstrel Thomas D. Rice. The human face is a major carrier of personal identity, engagement and mood. The negative caricature of facial features in blackface (in particular, of enlarged upper and lower lips) thus sends a message of bigotry, racism and hate. Neurological studies of White subjects found greater amygdala stimulation – with accompanying negative emotion and fear – when viewing darker rather than lighter-toned faces (Ronquillo et al., 2007).

Blindness

Children

A significant number of studies show that nonverbal communication for blind people bears similarities to those who are sighted. Using the Facial Action Coding

System (see *FACS*), for example, Galati et al. (2003, 418) found that "facial expressions of blind and sighted children were rather similar." This research supports Darwin's hypothesis that some expressions of emotion have biological and evolutionary roots. Iverson et al. (2000, 126) found that "blind children gesture at the earliest stages of word-learning, and they have the same types of gestures in their repertoires as sighted children." Blind children, however, may use fewer gestures than those who are sighted.

Adults

In 1998, Iverson and Goldin-Meadow examined videotapes of blind people and observed that they gestured despite the lack of a visual model. Moreover, they also gestured when speaking to another blind person. A study by Cohen in 1977 looked at the manner in which we use gestures. The study asked participants to give directions over an intercom and also face to face. Even when participants could not see the listener, they still used hand gestures, much as we do when speaking on the phone.

See also *Gesture*.

Blink

Sign

A rapid closing and opening of the eyes.

Usage

Our blink rate reflects psychological arousal in the manner of a polygraph test. The normal, resting blink rate of a human is 20 closures per minute, with the average blink lasting one quarter of a second (Karson, 1992). Significantly faster rates may reflect emotional stress, as aroused, for example, in the brain's emergency response (see *Fight-or-flight*).

Neuroanatomy

The blink reflex originates in paleocircuits of the midbrain (see *Amphibian brain*). Nervous impulses travel from vision centers of the superior colliculi to the facial nerve's motor nucleus, causing involuntary contractions in the eyelid portion of orbicularis oculi muscles.

Neuro-notes

We blink faster when excited because eyelid movements reflect bodily arousal levels established by the brain stem's reticular activating system (RAS). Emotion from the limbic system stimulates the RAS to act on our midbrain's substantia nigra, which releases the excitatory chemical, dopamine, to the superior colliculi.

See also *Facial flushing*.

Body action and posture coding system

Development and functions

The body action and posture coding system (BAP) (Dael et al., 2012) examines body movement at an anatomical level as different articulations of body parts; a form level, in direction and orientation of movement and a functional level as communication and self-regulation. It was developed using the Geneva Multimodal Emotion Portrayals (GMEP) corpus (Banziger and Scherer, 2010) and a set of emotional expressions rated as "recognisable and believable" (Dael et al., 2012, 101).

The study found patterns of body movement that were related to emotion in the GMEP corpus.

Blue jeans

Clothing cue

Usually close-fitting trousers of coarse twill, blue cotton cloth, worn to oppose the formality of dress slacks.

Usage

Debuting in the 1954 movie The Wild One, Marlon Brando's (1924–2004) blue jeans launched Levi's® as a medium of mass communication (see *Media*). Since The Wild One, Levi's have become a universal fashion statement of "independence," "rebellion" and "youthful" rejection of the formal business suit.

Media

Worn with boots in the 1955 movie Rebel Without a Cause, blue jeans reinforced the illusion that actor James Dean (1931–1955) had his feet solidly planted on the sidewalk (see *Antigravity sign*). Meanwhile, the rumpled fit of Dean's trousers sent a rebellious message in contrast to that of conformity suggested by gray-flannel business suits of the time. Blue jeans neither matched the gray corporate uniform of the day nor exhibited the formality of crisp creases worn in the boardroom.

Primatology

A curious sign emanates from Rebel's studio posters: James Dean conspicuously displays his derriere. He stands in the movie ad with his back turned and his hands thrust into his jeans' back pockets. If Dean were any other primate than a human, primatologists would say he was "presenting" his hindquarters. In monkeys and apes, presenting is a gesture of submission and sexual display (see *Submission*). The tiny red tag on the back of Levi's jeans is a feature designed to draw attention to a wearer's buttocks (see *Messaging feature*).

See also *Leg wear*.

Body adornment

Cloth

After its invention ca. 9,000 years ago: "Cloth would soon become an essential part of society, as clothing and as adornment expressing self-awareness and communicating variations in social rank. For good reason, poets and anthropologists alike have employed cloth as a metaphor for society, something woven of many threads into a social fabric that is ever in danger of unraveling or being torn" (Wilford, 1993, C1).

Wearable sign

1   The act of decorating the human frame to accent its grace, strength, beauty and presence, or to mask its less attractive features and traits.
2   Visually distinctive patterns of body piercing, dress, scarification and tattoos worn to express a personal, social, ethnic, military or national identity.

Bracelets

"Bracelets have nearly always been worn by females and it has been suggested that the custom originated as a way of exaggerating the gender signal of the slender feminine arm, the fine bracelets emphasizing the thinness of the arm diameter inside them" (Morris, 1985, 144).

Usage

What we place upon our bodies – arm wear, footwear, hats, makeup and tattoos – adds color, contrast, shape, size and texture to the basic primate form. Each day, myriad messages of adornment broadcast personal information in a continuous way, as "frozen" gestures, about one's ethnicity, status, affiliation and moods. "Social rank . . . has probably always been encoded through symbols in the material, design, color, and embellishment of the clothing" (Barber, 1994, 150).

Anatomy

Before pants, skirts and shoes, there was the unadorned primate body itself: eyes, teeth, skin, hair and nails, along with shapes formed of muscle, fat and bone. With the advent of clothing and shoes, the body's nonverbal vocabulary grew as shoulders "widened," ankles "thinned" and feet stood up on tiptoes (see *High heel*). As optical illusions, stripes, colors, buttons and bows accented or concealed natural signs and drew attention to favored – while diverting eyes from less favorable – body parts.

Fur and hair

As primates, we are also mammals for most of whom a dense mat of fur is an evolutionary birthright. Anthropologists do not know when or why humans lost their bodily hair, but it is clear that clothing originated as a "fur substitute" to cover the skin and genitalia.

Leather

Full-body dress originated in Africa or Eurasia to protect the body and keep it warm. The first clothes were made of prepared animal hides. Stone scraping tools from Neanderthal sites in Europe provide indirect evidence for hide preparation, suggesting that cold-weather clothing could be at least 200,000 years old (Lambert and the Diagram Group, 1987).

Flounce and weave

Unwoven skirts and shawls made of flounces of tufted wool or flax were worn by the ancient Sumerians 5,000 years ago (Rowland-Warne, 1992), although one of the earliest known textiles – a linen-knit bag from Israel found in the Nahal Hemar cave site, is thought to be 8,500 years old (Barber, 1994).

Fiber and fabric

More recently, the invention of the flying shuttle (1733), the spinning jenny (1764) and the 19th-century power-loom made cotton fabrics available in ever greater quantities as consumer products. Mass-produced clothing debuted in 1851 with the invention of the sewing machine and increased in production with the use of synthetic fibers (e.g., Orlon in 1952). As adornment media became subject to greater control, the diversity and number of clothing cues burgeoned (see *Messaging feature*).

Neuro-note

To the very visual primate brain, fashion statements are "real" because neurologically, "seeing is believing."

See also *Blue jeans, Business suit, Neckwear, Tattoo*.

Figure B.2 Body orientation

Body orientation

Nonverbal presence

When engaged in conversation, direct body orientation can create a strong sense of presence and immediacy (Palmer and Simmons, 1995; Barak et al., 1982). Forward leaning may be interpreted as a signal of interest (Coker and Burgoon, 1987). On the other hand, backward lean, facing away from the speaker or indirect body orientation may signal a reluctance to engage (Burgoon and Koper, 1984).

Body orientation can also change with unwanted proximity. Direct body orientation will change to indirect body orientation, and conversely, as a participant moves away, orientation becomes more direct again (Remland et al., 1995). In courtship, direct body orientation may signal interest (Givens, 2005). Direct orientation has also been connected to messages of dominance and success (Weisfeld and Beresford, 1982).

See also *Immediacy*.

Boot

Clothing cue

A usually heavy, protective covering for the foot, made of leather, rubber or vinyl. A conspicuous sign of authority and power designed to accent the foot's ability to stomp.

Usage

Nonverbally, boots suggest strength by adding stature (i.e., increasing a wearer's vertical standing height; see *Loom*) and stability (i.e., giving steadiness to stance; see *Antigravity sign*). For these reasons, police and soldiers often wear them as part of a uniform.

Anatomy

Boots enable a powerful gait and commanding stance. The boot shaft's snug contact with pressure-sensitive Pacinian corpuscles of the lower leg provides tactile reassurance while supporting the long tendons that drop into the feet from muscles above. Boots also stabilize the ankle joint.

Evolution

Boots evolved from leather sandals, as straps grew longer and thicker to support a human's congenitally weak ankles. Sandals reaching above the ankle (the oldest status symbol for feet yet discovered) were worn exclusively by Roman army officers. Gradually, the leather pieces widened until they enclosed the entire foot.

Media

By popularizing thick, buckled motorcycle boots, Marlon Brando (The Wild One, 1954) and Peter Fonda (Easy Rider, 1969) furthered the role of footwear as a fashion statement designed to figuratively "stomp" the establishment's powers-that-be.

Stomp

Blind and deaf-born children may stamp their feet in anger (Eibl-Eibesfeldt, 1971). "In man, stamping the feet in anger seems also to be a ritualized attack movement" (Eibl-Eibesfeldt, 1970, 96).

See also *Goose-step*.

Figure B.3 Bow

Bow

Bowing and dominance

It is argued that bowing in humans is akin to bowing in apes because of the similarities in context and gesture. As such, it falls within animal studies which examine body reduction (e.g., Keltner and Buswell, 1997). Such studies examine gestures of appeasement and dominance, with, for example, subordinate chimpanzees greeting more dominant ones by bowing their upper body (de Waal, 1989b).

Bowing and head movements

In their work on the meaning of "bowed" heads, Mignault and Chaudhuri (2003) conclude that "a bowed head connotes submission, inferiority emotions, sadness, joy in women, and an illusory smile" (Mignault and Chaudhuri, 2003, 128). de Meijer (1989) argues that bowing the head is also a predictor of fear, grief, shame and anger. For example, the Chinese expression "di tou ren zui" means to bow one's head when admitting to a wrongdoing and is used in the context of shameful admissions.

Bowing and culture

Culturally, bowing which involves bending the trunk and head is associated with traditional greetings in Asian cultures. Such bowing is undertaken to show respect for a high-status individual. Longer and lower bows are displayed for individuals who are highly respected. Sometimes such bowing is accompanied by bringing the hands together in front of the torso. In many instances, in East-Asian cultures, greetings which involve bowing are preferred over handshakes.

Posture

To bend, curl or curve the upper body and head forward.

Usage

Around the world, people bow to greet, to defer, to show courtesy and to pray. In some cultures, the bow is a formal gesture, as in Japan, for example, where people are judged by their bows. A casual hello to Japanese colleagues is a quick bend to a 15-degree angle; a respectful greeting to customers or superiors is a 30-degree bow; a formal apology involves a quick bend to a 45-degree angle, held to a count of three, with a slow return to upright posture.

Anatomy

Bowing the trunk forward starts with flexor muscles of the stomach's *Recti abdominis*, assisted by the backbone's *Erector spinae*. These muscle groups are supplied directly by spinal nerves rather than by more evolved nerve plexuses. The bow's submissive tone stems from the role these muscles and nerves originally played in curling the head and trunk forward into a protective crouch posture (see *Crouch*).

Culture. **1.** In Japan, the forwardness of one's bow reflects status; for example, those higher in status bow less deeply to those lower. It is considered bad form for westerners to bow too deeply to lower-status Japanese. **2.** Among the Mossi of Burkina Faso, the most servile gesture is the *poussi-poussi*. "To poussi-poussi, Collett [1983] explains, one takes off shoes and headgear (which add height), sits with the legs 'tucked to one side,' lowers the body, and beats on the ground. (Historically, men also threw dust on their heads.)" (Givens, 1983, 155). **3.** "In the Muslim world, the *body kowtow* – in which one kneels down and touches the ground with the forehead – is used in prayer to show humility before the deity (Morris, 1994, 11).

Antonym: *High-stand display*. See also *Body wall*.

Branch substitute

Artifact

Any of numerous and diverse consumer products (e.g., baseball bats, clothing irons and tennis rackets) designed to be held tightly in a power grip.

Usage I

Because the human hand was originally designed for climbing, we may find primal pleasure in gripping a handrail, steering wheel or golf club. Holding a hammer, for example, satisfies our inner primate's need to reach out and grasp, much as our ancestors once reached out to grasp tree limbs.

Usage II

Swinging a bat stimulates tactile nerve endings to refocus orienting attention inward, toward the grasping palm itself and away from potentially stressful future events "out there" in the wider world (e.g., tomorrow's dental appointment; see *Orienting reflex*). Thus, the power grip exerts calming effects through the physiological principle of shiatsu or acupressure massage, in the manner of anxiety-reducing worry beads, worry stones and stress balls (see *Self-touch*). Since the forebrain's thalamus cannot process all incoming signals at once, grasping a cylindrical object, smoothened shaft or other branch-substitute may reduce anxiety and block pain.

See also *Object fancy*, *Touch cue*.

Broadside display

Power cue

The act of enlarging or exaggerating the body's size to dominate, threaten or bluff an opponent.

Usage

To appear physically powerful, humans and other vertebrates display expanded silhouettes to loom larger than they truly are.

Pisces power

Early fishes may have turned the widest parts of their bodies toward rivals, as modern cichlid, puffer and cod fish do today.

Chameleon clout

Following pisces, amphibians (e.g., frogs) puff up fraudulently – or deceptively deflate, as the situation warrants – to threaten or yield. Of the toad, Porter states, "It will inflate its body with air, making itself appear much larger, or it will bow its head forward, thus forming its body into a crouched ball" (1967, 40).

Saurian size

Lizards stiffen all four legs in aggressive high-stand displays. Even limbless snakes may appear "bigger" or "smaller" through illusions of size. To threaten, the hognose snake, for example, rises vertically, widens its head like a cobra, thrusts its body forward and makes loud hissing noises (Porter, 1967).

Mammalian mass

Cats, dogs and other fur-bearing animals may enlarge with "big hair" (see *Hair cue*). Like fish and lizards, cattle turn a broadside when threatened to show a fearsome angle.

Primate punch

Our higher-primate relatives show dominance by straightening and holding their arms away from the body or submission by bending and pulling the arms into their sides. Mountain gorillas beat upon broadened chests as body hair stands on end.

Human hubris

A fashionable broadside display is tailored into every Brooks Brothers jacket (see *Business suit*).

Antonym: *Crouch*; see also *Loom*, *Swagger walk*.

Business suit

Chest display

A coat and matching pants or skirt designed to downplay personal identity and showcase upper-body strength. A tailored garment worn to suggest high status and power in business, government and military affairs.

Usage

Strength cues from the broadside display are tailored into every Brooks Brothers® suit. A coat's squared shoulders exaggerate the size and "strength" of an "expanded" upright torso. Dropped to fingertip level, the jacket's hemline visually enlarges the upper body to pongid proportions. Flaring upward and outward, lapels enhance the illusion of pectoral strength. Pads and epaulets cover inadvertent shrugs and slips of the shoulder blades to mask feelings of submission or uncertainty – in the boardroom or on the battlefield (see *Shoulder shrug*).

Evolution

Through a process of consumer product selection, business suits have become power uniforms. As a fashion statement, the broadside display may first have appeared in animal-hide clothing of the Neanderthals, ca. 200,000 years ago. The first solid evidence for the display, however, appears in the Roman toga. As early as 200 B.C., men in tunics draped wool or linen toga-cloths over their left shoulders to make the upper body look "thicker" and more formidable than when dressed in a tunic alone.

History

From togas to doublets (1300s), to shortcoats (1600s), court coats (1700s) and sport coats (1990s), clothing enabled men to seem "bigger" to present "larger" versions of themselves in public.

See also *Neckwear*.

Button

Clothing cue

A small, often rounded, wafer–thin artifact of plastic, metal, shell or wood sewn to a pliable material such as fabric, leather or vinyl. Buttons are often sewn on teddy bear faces as illusory "eyes." So nonverbally expressive are buttons that millions worldwide collect them (see *Collection*).

Usage

Most of today's buttons are used as fasteners to attach one piece of fabric to another through a specially stitched buttonhole. Nonverbally, the arrangement, color, shape, sheen, size and texture of buttons may be used to make fashion statements.

Form and function

While philosophers debate maxims of "form follows function" (FFF), the nonverbal communication of buttons reveals that function may also follow form. Buttons originated in ancient times as decorations (form) and later evolved as fasteners (function).

Eye spots

The size and Gestalt roundness of buttons address our primate sensitivity for eyes and eye spots (see *Eye contact*). Though small in size, their nonverbal impact may be quite large.

See also *Zipper*.

C

Candy cue

Fruit substitute

1 A rich confection, such as a strawberry sucker or chocolate mint, designed to communicate with human taste buds for sweetness and, secondarily, with receptors for sour, bitter and/or salty tastes (see *Taste cue*).

2 A food product designed to mimic the sweet taste of ripened fruit.

Usage

M&Ms®, Snickers® and Reese's Peanut Butter Cups® are among the best-selling U.S. candy products. Unlike marshmallows, which are merely soft, the above candies have crunchy textures that human primates find pleasing (see *Existential crunch*). Each sweet successfully combines fruitiness with nuttiness in a proven evolutionary formula for primates (see *Nutty taste*).

M&Ms

Colorful, nut-sized M&Ms are among the most popular fruit substitutes of all time. Their crisp candy coatings encase milk chocolate mixed with finely ground peanut powder. On average, U.S. citizens swallow ca. 11,000 M&Ms in a lifetime (Heyman, 1992), liking orange-colored M&Ms least. (N.B.: The primate brain decodes orange as a warning or aposematic coloration sign associated with poisonous snakes, insects and berries.)

See also *Coca-Cola*®.

Communication of Affect Receiving Ability Test

Designed by Buck (1976), the Communication of Affect Receiving Ability Test (CARAT) was created to test people's abilities to decode affect in others. It uses dynamic film clips of spontaneous nonverbal behaviors which are captured in a slide viewing technique. The slide viewing technique involves a "sender." The sender views emotionally loaded color images while seated alone. Examples of images include familiar people, unfamiliar people, unpleasant scenes, scenic scenes, sexual scenes and unusual scenes. Their spontaneous facial/gestural expressions in response to these images are filmed by an "unobtrusive" camera. On signal, the sender describes his/her emotional responses to each image. The slide is then removed, and the sender also rates their emotional response to the slide. Examples of emotional responses include sadness, happiness, disgust. "Receivers" look at the senders' facial expressions and guess what kind of image is presented on each clip. They judge the type of slide the sender viewed and also judge the sender's emotional response to the slide. These judgments are then compared to the actual slide viewed by the sender and the sender's self-rating of their emotional response to the slide.

The original CARAT test had 32 film clips (with each clip being 20 seconds long). These film clips were recorded in a 1.5-inch reel-to-reel videotaped recorder and were in black and white. The 32 clips for the test were chosen using item analysis techniques from an original collection of 600 clips which involved 40 senders viewing 15 emotionally loaded images.

See *CARAT-05*, *CARAT-SPR*.

CARAT-05

The original CARAT (Buck, 1976) was further developed by Buck et al. (2005) by continuing with the basic principles of the CARAT but by upgrading the film clips used. This was achieved by using digitized color Super-VHS clips. These clips were assembled from 680 video clips of 33 male and 35 female responses to 10 emotionally loaded color images.

Communication of Affect Receiving Ability Test – Spontaneous, Posed, Regulated

Introduction

Created by Buck et al. (2017) the Communication of Affect Receiving Ability Test – Spontaneous, Posed, Regulated (CARAT-SPR) measures human abilities to detect emotion from spontaneous displays. It also examines spontaneous, posed and regulated displays. It builds on previous versions of the CARAT (Buck, 1976) using digital recording from the outset. A total of 1,660 spontaneous, 160 posed and 128 regulated film clips were assembled.

Testing displays

The test examines three types of display.

Spontaneous displays which are "natural responses to emotional images" (Buck et al., 2017, 1)

1   Posed displays where the sender is asked to display "as if" responding to an image when no image is in fact present.
2   Regulated displays where the sender is asked to display "as if" responding to an image when an image of opposite valence is in fact present.

Accuracy scores

The test produces two accuracy scores within two domains:

1   Emotion communication accuracy. Here the participant (receiver) is tested as to their ability to accurately "detect" whether a sender (see *CARAT*) viewed a neutral, unpleasant or familiar image.

2   Expression categorization ability. Here the participant (receiver) is tested as to their ability to accurately judge whether an expression in a film clip was spontaneous, posed or regulated.

Certainty

Emotion

The inner, intuitive feeling that an observation, statement or proposition is correct, factual and true.

Bodily expression

Certainty may be evident in nonverbal cues suggestive of poise, assurance and self-confidence. Examples are chin-up (see *Head-tilt-back*), pronated hand gestures (see *Palm-down*) and squared-shoulders (see *Broadside display*). Note that such signs precisely oppose those for emotional uncertainty (see *Head-tilt-down*, *Palm-up* and *Shoulder-shrug*), supporting Charles Darwin's (1872) expressive principle of antithesis (see *Antithesis*).

Antonym: *Uncertainty*.

Chair

Consumer product

1   Typically, a piece of furniture with a horizontal seat, quadrupedal legs, an upright back and horizontal arms, designed to be occupied by a single person.
2   Perhaps *Homo sapiens'* most diversely styled furniture item.
3   Through their nonverbal decorations and design features, chairs have a great deal to "say."

Usage

Sitting is the preferred posture of primates, including humans. Office workers spend the majority of their working days seated in ergonomic swivel chairs.

Psychology

Inviting someone to "please sit down" reduces an opponent's standing height and diminishes effects of the high-stand (see *High-stand display*). Through the nonverbal principle of isopraxism, the arms, legs, back and seat of a chair suggest sitting down because the chair itself appears to be seated (see *Isopraxism*). On the bottom of chair legs, paws and hooves may suggest that a seated occupant has animal powers.

Throne

A throne is a decorative, ceremonial chair, usually of greater size to reflect the power of emperors, queens and religious leaders. Thrones may rest on stepped platforms to suggest that the leader is on a higher plain (see *Loom*).

Toilet seat

"The Posture Mold® seat designed by architect Alexander Kira is contoured and provides proper support for the thighs. This seat was selected for the design study collection of the Museum of Modern Art showing that good human factors can be aesthetically as well as functionally attractive" (Kantowitz and Sorkin, 1983, 482; see *Ergonomics of the mind*).

Figure C.1 Chest-beating

Chest-beating

Human chest-beating

1   A usually male nonverbal display in which one rhythmically strikes the upper torso firmly with the palmar surface(s) of open or fisted hand(s).
2   To beat upon one's own chest in a celebratory moment of triumph or victory in competition or sport.
3   Chest-beating is often accompanied by a widely opened mouth and vocal roaring.
4   The display draws attention as a nonverbal interjection of presence, viz., that "I am here!"

Gorilla chest-beating

Males of the mountain gorilla (*Gorilla gorilla berengei*) may use two cupped palms to chest-beat in a strident audio-visual display. Dominant silverbacks use chest-beating signs to attract female attention in courtship, beckon others to follow, celebrate victory in fighting and threaten rival males.

See also *Triumph display*.

Figure C.2 Chirality

Chirality

Right or left twist

Nonverbal communication often exhibits basic binary oppositions, such as yes/no, big/small and right/left. Chirality is a nonverbal sign that rotates or twists in a clockwise or counterclockwise direction.

Usage

Chiral body movements may be used to send diverse messages about, for example, negation (see *Head-shake*), certainty (see *Palm-down*) and uncertainty (see *Palm-up*).

Anatomy

Chirality is ubiquitous in physics, chemistry and biology. In communication, a right-hand-twist gesture may or may not contrast meaningfully with a left-hand-twist but will reflect the movement's anatomical bone structure. A right palm-up involves a chiral forearm-twist-right, while a right palm-down involves a twist left (see *Palm-up, Palm-down*).

Aroma and taste cues

Chiral aroma and gustatory molecules, and their mirror-image counterparts, may be distinctively decoded as separable sensations by the nose and tongue. Right-twisting carvone, for example, a terpenoid ingredient of caraway seeds (as in rye bread), smells distinctively different than its mirror image left-twisting carvone, an ingredient of spearmint (as in mint jelly; see *Herbs* and *Spices*).

See also *Handedness*.

Cingulate gyrus

Mammalian brain

1   The evolutionary new wing of the brain, in charge of grooming, nuzzling and cuddle cues.
2   The newest part of the limbic system, responsible for maternal caring, play and audiovocal signals.

Usage

As the brain's maternal and childcare center, the cingulate gyrus mediates many of the nonverbal cues we give to babies, small children and adults for whom we care (see *Love signal*).

Anatomy

Located on the medial surface of the cerebral cortex – in the frontal and parietal lobes (above the corpus callosum) – the cingulate gyrus receives subcortical signals from the thalamus (anterior nucleus) and cortical signals from modules of the cerebral cortex as well. "We cannot mimic easily what the anterior cingulate can achieve effortlessly" (Damasio, 1994, 141–142).

Neuro-notes

UCLA Psychologist Naomi Eisenberger found similarities between social pain (e.g., hurt feelings and being snubbed) and physical pain (being kicked in the stomach). She also found connections to the visceral brain (Eisenberger and Lieberman, 2004; see *Enteric brain*).

See also *Hypothalamus*.

CLEM

Gaze direction

1   An acronym for "conjugate lateral eye movement."
2   A nonverbal response, often to a verbal question, in which the eyes move sideward in tandem to the right or left.

Usage

CLEMs may signal information processing, reflection and thought. Because they reflect unvoiced doubt, as well, CLEMs may be used in interviews to probe (*Probing point*).

Creativity

In the classic study by Harnad (1972) of lateral eye movements of mathematicians during mental reflection, it was noted that rightward movement associated well with symbolic thinking, while leftward movement associated with visual thinking. Left-movers were thought to be more creative.

Research reports

Conjugate lateral eye movements are an index of brain-hemispheric activation (Gur, 1975). "People can be categorized as either 'right lookers' or 'left lookers' because approximately 75 percent of an individual's conjugate lateral eye movements are in one direction" (Richmond et al., 1991, 89).

Cognitive processing

Putting aside the issue of eye movements as signs of creativity, researchers continue to find that such movements are correlated with cognitive thought processes.

See also *Gaze-down*.

Clever Hans

In 1900, a man called Wilhelm von Osten purchased a horse called Hans in Berlin. When Von Osten was training his horse, he taught him to count by tapping his front hoof! Hans proved to be fantastic at counting. He was a fast learner. He also learned to add, subtract, multiply and divide and even moved on to solving problems involving fractions and factors! Needless to say, Hans couldn't talk, so the only way he could communicate his answer was by tapping his hoof. He could tell the time and use a calendar, and when Von Osten taught Hans an alphabet that could be coded into hoof beats, he began to use the German language. He could answer almost any question – either oral or written. It seemed he had an intelligence which was beyond the human mind.

And so Hans was brought to public audiences where he displayed this profound and unusual ability. People were agog. Needless to say, the world's media became aware of Clever Hans, and an investigating committee was established. Professors of psychology and physiology, veterinarians, the Director of Berlin Zoological Gardens and a number of others formed this committee to unlock the magical talents of Hans. Of course, they also wanted to unravel the gimmick at play. The committee decided they would set up an experiment with Hans, and as part of this experiment, Von Osten, his owner, was deliberately excluded. Now with Von Osten absent, how would Clever Hans perform? To everyone's amazement, Hans, once again astounded the intelligentsia with his answers. The committee announced there was no trickery involved. Hans was a sensation.

However, a second commission was established, this time with a new and very clever experiment in mind. Von Osten was asked to whisper one number into Hans' left ear while an experimenter whispered a number into his right ear. Hans was asked to add the two numbers. Neither the experimenter, Von Osten or the assembled crowd knew the answer in advance. Hans looked at the assembled crowd but tapped out the wrong answer. This marked the end for the celebrity status of Hans. More tests of a similar nature ensued and Hans continued to fail. Hans could only tap the answer when someone in his visual field knew the answer and was attentive to the situation. It emerged that Hans could detect human head movements as slight as one-fifth of a millimeter. Head movements accompanied by reduced body tension and a more relaxed disposition changed when Hans reached the correct number of taps. Put simply, he was able to read the body language of the crowd as a signal to stop when he reached the correct number of hoof taps.

Coca-Cola®

Drinkable sign

1   A sweet-tasting juice substitute with complex flavors and a carbonated "texture" that appeals to millions of consumers throughout the world.
2   A hand-held consumer product with an incredible presence in the media.
3   A usually refreshing beverage that encodes vast chemical information and has a great deal to "say."

Usage

As a nonverbal medium, Coca-Cola "speaks" through aroma, taste and touch channels. To the palate, for example, cola communicates with complex flavor molecules found in ripe fruit and broiled steak. Bubbly carbonation provides an interesting pseudo-texture to stimulate the tongue (see *Existential crunch*). In tandem with the sugary taste of sucrose (a crystalline carbohydrate suggesting the fruity sweetness of fructose, for which it stands) – and adept advertising (see *Media*) – its chemical messages have made Coca-Cola one of the most recognized brand names on earth.

Research reports

The carbohydrate sucrose ($C_{12}H_{22}O_{11}$) has a calming effect on infants. In concentrated amounts, it stimulates the release of natural opium-like substances (opioids) that can reduce pain and pacify crying (Blass, 1992). The alkaloid caffeine ($C_8H_{10}N_4O_2$) is a mild stimulant used to release norepinephrine into the brain (Restak, 1994; see *Pleasure cue*). That we crave sugar instinctively is suggested by babies who are born without a cerebral cortex and who respond to sweet but reject bitter tastes.

Evolution

A cola's sugary taste reconnects to our fruit-eating primate past. When Eocene primate ancestors took to the trees ca. 50 mya, they supplemented a basically insect diet with ripened fruit. Drinking a Coke, we are briefly absorbed in the primate's sense of the present moment.

See also *Candy cue*.

Cognitive valence theory

What is it?

Advanced by Andersen in 1985, cognitive-valence theory is a framework which examines intimate behaviors within dyad interactions. It uses both verbal and non-verbal criteria to examine behaviors. Changes in intimacy or immediacy behaviors in a relationship can prompt arousal changes which can have a valence value. Where the changes in behavior precipitate little or no change in arousal, then no behavioral adjustment occurs. On the other hand, if the partner's behavior causes a large increase or decrease in arousal, then negative behavior which seeks to compensate (as opposed to reciprocate) occurs.

Valence factors

When the arousal change is in the moderate category, six types of valence factors come into operation: (1) culture, (2) individual predispositions, (3) interpersonal evaluations, (4) relational expectations, (5) situational features and (6) transitory states. In these contexts, if any one of the aforementioned valence factors is negative, then the overall valence will be negative, and compensatory behaviors ensue. However, if all six factors are positive and if the arousal is of a moderate nature, the ensuing behavior of reciprocation occurs.

Collection

Alike like

Collections may encode nonverbal information germane to a collector's aesthetic sense, mental outlook and overall worldview. A collection is an assortment of artifacts, objects, plants or animals – for example, coins, rocks, meteorites, orchids and house cats – that have special meaning to an owner.

Usage

Displayed in homes, offices and museums, collections provide information about a collector's mindset and inner emotional state. The mindset of a gun collector, for example, may differ from that of one who collects dolls. A Faberge egg collector may have an artistic sensitivity, while a sword collector may have a more military frame of mind. Postcard, nutcracker and Depression glass collections may be considered "ordinary," while collections of naval lint, Pez dispensers and aluminum can tabs may be thought "unusual" and indicative of eccentricity.

Physical state

Collectors may prefer mint-condition, pristine items over those that are chipped, scarred, tattered, used or otherwise worn. The penchant for preservation over decay may be a property of the nonverbal brain's gestalt principle of closure, that is, to see complete – rather than incomplete – figures or forms.

See also *Barbie doll*.

Color cue

Light signal

A material substance such as a dye, ochre, paint, pigment, stain, tarnish, tincture, tinge, tint or wash that transmits a message about hue.

Usage

Color cues transmit information about emotions, feelings and moods. In fashion, wearing the same color suggests a social tie, such as shared membership in a club, gang, pack, school, sorority, team or tribe. States mark their national identities with colorful dyes affixed to banners, crests, flags and seals. Color plays a special role in **courtship**. It is estimated that about 10 million colors exist. According to Sharpe (1975), the normal human eye is capable of discriminating approximately 7 million different colors. Numerous research projects have found that red, yellow and orange are associated with excitement, stimulation and aggression. On the other hand, blue and green are associated with calmness, security and peace, while black, brown and grey are associated with melancholy and sadness. Yellow is connected with cheer, gaiety and fun, and, finally, purple is associated with dignity, royalty and sadness (Sharpe, 1975, 55). In short, people associate serenity and calm with the colors blue and green. On the other hand, red and orange are seen to be arousing and stimulating (Ball, 1965). Indeed, it would appear that any color which is bright is likely to be more stimulating and to get more attention than paler colors (Knapp and Hall, 2006).

Light and dark

Before color cues, light-sensitive eye spots perceived black and white. Photons striking a light-sensitive opsin protein in an eye spot triggered electrochemical signals addressed to the nervous system. Opsins are found in all life forms (for example, in algae, fungi, bacteria, jellyfish and vertebrates).

Research

1   We respond differently to color according to our age. Mahnke (1996) points out that children's acceptance or rejection of certain colors mirrors their own development. Perhaps one of the largest studies in this area was conducted by Heinrich Frieling (1957) of the Institute of Colour Psychology. He tested 10,000 children and young people from ages 5 to 19 years, from all corners of the world, in an effort to establish which colors are best suited to different age groups. While the work produced lengthy statistics and analyses, we can summarize the findings generally as follows:

   a   In the age group 5–8 years, black, grey, white and dark brown are rejected, while red, orange, yellow and violet are preferred.
   b   In the age group 9–10 years, grey, dark brown, black, pastel green and blue are rejected, with red, red-orange and green-blue being preferred.
   c   In the age group 11–12 years, black, white, grey, olive, violet and lilac were rejected.

   d   In the age group 13–14 years, the preferred colors were blue, ultramarine and orange.

2   In a study involving 21,060 participants, Eysenck (1981) found surprising consistency in the rank order of human adult's color preferences. These preferences covered gender and ethnicity, with the preferred color being blue, followed in order of preference by red, green, purple, orange and yellow.

3   Research suggests that colors which are "cool," such as blues and greens, have calming effects on humans, while colors which are warm, such as red, orange and yellow, produce an arousing effect (Davidoff, 1991).

4   Some of the great artists, such as Gauguin or Van Gogh, talked of using color to convey emotion and mood. Deborah Sharpe (1975, x) argues that "colour responses are more tied to man's emotions than to his intellect. In general people do not respond to colour with their minds." Using Freudian psychology to explain how we respond to color, Sharpe makes the point that color responses are normally under the control of the ego. They are controlled by the "self-preserving, socialised and conscience controlled energy system of the human" (Sharpe, 1975, xi).

4   Visible blue light is used in the treatment of infant jaundice (Mahnke, 1996).

5   Ultra-violet light is used to cleanse bacteria in operating theatres. Research by Escombe et al. (2009) also indicates that it can have significant value in approaches to preventing the transmission of tuberculosis.

Colors decoded

Introduction

Color cues may encode information about human emotions, feelings and moods. The decoded moods and symbolism of primary colors such as red, blue and yellow are succinctly summarized by Virginia Richmond and her colleagues (Richmond et al., 1991).

Black

Black is an achromatic color without hue. In the visible spectrum, it is the absorption of all colors. Prehistoric use of black pigments may be seen in France's Lascaux Cave, as charcoal outlines of bulls and other animals were made by *Homo sapiens* 18,000 to 17,000 years ago. Historically, ancient Egyptians considered black the color of Anubis, god of the underworld, who took the form of a black jackal.

Recognized moods for black include sad, intense, anxiety, fear, despondent, dejected, melancholy and unhappy; symbolic meanings include darkness, power, mastery, protection, decay, mystery, wisdom, death and atonement (Richmond et al., 1991).

Psychology. Our aversion to the sight of black may be innate (Thorndike, 1940).

Media. Black is used in movie titles more than any other color. Films such as Black Fury (1935), The Black Hand (1950) and Black Robe (1991) feature death and the darker meanings of black.

Blue

Blue is a shorter-waved hue than red. While the latter seems to advance and expand in size, the former seems to recede and diminish. Traditionally associated with the sea and sky, blue is a typically favored color. Identified moods include cool, pleasant, leisurely, distant, infinite, secure, transcendent, calm and tender; symbolic meanings include dignity, sadness, tenderness and truth (Richmond et al., 1991).

Media. Motion pictures such as Blue Hawaii (1962) and Blue Lagoon (1980) feature feelings of leisure and coolness associated with the color blue.

Picasso. In the Spanish artist Pablo Picasso's Blue Period (1901–04), his paintings featured somber blue and blue-green hues, likely reflecting his sorrow and psychological depression at the time.

Brown

The muted, composite color of brown is considered an earth tone; it may be a universal sign for the ground we stand on, its humus, soil and sod. The interior of human homes is often decorated in brownish earth tones, which are comforting, as they seem to bring the natural world indoors.

Brown's acknowledged moods include sad, not tender, despondent, dejected, melancholy, unhappy and neutral; symbolic meanings include melancholy, protection, autumn, decay, humility and atonement (Richmond et al., 1991).

Media. Brown is rarely used in movie titles.

Green

A priest clad in a white robe climbs the tree and with a golden sickle cuts the mistletoe, which is caught in a white cloth – Frazer (The Golden Bough, 1890, Vol. 2, 286).

Green is in the middle of the light spectrum, between yellow and blue. Its restful hue is likely a universal sign of verdant, natural greenery. In prehistoric times, mistletoe's green hue was worshipped. As Frazer noted in The Golden Bough, "From time immemorial, the mistletoe has been an object of superstitious veneration in Europe" (Frazer, 1890, 674). Its color and medicinal and sacred properties were especially esteemed by the early Druids.

Moods and meanings. Recognized moods include cool, pleasant, leisurely and in control; symbolic meanings include security, peace, jealousy, hate, aggressiveness and calm (Richmond et al., 1991).

Architecture. "Black Friars Bridge in London with its extensive black iron work was well known for its frequent suicides. When the city fathers painted it bright green, they were surprised to discover that suicides declined by more than one third" (Vargas, 1986, 153).

Consumer products. Bright green strongly attracts our attention and is used worldwide in traffic lights (as a sign for "Go"), under the first and last steps of escalators and in rented bowling shoes.

Media. Dramatic motion pictures such as Green Pastures (1936) and The Green Promise (1949) feature pastoral meanings of green and greenness.

Indigo

The color indigo gets its name from indigo dye, which is obtained from the plant *Indigofera tinctoria*. The color is close to the color blue and sometimes the color ultramarine. By comparison to blue, it is sometimes termed more sedentary (Logan-Clarke and Appleby, 2009). Indigo is located on the electromagnetic spectrum in the range 420 to 450 nanometers.

Sometimes described as the "colour that seduced the world, the colour indigo has for millennia been a very valued pigment" (McKinley, 2011, 1). In the middle ages, it was described by some Europeans as "blue gold." For color healers, the color indigo is associated with the forehead chakra and stands for intuition. This chakra is believed to influence the pineal gland (Mahnke, 1996, 35).

Consumer. Levi's jeans are frequently dyed in indigo.

Orange

"Orange is red brought nearer to humanity by yellow" – Wassily Kandinsky (1866–1944).

In the light spectrum, orange is the vibrant hue between red and yellow. Recognized moods include unpleasant, exciting, disturbed, distressed, upset, defiant, contrary, hostile and stimulating; symbolic meanings include sun, fruitfulness, harvest and thoughtfulness (Richmond et al., 1991).

Aviation. Commercial aircraft voice recorders known as "black boxes" are painted orange to be more visible to searching human eyes.

Interior design. "In another factory, employees were in the habit of standing around a drinking fountain and visiting. When the soft green walls of the area were repainted vivid orange, workers took a drink and left" (Vargas, 1986, 153).

Media. The 1971 film A Clockwork Orange features the disturbed, hostile meaning of orangeness.

Picasso. In the Spanish artist Pablo Picasso's Rose Period (1904–06), his paintings featured cheerful orange and pink hues, likely reflecting his romance with Fernande Olivier at the time.

Pink

"Psychologically, pink has been judged the 'sweetest' color" (Vargas, 1986, 144). Pink causes the hypothalamus to signal the adrenal glands to slow their secretions, thus reducing heart rate and blocking anger. Certain palettes of pink seem to be important in terms of their calming effects and the suppression of aggression. Studies reported by Pelligrini and Schauss (1980) and Schauss (1985) of people exposed to environments painted in "baker–miller" pink found that their heart rates, pulse and respiration decreased. These studies also found that pink aided the suppression of violent and aggressive behaviors in adult and juvenile correction centers, psychiatric hospitals and controlled laboratory studies. However, this is not always the case, and there are some exceptions. In a study undertaken in the county jail of San Jose in California, it was found that painting holding cells in the color shocking pink did not always have this calming effect. When prisoners were placed in these cells, they were calm for about 15 minutes, but then hostility began to increase, reaching a peak after 30 minutes.

Purple

Purple is the hue between red and blue. It has many variations, including mauve, pansy and mulberry. In ancient Roman times, Tyrian purple was a sign of royalty; derived from mollusks. Tyrian dye was too costly for common people to wear.

Acknowledged moods include depressed, sad, dignified and stately; symbolic meanings include wisdom, victory, pomp, wealth, humility and tragedy (Richmond et al., 1991).

Media. Films such as The Purple Heart (1944) and The Color Purple (1985) feature the tragic meaning of purple.

Red

Red is the longest-waved hue of the color spectrum. Traditionally associated with blood, red may be the most emotional of all primary colors. Identified moods include hot, affectionate, angry, defiant, contrary, hostile, full of vitality, excitement and love; symbolism includes happiness, lust, intimacy, love, restlessness, agitation, royalty, rage, sin and blood (Richmond et al., 1991).

Stimulation: "Knute Rockne tried to stimulate his [football] players by using a red-walled locker room, while the opponents were lulled in restful blue quarters" (Vargas, 1986, 152).

Media. Dramatic motion pictures such as The Red Badge of Courage (1951), Lady in Red (1979) and Reds (1981) feature, respectively, the hostile, sexual and political meanings of redness.

White

Acknowledged moods include joy, lightness, neutral and cold; symbolic meanings include solemnity, purity, chastity, femininity, humility, joy, light, innocence, fidelity and cowardice (Richmond et al., 1991).

Media. White is used in movie titles more than any color but black. Films such as White Mama (1980), White Hunter Black Heart (1990) and White Lie (1991) feature the darker racial meanings of whiteness.

Yellow

Yellow is a high-visibility hue. Black on yellow, the highest contrast known, is used worldwide on cautionary road signs and stoplights. As a color engineer noted, "Yellow Cabs are not as common as one may think. They simply stand out among other automobiles" (Vargas, 1986, 143). Identified moods include unpleasant, exciting, hostile, cheerful, joyful and jovial; symbolic meanings include superficial glamour, sun, light, wisdom, royalty (China), age (Greece), prostitution (Italy) and famine (Egypt) (Richmond et al., 1991).

Media. Motion pictures such as Yellow Submarine (1968) and Yellowbeard (1983) feature fanciful, light-hearted meanings of yellowness.

See also *Signal, Chinese lanterns.*

Combover

Hair cue

1   The historic, usually male practice of suggesting youth by covering hairless scalp areas on top of the head with hair from the scalp's back and sides. (N.B.: U.S. Patent 4,022,227 details a three-part methodology for sculpting the style; see *Consumer product*).

2   More recently, the masculine practice of wearing head hair noticeably longer on top, shorter on the back and sides and marked with a conspicuous lateral part.

Usage

1   In the historical sense, combovers have been used since Roman times (for example, by Julius Caesar) to make hair loss less visible than it otherwise might be (see *Invisibility*). Since hair enhances facial attractiveness and may be read as a youthful sign of virility, men often resist its loss in service to courtship (see *Love signal*).
2   In the more recent sense, combover-style manes attract notice and are similarly appealing in courtship.

Humorous hair

Viewers may judge conspicuous combovers for male pattern baldness as being somewhat sad or comical. Not only are combovers judged unattractive, but they also may reflect denial or borderline dishonesty (see *Deception cue*).

Trump hair

A case in point is the glowing yellow hue and gravity-defying shape of Donald J. Trump's combover, which seems to say, "See me – I am unique!" A key to decoding Trump hair may be found in the trademark mustache of surrealist artist Salvador Dali (1904–1989). Like the dramatic, curvilinear waxed hairs of Dali's upper lip, Trump's eye-catching combover makes a strong bid for attention. The meaning of both men's eccentric-hair displays is designed to announce a most wonderful presence: "ME."

   See also *Hair cue*.

Consumer product

Artifact

1   A material object deliberately fabricated for mass consumption and use (see *Artifact*).
2   An edible, wearable, drinkable (i.e., usable) commodity exhibiting a standard design (see *Design feature*).
3   An artifact bearing a brand name (see, e.g., *Big Mac*) promoted in the electronic and print media.

Usage

Like gestures, consumer products are informative, provocative and highly communicative. Shoes, hats and wristwatches, for example, have a great deal to "say" about gender, identity and status. The make, model and color of a new car may reflect a buyer's personal taste, individuality and moods.

Research report

The number of everyday artifacts encountered in our lives has been estimated to be between 20,000 and 30,000 manufactured objects (Petroski, 1992).

Neuro-notes

We eagerly covet, consume and collect material goods (see *Collection*), which beckon to us as "gestures" from billboards, catalogues and discount store shelves.

   See also *Object fancy*.

Contrapposto stance

Posture

1   A subtle or pronounced "twisting" pose of the human body suggestive of physical and psychic energy.
2   An energy-consuming deviation from standard anatomical position (SAP; see *Anatomical position*).

Usage

As it deviates from the body's relentless bilateral symmetry, a contrapposto posture may be used to present an attractive, energetic physical shape. As opposed to a static, flat-footed stance, the asymmetrical arrangement of body parts works to attract notice.

Anatomy

Contrapposto bodies seem to twist from head to legs to feet, even as they stand in place. The planes of the shoulders and hips, as well as those of the knees and feet, are held in a coordinated opposition that makes them more likely – and more lively – to behold.

Shoulders and hips

Placing a human's body weight fully on the right foot causes the right hip to raise and protrude and the right shoulder to dip. On the body's left side, the hip lowers, while the shoulder lifts. With its antithetical blend of limb extension, flexion and torsion, an otherwise frozen statue comes alive with movement and feeling (see Art cue subsequently).

Art cue

Contrapposto (Italian "counterpoise") has been used as an artistic device by painters and sculptors at least since 480 B.C. with the Greek statue Kritios Boy. Noteworthy later examples include the Roman Venus de Milo (ca. 100 B.C.) and Michelangelo's Statue of David (1504; see *Statue signs*).

Media

In 1949, a series of nude photographs of the soon-to-debut American actress Marilyn Monroe were taken, featuring her in supine, recumbent positions against red velvet (see *Velvet*) in pronounced contrapposto poses. One of the color photos – with knees sharply bent, hips twisted left and shoulders right – later appeared in the 1953 inaugural issue of Playboy magazine and on a 1955 wall calendar that has become the best-selling pin-up photo of all time (see *Reproductive imagery*).

See also *Nonverbal release*.

Costume

Identity signage

An often-coordinated ensemble of body adornment, clothing cues, footwear, hair cues and headwear (see *Hat*) that proclaim corporate membership, cultural identity, fantasy ideation, lifestyle or nationality.

Usage

Unlike spoken words that fade after utterance, costumes broadcast continuously through time. They may be worn to announce wearer identity at a glance.

Disguise

Costumes may be used deceptively in nonverbal signage to alter, mask or hide true identity.

Fantasy

Around the world, one may "dress up" in costumes to portray extinct animals (e.g., T-Rex), art objects (see *Statue*), historical figures (e.g., Cleopatra), mythical characters (fairies, leprechauns), objects (Helm of Darkness) and other idealized or mythological items or characters.

Everyday life

How we wear our hair and what we place upon our bodies on a daily basis may be considered our nonverbal costume, in service to what the American sociologist Erving Goffman's classic book, *The Presentation of Self in Everyday Life* (1959), persuasively chronicles.

See also *Parade*.

Courtship

Nonverbal negotiation

To send and receive messages in an attempt to seek someone's favor or love.

Usage 1

A significant measure of nonverbal communication is in service to courtship and reproduction (see *Reproductive force*). From gestures (e.g., shoulder-shrugs) to footwear (high heels) to clothing cues (puffy sleeves, cowl necks and prom dresses), nonverbal signs transmit information about sexuality.

Usage 2

In all cultures, human beings attain the closeness of sexual intimacy through courtship, an often slow negotiation based on exchanges of words and nonverbal cues. Vertebrates from reptiles to primates reproduce through mating – via fertilization of the female's body. In *Love Signals* (2005), anthropologist David Givens proposed that courtship advances in a series of five communicative phases: (1) attention, (2) recognition, (3) conversation, (4) touching and (5) lovemaking (see *Love signals I–V*).

Word origin

The English word "court" traces to the ancient Indo-European root *gher-*, "to grasp, enclose."

See also *Love signal*.

Crime signals

Red flags

Crime signals are nonverbal signs disclosing that someone has broken, or is about to break, the law. Like behavioral red flags (see *Verbalized nonverbal*), crime signals show that something bad is about to happen or already has. Criminals seldom verbalize their evil intentions beforehand. To the victim, treachery is more likely to be revealed in body movements and demeanor than in vocal comments. Research on chimpanzees thieving meat from peers indicates that theft as human beings know it has deep roots in animal psychology. The human grasping reflex may stimulate an urge to take, pick up and possibly steal.

Usage

Crime signals may be used protectively to prevent wrongdoing before it happens. In this sense, nonverbal cues may encode messages about otherwise hidden intentionality and emotion. Airport officials, for example, may be taught to watch for warning signs of anxiety, deception and ill intent as passengers move through terminal checkpoints (see *Deception cue*). A case in point is the U.S. Screening Passengers by Observation Techniques program (see *Spot*).

See also *Gangster garb*.

Cringe

Flight cue

A set of bodily, facial, postural, spatial and/or vocal signs that, in combination, signal a cowering, disliking, distasteful, fearful, guilty or servile state of mind.

Usage

We may cringe unconsciously to protect or remove our bodies from disliked people and their actions or words. Cringes may involve several body parts, such as the following:

Body movements

The upper body may suddenly recoil away, backward or to one side (see *Body bend*). One or both shoulders may lift (see *Shoulder-shrug*).

Facial expressions

One may squint and protectively lower the eyebrows (see *Eyebrow-lower*).

Posture

The body may bend forward (see *Bow*).

Voice quality

One may emit interjection-like, sudden vocalizations (see *Groan, Growl, Grunt* and *Sigh*).

Word origin

The English word cringe originates from Old English *cringan*, "to give way."
    See also *Freeze reaction*.

Crouch

Primeval posture

An originally protective body position of great age, in which the limbs bend and
the spinal column flexes forward to press the arms, legs and torso close to the
ground, as in cowering.

Canine crouch

In the dog: "Instead of walking upright, the body sinks downwards or even
crouches, and is thrown into flexuous movements; his tail, instead of being held
stiff and upright, is lowered and wagged from side to side; his hair instantly becomes
smooth; his ears are depressed and drawn backwards, but not closely to the head;
and his lips hang loosely" (Darwin, 1872, 56).

Paleontology I

The vertebrate crouch display is formed from ancient bending motions designed to
remove an animal from danger. A reflexive act controlled by the spinal cord, bending
the body moves it away from hazards, reduces its exposed surface area and makes it look
"smaller." Nonverbally, flexed body movements used to crouch lower to the ground
predate extension movements used to rise or lift above the terrestrial surface (see, e.g.,
High-stand display); thus, our remote ancestors crouched before they stood tall.

Paleontology II

Crouching can be traced to an avoider's response, which is tactile in origin rather
than visual as in the high-stand display. So primitive is the crouch posture's flexor
reflex that it exists even in immature fish and amphibian larvae. Stimulating the
skin of these simple creatures triggers side-to-side bending movements, which, in
a watery world, remove them from dangers
signaled by the touch.

Neuro-notes

The crouch is keyed to paleocircuits formed
of primitive, spinal-cord *interneurons* in
charge of tactile withdrawal.
    Antonym: *Antigravity display*.

Crying

Introduction

Crying is characteristically of a tonal nature,
involving the emission of voiced syllables,
typically in tandem with respiratory cycles.
It can have a harmonic quality but may also

Figure C.3 Crying

contain noisy segments (Lingle et al., 2012). It is estimated that the human makes between 15 and 30 gallons of tears each year.

Types of tears

There are three main types of tear:

1   Basal tears, which help lubricate, nourish and protect the cornea. They act as a type of barrier between the eye and the world, protecting it from items such as floating dirt.
2   Reflex tears are shed when the eye is trying to wash away irritants, for example, smoke or onion fumes.
3   Emotional tears are created as a result of an emotional state such as sadness or joy.

What are tears?

Tears are secreted from tear glands (lacrimal glands). They consist of salts, antibodies, antibacterial enzymes and water. Emotional tears may have a slightly different composition, with a higher concentration of stress hormones (e.g., leucine encephalin)

Human crying

The crying that is typically associated with humans has evolutionary roots (Provine et al., 2009). A number of studies indicate that, for many mammals, when an infant is separated from its mother, crying will ensue (Lingle et al., 2012; Provine, 2012a). Infants have a wide repertoire of crying sounds and at 2 years of age can use crying as a technique to get attention (Saarni, 1993). This matches with the argument that the function of tears is to kindle bonding and prompt assistance from others (Gračanin et al., 2018; Vingerhoets and Bylsma, 2016). Indeed, people who cry are perceived as friendlier, warmer and more helpless than those who don't cry (Stadel et al., 2019; Zickfeld et al., 2018).

Cue

Communication

A nonverbal sign used to prompt an event, behavior or experience. In psychology, a stimulus, consciously or unconsciously perceived, that elicits a type of behavior (for example, a soft touch may prompt a hug or a kiss).

Usage

Since nonverbal cues may suggest what might or could happen next, they often elicit a response (for example, a listener's shoulder-shrug reveals uncertainty, prompting the speaker to elaborate and further explain).

Figure C.4 Cut-off

Word origin

Cue is an ancient word derived from the 7,000-year-old Indo-European root word *kwo-*, for "who," "what," "when," "why," "where" and "how."

See also *Message, Signal.*

Cut-off

Body movement

A form of gaze avoidance in which one's head is turned fully away to the side.

Usage

In a conversation, a sudden cut-off gesture may indicate uncertainty or disagreement with a speaker. Sustained cut-off may reveal reluctance, shyness or disliking.

Shunning

Cut-off is a form of nonverbal shunning. To shun is "to avoid deliberately; keep away from" (Soukhanov, 1992, 1674). The English word comes from Old English *scunian*, to abhor.

Neuro-notes

The muscle that turns the head sideward – sternocleidomastoid – is controlled by the accessory nerve (cranial XI). As a special visceral nerve, accessory is emotionally responsive and automatically responds to stressful stimuli by turning the head away from the stressor.

See also *Angular distance.*

D

Dance

According to the American dancer Agnes de Mille (1905–1993), dance is the truest expression of a people, and dancing bodies never lie.

Figure D.1 Dance

Body motion

A repetitive series of usually rhythmic movements of the body and body parts (esp. feet, hands, hips and shoulders) to a musical beat, based on the alternating oscillations of walking.

Motions

The human form is more noticeable when moved. Thus, dancing couples not only attract the attention of their partners but of onlookers as well. Through principally palm-down motions, the arms may participate in dance as "walking" forelimbs.

Popular culture. When Joey Dee and the Starlighters played loud music with a beat at the Peppermint Lounge in New York in the 1960s, "even the waitresses were twisting" (Sutton, 1984, 33).

Neuro-notes I. The oscillating movements and rhythmic footsteps of dance are keyed to a two-point pedestrian beat. The natural rhythm of our upright, bipedal gait is coordinated by the same spinal circuits that programmed the oscillatory swimming motions of the earliest fishes (Grillner, 1996; see *Aquatic brain* and *Spinal cord*).

Neuro-notes II. Mirror neurons. Mirror neurons play a role in the synchrony of dance. "Almost instinctively we humans tend to synchronize our movements. I fold my arms, you fold yours, I look at you, you look away, you look back, I look away, I look at you, you start a new sentence, you look at me, I start a new sentence – it's quite a minuet we're dancing!" (Iacoboni, 2008, 130).

Benefits of dance

Dancing produces reward-related neurotransmitters, which can include endorphins and opioids (Boecker et al., 2008). It has also been found to enhance immunoreactivity (Wildmann et al, 1986) and cardiovascular health (Merom et al, 2016). Other benefits include "increased flexibility, increase in muscle strength tone, increased endurance, balance and spatial awareness, and a general feeling of well-being" (Alpert, 2011, 155). It is estimated that an actual dancing session over 1 hour can burn between 200 and 500 calories. Other benefits include improved socioemotional coping skills (Daniel et al, 1992) and increases in self-confidence (Aktas and Ogce, 2005). Morris observes that group dancing has a cohesive value "if the dancing actions performed by everyone together at the same time and at the same pace, emphasize the consensus of feeling in the group about patterns of living" (Morris, 2002, 264).

Research Reports

1   Some research has found that we have an innate capacity to dance owing to a common cognitive structure (Orgs et al., 2013), with infants as young as 3 weeks old synchronizing movements to a particular beat (Kohn and Eitan, 2016).

2   A somewhat misguided perception exists that human dance is primarily driven by seductive/mating motives. The main reason for such perceptions lies in comparisons with the animal world. While Darwin argued that dance was primarily concerned with courtship and mating, more modern discourse identifies its value as an "external system of autoregulation that aids in the maintenance of psychobiological and mental health" (Christensen et al., 2017, 9). As such, pleasure and sexual success are "correlates of the deeper psychobiological effects that drove the evolution of dance because they made it intrinsically rewarding" (Christensen et al., 2017, 9).

3   In some studies, point-light approaches are used to study dance, which show the emotions of surprise, fear, disgust, anger, joy and grief being expressed nonverbally (Dittrich et al., 1996). Work by Matsumoto (1987) found that movements connected with happiness were characterized by high speed and high energy, while dance moves associated with "lonely feelings" were typified by low energy and low speed. In their studies of emotional expression and arm movement, Sawada et al. (2003) used the lens of movement characteristics involving speed, force and directness to examine emotional expressions. The use of hands in dance has been identified as having an important communicative value (Godøy, 2010).

4   Other studies have made somewhat similar findings, with high velocity and force being connected with performances of joy (Camurri et al., 2003) and the portrayal of emotions such as grief being connected with slower and fewer changes in tempo (Lagerlöf and Djerf, 2000). Camurii et al. (2003) also found that anger is associated with many changes in actual dance movements. Dance movements have been shown to be more "impulsive" when in an induced "happy state" (Dyck et al., 2013).

5   Across cultures, the use of hands in dance can vary. In Asian and classical Indian dances, hand movements are of important value. Similarly, the traditional Khmer dance of Cambodia places important communicative value on hand movements (Wee, 2002).

See also *Music, Rapport.*

Deception cue

Dishonesty cue

A nonverbal sign of verbal deceit, untruth or lying.

Usage

A long-standing goal of nonverbal research has been to find reliable signs of deception. The quest is fuelled by popular and scientific observations that deceit is often accompanied by unconscious signals revealing anxiety, stress and shame while lying. Studies indicate that certain signs used when speaking, for example, (1) gaze-down and (2) the rate of head and hand movements – may accompany lies. At the least, deception cues present probing points with which to guide inquiry regarding possible lies, much as galvanic skin resistance (see *Sweaty palms*) in tandem with physiological breathing and heart rates are used to measure autonomic stress in a polygraph.

Chimpanzee deception

In the broadest sense of the term, "deception" is rife in the animal kingdom. Nonpoisonous flies and snakes, for example, may adopt the warning marks and coloration of poisonous species to seem, deceptively, more harmful than they are in fact. The ability to deceive is highly evolved in primates (see subsequently, Nonhuman Primates). Our close animal relative, the chimpanzee (*Pan troglodytes*), for example, is gifted in the art of deception:

1   A young male, Dandy, withheld nonverbal cues of excitement to deceive other chimpanzees as to the location of hidden grapefruit, which Dandy subsequently consumed all by himself (de Waal, 1989a).
2   A 9-year old male, Figan, withheld nonverbal food calls to conceal bananas, which Figan subsequently consumed all by himself (Goodall, 1986).
3   An adult male, Luit, pressed his lips together with his hand in an apparent attempt to hide the submissive fear grin he had given his rival, Nikki (de Waal, 1989a).

Sociopathy

People with antisocial personality disorder (once called "sociopaths") may not show behavioral signs of deception. According to the American Psychiatric Association's DSM IV-TR (2000), such individuals are characterized by deceptiveness and repeated lying, aggressiveness, absence of anxiety and nervous mannerisms and lack of remorse.

Research reports

1   Deliberate control of body movement and the mental energy required to fabricate a lie have been suggested as explanations for the research finding that fewer body movements occur with deception (Vrij et al., 1996, 2008).
2   Lower rates of head nodding "are associated with deceitful communication" (Mehrabian, 1972, 102).

3   "[E]xtensive reviews of the data . . . showed that several nonverbal cues are, in fact, consistently related to deception" (Burgoon et al., 1989, 270). "Deceivers display increased pupil dilation, blinking rates, and adaptors [i.e., self-touching], more segments of body behavior, and fewer segments of facial behavior" (Burgoon et al., 1989, 271).

4   People may make "fewer hand movements during deception compared to truth-telling" (Vrij et al., 1997, 97).

5   Masip and Sánchez (2019) argue that lies can be detected from non-behavioral information more often than from behavioral cues. Interestingly, unlike previous research (e.g., Novotny et al., 2018), they found that "suspicion is not triggered primarily from behavioral cues − rather, there is a trend in favor of non-behavioral information" (Masip and Sánchez, 2019, 481).

6   A meta-analysis by Bella DePaulo and colleagues which examined over 100 nonverbal cues in over 200 studies found that only 21 cues were related to deception. Indeed most of them were only loosely tied to deception. In fact, no single cue has been specifically linked to deception (DePaulo et al., 2003). Accuracy based upon perceptions of behavior which denote deception is only slightly above chance levels (Bond and DePaulo, 2006).

7   It seems the research is moving back toward verbal cues. "Many researchers are no longer interested in chasing elusive deception cues spontaneously displayed by liars. Such cues are weak and volatile" (Masip, 2017, 151). Since 2008, studies have drifted towards verbal cues of lying (meta-analysis show that verbal cues are more diagnostic than nonverbal cues).

See also *Eye-blink, Shoulder-shrug.*

Decision grip

Hand position

A manner of grasping an object securely between the fingertips' tactile pads and the palm.

A "proprietary" clasp intermediate between the precision grip and the power grip.

An indication that a customer has decided to purchase and take ownership of a hand-held consumer product such as a book, magazine or greeting card.

Usage I

The decision grip is a nonverbal sign showing that one's mind has decided to take possession of an artifact or object. After an exploratory waiting period reflected by holding a consumer product in the tentative precision grip, we unwittingly grasp the item in a decision grip. The latter maximizes contact between an item and the hand's sensitive tactile pads − as if it were now a personal possession or belonging.

Usage II

When a larger consumer product, such as a toaster or table lamp, is placed in a shopping cart, the prospective owner may grasp the cart's handrail in a decision (rather than the usual power) grip. Holding the cart in this "referred" manner reflects the emotional power exerted by a consumer product (see *Object fancy*).

Neuro-note

Using the sensitive fingertips as tactile antennae, we initially probe an object with the precision grip, keeping it "at a distance" – since, psychologically, it is not yet "ours." But as the mind takes ownership, we clutch the product between fingers and palm in a proprietary clasp before taking acquisition at checkout. In the retail-store world, approximately half of all purchases are impulsively based on a package's color, visual appearance and tactile smoothness (e.g., of its Mylar, foil or soft-touch coating). Handling objects in the decision grip stimulates tactile sensors for our pleasurable sense of "soft" touch and pleasure areas linked to grooming centers of the mammalian brain's cingulate gyrus.

See also *Hands*, *Touch cue*.

Deepfake

Media deception

An altered video of a public figure rendered deceptive through artificial intelligence (AI) software. Though the nonverbal head movements, facial cues and voice tones may closely resemble those of the personality they match, the images themselves are counterfeit.

Usage

Altered video images of public figures have been televised and shared in social media to portray misleading or deceptive verbal and nonverbal presentations of business, military and political leaders.

History

Deepfake's origin traces to 1997 and the Video Rewrite program of a Palo Alto, California, research organization that literally put one person's words into the vid-eoed mouth of another. Deepfake technology is currently available for amateur use and threatens to undermine the credibility of traditional media imagery.

Digital puppets

"Off-the-shelf video-editing and artificial intelligence software has made it easier than ever to create so-called deepfakes – advanced visual counterfeits that turn people into digital puppets, doing or saying things they never said or did" (Chakra-barti, 2019).

Differential emotions theory

General

Differential emotions theory (Izard and Malatesta, 1987) is grounded in the premise that a set of basic emotions seen in adults is also evident in infants. These emotions are considered discrete and include the following emotions: joy, interest, sadness, anger, fear, surprise and disgust. The theory labels these emotions as independent because they are not reliant on cognitive development processes for activation. Rather, they "achieve consciousness rapidly and automatically, and influence subsequent perception and cognition" (Ackerman et al., 1998, 87). From the ages of 2 to 4 months, the infant can express emotions such as interest, sadness, anger and joy, with fear appearing between 7 and 9 months. These emotions also have unique facial expressions which appear in early infancy and which are common to all humans. The theory argues that the "appearance" of these emotions is independent of cognition being the product of the maturation of neural circuits.

Maturation and development

Maturation and developmental factors play a role in the degree to which these emotions are evident in infancy and childhood. Proponents of the differential emotions theory (DET) also argue that in infancy, facial expressions of emotion match a corresponding discrete emotion. They point out that there is "an innate concordance between facial expression and emotion such that each infant emotion has a corresponding discrete facial expression" (Camras, 1993, 172).

DET tends to define emotion within a thin framework, arguing that it is more narrow than the typical emotional experience which may involve cognition. Rather, DET defines emotional feeling, as "a quality of consciousness that includes action-tendencies and readiness. The quality thus has non-random intentionality directed toward environmental objects and events" (Ackerman et al., 1998, 86)

Discrepancy arousal theory

General

This theory, proposed by Capella and Greene (1982) is an affect-based theory which propounds that when interacting, people have expectations about the communicative styles of the people with whom they are interacting. During an interaction, as discrepancies emerge between the expected and actual level of involvement, an arousal and consequent behavioral change is produced. Low to moderate levels of arousal produce positive affect, but as the arousal moves beyond moderate levels of arousal, the affect becomes increasingly negative. Positive affect produces reciprocity and/or approach, while negative affect produces compensatory or avoidance behaviors.

The theory argues that "arousal" alone is the critical mediator of nonverbal adjustments in contexts of human interaction. It also propounds that while interacting, behavioral changes and adjustments occur very rapidly, being a product of emotional arousal only, and as such move beyond active cognitive mediation factors, such as labeling (e.g., a smile from a friend would be cognitively labeled as liking).

Critiques

The model has been criticized for its assumption that discrepancy is a primary precursor of arousal, that arousal causes affective states and in turn that affective states cause "a reciprocal or compensating response" (Andersen and Andersen, 1984, 338). Other "exogenous variables" may also be at play.

Diagnostic Analysis of Nonverbal Accuracy

Designed by Nowicki and Duke (1994), this test is grounded in the participant's capacities to recognize basic emotions. The test measures individual differences in types of nonverbal receiving ability (facial expressions, postures, gestures and paralanguage) and in types of nonverbal sending accuracy (facial expressions, gestures and paralanguage). It comprises 24 subsets of emotional expressions – six expressions for each of the four emotions: anger, fear, happiness and sadness.

One of the aims in developing the Diagnostic Analysis of Nonverbal Accuracy (DANVA), was to construct a test which could help identify children who might have difficulties in using nonverbal signs and signals (dyssemia). The test assesses both visual and auditory nonverbal sensitivity to emotional expression. In so doing, the test makes use of spontaneous and posed expressions of emotions. The test is used in many contexts with both adults and children. It has also been further developed, for example, by Nowicki and Duke (2001).

Display Rule Assessment Inventory

General

Designed by Matsumoto et al. (1998, 2005), the Display Rule Assessment Inventory (DRAI) examines participants' responses when they experience different emotions in different social situations. The emotions examined were those generally agreed to be universally expressed and recognized and included fear, anger, contempt, sadness, disgust, happiness and surprise. Synonyms were also used for the aforementioned emotions and included hostility, defiance, aversion, worry, joy, gloom and shock. Participants were asked to "consider what they would do" if they felt each emotion in four social settings: with family members, close friends, colleagues and strangers (Matsumoto, 2006, 226).

Cultural differences

The first study by Matsumoto et al. (1998) examined responses from people from the following countries: the United States, Japan, South Korea and Russia. Results from this study showed that Russians exerted the strongest control over their expressions, with South Koreans next, then Japanese and Americans scoring lowest on their capacities to control emotions. Another study using the DRAI was undertaken in 2005 by Matsumoto et al. and found "consistent and predictable" differences among American, Russian and Japanese participants (Matsumoto, 2006, 226). For example, Americans and Russians expressed anger and contempt more than Japanese. Japanese participants "de-amplified" more than Americans and Russians (Matsumoto, 2006, 227).

Gender differences

Interestingly, gender differences have emerged from the use of the DRAI. For example, the study in 1998 by Matsumoto et al. which examined display rules across US, Japanese, South Korean and Russian participants found that males exerted more control over surprise and fear. It also found that females exerted more control over all emotions when with family members and that females also exerted more control over emotions connected with disgust, anger and contempt. A study in 2009 by Safdar et al. which examined display rules across Canadians, US Americans and Japanese participants found that "men expressed powerful emotions more than women and women expressed powerless emotions (sadness, fear) and happiness more than men" (Safdar, et al., 2009, 1).

Figure D.2 Disgust

Disgust

Emotion

A sickening feeling of revulsion, loathing or nausea.

Usage

Disgust shows in (1) a curled upper lip; (2) digestive vocalizations (e.g., "ugh," "yuck"); (3) narrowed, partly closed eyes; (4) lowered brows of the frown face; (5) backward head-jerks and side-to-side head-shakes and (6) visible protrusions of the tongue (see *Tongue-show*).

Media

Invented in 1971 by U.S. pediatrician Richard Moriarty, the fluorescent green "Mr. Yuk" face sticker is a familiar graphic symbol used as a nonverbal poison-warning label for children (cf. *Zygomatic smile*, <u>*Smiley face*</u>).

Evolution

Disgust is a mammalian elaboration of the *pharyngeal gag reflex*. The nerves and muscles used to close the mouth derive from the first pharyngeal arch, while those constricting the throat derive from the third and fourth arches. From the second arch, the facial nerve (cranial VII) contracts the orbital muscles to narrow the eyes, while corrugator and associated muscle groups lower the eyebrows, when we detect an offensive smell or taste (see *Aroma cue*, *Taste cue*).

Neuro-notes

In infants, a bitter taste shows in *lowered brows*, *narrowed eyes* and a *protruded tongue*. The noxious taste causes a baby to protectively seal off his/her throat and oral cavity, as *cranial nerves IX and X* activate the pharyngeal gag reflex. Cranial *V* depresses the lower jaw to expel the unpleasant mouthful, then closes the mouth to keep unpalatable food out as cranial XII protrudes his/her tongue. The sickening feeling we associate with disgust is mediated by the gut (see *Enteric brain*).

Dominance

Status sign

The exercise of influence, power or control over another.

Usage

Nonverbally, dominance may be encoded variously in the design of power uniforms (see *Business suit*), in lifted brows (see *Eyebrow raise*), arms akimbo (see *Hand-on-hips*) and pronated hand gestures (see *Palm-down*). Dominance cues also may be used to express a confident frame of mind.

Nonverbal dominance

"The role of nonverbal dominance is so important among some primate species that it at times eclipses real physical dominance in demarking social structure. Consequently, leading primatologists make use of the terms real dominance to describe when one ape physically dominates another (as in a fight) and formal dominance to describe the nonverbal rituals associated with dominant and submissive animals" (Ambady and Weisbuch, 2010, 467).

Evolution

Signs of dominance evolved from offensive body movements derived from the fight response (see *Fight-or-flight*) and are expressed through displays that make the body look more powerful, more threatening and "bigger" to the eye (see *Antigravity sign*, *High-stand display* and *Loom*).

Neuro-notes

The archistriatum ("most ancient" striatum; the amygdala of the basal ganglia) and paleostriatum (the basal ganglia's "ancient" striatum or globus pallidus) evolved to show reptilian dominance and submission through programmed movements and postural displays (MacLean, 1990; see *Reptilian brain*). In a dominant or aggressive pose, we unthinkingly square our shoulders and stand tall. The basal ganglia assist in this threatening posture through fiber links of the ansa lenticularis, which reach downward to hindbrain paleocircuits of the pontine reticular excitatory area, which descend, in turn, to spinal-cord circuits that excite antigravity muscles of our neck, back, shoulders and legs.

Research reports

1   A meta-analysis of various studies (Hall et al., 2005) which examined dominance found a few visible behaviors connected with trait dominance. These included smaller interpersonal distance, more open posture, more facial expressiveness and skill at posing emotions. Dominance tendencies were also found in people who "spoke more loudly, interrupted more (especially with successful interruptions), and had more relaxed sounding voices" (Hall et al, 2005, 914). Interestingly, there were "no credible trends" with regard to speech errors, rate of speech, vocal pitch, filled pauses, conversational overlaps, laughter or back-channel responses (Hall et al, 2005, 914).

2   People pay close attention to the face, with dominance being inferred from facial morphology and facial expressions (Oosterhof and Todorov, 2008; Sutherland et al., 2017). For example, baby faces and smiling faces can be perceived as weak. Alternatively, mature and or frowning faces with furrowed brows can be perceived as dominant (Montepare and Zebrowitz-McArthur, 1987).

3   The androgen testosterone, which is released by the endocrine system, has been linked with dominance (Cohan et al., 2003). As men have higher levels of testosterone, it has been argued that these higher levels result in higher levels of dominance among men as compared to women. Indeed, women with higher levels of testosterone have been found to be more dominant (Cohan et al., 2003). Some work by Mehta and Josephs (2010) found that the influence of testosterone on dominance was connected with levels of cortisol. Low levels of cortisol and high levels of testosterone increased dominance and higher social status. On the other hand, when levels of cortisol were high, high testosterone facilitated low dominance and social status.

4   Dominance typically has a social context. In considering the value of social context, Burgoon et al. (2016, 346) argue that dominance can be communicated "via a set of nonverbal behaviours that show social skill and competence." In their work, they group these socially skilled behaviors into three categories: (1) poise and self-assurance, (2) panache or dynamism and (3) conversational control. Each of the categories involves the following nonverbal behaviors (Burgoon et al., 2016, 347):

    a   Poise and Self-Assurance:
        Asymmetrical leg and arm positions, sideways leaning, open arms and body position, kinesic expressiveness, low amounts of swiveling, adaptors and random movement, fluent speech, facial pleasantness/smiling, eye contact, moderately fast and loud voice, increased talk time

    b   Panache or Dynamism:
        Close distancing, gaze and direct body orientation, forward lean, vocal and kinesic expressiveness, faster and louder speech

    c   Conversational Control:
        Attention-getting techniques (e.g., demure eye contact), fluent speech with unsmooth turn taking and interruptions, back-channeling and nodding, eye contact (especially when speaking), rejection and leave-taking behaviors (e.g., ignoring someone, increasing distance)

5   In considering other factors relevant to perceptions of power and dominance, the work of (Burgoon et al. 1998, 2002, 2016; Burgoon and Dunbar 2000) provides insights on the value of resources, physical potency and interaction control.

Antonym: see *Submission*.

E

Ear movements

Vestigial sign

To move the ears upward, forward or backward through contractions of the outer ears' auriculares muscles. The movements may go unnoticed by the naked eye, however, and thus have little to "say."

Usage

Though some human beings are able to "wiggle" their ears, the visible movements themselves may not be seen. When picked up by electronic measuring devices, however, the ears' vestigial muscle contractions may be decoded as signs of emotional arousal, as in anger, happiness or sorrow. Since a linkage exists between the smile's zygomatic muscle and the outer ears' auriculares muscles, a strong smile may visibly move the ears. These muscles are innervated by the emotional facial nerve, cranial VII (see *Special visceral nerve*).

Ear-flattening I

In addition to the previous ear movements – which originated to orient the ear flaps directionally to sound – ear-flattening originated to lower the ears protectively in dangerous or hostile conditions.

Ear-flattening II

Flattening occurs in many mammals, including lower primates (prosimians) such as the bush baby (*Galago* sp.) and has become a social sign of appeasement. In higher primates (monkeys, apes and humans), flattening has ceased to exist as a sign due to an evolutionary reduction in ear musculature, but part of the signal has been retained. Scalp-retraction, originally part of the ear-flattening complex, occurs in macaques and baboons as a stereotyped, exaggerated display (Andrew, 1965). Dominant members of some monkey genera (Macaca, Papio, Theropithecus, Mandrillus, Cynopithecus, Cebus and Cercocebus) raise the eyebrows in threat situations to expose light colored skin (van Hooff, 1967; see *Eyebrow-raise*).

See also *Eyebrow-flash*.

Education

Role of nonverbal communication in education

A number of studies indicate that nonverbal communication has an important role to play in the field of education. In particular, teacher "pzazz" (Neill and Caswell, 1993) and the teacher "X-Factor" (White and Gardner, 2011) have been identified as significant factors in the facilitation of pupil learning. In 2004, Klinzing and Aloisio analyzed a significant number of studies spanning almost half a century to examine correlations between teacher nonverbal expressiveness and pupil achievement. They came to the important conclusion that teacher nonverbal expressiveness is "comparable with other variables found to be related to achievement" (Klinzing and Aloisio, 2004, 9). In their trawl of the research, they found that there were significant positive effects on pupil achievement in those studies which examined frequent gesturing (Rosenshine, 1970), occasional teacher gaze (Breed, 1971), frequent teacher gaze (Otterson and Otterson, 1980), high rates of eye-contact (Driscoll, 1969), high rates of gesturing (Driscoll, 1969), dynamic voice tone (Driscoll, 1969) and high enthusiasm (Ware and Williams, 1977, 1977). Indeed, McCroskey et al. (2006, 425) argue that "the instructional research to date suggests that nonverbal factors may have a much stronger impact on learning than do verbal factors." They posit that the nonverbal communication of the teacher stimulates "affective meaning" whereby students develop an emotional connection with the subject and with the teacher.

Measuring learning outcomes and nonverbal communication

Measuring learning outcomes as a direct product of teacher nonverbal expressiveness is difficult. However, teachers with strong nonverbal communication skills have been found to influence learning outcomes in domains which are beyond the typically "measurable" learning objectives (McCroskey et al., 2006). Such teachers influence students' "affinity" for the teacher him/herself: the students have a greater liking for the subject being taught, and they have better perceptions of themselves as learners. Moreover, these teachers are seen as positive models and "task attractive" (McCroskey et al., 2006). Considerable work has been undertaken in the field of embodied cognition and in particular on pupils' use of gesture to process information. Such work is yielding notable findings in terms of nonverbal communication and learning.

See also *Embodied cognition, Gesture*.

Emblem

Use of emblems

The emblem can be described as a symbolic object or representation which presents a particular quality, message or concept. There are some who argue that emblems have etymological roots in the Ciceronian meaning of the word: something that can be detached and re-attached. Indeed, some esoteric theorists argue that the visual sign has its true beginnings with the Lingua Adamica: the language between God and man. They argue that traces of these signs and emblems can be discerned in the hieroglyphics of the Egyptians, and as such they present as "uncorrupted" by the human tongue – the purest form of communication.

In more modern times, it is generally agreed that the first book in English on emblems was entitled *Choice of Emblems* and written by Geffrey Whitey in 1586. The potency of emblems to provide a "network" of what McKeown (2010, xviii) calls "semiotic markers, signs, cognizances, devices, conceits and enigmas" has been discussed since renaissance times and certainly precedes the current technological age. While this network could not be termed a "world-wide web," early use of the emblem did provide a platform for understanding (a type of network of understanding) across cultures, and in so doing, it was assimilated and adapted across a range of civilizations. There are evident parallels with this century's world wide web.

Speech-independent gestures

With specific reference to the nonverbal world, Ekman (1976, 1977) described speech-independent gestures as emblems. Children are able to decode speech-independent gestures by the age of three, and this capability dramatically increases by the age of five (Knapp and Hall, 2006). Speech-independent gestures are typically culturally dependent, but some have universal currency, such as the nose wrinkle to express disgust. For example, the ring gesture (where the thumb and forefinger are used to create a circle) means "okay" in the United States, but in some parts of Italy, it means "asshole," and in parts of Turkey and Greece, it can be interpreted as a vulgar sexual invitation. Similarly, the thumbs-up gesture in the United States can be translated as "good" or "okay," but in the Middle East, it is decoded as an obscene gesture.

Embodied cognition

Cognition

The idea that our brain is like a computer which governs the body and which is largely detached from the actions of legs, arms, hands and all bodily movements has been criticized by exponents of "embodied cognition." They argue that our physical interactions with the world shape our cognition of the world (Glenberg, 2008; Semin and Smith, 2008). Our thoughts are shaped by the types of perceptual and motor experiences we have as we interact each day with the world, and as such, "cognition is for action" (Glenberg, 2008, 43). For example, strong links have been established between the use of gesture and language acquisition (Colonnesi et al., 2010; Iverson and Goldin-Meadow, 1997; Iverson and Goldin-Meadow, 2005).

Figure E.1 Embodied cognition

Body movements

As humans speak, their body movements are synchronized with what they are saying in "self-synchrony" (Dittmann, 1972). It is argued that such bodily movements, and in particular the use of gesture movements, can have benefits for the speaker in assisting them in retrieving information from memory and also to reduce the cognitive working load while speaking (Chawla and Krauss, 1994; Ping and Goldin-Meadow, 2010). It is also argued that the benefits of speaker gesturing lie in the assistance which such gestures provide for the listener in terms of understanding what is being said (Bavelas, 1994; Clark, 1996).

In particular, the value of gesture to assist human learning has been researched in a number of studies. First, the use of gesture by mathematics teachers has been found to assist the comprehension of concepts (Alibali et al., 2001; Hostetter, 2011; Koumoutsakis et al., 2016). Second, when children are asked to use gestures in solving equivalence problems, there is a greater likelihood they will benefit more from the teacher's instruction (Broaders et al., 2007; Wagner et al., 2003).

See also *Gesture* and *Education*.

Emoticons and emojis

Iconic mood signs

Any of diverse graphic signs, symbols and cues designed to inject emotions, feelings and moods into computer messages.

Usage

Nonverbal emoticons ("emotion icons") and emojis ("picture characters") may be used in isolation, together in narrative juxtaposition or in association with alphanumeric text to add emotion to written messages. In computers, the earliest emoticons – a punctuated :-) and :- (for, respectively, "smile" and "frown" – were used in the 1972 Plato IV computer system. Though iconic mood signs predate electronics, their prolific use began soon after the sale of personal computers (PCs).

Computers

In the early years, computers used Boolean logic to send and receive verbally meaningful alphanumeric information. Logical rules predominated, and verbal messages carried little about emotions, moods or feelings.

Nonverbal feeling

Since humans are very emotional creatures (see *Human brain*), the early PC emphasis on logic and verbal content was not likely to last. And, indeed, it did not. Emotion reasserted itself in 1972 in emoticons for "smile" (happy) and "frown" (angry or sad). In 2018, there were 2,823 emojis registered in the worldwide Unicode Standard, and the number is projected to grow.

Emoticons

Consisting of juxtaposed numerals, alphabetical characters and punctuation marks, emoticons suggest human facial expressions and gestures. These nonverbal shapes may be suggestive of emotions, feelings and moods. Emoticons have been largely replaced by the more expressive and colorful emojis.

Emojis

Emoji images began to appear in 1997 on Japanese mobile phones. They include pictographs of airplanes, animals, artifacts, buildings, people and other features, items and objects we see in everyday life. Emojis may stand alone; be grouped in narrative order like hieroglyphics to tell a story or accompany words to add emphasis, feeling or humor. That they are in worldwide use today gives testament to the power of nonverbal communication in the Computer Age.

See also *Isotype*.

Emotional contagion

Basic premise

The basic premise of the emotional contagion effect is that emotions can be caught. When communicating with another human, emotions such as joy, enthusiasm, fear and sadness are often "passed to the other person." This can happen in milliseconds. As we mimic the expressions and postures of the person we are talking to, we also "soak up" their emotions: "people automatically mimic and synchronise expressions, vocalisations, postures and movements with others and . . . as a result converge emotionally" (Hatfield et al., 1992, 156).

Catching emotions

There is some evidence that a convergent expression of the "absorbed" emotions may not always present for socially anxious individuals. In their work with socially anxious individuals, Dijk et al. (2018) found that such individuals tended to catch negative emotions from others but suppressed their expression by mimicking positive displays. Social anxiety was also found to be related to enhanced mimicry of smiling, but this was only for polite smiles and not for smiles associated with enjoyment. Dijk et al. (2018) argue that this may be explained by the tendency of socially anxious individuals to avoid conflict or rejection.

Interestingly, in recent years, the emotional contagion theory has been used in part to explain the feelings, thoughts and behavior of autistic children and religious fanatics (Hatfield et al., 2009, 26).

The Emotional Contagion Scale

The scale

The Emotional Contagion Scale was developed and validated by William Doherty (1997). The scale measures individual differences in "susceptibility to catching the emotions of others" (Doherty, 1997, 149). The scale has 15 items which examine participants' tendency to mimic the five emotions of love, happiness, sadness, anger and fear. Examples of items include:

- "If someone I'm talking with begins to cry, I get teary-eyed";
- "When someone smiles warmly at me, I smile back and feel warm inside";
- "I get filled with sorrow when people talk about the death of their loved ones."

Susceptibility

In developing the scale, Doherty (1997) found that susceptibility to catching the emotions of others was positively associated with affective orientation, emotionality, sensitivity to others, social functioning, reactivity and self-esteem. It was found to be more strongly associated with emotional rather than cognitive modes of empathy. Susceptibility was found to be negatively associated with "self-assertiveness, emotional stability, and alienation" (Doherty, 1997, 149). In short, an individual's personality influences the degree of susceptibility to catching the emotions of others.

Emotion

Neuro term

A pleasant or unpleasant mental state organized in the limbic system of the mammalian brain. Specifically, feelings of agreement, anger, certainty, control, disagreement, disgust, disliking, embarrassment, fear, happiness, hate, interest, liking, love, sadness, shame, surprise and uncertainty – as expressed nonverbally apart from words.

Meaning

Emotions are mammalian elaborations of vertebrate arousal patterns, in which neurochemicals such as dopamine, noradrenaline and serotonin step up or step down the brain's activity level as visible in body movements, gestures and postures (see *Emotion cue*).

Anatomy

Before the mammalian brain, life in the Nonverbal World was automatic, preconscious and predictable. Reptilian motor centers reacted to vision, sound, touch, chemical, gravity and motion sensory cues with preset body movements and programmed postures. With the arrival of night-active mammals ca. 180 mya, smell replaced sight as the dominant sense, and a newer, more flexible way of responding – based on emotion and emotional memory – arose from the olfactory sense. In the Jurassic period, the mammalian brain invested heavily in aroma circuits to succeed at night as reptiles slept. These odor pathways gradually formed the neural blueprint for what was later to become our limbic system (see *Mammalian brain*).

Neuro-notes I

Smell carries directly to limbic areas of the mammalian brain via nerves running from the olfactory bulbs to the septum, amygdala and hippocampus. In the aquatic brain, olfaction was critical for detecting food, foes and mates from a distance in murky waters. Like an emotional feeling, aroma has a volatile or "thin-skinned" quality because sensory cells lie on the exposed exterior of the olfactory epithelium (i.e., on the bodily surface itself). Like a whiff of smelling salts, a sudden feeling may jolt the mind. The force of a mood is reminiscent of a smell's intensity (e.g., soft and gentle, pungent or overpowering) and similarly permeates and fades. The design of emotion cues, in tandem with the forebrain's olfactory prehistory, suggests that the sense of smell is the neurological model for our emotions.

Neuro-notes II

Like aromas, emotions are either positive or negative (i.e., pleasant or unpleasant) – and rarely neutral. Like odors, feelings come and go, defy logic and clearly show upon our face in mood signs. It is likely that emotion evolved from paleocircuits for aroma.

Neuro-notes III: mirror neurons

Mirror neurons help us decode the emotions encoded in nonverbal cues: "The neural activity in the limbic system triggered by these signals from mirror neurons allows us to feel the emotions associated with the observed facial expressions – the happiness associated with a smile, the sadness associated with a frown" (Iacoboni, 2008, 112).

Physiology

There is some congruence across cultures in terms of the human's physiological (and accordant nonverbal and possibly verbal) responses to some emotions.

- Anger produces warmer skin temperature, tenser muscles and increased heart rate.
- Sadness produces a lump in the throat and tenser muscles.
- Fear produces tenser muscles, cold sweat and increased heart rate.

See also *Aroma cue*.

Emotion cue

Sign

A facial expression, body movement or tone of voice indicative of emotion. Specifically, for example, a fist of anger, a jaw-droop in surprise or a throat-clear of uncertainty.

Usage

1   Though our fingers, hands and arms show feelings as well, the study of emotion has focused mainly on facial expressions. From research on the face, six basic emotions – surprise, happiness, fear, anger, disgust and sadness – have been proposed (Ekman, 1994). "Thoughts and emotions are interwoven: every thought, however bland, almost always carries with it some emotional undertone, however subtle" (Restak, 1995, 21).

2   We have a rich vocabulary of emotion cues showing how we feel about ourselves and others. In the realm of emotional expression, words may be less trustworthy than nonverbal signs. This is because the latter cues are often unintentional, involuntary and unconscious. While some emotion cues, like

the frown and smile, are well known, others, such as the Adam's-apple-jump and tense-mouth, have neither common names nor listings in standard (i.e., verbal) dictionaries.

Anatomy I (face)

Eye, nose, mouth, throat and laryngeal openings are controlled by muscles and nerves from tissues of ancient pharyngeal arches. Thus, (1) we may close (i.e., constrict) our facial features to show negative emotion (e.g., frown, throat-clear) and (2) open (i.e., dilate) them to show pleasant feelings and moods (e.g., eyebrow-raise, laugh).

Anatomy II (body)

A powerful feeling may release neck reflexes of the asymmetrical tonic neck reflex (ATNR), resulting in hand-behind-head gestures or hyperextended reaching cues. Fear may show as the brain's amygdala activates the body's protective freeze reaction. Horror may show in the two-handed cheek-touch cue immortalized in Edvard Munch's 1893 painting The Scream.

Neuro-notes

Unlike fish, amphibians and reptiles, humans are strongly emotional mammals who run "hot" or "cold" and rarely feel neutral about the days of their lives. Emotion cues commence with activity in the limbic brain (see *Limbic system*). When stimulated, its septum – a pleasure area of the forebrain – may arouse facial expressions of happiness and joy. With those we love, the brain's cingulate gyrus inspires grooming, nuzzling and cuddle cues.

See also *Mammalian brain*.

En face gaze

Visual bonding

An intimate form of eye contact in which a mother positions her face within inches of her baby's face and aligns, eye-to-eye, in parallel, for optimal viewing. Family and people of all ages have been observed using the en face gaze with infants, frequently smiling and using high-pitched, cooing voice tones as well.

Usage

Nonverbally, en face may be used diagnostically as a sign of a mom's positive emotional relationship with her baby. In a study of child abuse, Givens (1978a) found non-abuser moms using en face while abusers omitted the cue.

Courtship

En face has been identified as a positive sign in human courtship (Givens, 1978b, 2005; see *Love*).

Research report

In a study of eye-contact behavior in babies, researchers found that "infants learn rapidly that the looking behaviors of others conveys significant information"

(Farroni et al., 2002, 9602). "The results show that, from birth, human infants prefer to look at faces that engage them in mutual gaze and that, from an early age, healthy babies show enhanced neural processing of direct gaze. The exceptionally early sensitivity to mutual gaze demonstrated in these studies is arguably the major foundation for the later development of social skills" (Farroni et al., 2002, 9602).

See also *Eye contact.*

Enteric brain

Neuro term

A vast collection of nerve cells and paleocircuits in the bowel area, of such complexity that it has been called the "second brain."

Usage

In many ways independent of the brain proper – that is, having a mind of its own – the enteric brain expresses itself nonverbally in visible "gut reactions." The "full" feeling of satisfaction, the "sick" feeling of nausea, the urge to vomit and abdominal pain, for example, may be telegraphed through familiar facial expressions and body movements.

Neuro-notes

"The gut is now recognized as a major regulator of motivational and emotional states. Our findings establish the vagal gut-to-brain axis as an integral component of the neuronal reward pathway (including dopamine cells of the substantial nigra)" (Han et al., 2018, 665).

Equilibrium theory

Equilibrium theory and interpersonal intimacy

Equilibrium theory (Argyle and Dean, 1965) examined interpersonal intimacy and argued that individuals signal their intimacy with others through nonverbal behaviors such as gaze, smiling, occupation of space and self-disclosure (verbal intimacy). The theory argued that over the course of an interaction, there is a necessity to maintain an equilibrium in the level of involvement. For example, if a stranger approached too closely, this might lead the partner to reduce smiling and avoid eye contact. This adjustment or "compensation" leads to a "rebalancing" of the equilibrium, with the reduction in gaze compensating for the stranger's close approach.

Ergonomics of the mind

Concept

The application of neuroscience principles to consumer-product design (see *Consumer product*). Design features adapted specifically to the brain and nervous system, intended to optimize product appeal, enjoyment and value (see *New car smell*). Emotional features added to make products more expressive, "lively" and fun to use (see *Messaging feature*).

Usage

Ergonomics of the mind means "user friendly to the brain." For the past 100,000 years, human beings have designed products to maximize their appeal to emotion. Today we form strong attachments to products that express themselves, show attitude and emote "personality" (see, for example, *Big Mac®, Blue jeans* and *Vehicular grille*).

Familiarity

We prefer products we have already seen, tasted, heard, felt or smelled to those not yet experienced. According to the American social psychologist, Robert Zajonc (1923–2008): "If subjects are exposed to some novel visual patterns (like Chinese ideograms) and then asked to choose whether they prefer the previously exposed or new patterns, they reliably tend to prefer the preexposed ones. Mere exposure to stimuli is enough to create preferences" (Zajonc's, 1980 statement, quoted in LeDoux, 1996, 53).

See also *Artifact, Object fancy*.

Figure E.2 Evil eye

Evil eye

Killing look

A lengthy, directed glance intentionally designed to be harmful. Any of several eye-like charms, fetishes or talismans designed to ward off the evil eye (see *Talisman*).

Usage

Evil-eye beliefs are widespread in traditional and peasant societies and in some urban areas today. With strong links to the sympathetic nervous system, eye contact often can be emotionally impulsive (see *Fight-or-flight*). A stare is often used by monkeys and apes as an aggressive threat. Given its emotional force and evolutionary roots in primates, it is not surprising that evil-eye messages have a widespread distribution in humankind.

Bone-pointing

In Aboriginal Australia, staring while pointing a short length of bone or wood at an enemy has been superstitiously linked to the premature death of this enemy. Nonverbally, for those who believe in the power of evil eye and sorcery, the threat of being targeted by enemies is psychologically "real," as in "voodoo death." A strong personal and physical orientation towards another may stimulate powerful emotion (see *Fear, Orienting reflex*).

Folklore

According to the American folklorist Alan Dundes (1934–2005), "The evil eye – the power to inflict illness, damage to property, or even death simply by gazing at or appraising someone – is among the most pervasive and powerful folk beliefs in the Indo-European and Semitic world" (Dundes, 1992).

See also *Eye contact, Point*.

Existential crunch

Tactile cue

A usually pleasant tactile sensation derived from chewing crisp vegetables, nuts, cookies and crackers (see *Nut substitute*). A crackling texture, conducted by sensory nerves of the jaws, teeth and tongue, often featured in the design of snack foods.

Usage

Along with nonverbal smell (see *Aroma cue*) and taste (see *Taste cue*), there is "mouth feel" (see *Touch cue*). We crave the crunchiness of nuts and extend the properties of crunching to crackers, nachos and corn chips, which are served crisp. For enhanced crunch, we may add sprinkles to cookies, chopped nuts to ice cream and salt crystals to pretzels. In breakfast cereals, the most advanced corn flakes stay crunchy in milk.

Evolution

Like their forest-dwelling Oligocene ancestors ca. 30 mya, the first humans on the African savannah ate nuts as well as fruit. The jaws and teeth of *Ramapithecus*, for example, reveal that early apes ate small, hard, nut-like foods ca. 15–8 mya in the Miocene.

Primatology

In Africa, chimpanzees shell panda nuts together under treetops in the Tai forest of Ivory Coast. The chimps socialize as they crack the hard shells with pieces of wood, carefully placing each nut in a knothole before smashing it. Similarly, humans gather to eat crunchy foods such as breadsticks and party nuts and enjoy eating peanuts and popcorn together at sporting events.

Candy messages

Varied commercial candy brands – including M&Ms®, Snickers® and Reese's Peanut Butter Cups® – contain nuts and are crunchy rather than merely soft. Each of these brands combines sweetness and nuttiness in a proven evolutionary formula for primates. The crisp candy coatings of M&Ms, one of the most popular candies of all time, encase milk chocolate mixed with finely ground peanut powder.

Chips

One of the most popular U.S. snack foods is neither a seed nor a nut but a crunchy nut substitute: the potato chip. Potato chips were accidentally invented in New

York in 1835 when a diner complained that his French fries were too mushy; the cook served them thinner and fried to a crisp, and by the 1960s, supermarket executives identified potato chips as necessity items. Potato, corn and other vegetable chips have the look and feel of primate finger food.

See also *Big Mac®*, *Coca-Cola®*.

Expectancy theory

Conceptual model

The hypothesis that a person's nonverbal communication unwittingly scripts a recipient's behavior, deportment or performance in the manner of a self-fulfilling prophecy.

Usage I

Displayed nonverbally, a teacher's eye, contact, smile and positive expectations for certain chosen students may encourage them to work harder and get better grades.

Usage II

A judge's body language (e.g., gaze cut-off, tense-mouth and tongue-show) may transmit negative feelings or attitudes which could inadvertently influence jurors to decide against a defense attorney's case.

Clever Hans

As human primates, we are highly responsive to nonverbal cues, and thus susceptible to the "Clever Hans" phenomenon. Once upon a 19th-century time, there lived a world-famous horse named Clever Hans, who displayed amazing "mathematical" ability. If someone asked him to add, say, five plus seven, Hans would faithfully stomp 12 times, astounding all present. For years, scientists were baffled by how the animal could add, subtract and compute square roots.

Pfungst

Eventually a German biologist, Oskar Pfungst (1874–1933), solved the mystery. According to Pfungst, Clever Hans looked closely at his human audience for subtle cues of the eyes, head movements and body postures telling him when to stop tapping his hoof. Kinesic signs alone – such as a slight lifting of the head – sufficed.

Eyes

Body parts

Paired organs of vision, the movements, lid positions and pupil size of which reveal a great deal about emotions, convictions and moods.

Usage

Gaze direction shows others where our attention lies. To gauge their feelings, we have developed an amazing ability to gaze into the eyes of our beholders. However, being looked at, so arouses the sympathetic nervous system (see *Fight-or-flight*) that we may feel compelled to glance away. Perhaps because the eye's retina is an outgrowth of the forebrain, peering into someone's eyes is not unlike seeing into the brain itself. This may be why the sacred Eye of Horus (the All-Seeing Utchat of Ancient Egypt) had so many complex meanings.

Anatomy

The resting position of an open eyelid is maintained by the levator palpebrae superioris muscle. Relaxed, the lower lid barely touches the bottom circumference of our iris, while the upper eyelid covers a good deal of its top. When excited, we widen our eye opening (palpebral fissure) and narrow it when we feel threatened. Sudden eyelid closure is part of a protective, mammalian facial grimace brought on by the startle reflex (Salzen, 1979). Widened eyes may reflect emotions of the fight-or-flight response (see *Flashbulb eyes*).

Fascination

We are enthralled by eyes. From the moment of birth, we respond to mother's eyes as if programmed to do so. Babies smile at black geometric spots – perceiving them as "eyes" by 6 weeks of age (Kandel and Jessell, 1991). In adults, eye contact shows personal involvement and creates intimate bonds. Mutual gaze "narrows" the physical and psychological gap between us.

Neuro-notes I

Suddenly narrowed or slitted eyes may reveal disagreement or uncertainty. Negative feelings associated with doubt or misunderstanding (i.e., cognitive dissonance) quickly pass from the limbic system to the hindbrain's facial nucleus (cranial VII), which triggers a brief narrowing of the eyes as if to protect against emotional pain.

Neuro-notes II

Rest-and-digest nerve fibers activate the irises' pupillary sphincter muscles to constrict the pupils. Fight-or-flight nerve fibers from the superior cervical ganglion activate dilator muscles to expand the diameter of the pupils.

See also *CLEM, Eye-blink*.

Eye-blink

Batting rate

A rapid closing and opening of the eyes.

Usage

One's blink rate reflects psychological arousal in the manner of a polygraph test. The normal, resting human blink rate is 20 closures per minute, with the average blink lasting one quarter of a second (Karson, 1992). Significantly faster rates may reflect emotional stress as aroused, for example, in the brain's alarm response (see *Fight-or-flight*).

Primatology

"Eye-blinking is another well-known primate movement. The moment you have the least little bit of stress, the eyelids blink, bang! bang! bang!" (Niko Tinbergen, 1964 *Psychology Today* interview)

U.S. politics

In the 1996 presidential debates, candidate Bob Dole averaged 147 blinks – seven times above normal. President Bill Clinton averaged 99 blinks a minute, reaching 117 when asked about increases in teen drug use, a sensitive issue of the day.

Neuroanatomy

The blink reflex originates in paleocircuits of the amphibian brain. Nervous impulses travel from vision centers of the superior colliculi to the facial nerve's motor nucleus, causing involuntary contractions in the eyelid portion of orbicularis oculi muscles (see *Amphibian brain*).

Neuro-notes

We blink faster when excited because eyelid movements reflect bodily arousal levels established by the brain stem's reticular activating system (RAS). Emotion from the limbic system stimulates the RAS to act on our midbrain's substantia nigra, which releases the excitatory chemical dopamine to the superior colliculi (Karson, 1992, 417). Thus, we bat our eyelids faster in courtship (see *Love signals III*), in public speaking (see *Stranger anxiety*) and in lying (see *Deception cue*).

See also *Facial flushing*.

Figure E.3 Eyebrow-flash

Eyebrow-flash

Brow-lift greeting

A widespread, possibly universal gesture in which both eyebrows lift briefly in greeting. Typically this lasts for approximately 1/3 of a second.

Usage

The eyebrow-flash is usually given in tandem by acquainted individuals engaged in mutual eye contact. It may be considered a sign of facial recognition and is often accompanied by smiling and a slight head lift. Morris (2002, 114) notes that the flash signals "a 'pleasant surprise' at seeing a friend."

Anatomy I

Paired, horizontally arched eyebrows are prominent facial features. Their movements and positions encode a variety of emotions, from anger to happiness and surprise (see *Eyebrow-lower* and *Eyebrow-raise*). The prime mover of eyebrow-flash is the forehead's frontalis muscle, which links to an emotionally responsive nerve, cranial VII, the facial nerve (see *Special visceral nerve*).

Anatomy II

Since the eyebrow muscle (frontalis) has connections with muscles of the eyelid (levator palpebral superioris), lifting the brows may also widen the eyes.

Research reports

The eyebrow-flash of greeting and recognition has been observed in many cultures, and according to German ethnologist Irenaus Eibl-Eibesfeldt (1970, 419), is an "inborn greeting" behavior: "I filmed this behavior even in stone age Papuans, who had only recently come into contact with government patrols (1970, 420).

Eyebrow–lower

Facial expression

To frown or scowl, as in anger, concentration, displeasure or thought. To depress, knit, pucker or wrinkle the brow by contracting the corrugator, procerus and orbicularis oculi muscles.

Usage

Lowering the eyebrows may be a sensitive indicator of disagreement, doubt and/ or uncertainty.

Research reports

1   "Many kinds of monkeys, especially baboons, when angered or in any way excited, rapidly and incessantly move their eyebrows up and down" (Darwin, 1872, 138).
2   In nursery school children, attacks "are often preceded and accompanied by fixating the opponent and by what looks like a frown with lowering of the eyebrows and rather little vertical furrowing of the brow ('low frown') and no conspicuous modification of the mouth expression" (Blurton Jones, 1967, 355).
3   Blind-and-deaf-born children frown in anger (Eibl-Eibesfeldt, 1973).
4   "Puzzlement was displayed by curving the mouth downward, lowering the eyebrows and eyelids, dropping the jaw, and constricting the forehead muscles" (Burgoon et al., 1989, 352).

See also *Eyebrow-raise*, *Hat*.

Eyebrow–raise

Facial expression

To lift the arch of short hairs above the eye, as in uncertainty, disbelief, surprise or exasperation. To elevate the eyebrow by contracting the occipitofrontalis muscle.

Usage I

Raising the brows adds emotional intensity to facial expressions. Brow-raising may, for example, strengthen a dominant stare, exaggerate a submissive pout or boost the energy of a smile. Occipitofrontalis elevates the eyebrows to form prominent, horizontal furrows in the forehead, making almost any gesture it accompanies look and feel stronger.

Usage II

In tandem with head-tilt-back, raising one or both eyebrows may suggest a supercilious air of disdain, haughtiness and pride. (N.B. "Supercilious" comes from the Latin word for eyebrow, supercilium.) We may unwittingly lift our brow as we give orders, argue key speaking points or make demands.

Research reports

Eyebrow-raise is a threat sign used by baboons, mandrills and cebus monkeys (Andrew, 1965; van Hooff, 1967). The eyebrow-flash of recognition is a worldwide friendly greeting (Eibl-Eibesfeldt, 2007; Morris, 1994). One eyebrow raised (as in the eyebrow cock) is a widespread sign of skepticism (Morris, 1994).

Eye contact

Sign

A visual connection made as one person gazes into the eyes of another. A highly emotional link established as two people simultaneously observe each other's eyes.

Usage

1   Gazing at another's eyes arouses strong emotion. Thus, eye contact rarely lasts longer than 3 seconds before one or both viewers experience an urge to glance away. Breaking eye contact lowers stress levels as measured by breathing rate, heart rate and sweaty palms.
2   People who make eye contact (but not excessive contact) are rated as more intelligent, credible, likable, pleasant and dominant (Kleinke, 1986).

Anatomy

The six muscles that cooperate to move each eyeball are ancient and common to all vertebrates. The muscles' nerves link to emotional as well as to "thinking" (i.e., rational) parts of the human brain. Levator palpebrae superioris, a muscle that raises the upper eyelid, arose from superior rectus, one of six muscles that rotate the eyeball itself. Note that because their connective tissue coats are fused, we automatically lift our eyelids when we look up.

Culture I

In Japan, listeners may be taught to focus on a speaker's neck in order to avoid eye contact, while in the United States, listeners are encouraged to gaze into a speaker's eyes (Burgoon et al., 1989, 194).

Culture II

After giving a talk, American speakers may look for raised hands to signify questions or comments. After speaking to Japanese listeners and seeing no hands, an American might assume the audience had little interest in responding. This assumption, however, would be wrong. In Japan one shows interest with direct eye contact – with "bright eyes," the Japanese cultural cue – rather than with the American cue of upraised hands.

Espionage

"If someone should surprise you, stay calm. Look him right in the eye – always maintain eye contact. That way you don't look shifty-eyed, but, more important, all he will notice is your eyes" CIA operative David Forden to Colonel Ryszard Kuklinski (Chelminski, 1999; see *Deception*).

Elevator eyes

In crowded elevators our eyes may not roam freely across others' faces, as they can, for example, when we watch faces pictured in magazines or on TV.

Primatology

"Thus, one interpretation of avoiding visual contact – which has been described in rhesus, baboons, bonnet macaques, [and] gorillas – is that it is a means of avoiding interactions" (Altmann, 1967, 332). "Facial expressions observed in threatening animals [e.g., wild baboons] consist of 'staring,' sometimes accompanied by a quick jerking of the head down and then up, in the direction of the opponent, flattening of the ears against the head, and a pronounced raising of the eyebrows with a rapid blinking of the pale eyelids" (Hall and DeVore, 1972, 169).

Research reports

1   We may generally begin an utterance by looking away and end it by looking back at the listener. While speaking, we alternate between gazing at and gazing away (Argyle and Dean, 1965; Kendon, 1967). There is more direct gaze when people like each other and cooperate (Argyle and Dean, 1965).
2   People make less eye contact when they dislike each other or disagree (Argyle and Dean, 1965).
3   Direct gaze (along with body alignment and smiling) is a trustworthy sign of good feeling between new acquaintances (Palmer and Simmons, 1995, 156).
4   Disturbed eye contact can be an indicator of psychiatric illnesses (Guillon et al., 2014)
5   In early childhood, the quality and quantity of eye contact between mother and infant is a telling indicator of psychiatric conditions in later life (Auyeung et al., 2015)
6   The pupils in the eye can play an important role in signaling attraction. When you make eye contact with a person you find attractive, your pupils widen (Hess, 1960, 1975). This happens outside of your control and has an evolutionary basis (the search for an appropriate mate).

Neuro-notes

Feelings of dominance, submission, liking and disliking pass from the limbic system and basal ganglia to the midbrain's oculomotor (cranial III), trochlear (IV) and abducens (VI) nerves. Acting in concert, these nerves lead our eye muscles to pull together in downward or sideward movements, depending on mood. Thus, for example, submissive and aversive feelings move our eyes subcortically through paleocircuits established long ago in vision centers of the midbrain (see *Amphibian brain*).

See also *CLEM*, *Eye-blink* and *Gaze-down*.

Eye-flash

Usage

The eye-flash involves a momentary widening of the eyelids, without movement of the eyebrows, revealing the white sclera surrounding the iris.

Timing

The eye-flash occurs in spoken conversation and, like voice intonation, serves to emphasize the particular word or phrase spoken at the time. It occurs more with adjectives than other parts of speech and is more common among women than men (Walker and Trimboli, 1985). Ekman and Friesen (1975) note that the eye flash typically lasts for a fraction of a second. Walker and Trimboli (1985) found that the eye-flash lasts on average for 0.75 seconds

Eye-rolling

Literature

An examination of literary works from the 14th century forward indicates that eye rolling was once associated with lust, flirtation and sexual desire. However, in more recent times, it has evolved in the passive-aggressive domain to be associated with disdain (Galen and Underwood, 1997). The semantic shift toward sarcasm today may have occurred recently, in the 1980s. That neurological wiring for intrinsic and extrinsic eye movements (for pupil size and eye-rolling, respectively) is deeply rooted in primitive spinal reflexes and emotion centers would seem to call the "recent semantic-shift" hypothesis into some question (see *Pupil size*, Neuro-notes).

Nonverbal pairing

Anthropologist David Givens notes that eye-rolling pairs well with a variety of negative nonverbal signs, signals and cues (see, e.g., *Disgust*, *Eyebrow-lower*, *Groan*, *Head-shake*, *Head-tilt-back*, *Lip-compression*, *Lip-retraction* and *Wan smile*).

Neuro-notes

Inward rotation (incyclotorsion) of the eyeball is due to superior oblique muscles mediated by the trochlear nerve (cranial IV). Outward rotation (excyclotorsion) is due to inferior oblique muscles mediated by the oculomotor nerve (cranial III), which also governs pupil dilation. A key facet of eye-rolling is its neural kinship with embryonic tactile withdrawal reflexes and protective movements designed to remove body parts from threatening circumstances (see *Flexion withdrawal*).

Eye rolling can be used to telegraph emotional contempt towards another individual (Worcel et al., 1999). It falls within the category of eye behavior, which involves efforts to exclude and or avoid eye contact with another individual (Eibl-Eibesfeldt, 2007).

Gender

Gender plays a role in eye rolling. Worcel et al. (1999) found that eye rolling was much more common in same-gender interactions. Eye rolling may also co-exist with other nonverbal expressions of aggression such as staring and tossing the head (Worcel et al., 1999). Eye rolling has been shown to have potent reverberations (Carrere et al., 2000). Its use has been shown to be a strong predictor of divorce (Carrere et al., 2000).

F

Figure F.1 Face

Face

Body part

At the front of the head, the human face includes 23 surface landmarks: (1) skin, (2) ears, (3) earlobes, (4) forehead, (5) eyebrows, (6) eyes, (7) eyelids, (8) eyelashes, (9) nose, (10) nostrils, (11) nostril bulbs, (12) cheekbones, (13) cheeks, (14) philtrum, (15) lips, (16) jowls, (17) hair, (18) wrinkles, (19) moles, (20) eccrine glands, (21) sebaceous glands, (22) apocrine glands and w. jaws.

Nonverbally, the most emotionally expressive part of the body (see *Facial expression*).

Usage

Our face (1) defines identity (see *Facial I.D.*); (2) expresses attitudes, opinions and moods and (3) shows how we relate to others. A face is every human's visual trademark and thus the most photographed part of the body.

Anthropology

For 99.99 percent of our existence as *Homo*, we watched other faces and rarely saw our own except as glimpsed in ponds or reflective pools. The phantom of facial personality is a dangerous and mystical experience in many cultures. Capturing a face in photographs or mirrors, for example, may be likened to capturing the soul. That in so many societies a face reflects the soul bespeaks the nonverbal power of its landmarks.

Primitive musculature

"In mammals the primitive neck muscles gave rise to two muscle layers: a superficial longitudinal layer, the platysma, and a deeper transverse layer, the sphincter colli profundus, which have come to extend well into the facial region" (Chevalier-Skolnikoff, 1973, 59). That sphincter colli profundus is a sphincter – that is, a muscle that constricts or widens a bodily opening – strengthens the contention that unpleasant emotions and stimuli lead cranial nerves to constrict the eye, nose, mouth and throat openings, while more pleasant sensations widen the facial orifices to incoming cues.

Facial schema

Perception of faces is rooted in the fusiform face area (FFA), located in Brodmann's area 37 of the temporal lobe. This proactive brain area is highly sensitive to facial templates. So actively does it seek out facial schema that we often see "faces" in cloud formations, shrouds (e.g., the Shroud of Turin), sandwiches and screen doors – and in our nearby celestial neighbor, the Moon.

See also *Blank face, Facial beauty, Facial recognition, Facial feedback hypothesis.*

Facebook

Using Facebook

Launched in 2004, Facebook is a social networking website that "allows users to create personal profiles, upload images, and post messages to friends, family members, colleagues, and others" (Montepare, 2014, 409). As such, it involves "self-construction" through an online platform (Gonzales and Hancock, 2008). Through this platform, users may communicate verbally (see *Word*) and nonverbally through emoticons, emojis, photographs and profile pictures (see *Emoticons and emojis*).

Faceism

Face/body index

Archer et al. (1983) created an index to measure facial prominence in drawings, photographs and other visual displays. Two measurements were used. The numerator was the distance from the top of the head to the lower point of the chin. The denominator was the distance from the top of the head to the lowest part of the depicted body. A result of 0 means no face is shown, and a result of 1 means that only the face is visible. In measuring a range of depictions of the face in American periodicals, publications from 11 cultures and artwork over six centuries, the researchers found that faceism was higher in visual depictions of men than in depictions of women. Proportionately more of the pictures were devoted to men's faces, while women's pictures showed more of the body.

Facial Action Coding System

Notation system

The Facial Action Coding System (FACS) is an alphanumeric scheme for classifying facial expressions. Based on work by Swedish anatomist Carl-Herman Hjortsjo, FACS was first published by Paul Ekman and Wallace Friesen in 1978. It describes actions of the entire facial anatomy and includes details regarding intensity and timing. It involves the careful determination of which muscles contract in various facially displayed emotions and then labeling these individual muscle movements as action units by number. "Retraction of the cheeks," for example, is "AU 12." The FACS was developed methodically and rigorously over more than a decade of research (Ekman and Friesen, 1978; Ekman et al., 2002).

Usage

FACS has been used extensively to observe human and nonhuman primate facial expressions and movements. It also includes codes for eye movements, head movements (such as the head-tilt) and a single entry for the shoulder-shrug. Intensity (amplitude) variables for a given facial expression or body movement are "trace," "slight," "marked or pronounced," "severe or extreme" and "maximum." FACS has undergone several revisions and updates, such as the recent F-M Facial Action Coding System 3.0 by Freitas-magalhães (2018).

See also *Kinesics*.

Facial Action Test (Directed)

Design

Designed by Ekman et al. (1983), this task(s) explores physiological responses to facial expressions. In the Directed Facial Action task, individuals are asked to move their facial muscles in certain ways but are not told the actual emotion they are expressing. Through the movement of the various facial muscles, participants form the prototypical emotional facial expression.

Research

Research by Levenson and Ekman (2002) has been consistent in discovering that facial expressions which involve anger, fear and sadness produce greater increases in heart rate than those expressions which show disgust.

Other research has found that the portrayal of fear compared with portraying calmness causes an increase in skin conductance and pulse rate (McCaul et al., 1982). The task has been validated across various cultures and age groups (e.g., Levenson et al., 1991, 1992).

Facial Affect Decision Task

Designed by Pell (2005), the Facial Affect Decision Task (FADT) investigates emotional associations between a speaker's voice and facial expressions. It involved 480 trials where one of four basic emotions was paired with an emotionally related or unrelated vocal prosody. Results from these trials revealed that prosodic features of communication aid the speed and accuracy of decisions about faces that are emotionally congruent with the prosody. The task also shows that "information about discrete emotions is shared across major nonverbal channels" (Pell, 2005, 45).

Facial appearance heuristic

Coined by Vrij (2004), the term facial appearance heuristic refers to people's tendency to judge another individual with an attractive face as more honest. As a result, perceptions of deception in daily life may be biased on appearance. Numerous studies have demonstrated this tendency (for example, Aune et al., 1993; Bull and Rumsey, 1988; Masip et al., 2004; Porter et al., 2002). In particular, females who are perceived as more attractive are judged as being less deceptive (Porter et al., 2002). Interestingly, work by Jones and Kramer (2015) found that the use of facial cosmetics has less effect on judgments of attractiveness than commonly assumed.

See also *Facial beauty*.

Facial beauty

Nonverbal perception

Qualities or features of the human face that may excite aesthetic admiration, attraction, desire and love.

Usage

Though facial beauty is "in the eye of the beholder," some qualities, features and proportions – such as those of the infantile schema – may be universally esteemed.

Eyes and cheekbones

Based on a study of Japanese and U.S. observer judgments of female attractiveness, high cheekbones, a thin lower jaw, large eyes and a shorter distance between the mouth and chin and between the nose and mouth, are usually preferred qualities in women's faces (Perrett et al., 1994).

Jaws

The size (a. normal, (2) vertically excessive ["too long"] or (3) vertically deficient ["too short"]) and placement (a. normal, (2) prognathic [protruding] or (3) retrusion) of the upper and/or lower jaws may affect perceptions of facial beauty. Cross-culturally, bimaxillary prognathism (protruding upper and lower jaws) is less attractive than either normal or bimaxillary retrusion. Vertical deficiency is more attractive than vertical excess, and normal jaw occlusion is more attractive than either retrograde or protruded lower jaws (Kiyak N.D.).

Love at first sight

A research team led by Knut Kampe of the Institute of Cognitive Neuroscience at University College, London, determined that eye contact with a pretty face – one judged to be attractive by the viewer on variables such as radiance, empathy, cheerfulness, motherliness and conventional beauty – activates the ventral striatum, a pleasure center of the brain.

Symmetry

Another preferred beauty trait involves facial symmetry between the right and left sides. In a review of symmetry in mate selection, researchers found that animals from scorpion flies to zebra finches showed a preference for symmetrical patterns and shapes (perhaps because asymmetry may be a sign of weakness or disease; Watson and Thornhill, 1994). College-student ratings of young adult faces reveal that vertical and horizontal symmetry are attractive features, at least in photographs. In another study based on the subjective ratings of judges: "The more symmetric twin of a pair was consistently rated as more attractive, and the magnitude of the

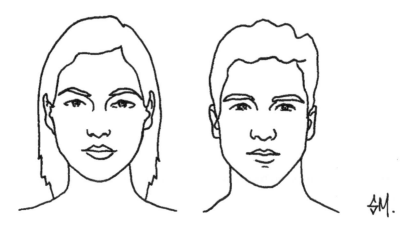

Figure F.2 Facial symmetry

difference between twins in perceived attractiveness was directly related to the magnitude of the difference in symmetry" (Mealey et al., 1999, 151).

Research report

In a study utilizing Asian, Hispanic and White judges, the most attractive female faces had larger, wider-set eyes; smaller noses; narrower facial breadths; smaller chins; higher eyebrows; larger lower lips; larger smiles; more dilated pupils and well-groomed, fuller hair (Cunningham et al., 1995).

Facial displays (syntactic)

Markers

These are facial expressions which serve as markers for words and or clauses in conversations. They can include grammatical information and help organize the structure of the conversation (Bavelas and Chovil, 2000, 2006). Examples include raising an eyebrow or widening the eyes to emphasize a word.

Facial displays (semantic)

Facial expressions that directly connect with what the speaker is saying. An example would be the use of widened eyes as an interjection when saying the word "amazing" in the sentence: "This wine tastes amazing."

Facial emblems

Coined by Ekman and Friesen (1975), facial emblems are facial displays which have a well-known verbal translation. Typically, facial emblems are performed by using only a part of the face (e.g., widening of the eyes). Examples of facial emblems include wrinkling of the nose to convey disgust, dropping the jaw and holding the mouth open to convey surprise, widening the eyes to convey surprise.

Facial expression

Visage sign

The act of communicating a mood, attitude, opinion, feeling or other message by contracting the facial muscles (see *Face*).

Usage

The combined expressive force of our mobile chin, lip, cheek, eye and brow muscles is without peer in the animal kingdom. Better than any other body parts, the face clearly reveals our opinions, feelings and moods (see *Emotion*). While we may learn to manipulate some expressions (see, e.g. *Smile*), many unconscious facial expressions (such as *Lip-pout*, *Tense-mouth* and *Tongue-show*) may reflect true feelings and hidden agendas or attitudes. Though some facial expressions are universal, others are shaped by cultural usage and rules.

Evolution I

In the Jurassic period, mammalian faces gradually became more mobile and far more expressive than the rigid faces of reptiles. Muscles that earlier controlled the primitive "gill" openings (see *Pharyngeal arch*) came to move mammalian lips, muzzles, scalps and ear flaps. Nerve links from the emotional limbic system to the facial muscles – routed through brain stem facial and trigeminal nerves (cranial VII and V) – enable the expression of joy, fear, sadness, surprise, interest, anger and disgust today.

Evolution II

That a nose-stinging whiff of ammonium carbonate may cause the face to close up in disgust shows how facial expression, smell and taste are linked. The connection traces to ancient muscles and nerves of the pharyngeal arches of remote Silurian ancestors. Pharyngeal arches were part of the feeding and breathing apparatus of jawless fishes; sea water was pumped in and out of the early pharynx through a series of gill slits at the animal's head end. Each arch contained a visceral nerve and a somatic muscle to close the gill opening in case dangerous chemicals were sensed. Early in Nonverbal World, pharyngeal arches were programmed to constrict in response to noxious tastes and smells.

Gag reflex

The Silurian pattern is reflected in our faces today. In infants, for example, a bitter taste shows in lowered brows, narrowed eyes and a protruded tongue – the yuck-face expression pictured on poison-warning labels. A bad flavor causes a baby to seal off the throat and oral cavity as cranial nerves IX and X activate the pharyngeal gag reflex. Cranial V depresses the lower jaw to expel an unpleasant mouthful, then closes it to keep food out, as cranial XII protrudes the tongue.

Research reports

1   Both happy and fearful faces have been shown to capture the attention of young children (Elam et al., 2010). In fact, by the age of 7 months, infants

can distinguish between happy and fearful expressions. At this age, infants look longer at the fear face (Bornstein and Arterberry, 2003; Nelson and Dolgin, 1985). By 7 months, infants can also discriminate between fear and anger but are unable to differentiate between fear and surprise (Serrano et al., 1992).

2   People from collectivistic cultures are more likely to inhibit facial expressions of negative emotions (Matsumoto, 2006). For example, people from South Korea and Japan can be "categorised" within collectivistic cultures. Such cultures can also find it difficult to identify facial expressions of negative emotions, more so than people from an individualistic culture (e.g., USA). People from Arab countries tend to be less inhibited in their expression of emotions, with more facial expressions, touching and energized gestures. A number of research studies show that people from the same culture are better at recognizing and interpreting the facial expressions of their own culture (Dovidio et al., 2006).

3   The study of the face can be divided up into two areas: "static features" of the face and "dynamic" features of the face. Static features, are, as the name suggests, features of the face which are "not moving." For example, the human makes a range of inferences from the static face such as gender, race, age. Moreover, inferences are also made about a person's personality from the static face. For example, females tend to prefer angular male faces when they are ovulating more than when they are menstruating (Penton-Voak et al., 1999). The term "dynamic" involves studying the movement of the face. Typically, this falls into two categories: "facial coloration change" and "muscular change." An example of facial coloration change is blushing. An example of muscular changes is smiling. The use of static/posed expressions in research has come in for some criticism, as researchers argue that facial expressions are complex and move in time: "compared to static presentation, dynamic presentation of facial expressions facilitates the ways in which the expressions are processed" (Sato and Yoshikawa, 2007).

4   Some scholars contend that the human is programmed to express emotion via facial expressions (e.g., Ekman, 1993). This is especially true for the "basic" human emotions, such as anger, sadness, contempt, disgust, fear, happiness, sadness/distress or surprise (Ekman, 1993; Ekman, 1994; Izard, 1994; Galati et al., 1997). However, there are only moderate correlations between facial expressions and emotion (Parkinson, 2005). Some argue that "the traditional focus on emotion as the way to explain our facial expressions is erroneous." Instead, they argue "that facial cues are better seen as "social tools" that modify the trajectory of our social interactions" (Fridlund and Russell, 2006, 299).

5   Research by Dimberg et al. (2000, 2002) shows that people respond unconsciously and spontaneously to "emotional facial stimuli" and that such responses involve the same facial muscles as those perceived in the "emotional facial stimuli." Moreover, these responses, while not necessarily visible to the naked eye, affect one's voluntary facial actions.

6   In processing threat and fearful facial images, the amygdala plays an important part in the processing of these stimuli. Such responses can even occur subconsciously (Le Doux, 1998; Gaffney, 2011; Suslow et al., 2006).

7   There is very significant research to show that "making the facial expressions associated with various emotional states triggers physiological responses similar

to how individuals would react if they were actually experiencing the emotion" (Afifi and Denes, 2013, 343). Work by Dimberg et al. (2000) found that even when people perceive a happy or angry face unconsciously, they will mimic this facial expression. (See *Mimicry*, *Emotional contagion theory*.)

8 Research by Behrens and Kret (2019, 513) found that "face-to-face" contact positively impacts "prosocial behaviour," even if the people in question "cannot verify whether their selfless acts are being reciprocated."

9 A range of studies show that fearful faces, and other threatening stimuli such as weapons and harmful animals, automatically capture the human's attention (Beaver et al., 2005; Carlson, 2016; Koster et al., 2004; Salemink et al., 2007). This bias towards socially relevant safety signals appears to extend beyond humans and has recently been observed in bonobos (Kreta et al., 2016).

10 Results from work by Torrence et al. (2017) indicate that human attention is captured and held by fearful faces at times earlier than approximately 300 ms.

Antonym: see *Blank face*.

Facial Expression Program

Discourse about facial expression

The Facial Expression Program (FEP) is a term used by Russell and Fernandez-Dols (1997) to encompass the various assumptions, theories and research that underpinned discourse and research on facial expression in the 1980s. Fundamentally, the FEP was underwritten by the belief that a list of basic emotions were the "cause of" and "signal received" from facial expressions (Russell and Fernandez-Dols, 1997, 10). Proponents of such beliefs undertook various research projects and discourse, with the belief that emotion is something measurable and understandable (Ekman and Friesen, 1975).

Key assumptions, premises and implications

The program has the following key assumptions, premises and implications, which are aptly summarized by Russell and Fernandez-Dols (1997, 11–12) as follows:

1 "There are a small number (seven plus or minus two) of basic emotions.
2 "Each basic emotion is genetically determined, universal, and discrete. Each is a highly coherent pattern consisting of characteristic facial behavior, distinctive conscious experience (a feeling), physiological underpinnings, and other characteristic expressive and instrumental actions. (Note that in this definition, cognition is not part of an emotion, although cognition might be one of the possible causes of an emotion.)
3 "The production (encoding) and recognition (decoding) of distinct facial expressions constitute a signalling system, which is an evolutionary adaptation to some of life's major problems. This premise predicts and relies upon similarity in facial configurations across species.
4 "Any state lacking its own facial signal is not a basic emotion. Therefore, discovering which facial expressions signal the same emotion universally provides a list of candidate basic emotions. The seven candidates found so far are

happiness, surprise, fear, anger, contempt, disgust, and sadness. There is some uncertainty over contempt and over the distinction between surprise and fear. Interest and shame might be added to the list. Candidates could then be tested against the criteria outlined in premise number 2.

5   "All emotions other than the basic ones are subcategories or mixtures (patterns, blends, combinations) of the basic emotions. For example, anger includes fury and annoyance as subcategories (which should therefore share anger's facial signal). Anxiety is a mixture of fear, sadness, anger, shame, and interest (and should therefore result in a facial blend).

6   "Voluntary facial expressions can simulate spontaneous ones. Voluntary expressions are deceptive in nature and culturally conditioned. Different cultures establish different display rules, which dictate when an expression can be displayed freely, and when it must be inhibited, exaggerated, or masked with a different expression. The true emotion "leaks" through the camouflage and can be detected through facial measurement.

7   "Any facial expression that deviates from the universal signals – either in an individual or in a cultural group – is a mixture of the basic signals or stems from the operations of culture-specific display rules.

8   "Emotional state is revealed by facial measurement. Thus, the emotions of newborns and of others unable or unwilling to speak truthfully become accessible. Verbal report can be bypassed. Great effort has gone into the development of scoring systems for facial movements. These systems objectively describe and quantify all visually discriminable units of facial action seen in adults or in babies. Scoring keys are available to translate the observed facial action units into emotion categories. Subtle or inhibited emotions can be revealed through facial electromyography. Expressions too brief to be seen by the unaided eye can be detected through high-speed photography.

9   "The subjective feelings associated with an emotion are due, at least in part, to proprioceptive feedback from facial movements. This "facial feedback hypothesis" has been offered as one means by which an individual "knows" which emotion he or she is feeling (and thus answers a question that has been central in the psychology of emotion since William James). The existence of these highly differentiated internal "cues" to an ongoing emotion would refute Schachter and Singer's theory that emotion consists of cognition plus undifferentiated arousal.

10   "Deliberately manipulating the face into the appropriate configuration creates the neurological pattern of the corresponding emotion. For instance, wrinkling the nose creates the neurological pattern of disgust. Facial manipulation can then be used in the laboratory to reveal the physiological signature of each emotion.

11   "The seven (plus or minus two) facial signals are easily recognized by all human beings regardless of their culture.

12   "The ability to recognize the emotion in a facial expression is innate rather than culturally determined. The ability is present very early, possibly at birth. In "social referencing" for example, young children use the emotion in their caregiver's face to decide how to handle ambiguous and potentially dangerous situations. The information obtained is more specific than simply whether the

caregiver feels positively or negatively about the situation. For instance, anger and fear expressions send very different messages to the child.

13   "The mental categories by means of which recognition occurs (in the self as facial feedback or in others through facial signaling) are genetically rather than culturally determined. The words happiness, surprise, fear, anger, disgust, contempt, and sadness thus designate innate and universal categories. Other languages may use other names, but the categories named are the same. These categories are natural kinds and semantic primitives. Like the emotions themselves, additional emotion labels designate mixtures or subcategories of the basic categories.

14   "Like encoding and decoding, the meaning ('signal value') of a facial expression is fixed by nature and invariant across changes in the context in which it occurs. Observers can thus recognize the emotion in another's facial expression, even when the other's context and behavior provide conflicting information. Observers can recognize the same emotion in the same facial expression across a range of modes of presenting the facial expression."

Many of the basic assumptions of the program have been criticized. For example, in Parkinson's work (2005), only moderate correlations can be found between facial expressions and emotion. The universality of facial expression has also been critiqued (Russell, 1994; Russell, 1995).

Facial feedback hypothesis

Emotion and facial feedback hypothesis

The facial feedback hypothesis is based on the idea that the act of engaging in a facial display of emotion stimulates physiological changes which are consistent with the emotion being expressed facially and which influence the actual emotional experience (Buck, 1980; Levenson, 1992; Capella, 1993). In short, "facial expression sends signals to the brain that produce feelings" (Burgoon et al, 2016, 312). For example, raising your cheeks can make an individual happier while furrowing your brow can make you angrier. Physiological responses involved in the display of an emotion closely resemble those involved in experiencing the emotion. For example, when displaying anger, sadness and happiness, increases in skin temperature have been found which were closely consistent with those involved in the "real" experience of these emotions (Ekman et al., 1983).

Research

Research indicates that facial feedback can modulate emotions currently being felt and also spark emotions (Adelmann and Zajonc, 1989; Cappella, 1993; Soussignan, 2004; McIntosh, 1996). This is especially true for facial expressions associated with happiness and anger (e.g., Dimberg and Soderkvist, 2011). It has also been established for expressions of fear and sadness (e.g., Flack et al., 1999) and for surprise and disgust (e.g., Lewis, 2012).

The facial feedback hypothesis has been interpreted in different ways. For example, the sufficiency hypothesis, which is widely supported, argues that facial expressions of emotion involving muscle activity alone can produce an emotional experience (Levenson and Ekman, 2002). The necessity hypothesis argues that there can be no emotional experience without facial feedback (Keillor et al., 2002). The modulation hypothesis holds that facial expression can modulate emotional experiences that have been elicited by an external stimulus. This stimulus is something other than the individual's facial actions. For example, a well-known study by Strack et al. (1988) asked participants to hold a pencil between their teeth and also between their lips (external stimuli). Those participants who held the pencil between their teeth (which activated smiling muscles) rated cartoons as funnier than those who held the pencil between their lips (which is linked with frowning movements).

How does it work?

How facial feedback actually works "remains unclear" (Soderkvist, 2018, 131). A number of studies using fMRI have found that facial feedback mechanisms modulate or attenuate activity in the amygdala (Hennenlotter et al., 2009; Kim et al., 2014). Skin sensory feedback has also been proposed (Tomkins, 1980), as has the vascular theory of emotional efference (Zajonc et al., 1989). The most common theory asserts that the activation of particular facial muscles results in afferent feedback produced by proprioceptive patterns which spark matching affect (Adelmann and Zajonc, 1989). Interesting work undertaken by Keillor et al. (2002) on a patient with bilateral facial paralysis tests the hypothesis that "an active face" is necessary to experience or process an emotion. In this case, the patient (despite bilateral facial paralysis) was able to engage with reported normal emotional experience.

Facial flushing

Emotion cue

Becoming red or rosy in the face from physical exercise, embarrassment, shyness, anger or shame.

Usage

Facial flushing or blushing is elicited by social stimuli, for example, as one becomes the focus of attention in a group, is asked to speak in public or experiences stranger anxiety. Suddenly the face, ears and neck – and in extreme cases the entire upper chest – redden, causing further embarrassment still.

Anatomy

Blushing is caused by sudden arousal of the sympathetic nervous system which dilates small blood vessels of the face and body (see *Fight-or-flight*).

Medicine

Some people blush uncontrollably in almost any social situation and suffer such embarrassment that they may undergo surgery to interrupt sympathetic nervous supply to the face. In a thorascopic sympathecotomy, an incision is made through the armpit into the thoracic cavity to sever a sympathetic nerve located close to the spine. (N.B.: Embarrassing sweaty hands may be controlled the same way; see *Sweaty palms*.)

Protoblush

One of the first signs of anger, arousal or embarrassment is a very visible, uncontrollable reddening of the ears.

See also *Eye-blink*, *Flashbulb eyes*.

Facial I.D.

Identification cues

Those definitive features of a face with which to establish age, sex, attractiveness and identity.

Usage

Despite an advanced ability to recognize and recall thousands of faces (see *Facial recognition*), we are unable to describe individual faces adequately in words. Witnesses at crime scenes, for example, may offer police few verbal clues of facial I.D.

Identity clues

Our brain's innate ability to recognize faces far exceeds that of any spoken language to describe them. Identity clues used by the Chicago Police, for example, consist of general, all-purpose words such as (1) high, low, wide and narrow foreheads; (2) smooth, creased and wrinkled skin; (3) long, wide, flat, pug and Roman noses; (4) wide, narrow and flared nostrils; (5) sunken, filled-out, dried, oily and wrinkled cheeks; (6) prominent, high, low, wide and fleshy cheekbones; (7) corners-turned-up, down and level for the mouth; (8) thin, medium and full upper and lower lips; (9) double chin, protruding Adam's apple and hanging jowls for necks and (10) round, oval, pointed, square, small and double chins.

Prehistory

That linguistic labels for the face pale in comparison to those for consumer products (see, e.g., *Footwear*) is because our primate face "speaks for itself" and has done so for millions of years. The need to describe faces in words is a recent development dating back only a few thousand years to adaptations for city life, urban crime and increasing numbers of strangers. (N.B.: Recognizing and remembering faces involves emotion centers of the brain that may be addressed only indirectly by speech centers.)

Evolution

Our face has become more "baby-like" and less intimidating through time. The wide jaws and broad dental arch of *Homo habilis* (ca. 2.3 mya), for example, belonged to a fearsome-looking face with great biting power. Our lower face's comparatively smaller features crouch today beneath an immense, bulbous, infantile forehead.

See also *Facial beauty*, *Facial expression*.

Facial masking

Hide and "speak"

Given the expressive magnitude of human faces (see *Face, Facial I.D., Facial recognition*), it was all but inevitable that *Homo sapiens* would find ways to increase or decrease the volume of its expressive features through material masks (see *Artifact*). Facial masking has a diverse and widespread distribution throughout the world.

Usage

A male thief may wear a bandana or face mask to conceal his facial identity (see *Invisibility*). A female Mardi Gras parader, in contrast, may leave most of her face uncovered while attracting notice to a mask's colorful, sexually expressive lines around the eyes. Nonverbally, face masks made of feathers, leather, leaves and wood have been used for at least 9,000 years to expressively "speak" in dramatic performances, Halloween gatherings, political celebrations, religious ceremonies and war dances.

Afikpo masks

Traditional Nigerian wooden masks cover the entire male face but add expressive eyebrows, eyes, cheeks, mouths, lips and chins, combining facial gestures that "speak" loudly in Afikpo secret ceremonies.

Amish no-masks

Facial masking is widespread among humans but not universal. Amish Americans, for example, dress plainly so as not to call attention to themselves, and masks are rarely seen. Amish women may not use cosmetics. Married men often wear very long beards below their cheeks and chins, leaving much of the lower face uncovered. Since mustaches may connote militance, passivist Amish men do not wear them.

Ceylonese masks

Traditional carved wooden masks from Sri Lanka are brightly colored (usually orange and yellow) for use in dancing (see *Dance*). Dances may be celebratory or curative and choreographed to drive away evil spirits. The masks themselves often possess dramatically ascending "hairpiece" elements (see *Hair cue*) and exaggerated, prominent ears that widen and lend authority to the facial plain. Ceylonese masks may have friendly smiling eyes and faces to greet onlookers in tandem with exposed, potentially hostile spatulate teeth to scare off evil ghosts and spirits.

Chinese masks

Facial masks originated in China ca. 3,500 years ago to scare away ghosts and evil spirits. Dark colors (see *Colors decoded*), angry facial expressions (see *Anger*) and biting teeth (see *Bite*) expressed frightful emotions. Today highly colorful masks may be used to observe and celebrate key life events such as birth, marriage and death. Chinese New Year and opera masks may have friendly eyes and happy smiles (see

Zygomatic smile). Colors are bright and symbolic; red, for example, connotes courage; yellow, evil and green, violence. Nonverbally, the diversity and high expressivity of Chinese face masks is a recognized art form (see *Art cue*, *Aesthetic messaging*).

See also *Saving face*.

Facial pattern recognition

Digital identification

Faces may be digitally identified by means of artificial intelligence (AI). While the human brain uses intuitive cortical modules to identify faces, AI identifies them through mathematics.

Usage I

AI computer programs use pattern recognition to identify distinctive features and landmarks on the facial surface. Features may include skin texture, eye width or jaw shape and size. Landmarks may include eyebrows, noses and chins. By connecting features and landmarks with straight lines, distinctive linear patterns emerge. Like fingerprints, the latter may be stored in an electronic database enabling comparative identification (see *Fingerprint*).

Usage II

Facial pattern recognition is in widespread use around the world as an identification tool for driver licensing, security systems and law enforcement. As AI draws from ever-expanding databases of facial image – from city surveillance cameras, licensing agencies and social media – usage of facial recognition technology is expected to grow.

See also *Facial I.D.*

Falsetto

Voice tone

A manner of calling, singing or speaking in a high-pitched tone of voice. A vocal register that contrasts with the normal modal voice and the lower-pitched, raspy voice known as vocal fry. The principal tone of the trademarked Tarzan jungle call.

Usage

Falsetto may be used to mark one's position or standing in society, as in working-class London's use of Cockney English. In music, a falsetto voice may be used to add emotion to the lyrical words of a song, as in vocal performances of the Bee Gees group and Queen. While selling fresh fish, a loud falsetto voice may be used to call attention to a fishmonger's stand.

Yodel

Falsetto voices may be heard in the yodeled sounds of traditional Hawaiian and U.S. country-western music. In a yodel, the singer's voice alternates rapidly between falsetto and modal (or "chest voice") tones. The piercing quality commands attention and may be audible over great distances, as in Alpine yodeled messages between isolated villages. Widely distributed – from Bavarian Germany to the Pygmies of African Congo – yodeling may be emotionally evocative of feeling and mood.

Anatomy

A falsetto voice quality is produced by vibrations of the lateral ligamentous edges of the vocal cords (see *Tone of voice*).

Antonym: see *Raspy voice*.

Familiarity

Same is safe

Nonverbally, familiar signs – aromas, art work, faces, footwear, gestures, hairstyles, hats, postures, smiles, tastes and voice tones – may be more pleasant and likable than those which are unfamiliar. Verbally, familiar phrases, rhymes, words and written characters may similarly sound or be more pleasing than those which are novel and new.

Usage

The familiarity effect may be used in advertising (see *Media*) to render a consumer product more likable through repeated exposure.

Mere exposure

The principle of mere exposure (Zajonc, 2001) holds that repeated exposure to, for example, a face seen in church, is enough to render that face more likable than a face previously unseen. A classic case of mere exposure involved Chinese ideographs. Western subjects exposed to a single Chinese written character, and later asked to choose the most liked character from an assortment of previously unseen ones consistently preferred the former. Merely being exposed to the one ideograph beforehand determined the preference.

Courtship

Research on social attractiveness consistently finds that the more one person sees and interacts with another, the more likable he or she becomes.

Biology

Neurologically, same is safe, and safe is same. Novel movements, smells and tastes, for example, may be interpreted cautiously with suspicion and avoided. Novel aroma, color, taste and touch cues may incur a neophobic food response as unusual gustatory, visual and textural (mouthfeel) stimuli lead to avoidance. Biologically, avoidance is a protective response against potentially dangerous food items.

Culture

A common response to unfamiliar foods, sights and sounds in different societies has been identified by anthropologists as "culture shock," an unpleasant, disoriented feeling experienced in exotic and foreign lands. Nonverbally, a low level of afferent sensory sameness may occasion anger, disgust, disliking and fear.

See also *Isopraxism*.

Fast motion

Chronemic cue

A sequence of audio or visual behaviors performed or recorded in faster-than-normal speed.

Usage

Fast motion may be used to call attention to or dramatize nonverbal units in the stream of behavior (see *Action unit*). Electronically recorded auditory cues, body movements, facial expressions and gestures may be played back in faster-than-normal time for purposes of teaching and macro-pattern recognition.

Teaching

Since the serial elements of nonverbal communication may take place over prolonged time periods, fast motion can be effective for use as a teaching tool. In faster-than-normal time, viewers are able to discern periodic and repetitive patterns of behavior that may not be visible in real time.

Macro view

Fast motion enables greater accuracy in recording macro – "big picture" – behaviors such as, for example, those involved in dyadic imitation, mirroring and synchrony (see *Isopraxism*).

Fast sound

A melody (see *Music*) may be rendered more cheerful and energetic when accelerated in allegro and presto modes.

Media

In a video, body motions may be momentarily speeded up or slowed down to add drama and emphasis or to showcase a nonverbal act or sequence in the behavioral stream. The sudden beginning and abrupt ending of a changed tempo call attention via contrast with real time.

See also *Slow motion*.

Fear

Emotion

A usually unpleasant, visceral feeling of anxiety, apprehension or dread.

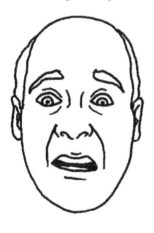

Figure F.3 Fear

Fear face

Fear may show prominently on the face in crying, increased eye-blink rate, a "fear grin," widely opened flashbulb eyes, lip-retraction, staring eyes with enlarged pupils, tense-mouth cues and yawning.

Additional signs

Fear may also show in an exaggerated angular distance, release of apocrine odor, increase in breathing rate, mandibular trembling ("chattering teeth"), crouching, displacement (self-touch) gestures, flexion withdrawal, the freeze reaction, bristling hair (piloerection), an accelerated heart rate, tightened muscle tension (esp. in muscles innervated by special visceral nerves, e.g., upper trapezius), screaming, squirm cues, staring eyes with enlarged pupils, sweaty palms, the throat-clear and an audibly tense tone of voice.

Art cue

Completed in 1893, the staring eyes and open mouth jaw-droop of the terrified face in The Scream, by Norwegian artist Edvard Munch, has become a cultural icon of humankind's ambient level of fear.

Media

We so enjoy vicarious fear that the world's most portrayed movie character is Bram Stoker's Count Dracula. Over 155 representations of the fearful character have appeared on the screen.

Neuro-note

Nuclei of the amygdala play key roles in the mediation and expression of fear (LeDoux, 1996).
    See also *Stranger anxiety, Facial expression.*

Feet

Pedestrian smart part

The terminal end organs below the legs, used for standing, walking, dance and display (see *Footwear*). Those body parts that make direct contact with the earth and ground; reveal dominance and submission by toeing out or toeing in, respectively (see *Shoulder-shrug display*, Constituents); link to sexual modules of the brain's sensory parietal lobe (as expressed, e.g., in foot fetishism); point toward or angle away from liked or disliked individuals, respectively and through men's and women's shoes, mark gender, identity and status.

Anthropology

Ca. 4 mya in Africa, after descending from trees to the savannah grasslands, human beings began upright walking. Hands were no longer needed for travel, and fingers continued their evolution as tactile antennae. At the same time – despite their own tactile savvy and prehensile IQ – feet were grounded and relegated to "foot duty."

Archaeology

Feet provide early signs of human presence. Evidence for human feet dates to ca. 3.5 mya to the tracks of three upright ancestors – probably australopithecines – who strolled across a bed of volcanic ash on the east-African savannah in what is now Laetoli, Tanzania. The footprints are nearly identical to those of modern humans today.

See also *Boot, Goose-step*

Fence

Barrier sign

A linear boundary marker, rising perpendicularly to a usually horizontal surface. Nonverbally, the meaning of a fence is its own presence, that is, its physical existence in space and time.

Usage

Fences may be used to keep people, animals, plants and mineral substances (e.g., sand) out of a space or, alternatively, keep them enclosed within. The opposed usages of fence structures – outer versus inner – are complementary and simultaneously function to regulate diverse movements. Fences may be used as safety devices, as in the white cast-iron, ribbed barriers lining the Ha'penny footbridge across the River Liffey in Dublin, Ireland.

Territory

Humans are very territorial primates and may erect fences to demarcate spaces claimed to be owned. The nonverbal message of a territorial fence may be supplemented by words such as "posted," "private property" and "keep out" (see *Word*).

Length

A fence's nonverbal narrative may be short, as in a chainlink gate between neighboring garages, or longwinded, as in the 14-mile U.S. border fence between San Diego, California, and Tijuana, Mexico, which is often newsworthy, with a great deal to "say."

Walls

Fences may evolve as higher, thicker, significantly enlarged walls, such as the Berlin Wall, Jerusalem's "Wailing Wall" and the Great Wall of China. Nonverbally, such walls take on symbolic meanings, respectively, of repression, religion and nationality.

Tunnels

The classic response to a wall is a secret tunnel (see *Invisibility*). Historically, a worldwide tradition of covert smuggler-tunneling exists, including dozens of long, underground passageways that secretly link Mexico and San Diego along the southern U.S. border.

See also *Space*.

Fight-or-flight

Ready response

An emergency reaction in which the body prepares for combat or escape from potentially dangerous situations, animals or people.

Usage

Many nonverbal signs, from sweaty palms to bristling hair, may be evident in stepped-up visceral feelings and body movements of the fight-or-flight response.

Evolution

Fight-or-flight is an ancient sympathetic response pattern which, in the aquatic brain, accelerated heartbeat rate, raised blood-sugar level and released hormones from the adrenal gland, preparing an alarmed fish to chase-and-bite or turn-and-flee.

Facial color

The sympathetic nervous system may telegraph its state of mind in the whiteness (pallor) or redness (flushing) of the human face. Pallor, associated with extreme fear or rage (see *Anger*), is caused by constriction of the facial blood vessels brought on by the release of adrenaline and noradrenaline. Associated with embarrassment or slight-to-moderate anger, a flushed face (which may begin with a faint blush at the top of the ears) is caused by dilation of the facial blood vessels due to adrenaline (see *Facial flushing*).

Neuro-notes

In the 1920s, American physiologist Walter B. Cannon (1871–1945) identified the sympathetic nervous system's emergency reaction, which prepared the body to exert high levels of physical energy. In the 1930s, while stimulating regions of cat hypothalamus, Swiss physiologist Walter R. Hess (1881–1973) identified the defense reaction, which included tendencies to fight or flee. The fight-or-flight response is coordinated by central command neurons in the hypothalamus and brain stem which "regulate the sympathetic outflow of both the stellate ganglion and the adrenal gland" (Jansen et al., 1995, 644).

Antonym: *Rest-and-digest*. See also *Freeze reaction*.

Fingerprints

Identity signs

Unique patterns of friction-ridged epidermal skin are found on the palmar (inner) surfaces of the human hand and foot. On the fingertips' tactile pads, friction ridges are called fingerprints or dermatoglyphs. Fingerprints encode unique nonverbal information about personal identity.

Arch, loop and whorl

Fingerprints form on hands in the womb before birth, and are fully formed – for the lifetime of an individual – by the prenatal sixth month. Friction-ridged skin aids in gripping and climbing, and is found in the hands and feet of lemurs, monkeys, apes and human primates, and in arboreal marsupials, such as the Australian koala. In humans, diagnostic arch, loop, and whorl patterns of fingerprints form as outer (epidermal) and inner (dermal) skin layers interact through physical processes of folding, compression and growth.

Usage

Nonverbal identity encoded in dermatoglyphs supplements more recent verbal and numerical identity of names and I.D. numbers. According to The Fingerprint Sourcebook (U.S. Department of Justice, 2014), fingerprints were first used as I.D. signs in 300 bc China, 702 ad Japan and the United States in 1902. The most extensive dermatoglyph collection is maintained by the U.S. Federal Bureau of Investigation.

See also *Facial I.D.*

Finger-snap

Auditory cue

A sharp, snapping nonverbal sound made when the middle finger's tactile pad suddenly releases from its tensed opposition with the thumb's tactile pad and strikes the palm with a slap. Snapping is a learned behavior children master through often-repeated trial and error.

Usage

Nonverbally, the finger-snap is a polysemous sign with diverse meanings, both within and across cultures. An audible snap may be used to summon a restaurant server, though as a sign of unequal status it may be considered rude. As an alternative to clapping, group usage may bond snappers together through the principle of same behavior (see *Isopraxism*). Finger-snapping may be used to mark rhythm in music and dance (see *Rhythmic repetition*).

Culture

In ancient Greece, finger-snapping (apokrotea) was used to synchronize rhythm in dance. Southern European flamenco dancers may finger-snap (pitos) synchronously as well. In the United States, repeated snapping may signal that one is searching his or her memory. In Latin America, the snap may mean, "Hurry up!" In the United Kingdom and United States, a spontaneous snap may be given when one has an inspiration or new idea.

Neuro-note

The combined sudden onset and abrupt ending of a finger-snap calls for attention – much like a beeping or clicking sound – by engaging a listener's midbrain auditory startle reflex (see *Beep, Lateral click*).

See also *Hand-clap*.

Fingernails

Gender sign

Flattened keratinous plates on the dorsal, distal ends of fingers and thumbs. Minor body parts with major nonverbal meanings. The color, length, shape and size of fingernails are often enhanced to mark gender contrasts.

Markedness

Verbally, the English word "dishonest" is a marked form of "honest." According to linguistic theory, marked forms have special meaning and may stand out to the mind. Nonverbally, colored fingernails are marked forms of plain nails and have meanings that similarly stand out as special (see *Color cue*).

Usage

Nonverbally, men's fingernails are most often unmarked, short, plain and unadorned with color. Men may use nails primarily as signs of cleanliness and good grooming. Women may shape and color their nails as beauty signs to attract notice and project glamour.

Gesture

In research on "The Language of Hands," Givens (2002) found that poor condition of fingernails can interfere with a hand's ability to communicate: a hand's negative appearance diminishes attention paid to its expressive shapes and gestures (see *Gesture*).

See also *Fingerprint*.

Finger of blame

Metaphorical gesture

One of many linguistic expressions that use the pointed human index finger as a metaphor. A similar noun phrases is "pointed finger of accusation." The "pointed finger of blame" phrase, itself, is widespread, for example, in Irish Gaelic ("an locht a chur ar dhuine"), French ("pointer un doigt de blame") and Spanish ("dedo acusador").

Usage

Verbally, the phrase may be used to describe a person's – or a group's – responsibility for mistakes, bad decision or wrongdoing. Nonverbally, an extended index finger may be used as a gesture to identify wrongdoing persons or groups. The widespread use of finger-of-blame locutions attests to the power of nonverbal pointing (see *Point*).

See also *Word*.

Fist

Hand signal

A gesture made with the hand closed, fingers flexed and tactile pads held firmly against the palm.

Usage

Clenched fists signal an aroused emotional state, as in aggression, anger, excitement (e.g., to cheer on a team) or fear. In a business meeting, unconscious fisting may be a visible sign of anxiety (see *Self-touch*) or unvoiced disagreement (see *Probing point*).

Thumb-over-fist

One may soften the impact of a fisted gesture by placing the thumb's rounded tactile pad atop the fist's flexed index finger. In the Lincoln Memorial in Washington, D.C., the 1922 statue of a seated Abraham Lincoln featured the president's curvilinear thumb pads to "humanize" the monumental, 19-foot-high, 120 ton statue's hands. In the same way, the thumb-over-fist gesture – first used by President John F. Kennedy in the 1960s – became an effectively assertive cue to emphasize speaking points without seeming overly aggressive in the process. After Kennedy, U.S. politicians, including Presidents Bill Clinton and Barack Obama, used thumb-over-fist to show strength, to humanize their political speeches and to connect emotionally with voters.

Antonym: *Palm-up*.

Flag

Symbolic wave

A usually rectangular, color-coded piece of cut fabric, replete with national, international, provincial, state or local-community signs and symbols. A key design feature of flags is their tendency to flap in the breeze and when waved by a standard bearer. Flags may be addressed verbally, as in pledging allegiance, and nonverbally with a hand salute (see *Gesture*).

Usage

Flags may be used as nonverbal signs to mark bounded territories and unite those residing within. They may be flown on high from flagpoles or waved from shorter staffs. As flags wave, they attract motion centers of the visual cortex and appear to be "alive."

Country cues

National flags originated in medieval times as preliterate battle standards in warfare. They later evolved as national emblems on sailing ships to identify country of origin. Today's country flags often entail diverse nonverbal protocols: tactile (for folding and handling), visual (for displaying and hanging) and audio (for singing an anthem; see *Singing*). How one communicates with a national flag is often decoded as being emblematic of patriotism.

Stars and stripes

The overwhelming majority of national flags proclaim their country's power through eye-catching color contrasts (see *Color cue*) and bold horizontal, diagonal and vertical straight (i.e., "unbending") lines. The human eye is highly responsive to linear designs, details and edges, possibly due to that organ's arboreal-primate past (see *Tree sign*). Most country flags feature blocky, rectangular shapes rather than more "friendly" curvilinear contours. Many showcase celestial designs, as well (for, e.g., the Moon, Sun and stars) to symbolically connect with cosmic powers.

See also *Proxemics*, National space.

Figure F.4 Flashbulb eyes

Flashbulb eyes

Facial expression

An involuntary and dramatic widening of the eyes, performed in situations of intense emotion, such as anger, surprise and fear. A maximal opening of the eyelids (i.e., a dilation of the palpebral fissure) which shows the roundness and curvature (i.e., protrusion) of the eyeballs.

Usage

When one is truly surprised, rather than feigning the emotion for effect, as, for example, in a conversation, two involuntary visceral muscles in the eyelids (superior and inferior tarsals) widen the eye slits to make eyes appear noticeably rounder, larger and whiter. Like dilated pupils, another visceral sign of emotional arousal, flashbulb eyes are controlled by impulses from the sympathetic nervous system's fight-or-flight division. As visceral signs, flashbulb eyes may be difficult to produce at will. Thus they are all the more trustworthy as nonverbal cues, especially of terror and rage. In angry individuals, flashbulb eyes may be a danger sign of imminent verbal aggression or physical attack.

Media

In the Dracula movies of 1931, 1973 and 1979, actors Bela Lugosi, Jack Palance and Frank Langella consciously widened their eyes before biting victims' necks to draw blood. Had they felt true emotion, their eyes would have opened wider still.

See also *Sweaty palms*.

Flexion withdrawal

Reflexive body movement

An automatic escape motion designed to remove a body part or parts from danger, for example, flexing the neck to lower and protect the head.

Usage

Flexion withdrawal underlies many negative and submissive nonverbal signs (e.g., cues of disagreement, disliking and fear; see *Body-bend*, *Bow*, *Crouch*, *Gaze-down*, *Head-tilt-side* and *Shoulder-shrug*).

Business

Around a conference table, colleagues may reveal unvoiced negative feelings in postures influenced by flexion withdrawal, for example, pulling the hands and arms backward, away from a disliked speaker.

Biology

In mammals, the most primitive protective response is a flexion withdrawal, which "takes the head and neck away from the stimulus" (Salzen, 1979, 130).

Embryology

The crouch posture is "a protective pattern characteristic of the early embryonic flexion response" (Salzen, 1979, 136). By 8 weeks, for example, the human fetus already "knows" to withdraw its head and neck when the mouth is touched. Defensive, coordinated flexing and withdrawing movements have been seen in immature fish larvae, in marine snails and in human embryos at 8 weeks of age. In four-legged animals whose brains have been surgically disconnected from the spinal cord, almost any tactile stimulus will cause flexor muscles to contract and withdraw a limb from whatever touched it (Guyton, 1996).

Anatomy

Human arms and legs have highly developed flexor reflexes. Automatic escape movements, coordinated by the spinal cord, can be triggered, for example, by a scalding pot handle – or by strong emotion from the amygdala.

See also *Nonverbal release*.

Fluctuating asymmetry

Measuring fluctuating asymmetry

The term fluctuating asymmetry (FA) refers to deviations from symmetry of bilaterally symmetrically traits (Moller and Pomiankowski, 1993). It is termed fluctuating, as the fluctuation is not controlled by genes (Kowner, 2001; Van Valen, 1962). Fluctuating asymmetry is measured by taking precise measurements of one side of the body (e.g., width of the foot) and comparing this measurement with the equivalent measurement on the other side of the body (i.e., width of the other foot). If there is a large discrepancy between these two measures (e.g., large discrepancy in the width measurement of two feet), then the result is a high fluctuating asymmetry.

Fluctuating asymmetry and health

Lower FA has been linked with greater health (Milne et al., 2003); greater disease resistance (Livshits et al., 1998); better fertility (Jasienska et al., 2006); increased masculinity in men (Gangestad and Thornhill, 1997) and positive personality traits such as sociability, confidence, balance and reduced anxiety (Fink et al., 2006).

See *Attractiveness*; *Facial symmetry*.

Footwear

Clothing cue

A consumer product, such as boots, shoes or slippers, to protect and decorate the feet. A highly expressive article of clothing designed to convey information about gender, status and personality (see *Information, Messaging feature*).

Usage I

Worldwide, shoes are among our most expressive nonverbal cues (see also *Hat*). This reflects the foot's primate evolution as a grasping organ and neurological "smart part," and the curious fact that our foot's sensory mapping on the parietal lobe abuts that of the genital organs – our feet are similarly sensitive, ticklish and sexy (see *Homunculus*).

Usage II

Feminine footwear may show personality and uniqueness – as if to say, "I'm someone special" – while masculine footwear is part of a uniform to mark membership in a group (to say, "I'm on the management team" or "I'm a cowboy").

Archaeology

Humans have been decorating their sandals and shoes at least since the beginning of the Neolithic Age, ca. 10,000 years ago. According to archaeologists who found them in homes, tombs and burials, the earliest sandals came in hundreds of designs. Thus, style in footwear was important from the very beginning, much as it is today.
See also *Goose-step*, *High heel*, *Sneaker*.

Freeze reaction

Posture

A sudden involuntary cessation of body movement, usually in response to a novel stimulus or fright (see *Fear*).

Usage

The freeze reaction is a protective reflex. The body may automatically tense up as the nervous system mobilizes for action (see *Fight-or-flight*), as in, for example, when we hear a rattlesnake or when the boss calls out our name.

Neuro-notes

The brain contains a "fear center" (see *Amygdala*) that activates the body's freeze reaction, and may stretch the mouth into a fear grin (see *Lips*).
See also *Orienting reflex*, *Startle reflex*.

Fringe

Clothing cue

Linear strips of fabric, flounce, leather, string or thread that add adornment and kinetic energy to clothing. Fringe attracts notice to apparel nonverbally by adding linear detail, movement and repetition (see *Rhythmic repetition*).

Usage

Fringe may be used as a decorative device to accentuate one's arm, chest, hip and leg movements. Fringed dresses may also call "see-through" attention to otherwise bared legs.

History

Fringe may date back ca. 5,000 years, as old as woven fabric itself. By removing several horizontal (weft) threads from vertical (warp) threads, the latter could then be braided and tied off to prevent the fabric from unraveling.

String skirts

At ca. 10,000 years old, the Neolithic string skirt, which revealed the body below the waist and accented its hip movements, was worn by women on behalf of fertility (see *Reproductive force*). Like string skirts, the Native Hawaii grass skirt emphasized hip movements in dancing, as well (see *Dance*). Fringed flapper dresses of the 1920s also accentuated motions of the pelvic area.

See also *Hair*.

Frown

Emotion cue

In the lower face, any of several usually negative displays of down-pulled lip corners. In the upper face, any of several degrees of lowered brows (see *Eyebrow-lower*). In anger, disagreement and other negative feelings, the two may show in tandem. In humans and primates, during times of aggression or protection, frowning involves a lowering of the brow which provides eye protection while simultaneously facilitating an opening of the eye (Morris, 1985).

Usage

The human frown may be used to encode a variety of emotions, feelings and moods from uncertainty to unhappiness to despair (see *Sadness*). While the frown is likely a cultural universal, its magnitude, meaning and use may be subject to societal shaping.Antonym: *Smile*.

See also *Ritualization*.

Fruit substitute

Consumer product

A foodstuff (e.g., a candy bar, cookie or donut) sweetened with sugar to resemble the taste of ripened ovaries of blackberry, raspberry, apple and other seed-bearing plants.

Usage

So successful have fruit substitutes become as "edible signs" – as foods suggesting the presence of ripe fruits and berries – that they are as common in the modern diet as fruit itself. A fruit substitute's sweetness may come from table sugar (sucrose), a crystalline carbohydrate that suggests the fruity sweetness of fructose for which, as a nonverbal sign, it stands. Fruit substitutes reconnect us to our frugivorous, primate past.

Juicy fruit

When primates took to trees ca. 50 mya in the Eocene, they supplemented a basically insect diet (see *Shellfish taste*) with ripened fruit. The evolution of our "sweet tooth" is reflected in ancestors' teeth. Insect-eaters had spiked cusps on their molar teeth, while fruit-eaters had flatter, rounder molars for grinding. Eocene-primate molars show a flattened adaptation for pulping fruit flesh, the better to taste its fructose. Our tricuspid teeth enable us to pulp grapes, bananas and Juicy Fruit® chewing gum.

Prehistory

Giving sweet gifts, for example, sugar cane, butter creams or chocolate-covered ants – may be a friendly gesture in every society. The earliest prehistoric candy may have been honey, which is still a popular commodity among living hunter-gatherers such as the !Kung Bushmen today.

Today

Earth's best-selling fruit substitute may be Life Savers®. Had they grown on trees, the colorful candies might have appealed to Miocene-primate tongues as well.

See also *Juice substitute*.

Functional model of nonverbal behavior

Functionality

The underpinning assumption of the functional model is that nonverbal behavior serves a pragmatic purpose (Patterson, 1982, 1983). In short, "people initiate patterns of nonverbal interaction to serve different social functions" (Patterson, 2019, 113).

Within this paradigm of thinking, nonverbal behavior can serve many functions, such as the expression of intimacy, exercise of influence, provision of information, regulation of interaction and management of impressions (Patterson, 1983, 1991, 2019). The construct argues that "people are doing more than managing their levels of nonverbal involvement in interactions. They are behaving, consciously or unconsciously, to achieve specific goals in interaction" (Patterson, 2019, 114).

Affect and goals

This model contends that emotions on their own do not determine all our nonverbal behaviors. It acknowledges that while emotions may influence the pursuit of goals, there are some goals which "over-ride"/replace emotional underwriting. For example, gaining compliance or deceiving someone can "over-ride" the role of affect in determining behavior. A smile or touch might be used to express intimacy with a partner or might be used to manipulate a partner. Both have differing underlying affect.

The functional model argues that biology, culture, gender and personality determine patterns of interaction. People who have similar biological hardwiring, culture, personality and immediate goals are "more likely to share common expectancies and behavioral predispositions" (Patterson, 2019, 114).

Fundamental attribution error

The fundamental attribution error (FAE), which is sometimes called the attribution effect or the correspondence bias, relates to the formation of impressions

(Ross, 1977). It is the tendency for people to overestimate the influence of dispositional factors and to underestimate situational factors. For example, if you think a person is trustworthy, then you are inclined to transpose this belief to the person being trustworthy in all situations. Emotion has been shown to influence fundamental attribution. Forgas (1998) showed that the fundamental attribution error applied more to people in a positive mood than a negative mood.

G

Gait

Walking style

A particular movement style in which the body is moved from one place to another while walking.

Vulnerability cue

There is evidence that indicates gait as a reliable indicator of vulnerability. People with high psychopathic tendencies can identify people who have suffered from assaults based on watching their gait alone (Wheeler et al., 2009; Book et al, 2013). Typical gaits of victims include: a. either long or short stride (proportional to the body); b. the weight of the body shifts laterality, diagonally or up/down rather than forward; c. the movement tends to be unilateral (first one side, then the other); (4) movements appear more gestural rather than postural (meaning the movement is initiated from the body's periphery) and e. walkers tend to lift their feet while walking rather than using a more fluid swing movement (Grayson and Stein, 1981). There is evidence that one can change one's gait to reveal less vulnerability (Johnston et al., 2004).

Personality

There is some correlation between gait style and aggressive traits. For instance, "When walking, the body naturally rotates a little; as an individual steps forward with their left foot, the left side of the pelvis will move forward with the leg and the left shoulder will move back and the right shoulder forward to maintain balance. Put simply, an aggressive walk is one where this rotation is exaggerated" (Satchell et al., 2017, 42–43).

Pathology

Gait can be a symptom or manifestation of a mental pathology. In depressed patient's walking style, there is a decrease in the length of the stride and in velocity (Lemke et al., 2000). Patients with Parkinson disease also show a reduction in the length of the stride and stride stability (Kim et al., 2018).

Sex

Gait is different in women and men. People can judge correctly the sex of the person while watching their gait, even using a point-light technique that masks the figure of the body and just allows the observer to see moving points (Kozlowski and Cutting, 1977). This is probably because swaying hips is a more likely characteristic of female walking, while shoulder swaying is usually more masculine (Johnson and Tassinary, 2005).

Emotions

Gait changes are noted when people are asked to walk to a particular emotion or while listening to different styles of music (Janssen et al., 2008). In one investigation, they have "identified several gait characteristics which differentiate sadness, anger, happiness, and pride revealed by gait. In particular, angry gaits were found to be relatively more heavy-footed than the other gaits, and sad gaits were found to have less arm swing than the other gaits. It was also observed that proud and angry gaits have longer stride lengths than happy or sad gaits. Finally, happy gaits appeared to subjects to be faster paced than the other gaits" (Montepare et al., 1987, 39).

Identity

People can identify a person by watching their gait (Cutting and Kozlowski, 1977)

Motion tracking software

The use of tracking software has enabled a closer and more elaborate examination of gait in the past two decades. For instance, a. shoulder angle while walking has significant influence when identifying affective states, and b. technology aspires to identify people based on their walking style (Karg et al., 2010).

Quote

1   "When young, healthy, vibrant people walk, they walk faster than older people, which results in theirs arms swinging higher in front and behind, and can even make it look as if they're marching. This is partly due to their additional speed and greater muscle flexibility. As a consequence of this, the army march evolved as an exaggerated walk to portray the effect that the marchers are youthful and vigorous. This same walk has been adopted by many politicians" (Pease and Pease, 2004, 210).

2   "The walking styles of different individuals and of different cultures have fascinated observers for many years. Personal differences are enormous and many famous people have such distinct walking actions they can be imitated with ease. One only has to mention Charlie Chaplin, Groucho Marx, James Cagney, Mae West or John Wayne to illustrate this" (Desmond Morris, 1985, 228–229).

Gangster garb

Clothing cue

A usually uniform style of adornment, fashion and footwear worn by diverse criminal-gang and organized-crime-syndicate members.

Usage

Despite openly announcing one's criminal affiliation to law enforcement, gang members tend to dress, groom, look and act alike in order to identify one another as members, to bond through the reptilian principle of mimicry (see *Isopraxism*) and to intimidate rivals.

Deciphering hats

Hats have long been favored signs of gang membership (see *Hat*). In the 1850s, members of New York City's Plug Uglies gang wore large plug hats – bowlers or top hats – stuffed with leather, rags and wood scraps. Like helmets, the padded hats protected heads in gang fights and announced gang affiliation on the streets.

Nonverbal notice

The visual theme of gang membership is to stand out clearly as a gangster. In the 1940s, Chicago gangsters wore dark pin-striped, double-breasted suits with wide, peaked lapels; double-pleated trousers and wide cuffs (see *Color cue*, Light and dark I-V). Jackets had tapered waist-fits and wide shoulders. Worn beneath jackets, tight-fitting, high-buttoned vests with satin backs and adjusters gave a vaguely sinister look.

Notice me

Earlier, in the 1930s, a Los Angeles gangster may have worn a "zoot suit." It, too had a wide-shouldered, narrow-waisted look (see *Broadside display*). The very long jacket, double-breasted with peaked lapels, gave a loose and casual drape. Its hem dropped well below a wearer's dangled fingertips. Fuller-fitting, baggy pleated pants were worn with a showy taper from the knee down. Accessories included suspenders, a glistening zoot chain, a very thin snake or crocodile belt, and a fedora with turned-down brim and pinch front crown. Conspicuous two-tone oxford "spectator" shoes completed the message: "Notice me."

See also *Business suit*.

Gasp

Audible cue

A usually sudden, brief, voiceless inspiration of breath given upon learning a disturbing fact or piece of upsetting information.

Usage

A nonverbal gasp may be used to communicate the sudden onset of astonishment, shock or surprise.

Media

In the 1954 film "Godzilla," Japanese onlookers exhaled vocal gasps upon sighting the monstrous 164-foot-tall reptile. The gasp expression has its own Japanese pictographic emoji (see *Emoticons and emojis*).

Physiology

Known as agonal respiration, gasping is a universal vertebrate behavior that may occur during ventricular fibrillation to resuscitate the heart and increase oxygen uptake. Emotional gasping in humans is found worldwide.

Neuro-notes

Responding to abrupt fear or surprise, the sympathetic nervous system may override our brain's speech production (see *Verbal center*) and produce a nonverbal sound in the vocal tract rather than a voiced word, phrase or sentence (see *Fight or flight*). The gasp may be decoded by mirror neurons that recognize its meaning intuitively – as if listeners themselves had gasped in surprise (see *Nonverbal brain*, Mirror neurons).

Gavel

Auditory cue

A usually wooden, hand-held mallet used to rap upon a table top or striking block to attract attention. Gaveling may be followed by a vocal edict, announcement or directive. Usually wielded by a leader, judge, auctioneer or other person in charge, a gavel's sharp, striking sound cuts through ambient vocal noises that may fill a crowded room. The nonverbal message of a gaveled sound suggests finality, as it abruptly pre-empts vocal verbiage at an auction or in a legislative chamber or court of law.

Similar wood-clapping sounds are used in Japanese kabuki theater and sumo wrestling. In the former, hardwood or bamboo sticks are clapped together to signal the beginning of a play, and call attention to key moments in its performance. In sum, the clacking noise of wooden hyoshigi sticks invites wrestlers to the ring and summons spectators to a momentary, altered-sensory state of consciousness.

Neuro-notes

The gavel's hardwood-striking cues are effective because they address the midbrain's auditory lobes, which are reflexively attuned to sudden changes in sound. Located just below the optic-center lobes, these pea-sized areas control our auditory startle reflex. Picked up by the cochlear nucleus, a loud noise received by the auditory lobes triggers the amygdala and circuits of the reticulospinal tract to activate the startle. Thus, attention paid to the gavel's woody call is a primal, subcortical response prompted by paleocircuits of the amphibian brain.

See also *Branch substitute*.

Gazebo

Architectural signage

Any of several small, usually circular – often octagonal – roofed structures seen in gardens, parks and public spaces. In a garden setting, the gazebo's symmetrical shape and radial symmetry stand in contrast to the verdant vines, grasses and trees, as if to send a message: "intelligently made by humans." A magnetically attractive pedestrian destination in which to find shade, solitude and quiet contemplation. Symbolically, the ring-like, circular shape may be suggestive of the infinite.

History

The earliest gazebos date to 5,000 B.P. in Egypt, and were popular in gardens of Classical Greece and Rome. Gazebos today have a worldwide distribution and provide pedestrians with places to sit and enjoy restful and often spectacular views.

Marriage

Often in service to courtship, gazebos are popular venues for wedding ceremonies in which to celebrate and showcase brides and grooms (see *Reproductive force*).

Rhythmic repetition

Nonverbally, the harmonic repetition of design features – such as columns, cupolas and horizontal-trim – serve to unify gazebo structure, add narrative flow and simulate a sense of motion. In gazebos with standing columns, children may circle the structure repeatedly, as if dancing through the circular arrangement of upright pillars and stones (see *Dance*).

Gaze

General

The significance of gaze in nonverbal communication is widely researched (See also *Eye contact*). As humans, we are able to discriminate between directed and averted gaze from infanthood (Farroni et al., 2002). Indeed, "mutual gaze" has been found to be important in infant social development (Flom et al., 2007; Fogel et al., 1999; Brooks and Meltzoff, 2005).

Burgoon et al. (2016, 131) summarize some of the early research on gaze as follows:

- The normal amount of gaze in an interaction ranges from 28 percent to 70 percent of the time.
- Under stress conditions, the range broadens to 8 percent to 73 percent of the time.
- Eye contact increases when listening (30 percent to 80 percent of the time) and decreases when speaking (25 percent to 65 percent of the time).
- Gaze increases when information is needed from another person, when monitoring another and when needing to be seen by another.
- Individuals are consistent in their looking patterns.
- Interactants coordinate their looking patterns.
- Gaze aversion is more frequent when discussing difficult topics, when uncertain, or when ashamed.
- Sex, race, personality and interpersonal relationship affect the amount of eye contact.

The study of gaze crosses into many domains of human behavior, such as attractiveness, deception, dominance, power, status and submission.

Averted/extended gaze and gaze direction

Direct intense eye gaze has been associated with dominance (Hall et al., 2005; Main et al., 2009). Kalma (1992) found that socially dominant people engage in more mutual gazing, while aggressively dominant individuals "look around" more and signal disinterest in others. In response to such directed gaze, Holland et al. (2016) found that people avert their gaze when another individual presents with dominant behaviors. In particular, highly anxious individuals use gaze direction as a cue and quickly avert their gaze in contexts of facial displays of anger (Rohner, 2002).

Some studies have established a link between the direction of one's looking and brain function. If you move your eyes to the left, then right hemisphere activity is inferred (e.g., spatial/emotional processing) while movement to the right infers left brain processing (e.g., intellectual/linguistic tasks) (De Gennaro and Violani, 1988; Weisz and Adam, 1993).

Gaze and liking

Gazing is also associated with "liking." As Argyle (1988, 162) observes, "people look more at those they like." We gaze more at romantic partners, friends, and people we like than people we dislike (Guerrero et al., 2007; Kleinke, 1986). Typically, increased gaze is associated with friendliness and affiliation, while averted gaze is associated with dislike and hostility (Burgoon et al., 1984). In conveying empathy and warmth, direct and continuous gaze is important (McAdams et al., 1984). Extended gaze has been connected with sexual interest (Thayer and Schiff, 1977). Absence of gaze has been identified as signaling inattentiveness, with mutual gaze signaling openness and attraction (Kleinke, 1986). Givens (1983) observes that gaze is one of the key cues in communicating attraction.

Gaze and culture

There are some differences across cultures with respect to degrees of gazing. Arabs engage in longer and more frequent gazes with their partners than Americans (Watson and Graves, 1966). While extended gaze is typically viewed as positive in American cultures, this may not be true of other cultures, where extended gaze can be interpreted as overly friendly. In his work, Watson (1970) found that contact cultures (where people engage in more physical touch and contact during interactions) have higher levels of gaze as compared to non-contact cultures. In India, gaze avoidance is a mark of deference when speaking to someone of higher status (Knapp and Hall, 1997).

Gaze and gender

It has been found that women receive more gaze than men. Some studies have found that women spend more time than men gazing (Fehr and Exline, 1987). Interestingly, females show a preference for males who gaze at them a lot, while males prefer a lower degree of gaze (Kleinke et al., 1973). Least gazing occurs when men engage with men and most gaze occurs when women engage with women (McCormick and Jones, 1989).

Gaze and status

Combined with particular head movements, Toscano et al. (2018) found that certain gazes can convey messages of "status-related traits" (Toscano, 2018, 285). Indeed, high-status individuals engage in greater and longer gaze patterns (Argyle, 1994; Dovidio et. al., 1988), especially at the end of utterances (Kalma, 1992).

Gaze-down

Sign

Rotating the eyeballs in their sockets to a downward position. Bowing or tilting the head forward so that the eyes face the ground or floor.

Usage

Gaze-down may convey a defeated attitude. It may also reflect guilt, shame or submissiveness, as when distorting the truth or telling a lie (see *Deception*). Gazing down while – or shortly after – stating "I am innocent," for example, shows that a speaker may not believe in his or her own innocence.

Anatomy

Gaze-down occurs as the inferior rectus muscle, innervated by the oculomotor nerve (cranial III), contracts as the prime mover.

Antonym: *Stare*. See also *Bow*.

Gaze (en face)

Emotional bond

An intimate form of eye contact in which a mother positions her face within inches of her baby's face and aligns, eye-to-eye, in parallel, for optimal viewing. Family and people of all ages have been observed using the en face gaze with infants, frequently smiling and using high-pitched, cooing voice tones as well.

Usage

Nonverbally, en face may be used diagnostically as a sign of a positive emotional relationship with a baby. In a study of child abuse, Givens (1978a) found non-abuser moms using en face while abusers omitted the cue.

Courtship

The en face gaze has been identified as a positive sign in human courtship (Givens, 1978b, 2005; see *Love*).

Research report

In a study of eye-contact behavior in babies, researchers found that "infants learn rapidly that the looking behaviors of others conveys significant information" (Farroni et al., 2002, 9602). "The results show that, from birth, human infants prefer to look at faces that engage them in mutual gaze and that, from an early age, healthy babies show enhanced neural processing of direct gaze. The exceptionally early sensitivity to mutual gaze demonstrated in these studies is arguably the major foundation for the later development of social skills" (Farroni et al., 2002, 9602).

Gesture

Nonverbal sign

A body movement, posture or material artifact that encodes or influences a concept, motivation or mood (thus, a gesture is neither matter nor energy but

Figure G.1 Gesture

information). Gestures may include facial expressions, clothing cues, body movements and postures. Many products contain messaging features designed to communicate as signs and may be decoded as gestures as well (see *Consumer product*).

Gesture can be defined as a "visible body action which communicates a message" (Knapp et al., 2014, 206). Gesture can happen in conjunction with speech but also without speech. Indeed, it has been shown to provide more information when the gesture provides information not relayed in the accompanying speech (Hostetter, 2011). Wagner et al. (2004), observe that gesture is an important feature of speech, as there are aspects of our thinking which are more grounded in images than words.

Children start to gesture at about 10 months (Beattie, 2004). It happens at a time in their development when they wish to express themselves but are limited in the words they can use (Goldin Meadow, 1999). There is significant evidence to show that children benefit more from gesture than adults Hostetter (2011).

History

Some gestures can be traced back to the year 690 BC in Italy, where the head toss was used to indicate "no." Roman orators and teachers were very interested in the behaviors associated with oratory and speech delivery. The Roman statesman Cicero argued that the body was like a musical instrument with an eloquence which involved gesticulation as well as speech. Indeed, there are some who argue that the ancient Greeks and Romans relied more on gestures in everyday life having a more "lively feel for the meaning of gestures" than we do (Wundt, 1921/1973, 66). Indeed, Wundt (1921) contended that they were better at reading these signals than humans of the 20th century.

Gesture and culture

Gestures can mean different things in different cultures. For example, the "okay gesture," which involves making a zero shape with the thumb and index finger can be understood as "worthless" in some cultures, as "all is well" in the United States and as an obscene gesture in other cultures (e.g., Middle East). Having your fingers crossed can be interpreted as a "good luck" gesture in some cultures and as a religious symbol in others. There is research to show that people from particular cultures use expressive gestures more frequently. For example, Italians and peoples from cities on the Mediterranean Sea use expressive gestures more frequently (Morris et al., 1979; Morris, 1994; Almaney and Alwan, 1982). Indeed, Beattie (2004) points to the "extravagant gesticulations" of the Italians compared with the "inhibited gesticulations" of the English. Indeed, it has often been noted that Arabs are the "world leaders" in terms of the vast variety of gestures they use. As Barakat (1973, 751) once wrote: "So intimately related are speech, gesture and culture, that to tie an Arab's hands while he is speaking is tantamount to trying to tie his tongue."

The use of gesture

Generally, two points of view are proposed on the use of gesture, with overlap between both points of view. Some say that it is used to promote understanding between the speaker and the listener (Bavelas, 1994; Clark, 1996). Others argue that gesture is chiefly of value to the person doing the gesturing. Here the use of gesture "confers a cognitive benefit on the speaker" (Wagner et al., 2004, 404), with gestures being used to help with the retrieval of lexical information (Butterworth and Hadar, 1989; Chawla and Krauss, 1994; Pine et al., 2007; Ping and Goldin-Meadow, 2010). In these instances, gestures help to "organise spatial and motor information into packages appropriate for speaking" (Wagner et al., 2004, 406).

Kinds of gesture

Deictic gesture

This type of gesture typically involves pointing and is often used by children. Indeed, children begin using these pointing gestures at around the age of 10 months. They are used to indicate objects and events and are context dependent, for example, a child pointing to a red square on the wall when discussing shapes.

Iconic gesture

This happens when we use a gesture which closely resembles a concrete object or event. They capture aspects of the form of the object. They may also communicate information about the object's characteristics, such as its speed or size. For example, a teacher may be explaining to children how to use paste to join together two butterfly wings. The teacher brings together the two hands in a joining motion to indicate gluing together. A number of studies suggest that, under particular conditions, the use of iconic gestures can communicate more semantic information than actual spoken words (Beattie and Shovelton, 1999a, 1999b, 2001, 2002; Holler et al., 2009; Riseborough, 1981)

Metaphoric gesture

This happens when gesture is used to present an abstract concept. These kinds of gestures are like iconic gestures in that they are essentially pictorial, but they differ in that the content is an abstract rather than a concrete object or event (Beattie, 2004). They can give an image of the invisible. For example, if discussing gravity, you bring your hand down from a height to indicate the downward force of gravity.

Gesture and conversation

Gesture used during conversation has been divided into three categories: emblems, illustrators and regulators (Ekman and Friesen, 1969b).

Emblems

Emblems typically have an explicit verbal meaning. They involve the use of gesture to communicate a message typically recognized by the community. For example, the thumbs-up signal to indicate approval or rubbing one's tummy to indicate hunger.

Illustrators

Illustrators are tied to speech and typically serve to elaborate and strengthen the verbal aspects of a message. For example, if talking about a missing bracelet, a speaker might point to his/her wrist. Work by Maricchiolo et al. in 2009 found that people who gesture when speaking were judged as more composed and competent than non-gesturers. Indeed, listeners have been shown to like people who gesture more as compared with those who do not gesture (Kelly and Goldsmith, 2004)

Regulators

Regulators are body movements which help in managing the flow of a conversation, for example, gesturing to a person when it is their turn to speak.

Gesture and beats

Beats are hand movements which follow the rhythm of speech. They involve the use of rhythmic, emphatic gestures like a baton while giving a public speech (Burgoon et al., 2016)

Anthropology I

"Gesture includes much more than the manipulation of the hands and other visible and movable parts of the organism. Intonations of the voice may register attitudes and feelings quite as significantly as the clenched fist, the wave of the hand, the shrugging of the shoulders, or the lifting of the eyebrows" (Sapir, 1931, 105).

Anthropology II

"[W]e respond to gestures with an extreme alertness and, one might almost say, in accordance with an elaborate and secret code that is written nowhere, known by none, and understood by all" (Sapir, 1927, 556).

Neuro-notes

We respond to hand gestures with an extreme alertness because dedicated nerve cells in our brain's lower temporal lobe respond exclusively to hand positions and shapes (Kandel et al., 1991). "Speech production and speech-related gestures are connected to such a degree that they have been considered as outlets of the same thought process, a view supported by the finding that hand and orofacial gestures are supported by the speech production area, i.e., Broca's region" (Nishitani et al., 2005, 66).

Muscles that today move the human larynx (for speech) and pectoral girdle (for hand gestures) evolved from hypobranchial muscles that originally opened the mouths and gill openings of ancient fishes. Paleocircuits that mediate our laryngeal and pectoral movements are connected in the posterior hindbrain and anterior spinal cord (Bass and Chagnaud, 2012).

Gesture and learning

The use of gestures can provide semantic value to the spoken word (Beattie and Shovelton, 1999a, 1999b). Research by Krauss et al., 1995; Hadar et al., 1998 and Wagner et al., 2004 in the field of gesture indicates that gestures are closely related to cognitive processing. They have an impact on your working memory and help you recall both visuo-spatial and verbal items. In particular, a number of writers in the field of gesture are united on the point that the nature of mathematical concepts lends them to the use of gesture (Goldin-Meadow et al., 1992; Perry et al., 1995; Goldin-Meadow et al., 1999). For example, when explaining mathematical concepts, teachers need to translate the concepts into many symbolic forms (Shavelson et al., 1988). The concept, where possible, needs a representational format.

A number of studies have found that in primary school, lessons which are characterized by the use of gesture are more effective than the same lessons without that usage (Perry et al., 1995; Valenzo et al., 2003; Goldin-Meadow, 2004; Church et al., 2004). There is also considerable research evidence to indicate that learners who gesture spontaneously on a task are more likely to retain what they have learned about the task than learners who do not gesture on the task (for examples: Alibali and Goldin-Meadow, 1993; Cook and Goldin Meadow, 2006). Moreover, teaching which includes gesture has been found to facilitate learning (Church et al., 2004; Singer and Goldin-Meadow, 2005 and Valenzo et al., 2003). When children use gestures to help them recall an event, they report more details about the event than children who are not instructed to gesture (Stevanoni and Salmon, 2005). Various reasons have been advanced for the value of gesture in learning, with embodied cognition which incorporates both motor and perceptual systems frequently being cited (Ping et al., 2014). Mayer's dual channel theory is also advanced given its emphasis on the presentation of information in both verbal and visual channels (Congdon et al., 2017)

See also *Facial expression*.

Gesture measurement

Assigned numbers

In gesture research, measurement involves assigning numbers to body movements and constituent parts. Numerical measures may be spatial or temporal (chronological) in nature.

Spatial

The simplest spatial measurements are observational. A researcher assigns a binary value, a "one" or a "zero," to a gesture to indicate its presence or absence, respectively, in the space of a communication venue such as a conversation. In signal detection theory, four values or outcomes are possible for each individual sighting.

Signal detection

Imagine a researcher observing the shoulder-shrug gestures of a man and a woman seated together at a small coffee table. At some level of precision, there will be uncertainty as to whether a shrug actually occurred. If the man coughs and shrugs, for example, should that be counted as a shoulder-shrug? For any communication venue, four observational outcomes are possible. In signal detection parlance (Peterson et al., 1954), the first is a "hit": a shoulder-shrug occurs and the researcher sees and records it. The second is a "miss": a shrug occurs but the researcher neither sees nor records it. Third is a "false alarm": a shrug does not occur, but the researcher incorrectly sees and records one. And fourth is "correct rejection": no shrug occurs and the researcher correctly notates its absence.

Size and magnitude

Regarding measurement of a gesture's size and magnitude, researchers have paid less attention to a signal's strength and amplitude than to the simpler binary metric of presence or absence. Four decades ago, the semiotician Paul Bouissac proposed that human body movements be studied in terms of the three-dimensional volumes they occupy in space (Bouissac, 1973). This focus was intended to improve upon earlier notation systems, such as the hieroglyphic-like kinesic system of Birdwhistell (1952), which accounted principally for the presence or absence of body-motion cues (see *Kinesics*). Though Bouissac's volumetric measurement scheme did not bear fruit, computers now make such measurements possible. Ning and colleagues, for example, have perfected a computerized motion detector that can be used to measure shoulder-shrug cues (Ning et al., 2006). Huazhong and colleagues (2006) have designed a realtime shoulder-shrug detector. Boker and colleagues (2009) have perfected a computerized avatar for use in measuring head movements in dyadic conversations.

Temporal

In temporal terms, the simplest gesture measurements are relative. A given body movement is observed to come before, during or after another body-motion unit or event. A shoulder-shrug, for example, may come before, during or after a spoken word or another nonverbal sign in the stream of behavior. The shrug's occurrence in time is measured not in absolute terms but in relation to its serial appearance in a timeline: preceding, coinciding with or following a spoken word or body movement.

See also *Point light*.

Gift

Presented item

A present proffered by one person or group to another. Items may include life forms (e.g., puppies, roses), property (automobiles, land) and other "things" (socks, necklaces, marbles and rings). Nonverbally, gifts may become highly valued possessions through their emotional connection to givers (see *Emotion*). As signs, gifts are more than simply material things – they are material means to social ends.

Usage

Usually accompanied by words (e.g., written on cards and tags or spoken face to face), nonverbal gifts may be used to express appreciation, mark anniversaries and show love. Used to strengthen social bonds, they are powerful emotional signs that may call for reciprocation and exchange.

Nonverbal exchange

Anthropologists study gift giving as a means of exchange. Gifts themselves communicate essential messages and meanings apart from words. Since the 1925 publication of Marcell Mauss' classic work, *The Gift*, ethnologists have recognized the power of giving in human relationships. Mauss taught that gifts are never free. Anthropologists today agree that when accepted, gifts may incur strong obligations.

Glasses

Introduction

Glasses, which are sometimes alternatively named eyeglasses or spectacles, are typically used to correct vision impairments. Such types of glasses involve the use of a lens and a frame which are placed in front of the eyes. Other types of glasses include safety glasses worn for protection (e.g., in the field of construction) and sunglasses which are used to protect the eyes from excessive light.

Historically

While there are accounts of glasses being used in Roman and Greek times, it is generally accepted that glasses were invented in Northern Italy c. 1290. In the past, the wearing of glasses was considered to hinder perceptions of attractiveness and even to be termed socially humiliating (Lundberg and Sheehan, 1994). A number of characteristics were attributed to people who wore glasses, with Thornton (1943) attributing stereotypical attributes such as intelligence, dependability, industriousness and honesty to those who wore glasses.

Glasses and attractiveness

Recent discourse and studies on the wearing of eyeglasses suggests that while perceptions of attractiveness can be reduced because of wearing eyeglasses, such perceptions are also reliant on the type of glasses being worn (Leder et al., 2011). For example, wearing glasses without rims makes the face less distinctive but not necessarily less attractive (Leder et al., 2011). Some research (Leder et al., 2011 and Terry, 1993) has found that wearing eyeglasses can hinder the observer's facial recognition abilities.

Glasses and perceptions of human attributes

Some recent studies echo past research, finding that people perceive those wearing glasses as having higher intelligence and being trustworthy (Hellstrom and Tekle, 1994; Terry and Krantz, 1993). In so doing, they conform to older stereotyping: "Thus, glasses affect how we perceive the faces of the people wearing them and, in accordance with an old stereotype, they can lower how attractive, but increase how intelligent and trustworthy people wearing them appear. These effects depend on the kind of glasses worn" (Leder et al., 2011, 211).

There is significant evidence to indicate that while there has been a positive shift in people's perceptions of those who wear glasses, adolescents with vision impairments still receive negative feedback from peers and report social isolation (Datta, 2014). Nonetheless, Pullin (2009) argues that there has been a shift in people's thinking about glasses. They are no longer perceived as devices associated with disability. Rather, they are now considered a fashion accessory, with some individuals wearing glasses purely for ornamental reasons.

Glasses and gender

In their research, Kinley et al. (2019) found some gender differences in perceptions of the wearing of eye glasses. Males who wore glasses were generally thought to be more reliable when wearing glasses but more "provocative" and "good-looking" without them. Females who wore dark-rimmed glasses were thought to be more reliable and jovial with these frames and, like their male counterparts, "more provocative and good-looking" without glasses (Kinley et al, 2019, 372).

Glitter

Sparkle sign

An assortment of colorful, reflective, loosely packed small particles that collectively shimmer as they reflect light from diverse angles.

Usage

Glitter has been used cosmetically and in artwork to attract notice since prehistoric times. As a nonverbal medium of expression, glitter has had – and continues to have – a widespread geographic distribution.

Prehistoric glimmer

Added to pigment, mica-flake glimmer has been used since ca. 40,000 years ago by *Homo sapiens* in Upper Paleolithic cave paintings. Illuminated by firelight, the painted images softly glowed.

Historic gleam

Historically, and to the present day, glitter has been used cosmetically on faces (see *Face*) and nails (see *Fingernails*) at least since ancient Egyptian times.

Media

In the classic 1972 film The Rise and Fall of Ziggy Stardust and the Spiders from Mars, singer-songwriter David Bowie (1947–2016) wore an other-worldly metallic and glitter medallion-third-eye on his forehead. As makeup artist Pati Dubroff commented, "Seeing his Ziggy Stardust character was the first time I understood and saw that makeup could be fantastical . . . that it could take you to magical places" (Valdesolo, 2016).

See also *Paisley*.

Glutamate

Taste cue

An amino acid used to enhance flavor and add a usually pleasant meaty taste to food products. The fifth basic taste after bitter, salty, sour and sweet, monosodium glutamate (MSG) is called umami ("pleasant savory taste") in Japan. A messaging molecule that prompts food items to "speak" nonverbally to the tongue as "meats."

Usage

With its rich meaty flavor, glutamate is a frequent additive to edible consumer products such as crackers, chips, seasonings, soup bases, sauces and "natural flavorings." Rich in free glutamate, parmesan cheese and tomatoes, for example, appeal to the carnivore tongue.

Comfort

Glutamate encodes a chemical "comfort." By 1966, the phrase "comfort food" appeared in print as a label for high-calorie – usually carbohydrate – dishes that provided feelings of contentment and well-being through the rest-and-digest (parasympathetic) division of the autonomic nervous system. Around the world, comfort foods (e.g., spaghetti, fried rice, macaroni and cheese) contain very high levels of glutamate. Consumers with acute or chronic anxiety may self-medicate with MSG to calm down.

Neuro-note

A study of the gustofacial reflex of newborns as young as 24 hours in age found that unseasoned soup stock produced an aversion response but that soup seasoned with MSG produced an acceptance response.

See also *Trigeminal taste*.

Golf

Introduction

At the 1981 Benson and Hedges golf tournament in Fulford, York, Bernhard Langer hit his ball onto the 17th green from atop the limb of a tree. At the 2013 Arnold Palmer Invitational in Orlando, Florida, Sergio Garcia climbed into an oak tree on the tenth hole to hit his golf ball from its arboreal, leafy lie 15 feet up in the oak's branches.

Hunting and gathering

An evolutionary correct game with which to rekindle the savannah experience our nomadic ancestors knew in Africa. A game enjoyed by small, face-to-face bands of players, wandering through artificial grasslands in pursuit of spherical prey, striking white/colored balls with high-tech branch substitutes called clubs.

Usage

Nonverbally, golf reconnects players to arboreal, savannah-grassland and hunter-gatherer roots. Golfers focus incredible attention on gripping the club, which in shape and thickness resembles a tree branch. Blending power and precision grips, they strike vinyl balls as if swatting small prey animals. Stalking through artificial grasslands in close-knit groups (see *Isopraxism*), sticks in hand – hunting for game balls and walloping them – people enjoy the same concentration, competition and camaraderie their ancestors felt 2 mya in Africa. (N.B.: No gas stations, subways or billboards disturb the "natural" view.)

Culture and the color green

"With this camaraderie, we were cut off from our ethnic roots, bias and prejudice. We were merely men against the course. We had transcended our race, color and ethnicity. The only color we saw was the color green" (Tharwat, 2000, 52).

Prehistory

Two mya in the Pleistocene, the first humans (genus *Homo*) lived in eastern Africa as hunter-gatherers on tropical, shrubby grasslands – in hot, flat, open countryside with scattered trees and little shade known as savannahs (from Taino *zabana*, "flat grassland"). *Homo habilis* would feel at home strolling the eighth hole at Pebble Beach, for example, with its cliffs, surf, boulders and tree-lined hills spanning the horizon. Its fairway resembles a game trail, its sand traps could be dried salt ponds and neither office buildings nor power poles disturb the "natural view."

Neuro-notes

Because the savannah experience took place during a critical time in human evolution – as *Homo*'s brain was expanding faster than any brain in the history of vertebrates – grassland habitats left an indelible mark on the species. We continue to find psychic comfort in open spaces. Indeed, neo-savannah grassland, with its scattered bushes and reassuring clumps of trees, is the landscaping theme of golf courses, college campuses, city parks and cemeteries.

See also *Lawn display, Nonverbal world*.

Goose-step

Bipedal display

An energetically marched or paraded version of the masculine stomp, in which the legs make sharp kicking movements from the hip, with the knees locked, as the soles and heels of military boots aggressively strike the ground. Troops may perform the marching step in unison to feel intra-group cohesiveness and uniformity (see *Isopraxism*).

History

The military goose-step began as the Stechschrift ("piercing or stabbing step") in Germany in the mid-18th century. The subsequent 1940s era goose-step of Nazi soldiers was visible a half-century later when, for example, North Korean soldiers marched on the 50th anniversary of the founding of the Workers Party in 1995. Nonverbally, a powerful physical demonstration of negative energy, the goose-step, a military version of the reptilian high-stand display, used to figuratively stomp an enemy to death. After WWII, the goose-step was outlawed in West Germany,

Figure G.2 Grab

making it one of the only human gestures to be officially banned by a state.

See also *Palm-down, Reptilian brain.*

Grab

Action unit

A usually sudden, forceful physical act of reaching for and clasping an object or living thing with the hand(s).

Children

Three-to-five-year-old children may grab toys from one another to take possession and assert dominance. Parents discourage such nonverbal aggression, and children may gradually learn to share.

Monkey grab

In the wild, dominant primates may grab food items from submissive peers.

U.S. presidential politics

On a May 25, 2017, tour of NATO headquarters in Brussels, Belgium, Donald Trump grabbed the right arm of – and pushed in front of – Montenegro Prime Minister Dusko Markovic to pose for NATO TV by squaring up to the camera, lifting his chin (see *Chin-jut*) and adjusting his suit jacket to embellish a dominant broadside display. The former leader may have been temperamentally unable to share the camera (see previously, Children).

See also *Dominance.*

Groan

Audible sign

A long, voiced, plaintive nonverbal exhalation emitted variously in disappointment, displeasure, grief, pain, stress or weariness.

Usage

An audible groan may be used to convey feelings – such as disappointment or loss – to listeners nearby. Groans are meant to be heard and are emitted less frequently in solitude. Thus, while not a linguistic word, groaning sounds may be considered socially meaningful as messages about feelings, emotions and moods.

Moan

A nasalized, usually quieter groan emitted in pain, mourning or sorrow. Soft moaning vocalizations may be expressive of sexual pleasure in courtship.

Sigh

An audibly soft, breathy, voiceless variant of groaning and moaning.

Nonverbally, a sigh may be used to convey regret or yearning.

See also *Growl*.

Growl

Vocal tone

A deep, raspy, low-pitched guttural sound made by an animal (esp. a dog) or human being, often expressive of displeasure, frustration or anger.

Usage

In spoken conversations, abrupt onset of a "hard" growling voice tone may be used as a nonverbal warning that one's tolerance limits have been exceeded or expectations unmet. Listeners may respond by amending or softening their comments or by growling in reply. "Soft" growling sounds may be used playfully (as in puppy tug-of-war), affectionately (as in courtship) and musically (as in U.S. singer Roy Orbison's 1964 rendition of "Pretty Woman").

Anatomy

In growling, the laryngeal epiglottis moves backward to partially cover the vocal cords. Expiration of air from the lungs causes the arytenoid cartilages to vibrate and produce a rolling vocal sound. A growl may be aggressive, loud and "hard" or playful, quiet and "soft" (see previously, Usage).

See also *Raspy voice*.

Grunt

Vocal tone

A usually short, guttural sound made by an animal (e.g., a gorilla or chimpanzee) or human being. In the latter, grunts may be expressive of disliking, displeasure, frustration or anger. A nonverbal sound that may express agreement, disagreement or misunderstanding in a spoken conversation.

Usage

While a grunted "uh-huh," "uh," "huh" or "huh?" may not be a word, the vocalization itself may be used as a shorthand cue to convey, respectively, "I agree," "I misunderstand," "I see" or "What are you saying?"

Huh? The "huh?" grunt has been found in a variety of national languages – from Spanish to Chinese to Icelandic – and in indigenous languages from Ecuador, Australia and Ghana.

See also *Growl*.

H

Figure H.1 Hair cue

Hair cue

Identity sign

The style, color, shape and sheen of the cylindrical, filamentous projections covering the scalp. Any of the visual, tactile and olfactory signs emanating from human head hair. Hair is of key value in the categorization and perception of human faces (Martin and Macrae, 2007).

Usage

Like the face, our hairstyle is a nonverbal signature display representing who, what and even "why" we are. Our hairdo is a badge of identity reflecting membership in a group and also showing an unvoiced desire to identify with (i.e., be like; see *Isopraxism*) other people. Like a baseball cap, for example, hair may be used to show membership in a corporate, military or religious "team" (see *Hat*).

Biology

We spend a great deal of time noticing, monitoring and commenting on each other's hair (or its absence). This is because, in mammals generally, clean hair is a sign of high status, good health and careful grooming. The biological equivalent of scales, feathers and fur, hair not only keeps our head warm and dry but protects the braincase from sunshine. Hair once provided camouflage, as well, to help ancestors blend into the natural landscape. Hairstyles help us blend into the social scene today.

Media

In the 1950s, magazine and TV images of Elvis Presley popularized the rebellious ducktail, in which hair sweeps back to meet in an upturned point at the rear of the head and the bangs ascend in a topknot, not unlike the tuft of a displaying male bird. In the 1960s, anti-establishment bushy hair for men was popularized by magazine and TV images of the Beatles, a British pop group whose members wore hair noticeably longer than male peers of the day. In the 1970s, very long straight hair for women was popularized by magazine and TV images of American folksinger Joan Baez, whose dark tresses contrasted with shorter, chemical-permanent styles of the time. In the 1980s, pop singer Madonna's TV-pictured soft-tousled blond hair popularized the sexy Marilyn Monroe look of the 1950s. In the 1990s, TV ads of Chicago Bulls basketball player Michael Jordan popularized the shaved-head look introduced by actor Yul Brynner in the 1956 movie The King and I.

See also *Facial I.D.*, *Facial recognition*.

Figure H.2 Hands

Halo effect

Perception of attractiveness

Coined by Thorndike (1940), the halo effect is the tendency to attribute characteristics to people based on perceptions of their attractiveness. An example is attributing superior intelligence to those who are physically attractive. Personal attributes of friendliness, ambition and likeability are often inferred as well (Hatfield and Sprecher, 1986).

Culture

The halo effect may be culturally immune and spontaneous and frequently occurs beneath conscious awareness (Langlois et al., 2000).

Negative halo effect

A negative effect (also called the horn effect) is the notion that a single negative attribute can bias personal judgments in a negative way.

See also *Attractiveness*.

Hands

Tactile antennae

"His hands are like antennae, gathering information as they flick outward, surveying the rock for cracks, grooves, bowls, nubbins, knobs, edges and ledges, converting all of it into a road map etched into his mind" (Karl Greenfeld [2001, 60] on Erik Weihenmayer, then 33, the first blind climber to scale Mount Everest (see subsequently, Anatomy).

Smart parts

The terminal end organs below the forearms, used to grasp and gesticulate (see Gesture).

Among the most expressive parts of the human body.

Usage

Their combined verbal and nonverbal IQs make hands our most expressive body parts. Hands have more to say even than faces, for not only do fingers show emotion, depict ideas and point to butterflies on the wing (see *Point*) – they can also read Braille, speak in sign languages and write poetry. Hands are such incredibly gifted communicators that they always bear watching.

Observation

So connected are hands to our nervous system that we rarely keep them still. Indeed, the First Law of Nonverbal Dynamics might read, "A hand tends to stay in motion even while at rest." When a hand is not moving or handling an object, it is busy scratching, holding or massaging its partner. This peculiar tendency of the digits to fuss and fidget intensified as fingers became major tools used to explore and shape the material world.

Anatomy

Hands are the tactile antennae we throw out to assay our material world and palpate its moods. Most of the 20 kinds of nerve fiber in each hand fire off simultaneously, sending orders to muscles and glands – or receiving tactile, motion and position information from sense organs embedded in tendons, muscles and skin (Amato, 1992). With a total of 100 bones, muscles, joints and types of nerve, our hand is uniquely crafted to shape thousands of signs. Watching a hand move is rather like peering into the brain itself (see *Human brain*).

Evolution

The 27 bones, 33 muscles and 20 joints of our hand originated ca. 400 mya from the lobe fins of early fishes known as rhipidistians. Primeval "swim fins" helped our aquatic ancestors paddle through Devonian seas in search of food and mates. In amphibians, forelimbs evolved as weight-bearing platforms for walking on land. In primates, hands were singled out for upgrade as tactile antennae or "feelers." Unlike flippers, claws or hooves, human fingers link to intellectual modules and emotion centers of the brain. Not only can we thread a needle, we can also pantomime the act of threading with our fingertips (see *Mime cue*) – or reward a child's successful threading with a gentle pat. There is no better organ than a hand for gauging unspoken thoughts, attitudes and moods.

Neuro-notes

Our brain devotes an unusually large part of its surface area to hands and fingers (see *Homunculus*). In the mind's eye, as a result (1) of the generous space they occupy on the sensory and motor strips of our neocortex and (2) of the older paleocircuits linking them to emotional and grooming centers (see *Mammalian brain*), almost anything a hand does holds potential as a sign. Today, our hands are fiber-linked to an array of sensory, motor and association areas of the forebrain, midbrain and cerebellum, which lay the groundwork for nonverbal learning; manual sign language; computer keyboard fluency and the ability to make tools of stone, silicon and steel.

See also *Feet, Palm-down, Palm-up*.

Handedness

Right vs. left

Nonverbally, an outer sign of the brain's inner asymmetrical motor function. In right-handed individuals, modules of the right-brain cerebral hemisphere are considered to be more nonverbal, holistic, visuospatial, intuitive and emotional than the verbal, analytic, sequential, and rational left-brain hemisphere(see *Nonverbal brain*).

Usage

Though we often picture handedness manually – as in which hand, right or left, we use to throw a ball – it is also involved in how we interpret incoming sensory information (see *Afferent cue*) encoded in auditory, aroma, taste, touch and vision cues. Thus, handedness (also called brain lateralization) provides important insight into nonverbal communication.

Auditory cues

Worldwide, ca. 90 percent of human beings are right-handed. Since sounds to the left ear are decoded by the right-brain cerebral hemisphere in these people (see *Human brain*, Right brain, left brain), emotional information encoded in paralanguage and tone of voice may be better decoded by this ear than the right. (The converse may be true for 10 percent of those humans who are left-handed.) Implication: To better hear emotional voice tones on the phone, listen through the more emotional ear.

Olfactory cues

Like auditory cues, olfactory reception is lateralized in the brain (see *Aroma cue*). In right-handers, smells received through the left nostril may have more salience than aromas received through the right.

Taste cues

While there is evidence for handedness and laterality in the human gustatory system, specific contralateral sensory nerve pathways have yet to be adequately traced. Research is ongoing.

Touch cues

Our nonverbal sense of touch is strongly lateralized. In right-handers, motor control is exerted by the left brain to render right-handed dominance. The left hand, meanwhile, addressing more emotional right-brain circuits, may better appreciate, for example, the smoothness of polished marble and the softness of silk.

Vision cues

Like the sense of touch, vision is strongly lateralized. The left visual field is processed by the right visual cortex and vice-versa. Thus, for right-handers, nonverbal items seen on the left may be more emotionally important and meaningful than those on the right and may lead viewers to orient leftward (see *Orienting reflex*).

See also *Hands*.

Hand-behind-head

Gesture

Touching, scratching or holding the back of the neck or head with an opened palm. In variant forms, reaching a hand upward to scratch an ear, grasp an earlobe or stimulate an ear canal and touching, scratching or rubbing the cheek or side of the neck.

Usage

In a conversation, hand-behind-head may be read as a potential sign of uncertainty, conflict, disagreement, frustration, anger, disliking or social aversion. It may reflect negative thoughts, feelings and moods. In counseling, interviewing and cross-examining, the gesture may telegraph a probing point, that is, an unresolved issue to be verbalized, explored and explained (see *Probing point*).

Culture

As used in Jewish communities, "The hand clasps the neck behind the ear" (Morris, 1994, 168), as if to say, "What a disaster!"

Asymmetry

Hand-behind-head is an asymmetrical gesture made with one hand only (see subsequently, Neuro-notes). In the United States, leaning back and placing both hands behind the neck in the bilateral head clamp posture is a nonverbal sign of superiority (Morris, 1994, 141).

Emoticon

For Japanese email users, in the phrase (^o^;>), "The triangular shape on the right apparently represents a protruding elbow and stems from the fact that an embarrassed or apologetic person will sometimes scratch the back of his or her head" (Pollack, n.d.).

Observations

Asked if he would like to have lunch with the group, a hesitant co-worker touches the back of his head with his hand. Sensing uncertainty, a colleague responds, "Maybe tomorrow?" Seeing his boss reach for her earlobe as he raises a sensitive point, an account executive proceeds with caution to resolve the issue. When Jones suggests a new idea at the weekly staff meeting, Smith glances away and clasps his neck. Sensing resistance – which could fester and eventually sabotage the proposal – Jones asks Smith to voice his opinion to the group in words.

E-commentary

"During interviews, I have observed people touching the back of the neck immediately after being told that they are suspect, and then followed up each time the investigators were accurate in describing something only the suspect knew about. I have also noted the speed at which the arm races to the back of the neck and head as being significant, and the amount of force applied once the hand reached the head or back of neck" (Joe Navarro, FBI [2/25/00 5:22:43 PM Pacific Standard Time]).

Neuro-notes

Hand-behind-head is a gestural fossil left over from spinal-cord circuits designed to keep the body upright in relation to gravity through neck reflexes (specifically, the asymmetrical tonic neck reflex [see *ATNR*]. Rotating or bending the head to the right, for example, produces bending (flexion) of the left arm, which may curl behind the back of the head (Ghez, 1991a) in a fencing posture. Negative opinions, feelings and moods stimulate defensive withdrawal – an avoider's response mediated by paleocircuits of the brain stem and spinal cord – as we unconsciously turn away from persons arousing the emotion.

See also *Flexion withdrawal*.

Hand-clap

Auditory cue

A rhythmically repeated, slapping sound often made when the right-hand palm and fingers percussively strike those of the left. The loudness, strength and tempo of clapping may reflect an audience's collective emotional response to a comedic, musical or stage performance.

Usage

The hand-clap is a polysemic nonverbal sign with multiple meanings and uses.

1   An individual may excitedly clap after winning a prize (see *Happiness*).
2   A group may collectively clap in approval at a concert, play or recital.
3   One may show allegiance to a group by standing and clapping when group members stand and applaud.
4   A camper may clap loudly to scare squirrels away from a picnic basket, tent or table.

High-five

A variant of clapping is the "high-five," in which two people extend and raise their arms triumphantly (see *Triumph display*) and audibly slap pronated palms (see *Palm-down*) in a dyadic clap.

Neuro-note

The combined sudden onset and abrupt ending of a hand-clap calls for attention – much like a beeping or clicking sound – by engaging a listener's midbrain auditory startle reflex (see *Beep*, *Finger-snap*, *Lateral click*).

See also *Table-slap*.

Handshake

General

Knapp et al. (2014) write that the handshake is about 150 years old, being preceded by a hand clasp which dates back to ancient Rome. Historically, handshakes are more associated with men than women (Chaplin et al., 2000). They are interpreted as signaling formality, trust, friendliness and hospitality (Hall and Hall, 1983).

Styles of handshake

Handshakes are frequently described within social etiquette discourse. In so doing, they are often described as firm, warm, cold, clammy, limp and so on (Vanderbilt, 1957). The style of handshake and its relevance to first impressions is important here. In western cultures, more positive first impressions are established when the person accompanies a firm handshake with direct eye contact (Chaplin et al., 2000; Stewart et al., 2008). Such handshakes have been shown to convey personality traits such as extraversion and openness to new experiences (Chaplin et al., 2000).

Gender and handshakes

Across gender, men's handshakes tend to be firmer than women's (Chaplin et al., 2000), and men tend to shake hands more frequently than women (Hall and Hall, 1983). Chaplin et al. (2000, 110) found that "a firm handshake may be an effective form of self-promotion for women."

Culture and handshakes

The manner and meaning of handshakes can vary across cultures (Hall and Hall, 1983; Mukherjee and Ramos-Salazar, 2014; Usmani, 2005). For example, in western cultures, handshakes are common; however, in East Asian cultures, they are less common, being replaced by greetings such as bowing (Singh et al., 1998). In Asian cultures, softer handshakes and less eye contact are more customary. In studies which examined handshaking in social interactions, Katsumi et al. (2017) found that it was perceived more positively by Caucasian than East Asian participants.

First impressions and firm handshakes

1   In deciphering what constitutes a firm handshake in first impression scenarios, Chaplin et al. (2000) found that a "firm" handshake had the following characteristics: strength, completeness of grip, duration, vigor and eye contact. Their work also found that when accompanied with direct eye contact, a firm handshake is rated more positively than a weak handshake.
2   Handshakes have been shown to influence first impressions in contexts such as business meetings (Dolcos et al., 2012) and negotiations (Schroeder et al., 2014). They have also been shown to be significant in doctor-patient greetings (Davis et al., 2007).

Power and handshakes

Webster (1984) argues that handshakes are typically initiated by the person of higher status. People develop a personally typical and consistent style of handshake

(Bailenson and Yee, 2007). Morris (1977) notes that the strength of an interaction between two people can be observed by watching the non-shaking hand!

Hands-on-hips

Origin

Hands-on-hips is an antigravity sign derived from pronated postures of the high-stand display. Resting the hands on the hips "locks in" the expansiveness of the gesture as a postural looming sign (see *Antigravity sign, Loom*).

Posture

An akimbo position in which the palms rest on the hips with elbows flexed outward, bowed away from the body.

Usage I

Hands-on-hips shows the human body is prepared to "take steps" to perform, take part in or take charge of an event, activity or work assignment. As a nonverbal cue, the posture reveals that the body is poised to "step forward" to carry out a superior's order, discipline or threaten a subordinate or defend against those who "overstep their bounds."

Usage II

Outward-bowed elbows – in tandem with the upper-arms' abducted position (held away from the torso) – widen, expand and visually "enlarge" the upper body, making it seem more powerful in size.

E-Commentary I

"I've always been fascinated with the Arms Akimbo gesture and use it all the time while on patrol. I've found that, in situational context, it usually means the person is in a negative state of mind. Thus if an officer can see this, it's a head's up there may be trouble. And I've even caught myself doing it when I'm upset. I've found it quite reliable in determining state of mind, which is important for any law enforcement officer" (Jeff Baile [7/29/00 9:24:45 AM Pacific Daylight Time]).

Neuro-notes

As a locomotive posture based on antigravity extension and pronation of the fore-limbs, hands-on-hips articulates as the limbic system instructs basal ganglia to prepare the limbs for movement.

See also *Boot, Goose-step, Reptilian brain*.

Hand signal

Manual sign

So expressive are human hands that we have created diverse specialized signal systems for use in a spectrum of activities, occupations and situations (see *Hand*). That human beings use hand-and-arm (i.e., pectoral) gestures to send nonverbal messages is rooted in incredibly ancient neurocircuits of the posterior hindbrain and anterior spinal cord (Bass and Chagnaud, 2012).

Army/police

The army (e.g., SWAT) teams and police make use of a wide range of signals. For example, the "OK gesture" (which involves making a zero between thumb and index finger) is used to signal "I understand," hand up to ear signals "listen" and the closed fist is used to say "freeze."

Basketball

Basketball referees make wide use of sign language. For example, rotating the fists indicates "travelling," and hands over the head with extended thumbs indicates "jump ball." Open palm of one hand supported by open palm of another hand at 90-degree angle indicates time-out.

Diving

Divers also make extensive use of sign language. For example, an opened hand with palm facing the other diver(s) indicates stop. A pointed index finger which is being moved in a circle (with the rest of the hand closed) indicates "turn around." An extended arm with clenched fist indicates "danger."

Fire fighters

Fire fighters who are attached to a search line make use of the OATH method of communication, which involves tugs as follows: one tug represents "O," which means "Okay"; two tugs represent "A," meaning "Advance"; three tugs represent "T," meaning "Take-up slack" and four tugs represent "H" for "Help."

Navy

On naval aircraft carriers, officers frequently use hand signals (e.g., touching the hands to the deck and then pointing straight is a signal to launch, while fists indicate "brakes on" and open hands mean "brakes off").

Sports: soccer

Referees use a wide range of signals. For example, when both arms are swung forward and upward, this means advantage. Hands pointing to the penalty spot indicates penalty; a whistle accompanied by a vertically raised arm indicates offside.

See also *Sign language*.

Happiness

Emotion

A pleasant visceral feeling of contentment, well-being and joy.

Usage

Happiness may show in digestive vocalizations (such as "Ahh, this orange tastes great" and "Mmm, this pizza is wonderful"), in joyful laughter and the "true" or zygomatic smile.

Evolution

Happiness is a mammalian elaboration of feelings of well-being and contentment related to parasympathetic digestion (see *Enteric brain*, *Rest-and-digest*) and of arousal from stimulation of pleasure areas of the brain (see *Pleasure cue*).

Neuro-notes

A happy, heartfelt or "true" smile is controlled by the anterior cingulate gyrus of the limbic system through paleocircuits of the basal ganglia.

See also *Happy sign*.

Happy sign

Emotion cue

Any of several nonverbal indications of joy, contentment or delight.

Usage

As incoming (afferent) cues, happy signs may reveal a sender's contented or happy state of mind. As outgoing (efferent) cues, they may be used to elicit or stimulate signs of happiness in a viewer.

Empathy

Our ability to feel what others feel is made possible as facial expressions register in mirror neurons. Seeing someone's glad eyes or smile, for example, may elicit a happy feeling in others. "The neural activity in the limbic system triggered by these signals from mirror neurons," neurologist Marco Iacoboni suggests, "allows us to feel the emotions associated with the observed facial expressions – the happiness associated with a smile, the sadness associated with a frown" (Iacoboni, 2008, 112).

Anatomy

Motion energy maps reveal that, facially, happiness is expressed primarily with the mouth (see *Zygomatic smile*).

Auditory cues

Happiness may be heard in nonverbal "oohs," "ahs" and high-pitched squeals of delight. Musical sounds, too, may connote or suggest happy feelings and moods. The ethereal piano of composer Wolfgang Mozart (1756–1791), for example, is suggestive of floating dreamily and merrily on puffy white clouds.

See also *Sad sign*.

Hat

Clothing cue

A highly expressive consumer product worn as a covering for the head. Distinctively styled head garb with varied markings, colors, shapes and fit, designed to communicate a wearer's identity, gender, occupation, mood or favorite sport.

Usage

Their prominence and proximity to the face enable hats to make impressive statements about social status, affiliation and personality (see *Hair cue*). Indeed, whatever we place atop our 15-pound head – which looms conspicuously above our upright bodies for all to see – will be decoded as a nonverbal sign.

Observation

In hat stores, shoppers may unwittingly reflect the power of head wear. After an uneasy smile, for example, hats that fit the head but not the persona are hastily removed. A proper hat, on the other hand, stays put and may ride out of the store atop the owner's head. Self-conscious thoughts that "everyone is noticing" soon fade (become "old hat") as the wearer assimilates to his or her "new personality."

Cap

For men, wearing a baseball cap may signify membership on a team. Although caps often display emblems of professional ball clubs, in a deeper sense, the group they most accurately refer to is the generic association of men. Unlike women's hats that show individuality, men's hats may be part of a uniform to show group affiliation – thus explaining the standardized design of turbans, fedoras, fezzes and military caps.

Brim

A hat brim may suggest masculine power by visually enlarging a man's bony brow ridges. The latter are natural signs of strength in the male skull (female brow ridges are smaller). Drawn down on the forehead, brims mimic eyebrows lowered in anger (see *Eyebrow-lower*). With its turned-down brim, the fedora worn by American film actor Humphrey Bogart (1899–1957) made him look "meaner," while its vertically ascending crown increased his standing height.

Neuro-notes

We respond to hat cues as we respond to natural cues of the face, via paleocircuits linked to the amygdala, and through modules of the primate brain's inferior temporal lobe, which respond to specific facial expressions.

See also *Eyebrow lower*.

Head-jerk

Aversive cue

Seen in verbal arguments, the head-jerk is an often-angry response visible when one strongly disagrees with another.

Energy outburst

A head-jerk is an abrupt, exaggerated tilt backward or to the side (see *Head-tilt*). It is more energetic than ordinary conversational head-tilts and may combine with an elevated upper-lip expression suggestive of emotional contempt (i.e., a sneer; see *Disgust*).

Research reports

Jerking the head rapidly upward, straight back or to one side, was described by Darwin (1872) as a component of sneering, scorn or defiance, accompanied by raising the upper lip and "uncovering the canine tooth" in a snarl or sneer. Izard (1971) included "throwing back" the head in his description of contempt-scorn. Eibl-Eibesfeldt (1973) observed head-jerking and frowning in situations of anger in a deaf-and-blind-born child.

Neuro-note

The prime mover of head-jerking is sternocleidomastoid, a neck muscle innervated by emotionally responsive nerves (see *Special visceral nerve*).

See also *Head-nod, Head-shake*.

Head-tilt-back

Gesture

Lifting the chin and leaning the head backward, dorsally, toward the shoulder blades (scapula bones).

Usage

Lifting the chin and looking down the nose may be used throughout the world as non-verbal signs of superiority, arrogance and disdain (Eibl-Eibesfeldt, 1970; Hass, 1970).

Anatomy

The prime mover of head-tilt-back (i.e., of extending the spine) is the erector spinae muscle group, components of which reach to the skull's occipital bone to produce extension movements of the head as well. These deep muscles of the back and neck are basic postural muscles innervated by the spinal nerves directly, without relay through the cervical plexus. Thus, we have less voluntary control of head-and-trunk postures than we have, for example, of hand-and-arm gestures. Gross postural shifts that involve back-extension and head-raising may express unconscious attitudes of superiority and dominance.

Origin

Head-tilt-back expresses superiority as a constituent of the primeval high-stand, a vertically looming stance in which, through extension of the limbs, the vertebrate body seems to "enlarge" (see *High-stand display*).

Politics

Political leaders who used the head-tilt-back gesture in public speeches include Benito Mussolini, Donald J. Trump and George Corley Wallace.

Chin jut

A derivative gesture of head-tilt-back is the "chin jut." As described by Desmond Morris (1994, 30), "The chin is thrust towards the companion" as an "'intention movement' of forward attack," which is a worldwide sign of threat.

Figure H.3 Head-tilt-side

The world's most exaggerated chin jut may have been that of Italian dictator Benito Mussolini.

See also *Head-tilt-side*.

Head–tilt–side

Gesture

Leaning the head over laterally toward the right or left shoulder.

Usage

Head-tilt-side may be used to show friendliness and foster rapport; to show coyness, as in courtship; to strike a submissive pose (e.g., of deference to a boss) or to respond to cuteness, such as immature cues, for example, from kittens, puppies or babies.

Anatomy

Head-tilt-side involves the scalene muscles, which connect the neck bones (cervical vertebrae) to the upper two ribs, as well as the trapezius and the sternocleidomastoid muscles. Controlled by "gut reactive" special visceral nerves (see also *Pharyngeal arch*), the latter two muscles are well equipped to express emotions, feelings and moods.

Origin

Head-tilt-side is one of several self-protective gestures stemming from the larger shoulder-shrug display (see also *Crouch*).

Research reports

Sideward head-tilts have been decoded as signals of shyness in young children (McGrew, 1972) and adults (Givens, 1978c). "This head [tilt] gesture may convey an attitude of coyness or submissiveness, but it is so common that one can almost always find such a head position in any group of women" (Key, 1975, 152).

See also *Head-tilt-back*.

Head–toss

Courtship cue

A sudden head-turn sideward, to flick or flip one's hair off and away from the face.

Usage

As a vision cue, the head-toss may be used to attract notice to one's face, hair and physical presence. Head-flips may given by men or women in the presence of others to whom they are physically or romantically attracted. The cue may be used unwittingly, as if to say, "Notice me – and my interest – in you."

Anatomy

The prime mover of head-toss is sternocleidomastoid, a branchiomeric muscle originally used for respiration and feeding. Head-toss thus may be emotionally responsive as a "gut-reactive" sign of romantic interest (see *Special visceral nerve*).

Neuro-notes I

Head-tossing gestures may be repeated in the presence of attractive others. Rhythmic repetition, which dates to ca. 500 mya in vertebrate spinal-cord, brain-stem and cortical-motor areas (Ghez, 1991a), may explain why head-tossing is a seemingly automatic and frequently used nonverbal cue in the opening stages of courtship. "Once initiated, the sequence of relatively stereotyped movements may continue almost automatically in reflex-like fashion" (Ghez, 1991b, 596).

Neuro-notes II

Vision centers of the amphibian brain – the midbrain's superior colliculi or optic lobes – are sensitive to moving body parts, as in the kinetic head-toss, and reflexively focus our attention on motions of the head and hair.

See also *Hair cue, Head-tilt-side*.

Height

Standing height is often associated with power, status and attractiveness. Romantic advertisements, for example, often refer to height (Cameron et al., 1978). Work by Lynn and Shurgot in 1984 found that romantic advertisements wherein men say they are tall receive more responses. Compared to shorter humans, taller people are often judged to be more socially attractive, dominant and powerful (Roberts and Herman, 1986).

Herbs and spices

Introduction

"Just a dash awakens dips, soups, salads, sauces, and entrees" (Label on a bottle of The Spice Hunters® "California Cayenne").

Aroma cues

Any of several aromatic plants (e.g., parsley, sage), trees (bay, cinnamon) or roots (ginger, sassafras) used in medicines, perfumes, deodorants and colognes and in food and drink as flavorings. Leaves, flowers (e.g., chamomile), bark or roots containing odor molecules specifically designed (like insectoid pyrazine molecules) as olfactory warning signs to deter insects and other invertebrate pests.

Usage

Though often bitter-tasting, we may use herbs and spices as seasonings to perk up the palate. In small amounts, their warnings put our sense of smell on alert, heightening food flavors with unconscious whiffs of "danger." In cologne, plant phytosterols (e.g., in incense) resemble animal steroids (male testosterone and female estrodiol; Stoddart, 1990) and thus may carry sexually suggestive messages.

Neuro-notes

Herbs and spices address pungency (trigeminal) sensory nerve endings (see *Taste cue*, Trigeminal "taste").

See also *Mint*.

High heel

Footwear

A woman's shoe with a thin, elevated heel designed to enhance the derriere, firm the leg and showcase the feminine ankle.

Usage I

Visually, high heels suggest that a woman's feet are delicate, submissive and ethereal – that is, destabilized and not planted firmly on the ground (cf. *Antigravity sign*, *Boot*) – and that her body weight defies earth's gravitational pull.

Usage II

Nonverbally, high heels stand wearers precariously on their tiptoes, shifting the body's center of gravity forward and causing a compensatory forward lean. The derriere – already prominent by primate standards – protrudes an additional 25 percent.

Evolution

Women's (and men's) elevated heels evolved from a 16th-century Italian high-platform shoe called a chopine. The original stilt-like design came to Italy from the Far East. Practical versions of the chopine, called pattens, made it easier to walk on muddy pathways before the advent of sidewalks and curbs. Because chopines raised both the heel and the toes above the ground, walking was difficult, and after two centuries on stilts, the sole was lowered while the heel was left standing. Thus the high-heel was born, an evolutionary hybrid.

See also *Leg wear*.

High-stand display

Introduction

"Looking as tall as possible and expanding the chest is universally employed by human beings as a means of intimidating an adversary, as witness the behavior of small boys" (Hass, 1970, 146).

Postural loom

A vertically looming stance in which the body "enlarges" through extension of the limbs (see *Loom*). A primeval "pushup" intended to lift the quadrupedal body higher off the ground.

Usage

The high-stand is an antigravity display often used to show a superior, confident or haughty attitude stance (see *Antigravity sign*). It is found in the aggressive push-up used by some lizards and in the assertive palm-down cue used by Homo sapient today.

Sea origin

It is likely that paleocircuits for "standing tall" developed in sea creatures before animals set foot on land. Fossil evidence is lacking, but in living fishes, such as gobies, status and rank vary in proportion to physical body size. The very big dominate the merely large, who in turn dominate the small. Gobies and other piscines, however, may appear "bigger" through an array of nonverbal illusions. To loom larger, a goby stiffens and raises its fins, lifts its head, puffs out its throat and flares its gill covers.

On terra firma

In land animals, forelimb extension lifts the body's front end to more vertically imposing heights. Doing a pushup makes living iguanas and lizards, for example, look "bigger" than they appear with their bellies lowered to the ground. The Australian frilled lizard rears and erects its frill, while the cobra rears and spreads its hood. Research confirms that an anole lizard's pushup to a high-stand is mediated by brain modules of the basal ganglia.

Mammals

Mammals push up in aggressive stiff-walk postures. Bulls, for example, take several stiff-steps to loom "large" before galloping at full charge. Bears, coyotes and wolves strut with a stiff-legged gait to carry their bodies higher off the ground. A dominant wolf stands over its submissive foe. Primates show dominance by straightening their legs and widening their arms.

Humans

To embody the vertebrate's natural weapon, sheer size, we may stand tall, bristle, square the shoulders, broaden the body with hands-on-hips gestures (*Hands-on-hips*), talk in deep tones and toe-out to military oblique.

Neuro-notes

Paleocircuits mediating the high-stand display consist of small networks of spinal-cord interneurons in charge of the muscle stretch reflex. These mini-networks mediate antigravity responses, that is, the muscular contractions that automatically extend the limbs to keep one standing upright without consciously deciding to do so.

See also *Basal ganglia, Reptilian brain*.

Homophily

Appearance

Homophily involves people's sensitivities to the appearance of others and, in particular, how they respond to others with an appearance similar to their own. It involves the extent to which people share significant similarities within domains such as age, appearance, culture, education, religion, social status, habits, beliefs, politics and interests. In short, the idiom: "birds of a feather flock together" summarizes homophily. Gorham et al. (1999) describe homophily as the degree to which "two people perceive themselves as similar to one another." It is argued that homophily can be valuable when seeking to influence others (Cialdini, 2001) and as a factor in affecting people's willingness to communicate with each other (Gorham, 1999).

Homunculus

Brain map

A distorted humanlike figure drawn to reflect the space body parts occupy on the brain's sensory and motor cortex. A misshapen "little man" whose swollen lips, hands and feet reflect the disproportionately large cortical areas they occupy. Areas of the body with less space on the homunculus – such as the neck, elbows and knees – are less communicative and may have little, nonverbally, to "say."

Usage

The comically enlarged tongue, lips, fingertips and feet of the human homunculus explain why these body parts play such key roles in nonverbal communication. The meaning of lip-touch, for example, as a self-stimulating gesture to relieve anxiety, is easily grasped from the "brain's-eye" view of the homunculus. Boots, high heels, self-touch gestures and the tongue-show may be similarly decoded from its viewpoint as cortically salient signs.

Neuro-notes

"Almost every region of the body is represented by a corresponding region in both the primary motor cortex and the somatic sensory cortex" (Geschwind, 1979, 106). "These cortical maps of the body surface and parallel motor maps are important and explain why neurology has always been a precise diagnostic discipline" (Kandel and Jessell, 1991, 372). "The finger tips of humans have the highest density of receptors: about 2500 per square centimeter!" (Kandel and Jessell, 1991, 374).

See also *Human brain*.

Human brain

Evolution

Collectively, those modules, centers and circuits of the brain that developed ca. 4 million to 200,000 years ago in members of the genus *Homo*. Specifically, those areas of the primate forebrain, midbrain and hindbrain adapted for emotional communication, linguistic communication, sequential planning, tool-making and rational thought.

Usage I

The human brain is both verbal (see *Speech* and *Word*) and nonverbal. Some time between 4 million and 200,000 years ago, human beings began to speak. And yet, despite the immense power of words, nonverbal signals are still used to convey emotions, feelings, moods and the contingencies of social status.

Usage II

Incredibly little is new in the human brain that cannot be found – perhaps on a simpler scale – in the aquatic, amphibian, reptilian, mammalian and primate brains preceding it. Yet, from a nonverbal perspective, what sets our brain apart are those highly specialized areas that control fine motor movements of the fingers, lips and tongue, all of which evolved as neurological "smart parts."

Right brain, left brain

Studies agree that as nonverbal cues are sent and received, they are more strongly influenced by modules of the right-side neocortex (esp. in right-handed individuals) than they are by left-sided modules. Anatomically, this is reflected (1) in the greater volume of white matter (i.e., of myelinated axons which link nerve-cell bodies) in the right neocortical hemisphere and (2) in the greater volume of gray matter (i.e., of nerve cell bodies or neurons) in the left. The right brain's superior fiber linkages enable its neurons to better communicate with feelings, memories and senses, thus giving this side its deeper-reaching holistic, nonverbal and "big picture" skills. The left brain's superior neuronal volume, meanwhile, allows for better communication among the neocortical neurons themselves, which gives this side a greater analytic, intellectually narrower focus (see, for example, Gur et al., 1980).

Neuro-notes I

To the primate brain's hand-and-arm gestures, our brain added precision to fingertips by attaching nerve fibers from the primary motor neocortex directly to spinal motor neurons in charge of single muscle fibers within each digit. Direct connections were made through the descending corticospinal tract to control these more precise movements of the hand and fingers.

Neuro-notes II

With practice, we can thread a needle, while our closest animal relative, the chimpanzee, cannot. No amount of practice or reward has yet trained a chimp to succeed in advanced tasks of such precision; the primate brain itself simply lacks the necessary control.

Neuro-notes III

As our digits became more precise, so did our lips and tongue. These body parts, too, occupy more than their share of space on the primary motor map (see *Homunculus*).

Neuro-notes VI

Humans are what they are today because their ancestors followed a knowledge path. At every branch in the 500-million-year-old tree of vertebrate evolution, the precursors of humanity opted for brains over brawn, speed, size or any lesser adaptation. Whenever the option of intelligent response or pre-programmed reaction presented itself, a single choice was made: Be smart.

See also *Nonverbal brain*.

Hypothalamus

Neuro structure

A subcortical group of nuclei in the forebrain that serves the limbic system, the autonomic nervous system (see *Fight-or-flight*) and the endocrine system. A thumbnail-sized neuro structure that organizes basic nonverbal responses, such as aggression, anger, sexuality and fear.

Evolution I

The hypothalamus has deep evolutionary roots in the chemical sense of smell (see *Aroma cue*).

Evolution II

As the forebrain's main chemical-control area, the hypothalamus regulates piscine adrenal medullae, chemical-releasing glands which, in living fish, consist of two lines of cells near the kidneys. The adrenal medullae pump adrenaline into the bloodstream, from where it affects every cell in the fish's body. (N.B.: In humans, adrenaline speeds up body movements, strengthens muscle contractions and energizes the activity of spinal-cord paleocircuits.)

I

Immediacy

General

Nonverbal immediacy has been found in research covering many disciplines and fields, such as health care (for example, see Robinson, 2008; Larsen and Smith, 1981), relationships (see Givens, 1978a, 1983) and education (see White and Gardner, 2011; Andersen and Andersen, 1982). It involves degrees of "perceived physical or psychological closeness between people" (Richmond et al., 1991, 205). This closeness can be characterized by immediacy behaviors which involve "approach or avoidance" and, in the process, affect the level of sensory involvement of the participants (Burgoon et al., 1989, 100).

Emotion cue

The degree to which a nonverbal message conveys liking or disliking. Nonverbally, an expression of emotional *attachment* (or a feeling of closeness) to another person.

Usage

Immediacy – which most often refers to friendly rather than unfriendly cues – may show, for example, in minimal angular distance, direct body alignment, mutual eye contact, isopraxism, love signals, palm-up signs, perfume cues and zygomatic smiles.

Mehrabian and immediacy

Immediacy was first defined in 1967 by the American psychologist Albert Mehrabian (1939–) as the directness and intensity of social action. Immediacy promotes psychological closeness (Andersen et al., 1979). Mehrabian's work led to the "immediacy principle," which argues that "people are drawn toward persons and things they like, they evaluate highly, and prefer; they avoid or move away from things they dislike, evaluate negatively, or do not prefer" (Mehrabian, 1971, 1). Mehrabian's work identified the following aspects of nonverbal communication which are connected with immediacy: forward leaning, close proximity, eye contact, openness of arms, possible exposed palms, openness of body, postural relaxation and positive facial expressions. Much of this work is grounded in the view that internal emotions provide the stimulus for immediate behaviors. "In short, immediacy behaviors express approach or avoidance and, in the process, affect the level of sensory involvement of the participants" (Burgoon et al., 1989, 100).

Emotion cue

1   The degree to which a nonverbal message conveys liking or disliking.
2   Nonverbally, an expression of emotional attachment (or a feeling of closeness) to another person.
3   Signs that show heightened sensory stimulation, attentiveness and liking (Mehrabian, 1971).
4   In considering whether emotion is always present when immediate behaviors are evident, Richmond and McCroskey (2000a) argue for a corollary to Mehrabian's work which is termed the "principle of immediate communication." Here immediate behaviors are considered as being under the control of the communicator, somewhat like tools, where "the more communicators employ immediate behaviours, the more others will like, evaluate highly, and prefer such communicators" (Richmond and McCroskey, 2000a, 212). Conversely, lower employment of immediacy behaviors results in more negative evaluations and a greater possibility of "dislike" of the communicator.
5   While much of the discourse on immediacy presupposes nonverbal behaviors associated with "liking" and "positive affect," there are some who argue that affect may not necessarily always be associated with immediacy. Rather, as immediacy involves approach behaviors, one cannot presuppose that such approach behaviors can always be described with terms such as "liking" or "positive affect." For example, Burgoon (1994) points out that approach behaviors involving forward lean, vocal expressiveness and direct body orientation can be characteristic of communication which involves negative affect (e.g., a heated argument).

Channels of immediacy behaviors

Immediacy – which most often refers to friendly rather than unfriendly cues – may show in (1) angular distance, (2) body alignment, (3) body-lean, (4) cut-off, (5) eye contact, (6) hand-reach signs, (7) isopraxism, (8) love signals, (9) palm-up signs, (10) perfume cues, (11) personal distance, (12) pupil size, (13) rapport, (14) tone of voice, (15) touch cues and (16) zygomatic smiles.

In examining the "constituents" of immediacy behaviors, the work of Andersen (1985) provides valuable insights. Andersen (1985) argues that immediacy behaviors (which involve an exchange of warm, involving, affiliative behaviors) can be defined with the following four characteristics:

1   They involve approach as opposed to avoidance.
2   They signal availability as opposed to unavailability.
3   They induce stimulation and physiological arousal in a receiver.
4   They are perceived as warm messages that convey interpersonal closeness (except in contexts of conflict).

In discussing channels of immediacy, Andersen and Andersen (2004) note that it is typically perceived in a multi-channel manner. Perceptions of immediacy are based on combined perceptions of a number of nonverbal behaviors (such as gaze and spatial closeness), rather than judgments based on an individual nonverbal behavior (e.g., perceptions of immediacy based on gaze only). In breaking down the various channels of immediacy, Andersen and Andersen (2004) identify the following:

1   Proxemics. Close interpersonal distances signal friendship, agreement and warmth. Body orientation, such as face-to-face positioning similarly conveys warmth. Level of eye contact is also relevant here, with warmth and availability being enhanced if interactants are at similar eye level. Forward leaning also contributes to perceptions of immediacy.
2   Eye Behaviors. Higher levels of eye contact, gaze and pupil dilation can convey immediacy.
3   Kinesic Behaviors. A number of kinesic behaviors contribute to perceptions of immediacy. These include head nodding, smiling, facial expressiveness, increased gesturing, relaxed body posture and interactional synchrony.
4   Vocalics. Vocal variation in pitch, rate and volume can convey enthusiasm, warmth and optimism. Listener responses in the form of "ah-huh" can also enhance immediacy.
5   Chronemic Behaviors. Spending time with another person contributes to immediacy. Also, on-time arrival, "not seeming rushed, being in the present, appropriate pauses and silences, and sharing talk time are all potentially important chronemic immediacy behaviors" (Andersen and Andersen, 2004, 116).
6   Haptics. Touch can be used to signal warmth, availability and immediacy.

Immediacy: measurement

Andersen et al. (1979) devised three types of schemes for measuring nonverbal immediacy:

1   *The Behavioral Indicants of Immediacy Scale*, which measures an interactant's perception of a partner's immediacy. This scale had two Likert-based (factor-based) versions. One version was designed for instructional settings which measured 15 perceptions of immediacy. Examples of items include:
    This instructor has a more tense body position while teaching than most other instructors.

    This instructor gestures more while teaching than most other instructors.
    This instructor engages in less movement while teaching than most other instructors.
                                        (Andersen and Andersen, 2004, 121–122)

The other version is an interpersonal version which measures perceptions of 20 immediacy or non-immediacy behaviors as perceived by the receiver. Examples of items include:
    This person has a more relaxed body position than most other people.
    This person directs his/her body position more toward me than most other people usually do.
    This person smiles more than most other people do.
                                        (Andersen and Andersen, 2004, 124)

2   *The Generalized Immediacy Scale,* which is a gestalt measure of a person's global impression of general immediacy. Examples of items include:

Please place an "X" in each of the following scales to indicate the word that best describes the conversational style of the other person:
Cold – – – – Warm
Close – – – – Distant

(Andersen and Andersen, 2004, 123)

3   *The Rater's Perception of Immediacy Scale* which is used by a trained observer to assess immediacy.

A The Nonverbal Immediacy Measure

Designed by Gorham and Zakahi (1990), this measure of immediacy drew on the work of Andersen (1985) and also included some of its own items. The measure was primarily designed for instructional settings. It involved the use of 13 non-verbal items (later reduced to 10 by McCroskey et al., 1996) and 17 verbal items. Examples of nonverbal items include: "Sits behind desk while teaching"; "gestures while talking to class"; "uses monotone/dull voice while talking to class" (Gorham and Zakahi, 1990, 358).

B Observer Ratings of Nonverbal Involvement and Immediacy

Guerrero (2005) provides a coding scheme which can be used to record specific behaviors related to nonverbal involvement and immediacy. Her scheme is grounded in the following constructs of nonverbal involvement and immediacy: 1. Touch, 2. Proxemic Distancing, 3. Forward Lean, 4. Gaze, 5. Body Orientation, 6. Kinesic Animation, 7. Vocal Animation, 8. Altercentrism (focusing on head–nodding, general interest and attention), 9. Smooth Interaction Management (focusing on speech fluency, response latencies, interactional fluency), 10. Composure (focusing on vocal and bodily relaxation, lack of random movement) and 11. Positive Affect (focusing on smiling, facial pleasantness, vocal pleasantness). Examples of items include:

The target: never looked at the partner 1 2 3 4 5 6 7 always looked at the partner exhibited unsteady gaze 1 2 3 4 5 6 7 exhibited steady gaze gave no eye contact 1 2 3 4 5 6 7 gave constant eye contact
The target: leaned away from the partner 1 2 3 4 5 6 7 leaned toward the partner faced away from the partner 1 2 3 4 5 6 7 faced toward the partner

(Guerrero, 2005, 234)

C Nonverbal Immediacy Scale

Designed by Richmond et al. (2003), the Nonverbal Immediacy Scale (NIS) can be used as either a self-report or an other-report measure of nonverbal immediacy. The scale involves a total of 26 items which have an even distribution of positive and negative wording (i.e., 13 items are positively worded and 13 items are negatively worded). The items are presented in a 5-point Likert-type response format. The scale has high reliability estimates (0.90). Examples of items include:

"I use my hands and arms to gesture while talking to people";
"I touch others on the shoulder or arm while talking to them";
"I use a monotone or dull voice while talking to people";
"I am animated when I talk to people"

(Richmond et al, 2003, 509)

See also *Affiliative cue, Aversive cue, Percent nonverbal, Education; Courtship; Love.*

Infantile schema

Cute-face design

Figure I.1 Infantile schema

A nonverbal set of appealing, attractive and youthful features included in the facial design of vertebrate hatchlings and new-borns. A pattern of "baby face" physical traits that combine to suggest harmlessness and appeal for social bonding, emotional closeness and parental nurture.

Cuteness I

In the 1930s, researchers isolated specific "cute" features in the resting human face, seemingly favored by people in every society. A set of youthful traits and proportions – for example, wide-set eyes and full lips set upon soft, smooth, unblemished skin – appears to be attractive both in male and female faces. Existence of an infantile schema was originally identified in mammals (including *Homo sapiens*) by Konrad Lorenz in 1939.

Cuteness II

"The infantile/diminution response could have evolved from the responses of adults to infants. It is a fact that youngsters are cared for and protected in virtually all mammalian and bird species, some amphibian, reptilian, and fish species, and among the social, and possibly nonsocial, insect species" (Omark, 1980, 56).

See also *Facial beauty.*

Information

Concept

Nonverbal communication is about sending and receiving information apart from words. Information itself consists of knowledge, facts and data derived from communication. Information includes answers to questions and is fundamentally about the resolution of uncertainty. As Norbert Wiener (1950) pointed out, information differs from matter and energy.

Primordial model

The first informational signs precede life and date to ca. 13.8 bya – the beginning of the universe. Specifically, they consist of photons emitted by individual electrons to communicate presence ("I am here") to fellow electrons. Upon receipt of a photon message, a recipient electron would divert its course to avoid collision with the sender. Photon communication may be the primordial model for all subsequent nonverbal communication, from bacterial quorum sensing to the human smile.

Usage

The meaning of a sign, signal, or cue is the information it transmits to receivers. Nonverbal signs convey information about social status (see, e.g., *Dominance* and *Submission*), feelings (*Anger* and *Fear*) and thoughts (*Certainty*, *Deception* and *Uncertainty*). Nonverbal information ranges from low level signs of physiological arousal (e.g., facial flushing) to higher-level signs of conceptual thought (see *Mime cue*).

Neuro-notes

Nonverbal information flows in two directions simultaneously, as our nervous system sends outgoing and receives incoming signs (see *Efferent* and *Afferent cue*).

Insignia

Identity emblem

Any of diverse visual markers – often made of cloth, metal or plastic – with which to proclaim one's social I.D. Examples include arm patches, badges and military pins that combine verbal and nonverbal information in succinct, eye-catching coded signals (see *Lapel pin*).

Usage

Insignia may be used "at a glance" to convey membership, rank or status in a group. They include color-coded designs, graphic images (e.g., of lions, tigers and bears) or symbolic elements such as national flags, the Star of David and the medical Staff of Hermes.

Power signs

The nonverbal potency of insignia was revealed in Philip Zimbardo's classic 1971 Stanford University prison experiment. Student volunteers were asked to play roles of either "prisoner" or "guard" in the basement of Stanford's Psychology Department. Guards wore boots and khaki uniforms, carried billy clubs, had whistles fastened around their necks and masked their eyes with mirrored sunglasses. These visible, insignia-like signs of power contrasted markedly with the more submissive accouterments of prisoners: calf-revealing "dresses," rubber sandals and stocking caps that simulated "shaved heads." Powerfully bonded by the uniformity of their dress code and accessory insignia (see *Isopraxism*), the student guards became so dangerously militant and aggressive that the experiment had to be halted after just 7 days.

Intention cue

Body movement

A gesture, motion or posture of the fingers, hands, arms, feet, legs, face, head, neck, shoulders or torso that is preparatory to an action such as leaving a room, rising from a couch or attacking an enemy.

Usage

An intention cue – such as angling the feet away from someone we dislike – is an unconscious signal of how we truly feel about another. Intention cues may reflect inner attitudes, unvoiced opinions and emotion.

Animal behavior

"These are the incomplete or preparatory movements which often appear at the beginning of an activity" (Hinde, 1970, 668). "Intention movements of biting or striking are a common source of the components of threat movements: the upright threat posture of the herring gull provides several examples. In other cases intention movements of preening, nesting, self-protection, copulation, and many other types of behaviour have given rise to display movements" (Hinde, 1970, 668).

Arm-reach

Sitting across a table from an attractive stranger, we may unwittingly extend our arms toward that person as if in preparation to touch (see *Love signals IV*). As with other intention cues, the preparatory action may not be completed, that is, may stop short of physical contact.

Knee clasp

In the seated position, leaning forward and clasping "both knees with the hands" means, "I am about to leave" (Morris, 1994, 149).

Snarl

"When your dog lifts his lips and shows you his teeth because you reached for the bone between his paws, you've witnessed an intention display. Rather than bite you there on the spot, your dog shows the beginning phase of the biting sequence to bluff you away" (Givens, 1983, 43).

Interaction adaptation theory

Proposed by Burgoon et al. (1995) interaction adaptation theory "attempts to take into account the complexities of interpersonal interaction by considering people's needs, expectations, and desires or goals as precursors to their degree and form of adaptation" (Burgoon et al., 2016, 400). Biological drives and needs are also relevant (Patterson, 2019, 114). The theory provides for the complexities of inter-personal interaction by examining people's needs, goals, expectations, and desires as precursors to how they adapt when communicating. Within communication contexts, the "communicator observes the other person's behaviours and decides how to respond by assessing the alignment between the other person's behaviours and the interlocutor's own interaction position" (Bernhold and Giles, 2020, 47)

As such, the theory is grounded in the following principles (Burgoon, 2016, 399):

1   People are innately programmed to adapt and synchronize.
2   Biological and social forces predispose people to coordinate interactions through similar behaviors.
3   At the communication level, both reciprocity and compensation may occur.
4   Several factors may limit interaction adaptation: (1) internal causes of adjust-ments, (2) individual style, (3) poor self-monitoring, (4) poor skills and (5) cultural differences.
5   "Biological, psychological, social, and communicative forces set up boundaries within which most interaction patterns will operate, producing mostly match-ing, synchrony, and reciprocity" (Burgoon, 2016, 399).
6   Patterns of adaptation are quickly predicted for constellations of interrelated behaviors rather than individual ones.

Interior design

Humane habitat

The nonverbal practice of decorating an indoor space with lights, colors, land-scapes, textures, animals, plants and other natural objects found in the great out-doors. The unconscious or deliberate act of bringing inside the world's outside cues (see *Nonverbal world*).

Usage

Nothing in our evolutionary past prepared us for a life lived almost entirely indoors – so we bring the outdoors in. Through ingeniously designed consumer products, we make home and office spaces look and feel more like the outside world our forebears knew.

Color

"An East Coast [U.S.] factory gave its cafeteria a face-lift by painting its previ-ously peach-colored walls a light blue. Patrons responded with complaints of being cold. . . . When the room was painted peach again, complaints stopped" (Vargas, 1986, 151; see *Color cue*).

Nonverbal reminders

People may be most happy when their work and play spaces duplicate features of the ancestral African plain. The best offices, for example, provide obvious replicas as well as more subtle reminders of the original savannah habitat, including its warmth, lighting, colors, vistas, textures and plants. Flowers, cacti, palms, ivy vines, leafy shrubs and fig trees may be cultivated indoors today for the reassuring outdoor look of yesterday.

Sky and sun signs

We may keep homes heated (or cooled) to 72 F – the savannah average – and decorated with travel posters of oceans, mountains and trees. We may paint ceilings in light colors to suggest the sky, leaving them unadorned to seem "bigger," "higher" and less enclosing.

Windows I

After sunlight comes the wish for a window to see outside. Without reference to landscapes or the far horizon, workers in windowless offices may feel emotionally disoriented and disheartened. Industry studies suggest that staff members without scenic vistas are more apt to display art prints depicting natural earth scenes and to feel lower in status than colleagues with vistas and views.

Touch cues

Too much smoothness in surfaces may create a peculiar feeling of unreality. Foreign visitors to the United States, for example, have been advised to carry unfinished stones or pieces of natural wood to satisfy their primate cravings for texture, which much of urban America lacks.

See also *Lawn display*.

Interpersonal Perception Task

Spontaneous behaviors

This test was designed by Archer and Costanzo (1988) and Costanzo and Archer (1989). The Interpersonal Perception Task (IPT) was designed to examine spontaneous behaviors, being grounded in "real life"/"naturalistic events" which are grounded in human relationships. As such, situational and nonverbal (and verbal) cues are examined which include scenes related to deceit, competition, intimacy, status and kinship. The test comprises 30 video items (with audio), with each item being about 60–90 seconds in length. While the text uses both verbal and nonverbal channels of communication, the verbal component is sufficiently ambiguous to ensure that "words alone" do not reveal the communication messages. Examples of video clips include scenes where two players discuss a tennis game (who was the winner?) or a scene where one has to try to determine the length of a couple's dating relationship. After watching the clip, the viewer has to choose the correct interpretation of the scene.

In comparing the IPT to the PONS test, (Ambady et al., 1995, 526) note that "the PONS may tap skills that differentiate good male decoders from poor male decoders and that the IPT may tap skills that differentiate good female decoders from poor female decoders in real life situations such as the peer-rating situations."

Social intelligence

The test seeks to be "socially intelligent" (Archer et al., 2001), examining relationship areas such as dominance, intimacy, truth and deception, and in so doing takes account of the subtle yet complex skills which people use in everyday life. Indeed, interpersonal perception is closely linked with "healthy psychological functioning that is manifested in both intrapersonal and interpersonal domains, including work settings" (Hall, 2009, 161). A study by Archer et al. (2001) found that those who score higher on the IPT are more socially competent and socially aware. The IPT has been valued for its use of naturalistic interactions and its provision for sophisticated nonverbal decoding (Bernieri and Gillis, 2001; Bernieri and Rosenthal, 1991).

See *PONS* and *IPT-15*.

Interpersonal Perception Task-15

Created by Costanzo and Archer in 1993, the Interpersonal Perception Task-15 (IPT-15) is an adaptation of the Interpersonal Perception Task (Archer and Costanzo, 1988; Costanzo and Archer, 1989). This test is much briefer, using 15 short video scenes (as opposed to 30 video scenes) to measure an individual's nonverbal sensitivity (Costanzo and Archer, 1993; Archer et al., 2001). Participants view a short video scene (approximately 1 minute long) and then answer questions which require them to decode nonverbal behaviors in the scene. Each scene draws on one of five areas: status, competition, lies, kinship and intimacy.

Invisibility

Not seen

Nonverbally, the condition of being difficult or impossible to see, as in the use of camouflage, concealment, flatness, thinness, hiding or transparency.

Usage

Animals from jellyfish to humans have devised ingenious ways to be stealthy and avoid detection.

Jellyfish

In the featureless ocean depths, jellyfish have no place to hide and thus rely upon transparency to become functionally "invisible." Their clear, gelatinous bodies allow from 20 to 90 percent of light to pass through, enabling them to sneak up on prey while avoiding detection by sighted enemies.

Human beings

In the corporate world, one may become functionally invisible by keeping a low profile, remaining silent and concealing the body within a conformity-proclaiming uniform (see *Business suit*). The latter garment offers camouflage so wearers do not stand out in the crowd. In private life, we spend a great deal of time in seclusion in backyards, bathrooms and bedrooms and behind partitions designed to shield us from prying eyes. Too much visual monitoring may be harmful to human health.

See also *Silence*.

Figure I.2 Isopraxism

Isopraxism

Imitation

"A non-learned neurobehavior in which members of a species act in a like manner" (Soukhanov, 1993, 135). A deep, reptilian principle of mimicry, that is, of copying, emulating or aping a behavior, gesture or fad. An impulsive tendency to, for example, stand and clap as audience members nearby stand and applaud or wear the same style of jewelry, clothing or shoes. (Isopraxism also may be known as behavioral imitation or the chameleon effect.)

Usage I

Isopraxism explains why we dress like our colleagues and adopt the beliefs, customs and mannerisms of the people we admire. Wearing the same team jersey or franchise cap to look alike suggests like thinking and feeling, as well. Appearing, behaving and acting the same way makes it easier to be accepted, as behaviorally, "same is safe."

Usage II

The word isopraxis (Greek iso-, "same"; Greek praxis, "behavior") was introduced by the American neuroanatomist Paul D. MacLean (1913–2007), who first used it in print in 1975. Examples include the simultaneous head-nodding of lizards, the group gobbling of turkeys and the synchronous preening of birds. In human beings, isopraxism "is manifested in the hand-clapping of a theater audience and, on a larger scale, in historical mass migrations, in mass rallies, violence, and hysteria, and in the sudden widespread adoption of fashions and fads" (Soukhanov, 1993, 135).

Media

One of the most dramatic isopraxic events in human history was featured as a "Classic Moment" by Life magazine (1990). The two-page photograph by Ken Regan of the (Rev. Sun Myung) Moon Wedding (January 1983) shows parallel rows of 2,074 white-clad brides (all wearing Simplicity gown pattern No. 8392), and 2,074 dark-suited men, standing with serious (see *Blank face*) expressions in Madison Square Garden, New York, waiting to be joined in the largest mass wedding on Earth.

Painting

Nowhere is isopraxism better exemplified than in Western civilization's Cubist art tradition, founded by French painter Georges Braque (1882–1963) and Spanish artist Pablo Picasso (1881–1973) in 1907, with the latter's oil painting, *Les Demoiselles d'Avignon*. Picasso and Braque were influenced by the flattened-perspective painting style of French artist Paul Cezanne (1839–1906) exemplified in Cezanne's 1895 oil-on-canvas *Bibemus Quarry*. Cubist paintings also show flattened, fragmented perspectives with intersecting lines and angles, flattened planes; squared-off, triangular and rounded shapes and abstract, solid-geometric forms such as spheres, cylinders and cones. Abruptly, from 1907 onward, Cubist-imitative art and architecture has flourished.

Neuro-note

Our tendency to imitate clothing styles and pick up nonverbal mannerisms and signs is rooted in paleocircuits of the reptilian brain. "The major counterpart of the reptilian forebrain in mammals includes the corpus striatum (caudate plus putamen), globus pallidus, and peripallidal structures [including the substantia innominata, basal nucleus of Meynert, nucleus of the ansa peduncularis, and entopeduncular nucleus]" (MacLean, 1975, 75; see *Reptilian brain*).

Isotype

Pictorial sign

Isotype (International System of Typographic Picture Education) was introduced in 1936 by Otto Neurath. Isotype is a set of pictographic characters used "to create narrative visual material, avoiding details which do not improve the narrative character" (Neurath, 1936, 240). Isotype was designed to be an alternative to written script adapted to the child's mind as a pictorial means for communicating information about actions, directions, events and objects and complex relationships in space and time.

Usage

Though Isotype ultimately failed as a means of communication (in part because educators favored written words over pictures), Neurath's "international picture language" laid the foundation for international graphic symbols, the pictographic signals of airport, train-station and highway signs. Today, the use of graphics at the human-computer interface further demonstrates the power of pictographic communication.

Research reports

"The first step in Isotype is the development of easily understood and easily remembered symbols. The next step is to combine these symbolic elements" (Neurath, 1936, 224–225). "Simple [pictographic] elements can be made to show the most complicated facts and relationships. The visual method, fully developed, becomes the basis for a common cultural life and a common cultural relationship" (Neurath, 1936, 226).

Future

Semiotic principles of isotype are included in a U.S. Department of Energy WIPP warning system, designed to send a cautionary message to human beings 10,000 years in the future about the dangers of nuclear waste.

Neuro-note

"Pictographic traditions – both protowritings and true pictographic scripts – rest on semiotic principles which seem to have deep roots in human perception and cognition" (Givens, 1982, 162–163).

See also *Nonverbal learning*.

J

Japanese and Caucasian Brief Affect Recognition Test

Designed by Matsumoto et al. (2000, 179), the Japanese and Caucasian Brief Affect Recognition Test (JACBART) measures individual differences in "emotion recognition ability" by assessing participants' sensitivity to micro-momentary expressions (see *Microexpression*). Participants are shown photographs of facial expressions of white American and Japanese adults in fraction-of-a-second bursts. Each burst is preceded and followed by a neutral expression (see *Blank face*). Studies using this test would suggest a correlation between emotion recognition ability and the "personality constructs of Openness and Conscientiousness" (Matsumoto et al., 2000, 179).

Jargonics

Academic categories

In college classrooms the following suffixed "-ic" words – modeled after the English word, "phonetic" – are used to classify the subfields of human nonverbal communication:

Chronemics

This field involves the role of time (see, e.g., *Waiting time*).

Deictic

Deictic gestures may be used to indicate objects and events, such as pointing to a bird in flight (see *Point*).

Gustorics

Gustorics studies the communicative role of taste (see *Taste cue*).

Haptics

This subfield studies touch (see *Touch cue*).

Heuristics

Any of several usually non-rational human short-cut approaches to explaining, decision-making or problem-solving. Nonverbal and/or verbal, such gut-reactive, rule-of-thumb, snap-judgment heuristics may be used to simplify mental uncertainty (see *Uncertainty*). The heuristic of seeing a man in an expensive car, for example, would be to imagine a man of wealth.

Iconics

Iconic gestures are body movements that bear a close physical resemblance to the objects or actions being described. An example is bringing the fists together to indicate "glued together" (see *Mime cue*).

Kinesics

Founded by anthropologist Ray Birdwhistell (1952, 1970), kinesics is the study of nonverbal communication using the methods and concepts of American descriptive linguistics of the late 1940s.

Metaphorics

Metaphoric gestures are used to present abstract concepts rather than concrete objects or events. Moving a hand up and down, for example, when discussing the concept of gravity.

Objectics

This field studies artifacts as nonverbal cues (see *Artifact*).

Occulesics

Occulesics is about visual signs, signals and cues (see *Vision cue*).

Olfactics

This field studies smell signs (see *Aroma cue*).

Prosodic

Prosodic is an adjective derived from the term prosody. It involves the description of vocal variations (and possibly nasal sounds) which may change the meaning of what is said (see *Prosody*).

Proxemics

Proxemics studies space and territoriality.

Semiotics

Semiotics is the study of signs and symbols and how they are interpreted (see *Emblem*).

Vocalics

Vocalics is about paralanguage (see *Tone of voice*).

Analysis

A strength of these academic categories is their clear focus on the primary sub-fields of nonverbal communication. A weakness is that they are neither pleasantly euphonic nor all inclusive (see, e.g., *Balance cue*, *Enteric brain*).

Jaw-droop

Slightly drooping jaw

"Darrell Ehrlich scanned the crowd of airport travelers for the look. The wide eyes. To identify and help passengers find their way through crowded airports, airport personnel may watch for "rubbernecking"— scanning wide eyes and slightly drooping jaws. Seeing these non-verbal signs of puzzlement, employees may then ask, "Can I help you find your way?""

Facial expression

A sudden, frequently sustained opening of the mouth visible in parted lips and dangling jaw, given in excitement, surprise or uncertainty. An open-mouth position often seen in sleep. A sometimes aversive nonverbal sign used to mock, challenge or confront a foe. A chronically open position of the mouth and jaw observed in the mentally challenged.

Usage

The jaw-droop expression is often seen in adults and children who have lost their way (e.g., in airports) or are entering or walking through unfamiliar, crowded or potentially threatening places (e.g., taverns, bars and darkened alleys; see *Alley*).

Media

The jaw-droop is a staple of science-fiction thrillers as a sign of disbelief or horror while confronting colossal apes, giant lizards and alien spacecraft. Classic jaw-droop faces were filmed, for example, in *King Kong* (1933), *Godzilla, King of the Monsters* (1956) and *Close Encounters of the Third Kind* (1977).

Anatomy I

In standard anatomical position, the mouth is closed as tone in masseter, temporalis and medial pterygoid muscles is stimulated, in the awake state, by brain-stem impulses from the ascending reticular activating system to the trigeminal nerve (cranial V). In sleep, the chewing muscles relax and the jaw may droop of its own weight (see *Blank face*).

Anatomy II

Platysma, lateral pterygoid and digastric muscles reflexively open our mouth should we gasp for air in shock or surprise.

Neuro-notes

Emotional stimuli related to surprise, fear or horror travel downward from the limbic system through the brain stem to the trigeminal nerve to contract the lateral pterygoid muscles and open the mouth. Trigeminal is an emotionally responsive (i.e., "gut reactive") special visceral nerve.

See also *Flashbulb eyes*.

Jump

Body movement

To suddenly lift or spring off the ground through combined muscular contractions of the arms, legs and feet.

Nonverbal usage

In addition to jumping's role in locomotion (e.g., in hurdles and steeplechase), jumping may be used to express strong emotions as in anger and joy. When told to turn off his smart phone, a child may jump up and down in anger and beat the air with fisted hands. When told she just won a new car, a woman may jump up and down for joy and clap her hands.

Freudensprung

Excited jumping has been studied in chimpanzees, dogs and rats. Known as freudensprung ("joy jumps"), the jumping behaviors may be glossed as intention cues of quadrupedal locomotion (see *Intention cue*).

Neuro-notes

Sudden anger may release noradrenaline into the bloodstream to stimulate angry jumping outbursts. Sudden joy – as when one's soccer team scores a goal – may release dopamine to boost bodily energy and release excited jumping. U.S. baseball teams triumphantly jump up and down in joyful unison after winning a playoff game (see *Isopraxism*).

See also *Triumph display*.

K

Kinesics

Linguistic analogy

Founded by anthropologist Ray Birdwhistell (1952, 1970), kinesics is the study of nonverbal communication using the methods and concepts of American descriptive linguistics of the late 1940s.

Usage

Students of kinesics searched for a grammar of body movements, facial expressions and gestures, much as descriptive linguists formulated a grammatical structure of words.

Research reports

"I suggest that this separate burgeoning evolution of kinesics and paralanguage alongside the evolution of verbal language indicates that our iconic communication serves functions totally different from those of language and, indeed, performs functions which verbal language is unsuited to perform" (Bateson, 1968, 615). "Not everyone agrees with Birdwhistell that kinesics forms a communication system which is the same as spoken language" (Knapp, 1972, 96). "So as you can see, Birdwhistell based his category system of behaviors on a model taken from the categories of verbal communication (allophone, phone, phoneme, morpheme)" (Richmond et al., 1991, 55).

See also *Paralanguage*, *Proxemics*.

Kinda sorta

Vocal shrug

In English speakers, the verbal practice of inserting a "kind of" or "sort of" phrase into a sentence to hedge its accuracy or truth. Nonverbally, abbreviated versions of the phrases – used as "throw away" comments – may be likened to shoulder-shrugs of uncertainty.

Usage

Kinda-sorta phrases may be used in political talk shows to suggest that a pundit's vocal comments may not be entirely true as stated, providing an opportunity to change course, recant, restate or rephrase. The verbal remarks may be accompanied by nonverbal hedge cues derived from the shoulder-shrug display (see *Shoulder-shrug*).

Neuro-notes

That we live in a perennially uncertain world is reflected by the brain's innate ability to function – verbally as well as nonverbally – despite prevailing cognitive doubt and gaps in certitude (see *Certainty*).

See also *Verbal pause*.

Figure K.1 Kiss

Kiss

Touch cue

To caress, touch or gently feel with the lips. To press one's lips against those of another.

Usage

We kiss to show affection, as in kissing a child, parent, friend or lover.

Culture

In Latin countries, a man may kiss the back of a woman's hand to greet her with respect. His hand kiss should be "effortless, noiseless and moistureless" (Morris, 1994, 113). In many Mediterranean countries people often greet one another by kissing cheeks. This typically involves kissing one side of the face and then the other.

Primatology

Chimpanzees may kiss and embrace after a fight.

Research reports

"Our kiss originates from a mammal-wide sucking reflex" (Givens, 1983, 93). "Mouth-to-mouth contact with the lips" is a worldwide sign of love (Morris, 1994, 155). There is significant research to contend that kissing can strengthen the immune system and can also have stress-alleviating effects (Burgoon et al., 2010b). Across the genders, there is evidence that certain types of kissing can be interpreted differently by men and women. With a male partner, women may interpret kissing as an act of playfulness or a sign of warmth or love, in comparison to men, who are more inclined to see such behaviors as indicative of sexual desire (Pisano et al., 1986). Some studies show that individuals turn their heads proportionally more to the right when kissing (e.g., Güntürkün, 2003). However, more recent research by Sedgewick et al. (2019), suggests that such head turns are context specific. For example, they found no head turning bias among non-romantic kisses.

Neuro-notes I

The most sensitive area of our face is the perioral area (which includes the lips and nose). Kissing sensations travel through the trigeminal nerve (cranial V), which carries impulses received from the lips. Reflecting its importance, the trigeminal is served by three sensory nuclei, extending from the upper spinal cord through the brain stem to the amphibian brain. Pleasurable light-touch sensations travel from the principal and spinal nuclei through evolutionary-old pathways to the thalamus, then to areas of the mammalian brain (including the cingulate gyrus, prefrontal cortex and basal forebrain), as well as to primary sensory areas of the parietal cortex (see *Homunculus*).

Neuro-notes II

Mirror neurons are incredibly powerful; "vicarious" would not be a strong enough word to describe their effects. When we watch movie stars kiss onscreen, some of the cells firing in our brains are the same ones that fire when we kiss our lovers (Marco Iacoboni, 2008).

Neuro-notes III

Mirror neurons: "Even so, when moving heads together for a kiss, even a first time, sudden, passionate kiss, we rarely end up breaking our front teeth. There is usually a soft landing. The essential point is that when people move synchronously or in temporal coordination, they are participating [via mirror neurons] in an aspect of the other's experience" (Stern, 2007, 38).

See also *Emotion cue*.

Kneel

Posture

The act of placing one or both knees downward on the ground. A kneeling posture may connote a submissive social stance or frame of mind, as in genuflecting before religious leaders or royalty.

Usage

Kneeling may be used as a symbolic lowering of the body in deference, worship or prayer.

Religion

Religious displays may involve kneeling which symbolize "submissive acts performed towards dominant individuals called gods" (Morris, 1977, 148).

Semantic shift I

In 2016, another meaning attached to the kneeling posture when American football quarterback Colin Kaepernick of the San Francisco 49ers knelt rather than standing for the country's national anthem (see *High-stand display*). Broadcast live on national television (see *Media*), the posture became a nonverbal sign of opposition to racism, not unlike the raised-fist Black Power salute given by American athletes at the 1968 Olympic Games.

Semantic shift II

On May 25 2020, American police in Minneapolis arrested George Floyd, a 46-year-old black man, and pinned him to the ground. One officer knelt with his knee on Floyd's neck, contributing to the latter's premature death. Videos of the police officer kneeling led to demonstrations around the world for racial justice.

Neuro-notes

The Principle of Antithesis, proposed by Charles Darwin (1872), is the idea that opposite emotions such as happiness and sadness may evoke precisely opposite bodily responses (see *Antithesis*). As nonverbal opposites, kneeling and standing may elicit strong emotions, mostly negative, when the one is expected but the other appears. The unexpected kneeling posture may register as a negative or positive emotion in the brain's amygdala (see *Amygdala*).

See also *Bow*.

L

Language origin

Deep nonverbal roots

Rather than arising spontaneously, sui generis, as a self-contained entity in itself, verbal language gradually evolved from pre-existing patterns of nonverbal communication. Nonverbal messaging preceded linguistic expression by ca. 3 billion years. The former not only came before but also established the patterns and standards of linguistic communication through body movement, gesture and vocalization.

Nonverbal steps

The Routledge Dictionary of Nonverbal Communication proposes that human language – in both its vocal and gestural forms – was superimposed upon the older nonverbal medium of expression. Today's verbal communication reflects the earlier medium's role in (1) self-assertion, (2) species recognition, (3) genetic reproduction, (4) emotional expression and (5) attention to objects and the environment (Givens, 2020).

Lapel pin

Identity sign

A usually small, often circular badge – pinned to a carry bag, jacket or other piece of fabric – that graphically and symbolically suggests allegiance to a political, religious, social or sporting group.

Usage

Nonverbally, lapel pins may be worn to show affiliation (see *Affiliative cue*) and like-mindedness (see *Isopraxism*).

Placement

Worn on the left lapel of one's jacket, a lapel pen's asymmetric placement attracts notice, as it contrasts with the human body's relentless bilateral symmetry.

Hue

Pins may be multicolored to engage the human primate's highly evolved sense of color (see *Color cue*). They may be reflective to attract further notice.

Brooch

Significantly larger and more expensive are brooches, women's jewelry designed as very visible pins to be worn on fabric. Brooches may be purely decorative or decorative and political. Notable cases in point are the whimsical brooches worn by former U.S. Watergate prosecutor Jill Wine-Banks in TV interviews during the 2019 impeachment of U.S. president Donald Trump.

"I had an old celluloid eagle above a shield that said 'Defend America,' and I thought, No one will notice it – it didn't stand out. But someone on Twitter saw it, and I realized I was sending a message" (Yaeger, 2018).

See also *Collection, Media*.

Laugh

Rhythmic vocalization

Figure L.1 Laugh

Human laughter varies greatly in form, duration and loudness. A common form of laughter includes sudden decrescendo (i.e., strong onset to soft ending), forced-expiration bursts of breathy vowel sounds (e.g., "hee-hee," "heh-heh," "ha-ha" or "ho-ho-ho") given in response to embarrassment, excitement or humor. In extreme form, an involuntary spasm of the respiratory muscles, accompanied by an open-mouth smile, flared nostrils, tearing eyes, facial flushing and forward bowing motions of the head and torso. In mean-spirited form, laughter (esp. group laughter) may be directed at enemies and persons with whom one disagrees or dislikes, as a form of aggression-out. (N.B.: Shared aggression directed at another works to bond aggressors as a cohesive unit.) Mocking-aggressive laughter resembles the group-mobbing vocalizations of higher primates.

Usage

To laugh is human ("Man is the only animal who laughs," noted the French philosopher Henri Bergson; but see subsequently, Primatology). Chemically, laughter may provide relief from pain or stress by releasing endorphins, enkephalins, dopamine, noradrenaline and adrenaline. Socially, laughter may bind us as allies united against outsiders and against forces (e.g., mortality, as in dark humor) beyond our control. Psychologically, the comic laugh (in response, e.g., to jokes, puns and satire) may be a recent development linked to the evolution of speech. Laughter has a rhythm, with vocalizations of about five syllables per second (Bryant and Aktipis, 2014).

Exhilaration

Laughter may be associated with – and thus may be a sign of – the emotion of exhilaration. According to Ruch (1993, 607), exhilaration is a "pleasurable, relaxed excitement" which begins with a "sudden and intense increase in cheerfulness, followed by a more or less pronounced plateau and a prolonged fading out of the emotional tone."

Types of laughter

Different types of laughter have been identified in research, with laughter typically falling into the following domains: shared laughter (Kurtz and Algoe, 2015, 2017; Provine, 1992), volitional laughter (Bryant and Aktipis, 2014), spontaneous laughter (Bryant and Aktipis, 2014), voiced and unvoiced laughter (Bachorowski and Owren, 2001) and genuine laughter (Keltner and Bonanno, 1997).

Shared laughter

Connections have been found between relational closeness and the production of laughter (Smoski and Bachorowski, 2003), with shared laughter being shown to help relationships (Kurtz and Algoe, 2017). Research by Kurtz and Algoe (2017, 45) found that "shared laughter promotes relationship well-being, with increased perceptions of similarity most consistently driving this effect."

Contagious laughter

"Consider the bizarre events of the 1962 outbreak of contagious laughter in Tanganyika. What began as an isolated fit of laughter (and sometimes crying) in a group of 12- to 18-year-old schoolgirls rapidly rose to epidemic proportions. Contagious laughter propagated from one individual to the next, eventually infecting adjacent communities. The epidemic was so severe that it required the closing of schools. It lasted for six months" (Provine, 1996, 38).

Laughter and speech

"One of the key features of natural laughter is its placement in speech. Laughter is not randomly scattered throughout the speech stream. The speaker and the audience seldom interrupt the phrase structure of speech with laughter. In our sample of 1,200 laughs there were only eight interruptions of speech by laughter, all of them by the speaker. Thus a speaker may say 'You are going where? . . . ha-ha,' but rarely 'You are going . . . ha-ha . . . where?' The occurrence of laughter during pauses at the end of phrases suggests that a lawful and probably neurologically based process governs the placement of laughter in speech – a process in which speech has priority access to the single vocalization channel. The strong and orderly relationship between laughter and speech is akin to punctuation in written communication (and is called the punctuation effect)" (Provine, 1996).

Anatomy

In laughing, diverse facial, jaw and throat muscles are involved, including levator labii superioris, risorius, mentalis, depressor anguli oris (the "frown" muscle), orbicularis oris, buccinator and depressor labii inferioris (Ruch, 1993). Laughter may be accompanied by a general lowering of muscle tone and an increase in bodily relaxation, leading one, for example, to "collapse in laughter" (Ruch, 1993). The abdominal muscles and diaphragm contract in a respiratory "fit," not unlike sneezing or crying. Zygomatic and risorious muscles of the face contract in a grimacing smile; mandibular muscles may rhythmically contract as the lower jaw quivers. In a "belly laugh," heartbeat accelerates, blood pressure rises and the vocal cords uncontrollably vibrate.

Primatology

Stimulated by the mammalian brain, laughter has much in common with animal calls. Gorillas and chimps "laugh" (i.e., give breathy, panting vocalizations), for example, when tickled or playfully chased. Indeed, research by Ross et al. (2010) indicates that "tickle induced vocalisations" in orangutans, gorillas, chimpanzees, bonobos and humans are similar, creating grounds for the hypothesis that laughter is common to humans and these creatures. This work suggests that "Laughter therefore is not an anthropomorphic term, and can instead arguably be traced as a vocalization type back to at least the last common ancestor of modern great apes and humans, approximately ten to sixteen million years ago" (Ross et al., 2010, 192).

Neuro-notes

Visual, auditory, tactile and vestibular (but rarely smell or taste) cues stimulate laughter's complex, reverberating chain of events involving areas of the brain stem, hypothalamus and frontal lobes, as well as centers of the motor and cognitive cerebral cortex.

Mirror neurons

"Rapid facial mimicry (RFM) is an automatic response, in which individuals mimic others' expressions. RFM, only demonstrated in humans and apes, is grounded in the automatic perception-action coupling of sensorimotor information occurring in the mirror neuron system. In humans, RFM [as in laughing] seems to reflect the capacity of individuals to empathize with others. Here, we demonstrated that, during play, RFM is also present in a cercopithecoid species (*Theropithecus gelada*) [in the "play face," thought to be homologous with human laughter]" (Mancini et al., 2013).

Research reports

1   Laughter is more social than humorous (Van Hooff, 1967, 59).
2   In contexts of dominance, people who are submissive will laugh more at the humor of more dominant individuals, and conversely, the dominant individual laughs less at the submissive person's humor (Provine, 2001).
3   Human laughter "seldom exceeds 7 seconds" (Ruch, 1993).
4   Laughter may be vocal or voiceless, may include all vowels and many consonant possibilities; it frequently begins with an initial "h" sound, most usually as "he-he," grading into "ha-ha" (Ruch, 1993).
5   Anikin at el. (2018, 57) claim that laughter is innate – "that is, their acoustic form and, to some extent, meaning are predetermined by our genetic endowment."

6   Bryant and Aktipis (2014, 327) point out that "spontaneous laughter is an honest signal of cooperative intent" and may have roots in human "phylogenetically older vocal control mechanisms"

7   Typically, people laugh, on average, approximately 18 times per day, with the majority of these laughs occurring in the presence of another human. However, there is variation in these amounts (0–89 incidents per day) (Martin and Kuiper, 1999). Martin and Kuiper (1999) found that laughter increases as the day progresses, being more "pronounced" in evening. Their work also found that the most "prominent" form of laughter was spontaneous situational laughter.

8   Research indicates that women laugh more than men (Bilous and Krauss, 1988). In dyadic contexts, the gender make-up is also relevant. Women's laughter is more pronounced when interacting with a male, and men's laughter is lower when interacting with another male (Bilous and Krauss, 1988).

9   Provine (1996?) found that

   a   laugh vocalizations last about 75 milliseconds, separated by rests of 210 milliseconds;
   b   on average, speakers laugh 46 percent more than listeners;
   c   male speakers laugh only slightly more than male listeners;
   d   female speakers laugh considerably more than female listeners;
   e   male speakers laugh 7 percent less than female listeners;
   f   female speakers laugh 127 percent more than male listeners
   g   speakers usually laugh at the end of complete phrases (rather than in the middle), as a kind of nonverbal punctuation.

See also *Zygomatic smile.*

Lateral click

Auditory cue

A voiceless nonverbal clicking sound of ingressive air, released when the side of the tongue suddenly pulls away from the mouth's palate and/or alveolar ridge.

Usage

Used verbally, the lateral click is a consonant in some African languages, for example, in Hadza, Khoisen and Sandawe. Consonantal clicks may be voiced or nasalized. Lateral clicks also may be used nonverbally to communicate with animals, as in prompting horses to move forward or accelerate. Such clicks may be used in echolocation, for navigation by the blind.

Auditory startle

The combined sudden onset and abrupt ending of a loud click calls for attention – much like a beeping sound – by engaging a listener's auditory startle reflex (see *Beep*).

See also *TSK.*

Lawn display

Spatial cue

A plot of carefully groomed grass, and any of several decorative artifacts (e.g., white pickets or plastic pink flamingos) emplaced upon its surface.

Usage

Lawns mark territory and betoken status. Each year, Americans buy an estimated 500,000 plastic pink flamingo ornaments to mark their yard space – and to provide tangible evidence that "This land is mine."

Evolution

Two mya, the first humans lived in eastern Africa on hot, flat, open countryside with scattered trees and bushes and little shade, known as savannah grasslands. (N.B.: At this time, the human brain was expanding faster than any brain ever had in animal history and in the growing process seemingly locked in a fondness for level grassland spaces.)

Verbal prehistory

The English word "lawn" may be traced to the 7,000-year-old Indo-European root, *lendh-*, "open land."

Today I

To make earth more to our liking, we flatten and smooth its surface to resemble the original rolling plains our ancestors walked upon during the critical Pleistocene epoch 2 mya. Neo-savannah grassland – with its scattered bushes, trees and lawns – is the dominant theme of housing tracts, campuses, cemeteries, entertainment parks and shopping malls in almost every city today.

Today II

So important are lawns as consumer products that, at the University of Florida, a $700,000 campus laboratory – known as the TurfGrass Envirotron – was fabricated so horticulturalists could watch grass grow.

Flatland, China

In 1999, Chinese leaders planted a few hundred square yards of grass from seed (shipped from USA's Inland Northwest) on Tiananmen Square. "Across China, cities are planting thousands of acres of lawns, parks and golf courses ['to reverse decades of environmental ruin and make drab cities more livable']" (McDonald, 1999). (N.B.: On Tiananmen Square, knee-high metal signs warn visitors: "Please don't enter the grass.")

Neuro-notes

Like the cylindrical, filamentous projections covering our scalp, we respond to grass blades as we do to hair. The compulsion to feed, clip and groom our yard space is prompted by the same pre-adapted modules of the mammalian brain that motivate personal grooming and hair care (see *Cingulate gyrus*). Like thick, healthy locks, well-groomed lawns bespeak health, vigor and higher status.

See also *Golf*.

Leg wear

Fashion statement

Clothing worn to cover and to modify the color, thickness, length, shape and texture of the legs (see, e.g., *Blue jeans*). Ornaments (e.g., anklets and cuffs) worn to attract notice and accent the legs' masculine or feminine traits.

Usage

What we place upon our legs accents their thickness or taper. Trousers may "widen" the legs, for example, while dresses may bare the turn of an ankle. Skirts reveal, while pants conceal, vulnerable landscapes of skin.

Media

While fleeing from gorillas, giant lizards and Martians in vintage films, leading men (in pants and boots) may help leading women (in skirts and high heels) as the latter twist their ankles, stumble and fall to the ground.

Skirts, women

Though early skirts may have been made of thong-tied animal hides, the oldest-known skirts were more provocative and revealing than leather. Evidence for the ancient string skirt consists of detailed carvings on Upper Paleolithic Venus figurines from Lespugue, France, estimated to be ca. 23,000 to 25,000 years old (Troeng, 1993). The string skirt (not unlike the filamentous grass skirts of old Hawaii) revealed the legs and ankles and, when a woman walked, made sexually suggestive movements of its own as well (Barber, 1994).

Skirts, men

Japanese men may wear kimonos, Samoan men may wear sarongs and Bedouin men may wear flowing robes. Men from Amazonia, Bali, Egypt, Fiji, Ghana, Greece, Hawaii, India, Kenya, Korea, Scotland and Tibet also may wear skirts.

Stance

Leg wear suggests how solidly – or lightly – we tread upon the earth. In tandem with heavy shoes, for example, masculine cuffs define a solid connection with terra firma, as if a man "had both feet on the ground." In thinner shoes and higher heels, feminine bared legs seem to lift a woman, ethereally, above the earthly plain. (N.B.: In the corporate world, women may need to balance femininity against the stability of their stance.)

See also *Arm wear*.

Lip-compression

Facial expression

A usually negative cue produced by pressing the lips together into a thin line.

Usage

Lip-compression is a specific version of the tense-mouth display. A sudden lip-compression may signal the onset of anger, discomfort, disliking, grief, sadness or uncertainty.

Observation

Barely noticeable lip-clenching may signal unvoiced opposition or disagreement. Like other lip cues, in-rolling is controlled by "gut reactive" special visceral nerves.

Anatomy

At rest, the upper and lower lips make gentle contact, and the upper and lower teeth are slightly separated (see *Blank face*). In lip-compression, the prime mover is orbicularis oris (contraction of both pars peripheralis and marginalis; see *Lips*); the teeth may or may not occlude.

Research reports

In rage, "The mouth is generally closed with firmness" (Darwin, 1872, 236). Apes express anger by staring, clenching the jaws and compressing the lips (Chevalier-Skolnikoff, 1973, 80). In chimpanzees, a compressed-lips face "typically accompanies aggression" (Goodall, 1986, 123). "In an aggressive mood, the [bonobo chimpanzee's] lips are compressed in a tense face with frowning eyebrows and piercing eyes" (De Waal and Lanting, 1997, 33). In the Highlands of Papua New Guinea, when men were asked to show what they would do when angry and were about to attack, "They pressed their lips together" (Ekman, 1998, 238).

Neuro-notes

Lip-compression is an unconscious sign controlled by the limbic system acting through emotionally responsive paleocircuits of the facial nerve (cranial VII).
   See also *Lip-pout, Lip-purse*.

Lip-frown

Facial expression

A nonverbal "antonym" of the human smile, in which lip corners trend downward rather than upward in a grin. The mouth portion of a frown face may include lowered eyebrows as well.
   See *Eyebrow-lower*.

Usage

Down-trending lips may signal sadness, as in disappointment, unhappiness or loss.

Observation

A colleague orders a tuna sandwich for lunch. When she opens her take-out bag, she finds a pastrami sandwich instead. Disappointment shows in her lip-frown.

Anatomy

The lip-frown's prime mover is depressor anguli oris, which contracts to pull the lip corners downward. Also involved are risorius and platysma muscles, which stretch the lip corners laterally sideward and protrude the lower lip, creating a diagnostic horizontal crease beneath the latter's margin.

Neuro-notes

Lip-frown is controlled by the facial nerve (cranial VII), an emotionally responsive special visceral nerve. When we feel disappointment or loss, efferent nerves from the limbic system automatically produce the cue. Afferent nerves linked to mirror neurons decipher the cue's meaning.

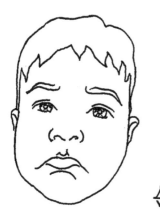

Figure L.2 Lip-pout

Lip-pout

Facial expression

To push the lower lip against the upper in a protruded look of disappointment, displeasure, sadness or uncertainty.

Usage

Children throughout the world may pout in sadness, frustration and uncertainty. Adults unthinkingly pout – or show fragments of the pouting cue (esp., contractions of the chin muscle's mentalis) – when disagreeing with comments presented across a conference table.

Evolution

The lower lip everts and pushes upward in a familiar movement used first in nursing and later in drinking from cups, glasses and straws. As a feeding-related sign, pouting has roots in the mammalian sucking reflex. The lip-pout, as well, is often a component of the shoulder-shrug display (see *Shoulder-shrug*).

Research reports

"[P]rotrusion of the lips, especially with young children, is characteristic of sulkiness throughout the greater part of the world" (Darwin, 1872, 237). The lip-pout has been observed as a mood sign in old-world monkeys and apes (van Hooff, 1967). Pouted lips are used as submissive signals in Bushman and deaf-and-blind-born children (Eibl-Eibesfeldt, 1970, 1973) and in adults expressing shameful moods (Izard, 1971). A brief pout or mouth shrug (Morris, 1994) reveals doubt or uncertainty (even as one says, e.g., "I am absolutely sure").

Neuro-notes

The lip-pout's feeding connection suggests control by diverse areas of the hindbrain (medulla and pons), midbrain and forebrain (amygdala and hypothalamus). Electromyographic studies show "fairly continuous activity" in the chin's mentalis (Gray, 1995, 795), reflecting a close link between this muscle and emotions of the mammalian brain.

See also *Lip-compression*, *Lip-purse*.

Lip-purse

Facial expression

To evert, pucker and round the lips in a look of disagreement, scheming or calculated thought.

Usage

The paramount message of lip-pursing is "thoughtful dissentience" – as if to say, "I disagree." The tightly screwed-out lips of the "pig snout" show that a listener has gone beyond the lip-pout of uncertainty to a more dissenting frame of mind. As a mood sign, a lip-purse may reflect an alternative verbal reply forming in the brain's speech-production center, Broca's area.

Anatomy

In the lip-purse, orbicularis oris, buccinator and direct labial tractor muscles of the lips contract. The principal muscle, orbicularis oris, is a sphincter consisting of pars marginalis (located beneath the margin of the lips themselves), and pars peripheralis (located around the lips' periphery, from the nostril bulbs to the chin). Pars marginalis, which is uniquely developed in human beings for speech, is a key muscle in the lip-purse cue.

Observation

Because the lip-purse signals mental resistance, speakers should immediately ask if listeners disagree before continuing the verbal argument. Clearing unspoken resistance beforehand facilitates understanding. (N.B.: Listeners may appreciate a speaker's seemingly "intuitive" grasp of their thought processes.)

Primatology

In the brain of our closest living relative, the chimpanzee, a motor area analogous to Broca's controls the rounded, pursed-lip movements used to make facial grimaces and emotional calls (Lieberman, 1991). The pant-hoot cry of excitement is a case in point (Goodall, 1990).

Research report

"Apprehension, scheming, or mere disinclination to speak may be betrayed by tightly screwed [i.e., 'pursing of the'] lips" (Peck, 1982, 254).

Neuroanatomy

Pursed-lips is a gestural fossil from the primate brain that unwittingly appears when we disagree. As quarrelsome words form in Broca's area, a call goes out through limbic system circuits to the brain stem's facial nerve (cranial VII). Forwarding the call, motor branches of the facial nerve instruct the lips to round and purse in preparation to disagree.

Neuro-note

Pursed-lips is an orofacial gesture controlled, in part, by Broca's area, a finger-sized patch of neocortex involved in the production of words. It is often the first sign of disagreement.

See also *Tense-mouth.*

Lip-retraction

Facial expression

To pull the lip corners horizontally and laterally backward in a nonverbal sign of annoyance or regret.

Annoyance

English "annoy" derives from Latin odium, "hatred."

Regret

Regret stems from the emotion of sadness. English "regret" derives from Old French *regreter,* "to weep," that is, cry (see *Cry*).

Anatomy

Lip-retraction is produced by the contraction of risorius muscles, assisted by mentalis muscles. Risorius may be a purely expressive (mimetic) facial muscle, without additional structural or functional roles. Perhaps the most recently evolved muscle in the human face, risorius is found exclusively in gorillas, chimpanzees and humans. The muscle may be misnamed (derived from Latin *risus,* "laugh"), as it is not a principal muscle in involved in laughing or smiling.

See also *Lip-frown.*

Lips

Mood signals

The muscular, fleshy, hairless folds surrounding the mouth opening, which may be moved to express emotion, pronounce words and kiss. Among the most emotionally expressive parts of the human body.

Usage

Lips give off telling cues about inner feelings and moods. So connected are lips to the visceral nervous system and to companion muscles of our lower face that we rarely keep them still. Like hands, lips are incredibly gifted communicators that always bear watching (see *Hands*).

Anatomy I

Lips may be moved directly by orbicularis oris and by direct labial tractor muscles in the upper and lower lips. Contraction of levator labii superioris alaeque nasi, levator labii superioris and/or zygomaticus minor, for example, elevate and/or evert the upper lip. Depressor labii inferioris and/or platysma par labialis depress and/or evert the lower lip. The complexity of muscle interactions may thus reflect the complexity of emotion blends.

Anatomy II

Lips may be moved indirectly, as well, by nine or more additional facial muscles (e.g., by zygomaticus major in laughing) through attachments to a fibromuscular mass known as the modiolus. That so many facial muscles interlink via the modiolus renders human lips extremely expressive of attitudes, opinions and moods.

Lip-reading

From fMRI studies, researchers find that linguistic visual cues afforded by lip movements activate areas of auditory cortex in normal hearing individuals (Calvert et al., 1997).

Primatology

Beginning with muscular contractions for suckling breast milk, our primate brain added the ability to grasp food items with everted lips. Chimps, for example, use prehensile lips to pluck termites from twigs. (N.B.: Humans may use prehensile lips to pluck French fries from a bag.)

Neuro-notes I

The facial nerve's (cranial VII's) lower nucleus controls the pouted-, curled- and tightened-lips expressions that unintentionally reveal our moods. Instructions for these signals come from limbic modules such as the amygdala and cingulate gyrus by way of the brain stem. Because there is little or no conscious control from higher brain centers, lip movements may provide trustworthy nonverbal cues.

Neuro-notes II

The human brain added precision to lip movements through nerve fibers linked to the primary motor neocortex. Today, fiber links from this area descend through the corticobulbar tract to motor neurons of the facial nerve, whose branches take charge of specific muscle fibers of the lips. That we can whistle a tune – and that whistle languages are "spoken" in some areas of the world – testifies to our lips' high nonverbal IQ as neurological smart parts (see *Whistle*).

See also *Disgust, Lip-compression, Lip-pout, Lip-purse* and *Tense-mouth*.

Lip-touch

Self-touch cue

A brief or sustained tactile stimulation of the hypersensitive fleshy folds around the mouth. A touch delivered to one or both lips with the knuckles, fingers or tactile pads of the fingertips, or with an object (e.g., a pencil or pen) held in the hands.

Usage

One of our most common self-touch cues, the lip-touch may signal a variety of moods and mental states including anxiety, boredom, excitement, fear, horror or uncertainty. Stimulating the lips diverts attention, for example, from disturbing thoughts and from people who may upset us. As a self-consoling gesture, the lip-touch is equivalent to infantile thumb-sucking.

Probe

In a conversation, cross-examination or interview, the lip-touch may mark a non-verbal probing point – an unexpressed feeling, opinion or thought to be explored (see *Probing point*).

Neuro-notes

Touching the mouth is emotionally analgesic and may help relieve physical and psychic pain. Our brain's cerebral neocortex devotes a disproportionately large part of its sensory surface area to fingers, hands and lips (see *Homunculus*). Thus in the mind's eye, pressing mentally "huge" fingertips against "enormous" lips is an efficient form of acupressure massage.

See also *Fingertip cue*.

Loom

Size display

Gestures and messaging features which appear massive, magnified and powerful – and often dangerous or imminently threatening to the mind.

Usage

The looming phenomenon gives innate meaning to nonverbal cues of size (see, e.g., *Antigravity sign*, *Broadside display* and *High-stand display*). Impressive mountains, large stones and tall trees are often viewed with wonder and may be considered sacred.

Architecture

Looming height "speaks" to us nonverbally, eliciting emotional reverence and awe. In prehistoric times, for example, Ireland's Hill of Tara, Australia's Uluru and Washington state's Mt. Rainier in the United States have been perceived reverentially, as sacred grounds worthy of respect and special treatment. Meanwhile, at 1,142 ft, the sandstone monolith of Uluru projects starkly above the desert floor below. Inspired by its looming size, the aboriginal Anangu people consider Uluru a spiritual site. And, rising to 14,411 ft. above sea level, Mt. Rainier (originally known as Tacoma) was believed by Native people to contain a spiritual lake of fire on top. The Hill of Tara, a limestone-cored, loaf-shaped mound of limestone standing ca. 180 ft above the flatlands of Meath Co., looms large over the landscape. Reputed home to ancient kings of Ireland, the Hill displays a dense concentration of burial and ceremonial sites and mounded earthworks.

Evolution

Looming is more recent in evolution than the tactile crouch and is at base a visual response. Without eyes to see it, the loom literally would make no sense. But to those with eyes, the movements and postures of expansion evoke strong, automatic reactions. Big is innately threatening to the vertebrate eye itself.

Neuro-notes

Movements and postures of expansion evoke a strong, automatic reaction known as the looming response, seen in birds 3 hours after hatching, and in puppies at 2 weeks of age. At 14 days, human babies avoid a rapidly dilating shape projected to "loom" on a screen – as if they already knew the danger portended by large, moving objects.

Antonym: *Crouch.*

Love

General

Like an avalanche where you have to run for your life. – Roger (age 9)

Emotion

1 A feeling of affection, devotion and fondness for a person, place or thing.
2 A feeling of attachment to a family member, esp. to a baby or young child.
3 A strong desire to be near a person who is the object of sexual passion.

Usage

As intangible as it is illogical, love is thought to be our noblest and strongest emotion. Nonverbally, love may show in

1 arousal cues (see *Hypothalamus*),
2 breathing rate,
3 courtship,
4 the en face gaze,
5 facial flushing,
6 head-tilt-side,
7 heart rate,
8 the hug,
9 isopraxism,
10 the kiss,
11 love signals,
12 personal distance,
13 pupil size,
14 synchrony and
15 tone of voice.

Parental care

Love has deep biological roots in mammalian parental care of the young and shows in such nonverbal behaviors as feeding, grooming, licking and nuzzling. Parental cues are not often seen in fish (see *Aquatic brain*) or amphibians (see *Amphibian brain*) but are evident in some reptiles (possibly including dinosaurs) and plentiful in birds; see *Reptilian brain*).

Research reports

1   "Although the emotion of love, for instance that of a mother for her infant, is one of the strongest of which the mind is capable, it can hardly be said to have any proper or peculiar means of expression" (Darwin, 1872, 212).
2   "I agree with Darwin that there is no distinctive facial expression for love" (Ekman, 1998, 212).

Neuro-notes

Love evolved from paleocircuits of the mammalian brain (specifically, modules of the cingulate gyrus) designed for the care, feeding and grooming of offspring. (N.B.: There is a strong tendency to take care of, feed and groom the people [and objects, e.g., automobiles] we love.)

See also *Love sign*, *Object fancy*.

Love sign

Sexual icon

Nonverbally, a male or female sexual trait encoded in an artifact, drawing, photograph, statue or sculpted figurine. Despite her missing arms, the ancient Greek marble sculpture Venus de Milo, for example, with her smooth, curvilinear right shoulder and hip and partially bared buttocks, has communicated femininity for ca. 2,000 years. Similarly, completed in 1504 by Michelangelo, the statue of David today encodes attractive masculine signs such as muscular hands and wrists, squared shoulders and an overall athletic build, as it has for centuries.

Usage

Easily aroused by visual cues, men enjoy erotic pictures, images and videos more than women do. *Playboy*, a magazine founded in 1953 that pictures idealized features of the female form, outsells *Playgirl*, founded in 1973, which features iconic images of male anatomy. Both are viewed predominantly by men.

Prehistory I

The earliest sexual illustrations were realistic and abstract renderings of female and male sexual organs painted on Upper Paleolithic cave walls in western Europe between 34,000 and 12,000 years ago. (N.B.: The most common themes depicted on Paleolithic cave walls are food and sex, in that order.)

Prehistory II

Dating to ca. 25,000 years ago, female Venus figurines with exaggerated breasts, buttocks and presumably pregnant tummies have been found across Europe from Spain to Russia. The figurines had less to do with beauty than fertility. Carved from mammoth ivory, the German Venus of Hohle Fels (ca. 38,000 BP) is presumably headless with enormously swollen breasts, an enlarged abdomen and exaggeratedly incised genitalia. The 2.4-inch-tall figurine is arguably the oldest iconic sign of a human body yet discovered.

Media

In U.S. college bookstores of the 1990s, the number one, two and three best-selling magazines, respectively, were *Cosmopolitan*, *Glamour* and *Vogue*, read by women seeking to enhance their sex appeal. Launched in the United States in 1892, *Vogue* (from French, "style") has become one of the world's most influential fashion magazines.

Trust the force

Love signs are in service to reproduction (see *Reproductive force*). After RNA and DNA appeared ca. 3.7 bya to encode information, via codons, about how to replicate, reproduction became a dominant force, joining the four physical forces – gravitation, the weak, the strong and electromagnetism – as a fundamental force to be reckoned with. The reproductive force remains a potent motivator in humans today, in their automobiles (see *Vehicular grille*), magazines, art, music, media and clothing.

See also *Barbie doll®*.

Love signal

Attraction cue

A nonverbal sign exchanged in the process of courtship (see *Courtship*). A nonverbal message emitted to attract a sexual partner. Presented less flirtatiously, a sign to help build familiarity, trust and rapport (see *Rapport*).

Figure L.3 Love signal

Usage I

A significant portion of interpersonal and small-group communication is about sexuality. Despite our ability to speak, courtship is often transacted in an unspoken medium of facial expressions and gestures including lip-pouts, sideward head-tilts and shoulder-shrugs. To bluntly state "I love you" in words before showing love suggestively in nonverbal signs, cues and deeds may scare a partner away.

Usage II

Loving feelings are powerful yet intangible emotions housed in the mammalian brain. Love signals themselves, however – from a shy head-toss to a subtle display of toe cleavage – are tangible signs that can be seen and identified. While love itself may be intangible, courtship runs on tangible mood signals.

Usage III

Love signals are nonverbal messages about physical proximity and psychic closeness. We trade gestures to tell each other – apart from words – to come nearer and nearer until we touch. Facial nuzzles, kissing with the lips, and caressing smooth, hairless terrains of skin with the fingertips used as tactile antennae (see *Fingertip cue*) are the preliminary signs that could lead to romance.

Research report

"Two of the most detailed analyses of the courtship process come from Givens (1978a) and Scheflen (1965). Givens' conclusions come from an examination of commonalities between humans and other species in the basic courtship sequence and signals" (Burgoon et al., 1989, 325).

Lullaby

Musical voice tones

Usually maternal, soothing vocal tones and prosodic voice qualities softly sung to infants, young children and often to adults in the early stages of courting (see *Courtship*).

Usage

Sung at close quarters, lullabies may be used to calm the nerves of physically or mentally upset youngsters, helping them relax and transition from alertness to sleep. Due to the softer voice needed to sing a lullaby, physical proximity is needed. This enhances psychological closeness through immediacy cues of warmth and affection (see *Immediacy*).

Culture

Though lullaby words differ variously in Iceland, Ireland, Italy and the Philippines, nonverbal sounds of lullabies may be culturally universal. Higher-than-normal pitches and pitch ranges; hypnotic, rhythmic repetition and slower, softer tempo. The singer's lips may be visibly closer to the listener's ear, as if in readiness to kiss (see *Intention cue*).

See also *Music*.

Lunch

Midday meal rite

The usually friendly ritual of eye contact, gestures and words exchanged at midday while consuming foods and food products (see *Consumer product*).

Usage

We "do lunch," schedule luncheon meetings and conduct business over lunch because eating together reduces anxiety as the parasympathetic nervous system switches to rest-and-digest and promotes sociability through the reptilian principle of "acting alike" and "doing the same thing" (see *Isopraxism*).

Courtship

Since lunch is conducted in the light of day, it is an effective venue for the early exchange of love signals. As in the more serious dinnertime rite conducted after dark (see subsequently, Media), couples may find eating together less stressful than conversing without the shared focus of utensils, food and drink.

Media

"The next day, Vicki offers to cook Gary dinner at his apartment. Thinking quickly, Gary says his place is too messy; they decide to have lunch at the ranch instead." – Young and Restless (*Soap Opera Digest* synopsis, May 2, 2000, 114)

Corporate culture

Office rituals invariably involve eating and drinking together. Nonverbally, food consumption allies staff and draws employer and employees closer. But note that food is rarely served at annual performance reviews.

Ancient history

Food is a powerful nonverbal symbol, as the Egyptian artists who drew ritual offerings of food and drink on tomb walls understood 2,500 years ago.

Prehistory

Unlike other primate species, human beings have been sharing edibles for at least 2 million years, as evidenced by arrangements of cut and broken big-game bones found in sites at Olduvai Gorge, Tanzania. The earliest-known ritual involving food is found in Upper Paleolithic cave paintings dated to between 34,000 and 12,000 years ago. The cave walls show big-game animals speared or caught in what may have been "magical" traps (Wenke, 1990).

Neuro-notes

In primates, including human beings, there appear to be highly developed nervous-system pathways and accompanying mirror neurons involved in bringing food to the mouth with the hands. This may explain why people so closely monitor the eating and drinking actions of others at county fairs and other public places, in cafeterias, diners, waiting rooms and cafes. Thanks to mirror neurons, watching a fellow human being eat a burger brings more than a little vicarious pleasure: It is as if we, ourselves, were eating the sandwich.

See also *Taste cue*.

M

Mammalian brain

Evolution

Any of several parts of the human brain to emerge during the mammalian adaptation to nocturnal (i.e., night) life and to competition with reptilian foes. A great deal of our nonverbal communication is rooted in modules and circuits of the mammalian brain, specifically in forebrain areas at the heart of the limbic system, which generate emotions for parental care, playfulness and vocal calling (MacLean, 1990; see *Emotion*).

Usage I

By ca. 150 mya, our mammalian forbears had entrusted their evolutionary future to a new and powerful form of arousal: emotion. In significant measure, the nerve network for emotions, feelings and moods evolved from neural structures earlier committed to smell (see *Aroma cue*).

Usage II

That emotions are like aromas – pleasant or unpleasant – is because they were designed from an olfactory model. This shows nonverbally, for example, in the curled-upper-lip display, which reveals nausea, should we smell a foul odor, and disgust as we listen to a colleague's "rotten" idea. When something looks, sounds or smells "fishy," emotional muscles of the face telegraph a nonverbal response for all to see.

Usage III

The fourth great epoch of nonverbal communication took place during evolution of the mammalian brain. In earlier vertebrate brains, body movements appeared as reflexes. Neither learning nor memory was required, for example, to crouch from a looming object, startle to a sound or withdraw from a painful bite.

Research reports

In proportion to brain size, humans have the largest limbic system of any vertebrate (Armstrong, 1986), making them the most emotional creatures to walk the earth. The earliest mammals "were 'reptiles' that were active at night" (Jerison, 1976, 11). "The evolution of hearing and smell to supplement vision as a distance sense is sufficient reason for the evolution of an enlarged brain in the earliest mammals" (Jerison, 1976, 11–12).

Nonverbal consciousness

Consciousness first appeared in vertebrates ca. 200 mya in mammals, according to neurophysiologist John Eccles of the Max Planck Institute for Brain Research in

Frankfurt. To seek primordial self-awareness, human beings go to great lengths to quiet the verbal dialogue – through meditation, chanting or yogic breathing – to re-enter the original, nonverbal state of consciousness. Pre-verbal consciousness lies in a region of the brain stem called the thalamus, below the chatty stream of consciousness in the cerebral cortex above.

Neuro-notes I

"The paleomammalian brain is represented by the limbic system" (MacLean, 1975, 75). "The neomammalian brain is represented by the rapidly evolving neocortex and structures of the brainstem with which it is primarily connected" (MacLean, 1975, 75).

See also *Primate brain*, *Reptilian brain*.

Figure M.1 Mask

Mask

Face concealer

A material artifact or consumer product that partially or completely covers the human face and conceals one or more of its 23 nonverbal landmarks (see *Face*).

Usage

Masks are worn around the world in ceremonies, as disguises and in performances and rites of passage. Since the human brain closely attunes to facial features and movements (see subsequently, Neuro-notes), masks are among the most expressive artifacts designed by *Homo*. Colorful and evocative of emotional response, traditional masks are collected and displayed in museums around the world.

Prehistoric masking

The origin of masks is unknown. The practice of masking may have begun thousands of years ago in Upper Paleolithic face painting with sediments of clay and pigments of red ochre to mark the facial plain. Dating to ca. 17,000 years ago, the painted Birdman, of France's Lascaux Cave, likely depicted a stick-figure human being wearing a mask.

War paint

In the mid-1800s, Native American warriors of the Great Plains wore face-paint designs to proclaim ceremonial and ritual strength and to intimidate enemies in battle. Popular designs included black and red lines drawn on chins, cheekbones and foreheads to emphasize masculine size and strength. Red often symbolized blood and black aggression and power (see *Colors decoded*). Zig-zag lines above the brows suggested lightening, and hand symbols drawn on the cheeks betokened success in hand-to-hand combat.

Emotion: damper/enhancer

Around the world, traditional face masks downplayed or emphasized expressive facial features such as lips, eyes and eyebrows (see *Emotion cue*). Dampening masks like those of the Congo's Yaka show a human face devoid of emotion. Neutral visages may be judged as "angry" or "unfriendly" (see *Blank face*). Enhancing masks like the Japanese Noh mask's angry frown (see *Eyebrow-lower*) and the Javanese Topeng mask's friendly smile and lifted brows (see *Eyebrow-raise*) emphasize the face's expressive topography for all to see.

Going viral

With the 2020 coronavirus pandemic, surgical face masks were worn worldwide for protection against the disease. So expressive has the human face become through time that the utilitarian surgery mask inevitably became a fashion statement. In a matter of months, the homely medical garment, which covers the mouth and nose, was available in attractive colors and patterns, some featuring friendly images of the lower face to replace what it masked.

Neuro-notes

Our perception of faces is robust and rooted in the fusiform face area (FFA) located in Brodmann's area 37 of the temporal lobe. This proactive brain area is highly sensitive to facial templates, artifactual or real. Seeing a masked face with distorted, obscured or unusual features may elicit strong emotional responses, often fearful, in viewers (see *Amygdala*).

See also *Blackface*.

Meaty taste

Introduction

According to Bob Schwartz, VP of Sales, Vienna Beef in Chicago, "It's a fun product. When I meet someone at a party and tell them where I work, they smile. People love hot dogs" (Jackson, 1999, 106).

Flavor cue

The usually pleasant aroma and taste of cooked animal flesh. Intensely flavorful molecules created as myoglobin, the red pigment of raw steak, turns brown and a flavor-rich coating forms as juices evaporate from the meat's surface, and as the browning reaction releases furans, pyrones and other carbon, hydrogen and oxygen molecules which provide the complex oniony, nutty, fruity, chocolate and caramel-like tastes we prefer to the bland taste of uncooked meat and raw vegetables (McGee, 1990).

Usage I

The aroma of sizzling beefsteak basted with sage and garlic sauce is a chemical signal transmitted when a chef brushes the meat with seasonings and sears it with flame. According to McGee (1990, 304), "All cooked foods aspire to the [rich and flavorful] condition of fruit."

Usage II

In Nonverbal World, the essence of charbroiled steak evokes an emotional desire to approach the aroma. Among the most evocative of all chemical signals processed by the brain are those emanating from meats and meaty consumer products, such as baked ham and fried Spam® (see *Big Mac®*).

Evolution

As did late-Devonian amphibians, early mammals of the Cretaceous and early primates of the Paleocene epoch passed through a predominantly flesh-eating stage. Acting in accordance with a primeval chemical code, amphibians pursued fish (and fellow amphibians), while mammals and primates pursued mainly insects. With so many carnivores and insectivores on the family tree, we respond to meats with an extreme alertness, as if scripted to do so by the ancient code.

Neuro-notes

We crave meaty taste because the amphibian brain's hunger for flesh is older than the primate brain's "acquired taste" for fruit and nuts. As it influenced the pursuit, handling and killing of game, the amygdala also stimulated the release of digestive juices in preparation for eating the kill (see *Amygdala*). Thus, today, hidden aggressiveness in the meat-eater's code makes a sizzling steak more exciting than a bowl of fruit. This explains, in part, why, when possible and affordable, meals throughout the world are planned around a meat dish.

See also *Glutamate, Herbs and spices, Shellfish taste*.

Media

Introduction

In his 1961 speech, FCC chairman Newton Minow called television nothing more than a "vast wasteland" (Jankowski and Fuchs, 1995, 125).

Electronic signals

The great, bristling background noise of television, radio, social media, print and computerized sounds, words and images filling the world's computer servers, transmission lines and air waves.

Usage I

As the ancient world resonated with natural sound – animal cries, storms, flowing waters and whistling winds – ours today blusters with media. Media has become a seamless electronic web for the display of consumer products and services, and for the shaping of attitudes, tastes and worldview.

Usage II

Nonverbally, video images are seductive, addictive and immediate (see *Immediacy*). Viewers may share eye contact with TV personalities and read their facial expressions, shoulders and hands. Close-ups of body movements render their non-verbal signs more dramatic. Similarly, sound technology may dramatize voice tones, and music may imbue body language and words with stronger emotion.

Images and words

Promotion of consumer products is a dominant theme in the background noise of media. Commercial spots, print ads and digitally enhanced billboard designs, for example, rely on a partnership forged in prehistory between nonverbal images and words. As the original medium through which we communicated about bone, stone and shell implements, the combination of images and words – which synergistically reinforce each other – is the most powerful venue for selling products today.

TV laughter

Invented in 1953 by CBS electrical engineer, Charles Douglass, canned laughter stimulates an unconscious contagion of chuckling in viewers (see *Isopraxism*, *Laugh*). Douglass called his invention "audience reaction."

See also *Blue jeans*, *Coca-Cola*.

Men's shoes

Clothing cue

A masculine style of footwear marked with messaging features designed to contrast with those of feminine footwear (see *Women's shoes*).

Usage

In expressive style, men's shoes may be dominant, submissive or neutral.

Stomping I

Dominant shoes are typified by thick, crepe-soled "beetle crushers" worn by English Teddy boys of the 1950s; middle-class Desert Boots® of the 1950s and 1960s; urbane Timberland® boots of the 1970s and aggressive Doc Marten® boots worn by alienated young men and women of the 1990s. Dominant styles are robust – wide, thick and heavy – to accent the size of the foot and its ability to stomp (see *Goose-step*).

Stomping II

The oldest stomping shoes are sandals from ancient Egypt with pictures of enemies painted on the soles. More recently, by popularizing thick, buckled motorcycle boots in the media, Marlon Brando (The Wild One, 1954) and Peter Fonda (Easy Rider, 1969) furthered the role of footwear as a fashion statement with which to figuratively stomp the powers-that-be.

Mincing

Men's submissive shoes are narrow, with lightweight uppers, thin soles and tapering toes. Styles include pointed "winkle-pickers" worn by British Mods of the 1950s;

pointed-toe Beatle boots of the 1960s and Gucci® loafers, the late-20th century's premier power slipper. Submissive styles are gracile to suggest vulnerability and downplay the foot's size and bluntness. Moreover, they stand wearers precariously on their metatarsals in a tip-toed position. Unstable, high-heeled styles (e.g., the Beatle boot) make stomping difficult.

Hushing

The third prototype in men's footwear is the neutral shoe, neither dominant nor submissive but fashionably introverted and bland. Stylistically neither wide nor narrow, pointed nor blunt, the sole is neither thick nor thin, nor obviously masculine or feminine. The neutral shoe is personified by dark-gray, brushed-pigskin Hush Puppies® (1950s to 1990s [see below, Media]), and by Ivy League saddle shoes and penny loafers (1950s to 1990s), worn by both men and women.

Media

"When those technicolor [e.g., bubble gum pink, lemon yellow] Hush Puppies appeared on the New York runway, fashion wags went berserk. The shoes began appearing in *GQ* magazine. Stylists snapped them up to dress musicians for videos. They were used to accessorize pricey clothes with puffed-up designer labels. Forrest Gump wore them. Fashion insiders began publicly proclaiming their love for Hush Puppies" (Givhan, 1995, C2).

See also *Boot*.

Message

Communication

A transmittal of information by signs, signals, cues from one living thing to another (see *Information*).

Usage

Regarding nonverbal messages, all cues are signals, and all signals are signs – but not all signs are signals, and not all signs and signals are cues. Regarding verbal messages, words may be spoken, whistled, written or manually signed (see *Word*).

See also *Messaging feature*.

Messaging feature

Sign

A usually brief message crafted into the design of a plant, animal or consumer product. A meaningful mark, line, shape, pattern, brand, label, seal, banner, badge, decoration, symbol, gloss, feel, flounce, color, aroma, spice, cadence, tone, edging, spangle or appliqué added to a product to transmit information rather than to provide functionality, durability or strength (see *Information*).

Usage

Messaging features, for example, the hem, lapels and shoulder pads of a business suit, "speak" to us nonverbally as gestures. In manufactured retail goods, messaging features evolve through a process of product selection, which gives voice to seemingly innate preferences for items that not only function well but also "express themselves."

Biology

Millions of years before the advent of products, messaging features were prominent in biology. Peculiar features of the orangutan's face, for example, are its cheek flanges – prominent fleshy flaps on the right and left sides of a mature male's face. Without practical function, cheek flanges visually "enlarge" an orangutan's face to signal dominance, rank and seniority, much as the graying "silverback" saddle cue bespeaks dominance in male gorillas.

Botany

In plants, messaging features are called secondary products. In the tobacco plant, for example, nicotine is a secondary product (see *Nicotine*).

Automobile tail fins

Exotic tail "fins" decorated American automobiles in the 1950s. The conspicuous fins added nothing to automotive safety, durability, efficiency or speed but were popular nonetheless, suggesting, in tandem with tail lights, that 1950s-era cars were "jet propelled." The most exaggerated tail fins may have been those of the 1959 Cadillac.

See also *Vehicular stripe*.

Microexpression

Hypothesis

Microexpression is a fleeting facial expression that may last less than a second before disappearing from the human visage. The underlying idea is that a true emotion or emotional blend triggers the microexpression, followed by a voluntary attempt to mask or cover-up the initial display.

History

The term was introduced in 1966 by E. A. Haggard and K. S. Isaacs. Subsequently, Paul Ekman and Wallace Friesen (1969b) introduced "micro affect displays." Ekman later created a seminar for nonacademic consumers to be certified as trained observers of microexpressions for detecting deception. Today, Paul Ekman International (PEI) Training Services offers classes leading to certification as an "Ekman Approved Associate."

Validity

The scientific status of microexpressions in human nonverbal communication remains in question. In her 2018 article, "Microexpressions are Not the Best Way to Catch a Liar," for example, Judee Burgoon criticizes six of the basic principles upon which microexpression theory (MET) rests.

Mimicry

Mimicry, mirroring and chameleon effect

Sometimes called the "chameleon effect" (Chartrand and Bargh, 1999), the manner in which people often change their body movements (but obviously not their color!) and mannerisms (e.g., posture and gestures) to match those of the person with whom they are interacting is termed mimicry. For example, it can involve matching the nonverbal communication of the other interactant by crossing the legs, crossing the arms, sitting in a particular position (postural congruency), rubbing the face, moving the foot, leaning and head propping. When the listener's behavior becomes a "mirror image" of the speaker, this is termed mirroring.

Domains of mimicry

Typically, mimicry is examined in the research within two domains: intentional mimicry and spontaneous mimicry. Intentional mimicry occurs when the individual deliberately copies the behavior/actions of another person (for example, dressing in a similar manner or waving). On the other hand, spontaneous mimicry occurs when one observes another person and unintentionally copies their behavior/actions.

Research reports

1   Burgoon et al., note that "synchronous and motor mimicry" may well be innate, rhythmical and cyclical, suggesting that "humans are inherently predisposed to synchronize their rhythms and behaviors to one another" (Burgoon et al., 2016, 416).

2   Arnold and Winkielman (2020) make the point that, within atypical social cognition contexts, there are some factors which are influential. For example, people presenting with autism spectrum conditions, loneliness and alexithymia may "misshape" mimicry responses. As they state: "it appears that atypical reward processing, interoception, and alexithymia may function as individual difference variables that (mis)shape mimicry responses, in part based on changes in one's own capacity to feel and label internal states" (Arnold and Winkielman, 2020, 207)

3   Hess and Fischer (2013) observe that spontaneous facial mimicry can be affected by social factors. Here interaction goals, situational factors and emotional judgments combine to influence the perceiver's facial response, for example, facial responses in contexts of power and perceived higher/lower social hierarchy.

4   Within the context of emotional contagion theories, when humans are communicating, they "pass on emotions" via the mimicry of expression and body movements (e.g., postures, gestures). Hatfield et al. (1992, 156) argue that "people automatically mimic and synchronise expressions, vocalisations, postures and movements with others and . . . as a result converge emotionally." It is important to note there is some evidence that "socially anxious" may well "catch" negative emotions from others, but they tend to suppress this mimicry and instead opt for the mimicry of positive displays (Dijk et al., 2018).

5   Within theories of embodied cognition, the argument is made that our physical interactions with the world shape our cognition of the world (Glenberg, 2008; Semin and Smith, 2008). Our thoughts are shaped by the types of perceptual and motor experiences we have as we interact each day with the world and, as such, "cognition is for action" (Glenberg, 2008, 43). Accordingly, mimicry is a fundamental feature of how humans learn and can take place at a variety of levels, both in the physical manifestation of actions (e.g., smiling/posture) or at an "un-observable" level as embodied simulation (e.g., neural activity, salivation, which "run" "within" the human). For example, functional magnetic resonance imaging reveals that simply observing a facial expression can lead to increases in neural activity in those somatosensory regions of the brain which deal with the face (Molenberghs et al., 2012)

6   Researchers such as La France (1985) and Trout and Rosenfeld (1980) note that postural congruency (where the postures of the interactants are mirrored) occurs during periods of positive speech and is rated as an indicator of cooperation and rapport.

See *Embodied cognition, Emotional contagion effect, Rapport, Dominance.*

Figure M.2 Mime cue

Mime cue

Gesture

A position or movement of the hands used to depict the shape, motion or location of a person, place or thing. A speaking gesture in which the hands and fingers mimic physical, spatial and temporal relationships among objects, activities and events. A hand gesture with neurological circuits as complex as those for speech.

Usage

Because they reveal the presence of conceptual thought, mime cues may be our most intellectual gestures. Unlike palm-down, palm-up and self-touch cues, which convey mainly emotion, mime cues express narrative thinking, relationships among objects and associations of ideas. In this regard, mime cues resemble the spoken words they often accompany.

Evolution

Mimicking complex sequences of acts – demonstrating the body movements used, for example, to make stone tools, build brush shelters and topple trees – mime cues represent an advanced conceptual form of nonverbal communication. Given in serial order, miming may have been our species' first step on the intellectual path leading to nonverbal narrative, precursing the verbal sign (e.g., American Sign Language) and vocal languages (e.g., English) used today.

Semantics

In a conversation about throwing a baseball, for example, we may pantomime the motion with our hands. Mime cues depict relationships among objects (e.g., "closer than," "as big as," "heavier"), attributes ("flat," "long," "rounded") and action sequences ("I pick up snow," "form a snowball" and "throw it at you"). A typical mime cue is the walking-figure, in which two fingers are used to mimic the body's rhythmic, strolling gait.

Neuro-notes I

To mimic an act such as changing a lightbulb, mime cues use the same brain modules to move the same muscles as the physical activity itself. Neurologically, swinging a bat, for example, is nearly the same as gesturing the act of batting. Computer imaging studies show that mentally rehearsing an activity involves the same brain areas as well (Sirigu, et al., 1996, 1564).

Neuro-notes II

Miming in temporal order and tracing shapes in space involve a highly evolved area of the neocortex's parietal lobe. The posterior parietal's left side is specialized for language. Its right side helps us process relationships among objects in space, along with information about the position of our hands and our motivational state, all at the same time.

See also *Point, Steeple*.

Mini-PONS

This test, developed by Banziger et al. (2011) is a shortened version of the Profile of Nonverbal Sensitivity (PONS) developed by Rosenthal et al. in 1979. It is a multichannel version of the PONS test consisting of 64 items which provides for swift screening of emotion recognition ability.

Mint

Aroma cue

Any of several plants of the aromatic genus *Mentha* used in diverse consumer products (e.g., cakes, candies, cookies and toothpaste). Mint addresses nonverbal messages to smell, taste and tactile receptors of the brain.

Usage

Peppermint is used to flavor sweets, candies and various liquor drinks. Spearmint is often used in cooking.

Evolution

Many plant-odor signals (e.g., pyrazines) evolved as nontoxic warning signs to deter predators (McGee, 1990, 311). Ever-popular true mints, including sage, rosemary, marjoram, oregano and thyme, evolved strong odors of camphor, eucalyptol and limonene to keep insects at bay.

Anatomy

Menthol – a crystalline alcohol obtained from peppermint oil – tricks heat-sensing organs (thermoreceptors) of the tongue and skin into sending messages to the brain that the sensation tastes and feels "cool" (Feldman, 1991, 192).

Neuro-notes

Mint sends a multimodal message to aromatic (smell), gustatory (taste), and pungency (trigeminal nerve) sensory nerve endings (see *Taste cue*, Trigeminal "taste").

Mirror neurons

Decoder cells

On the encoding side of nonverbal communication, researchers have traced the origin of many wordless signs, signals and cues to specific paleocircuits of the human brain and nervous system (see *Efferent cue*). These neural circuits predate newer, cerebral circuits that today enable speech and sign language. On the decoding side, however, how we attribute meanings to nonverbal cues (such as the tongue-show and shoulder-shrug) has remained a mystery (see *Afferent cue*). With the discovery of mirror neurons, researchers now have a tool to explain how certain gestures may be decoded intuitively apart from learning and experience.

Monkey brain

In the early 1990s, mirror neurons were discovered in the premotor cerebral cortex of macaque monkeys. Vittorio Gallese, Giacomo Rizzolatti and colleagues at the University of Parma, Italy, identified neurons that activated when monkeys performed certain hand movements (such as picking up fruit) – and also fired when monkeys watched others perform the same hand movements.

Baby see, baby do

In *The Imitative Mind* (Meltzoff and Prinz, 2002), Andrew Meltzoff used mirror neurons to explain how human newborns from 42 minutes to 72 hours old (mean = 32 hours) could imitate adult facial acts (tongue protrusion, lip protrusion, mouth opening, eye blinking, cheek and brow movements and components of emotional expressions), head movements and hand gestures. Human mirror neurons have been located in Brodmann's area 44 (Broca's area) of the brain's cerebral cortex.

Like me

"I propose," Meltzoff (2012) wrote, "that young infants' fundamental recognition of others as 'like me' provides a connection to others that is used to bootstrap learning about intentions, emotions, perspectives and other minds."

A blueprint in the brain

In the context of nonverbal communication, mirror neurons provide brain circuitry that enables us – intuitively – to decode and understand the meaning of unspoken signals and cues. When we see a hand gesture, for example, or hear an angry voice tone, mirror neurons set up a motor template, a prototype or blueprint in our own brain, that allows us to mimic the particular hand gesture or vocal tone. Additionally, through links to the limbic system, there are mirror neurons to help us decode emotional nuances and meanings of the hand gestures we see and the tones of voice we hear. We are seemingly wired to interpret the nonverbal actions of others as if we ourselves had enacted them.

Motion energy map

Observation tool

A computerized rendering of facial energy patterns used to read emotions, feelings and moods. A digitalized camera image with which to display the facial-muscle contractions of specific emotions (e.g., of sadness, anger and fear).

Usage

Motion energy maps show which areas of the face move to express emotions. They may someday enable computers to recognize and respond to emotion cues of the face.

See also *Face*.

Motivation impairment effect

Motivation and lying

The motivation impairment effect (DePaulo and Kirkendol, 1988) is fundamentally a hypothesis which argues that when people are highly motivated "to get away with their lies (relative to those who are less highly motivated), they are less successful at doing so, whenever observers can see or hear any of their nonverbal cues" (De Paulo et al., 1988, 177). The hypothesis propounds an inverse effect. One would imagine that motivated liars would be better at lying than "unmotivated" liars. However, this hypothesis predicts the opposite, where motivated liars are more easily identified once their nonverbal cues can be seen or heard.

Critiques

The hypothesis has been criticized, with Burgoon (2005) arguing that the only main example of the motivation impairment effect occurs when verbal and nonverbal channels are affected by extreme motivation or jeopardy. Indeed, work by Burgoon et al. in 1995 found that "liars" who were highly motivated were judged more credible than "liars" who were less motivated. Interestingly, within the worlds of computer-mediated environments, Woodworth et al. (2005) found that "motivated liars" in these environments were "immune" to the motivational impairment effect, being judged more successful in their deceptive endeavors. They in fact suggested that computer-mediated environments facilitate motivated liars and that in this instance, rather than impairing deception, they suggested being motivated to lie (within the computer-mediated environment) has an enhancing effect – the motivational enhancement effect.

Music

Artistic auditory signals

An aesthetically pleasing, sequential arrangement of vocal or instrumental sounds. English "music" derives from the 7,000-year-old Indo-European root word *men* – "to think."

Usage

Music encodes a highly evocative, emotional message through its compositional harmony, melody, rhythm and timbre. Words set to music evince more feeling than when spoken or manually signed apart from melody.

Amusia

"Cases of amusia, i.e., loss of ability to produce or comprehend music – an abnormality as regards music analogous to aphasia as regards the faculty of speech – conclusively demonstrate that the musical faculties do not depend on the speech faculty [i.e., one may suffer from amusia without aphasia, and vice versa, though some may suffer from both]" (Reiling, 1999, 218).

Anthropology

So diverse are the world's musical "languages" that some sociocultural anthropologists specialize entirely in ethnomusicology.

Symphony

A symphonic composition is an extended, intensely emotional musical piece performed by an orchestra."The highs and lows of emotional experiences are touched in an ever-changing pattern that cannot be experienced in everyday life" (Eibl-Eibesfeldt, 1970, 440).

Neuro-notes I

Research on amusia suggests "that there is only one musical center in the cerebrum, and that it is situated in the anterior two-thirds of the first temporal convolution and in the anterior half of the second temporal convolution of the left lobe, i.e., in front of the [speech-comprehension] center of Wernicke" (Reiling, 1999, 218).

Neuro-notes II

PET studies of listening to familiar melodies show involvement of the right superior temporal cortex, the right inferior temporal cortex and the supplementary motor area (Halpern and Zatorre, 1999). Retrieval of a familiar melody activates the right frontal area and right superior temporal gyrus (Halpern and Zatorre, 1999). No significant activity was observed in the left temporal lobe (Halpern and Zatorre, 1999).

See also *Dance, Singing*.

N

Neck dimple

Body part

A visible indentation at the front of the neck, below the Adam's apple (laryngeal prominence) and above the collar bones. A fleshy hollow area of skin in the neck, surgically known as the suprasternal notch, through which the windpipe's tracheal cartilages may show.

Usage

The neck dimple is a frail body part revealed by upright posture and hairless skin. As an expressive feature, its fragility is either left uncovered for display or concealed by neckwear. In courtship, for example, the neck dimple is revealed to suggest harmlessness and vulnerability, as if to say, "You may approach" (see *Love signal*). In business, government and military affairs, the neck dimple is often masked by button-up collars, scarves and knotted ties that suggest formality, strength and reserve, as if to say, "Step back."

Media

"The idea that body language taps into non-conscious thought is not a new one. It has spawned generations of self-help books on how to succeed in interviews, or read the signs that your boss fancies you. Consider the indentation at the base of the neck, says David Givens, director of the Center for Nonverbal Studies in Spokane, Washington. Revealing it is a universal sign of submission and approachability in all mammals and a courtship cue in humans. So a man who loosens his tie in the presence of a potential mate may unwittingly be expressing his attraction" (*New Scientist*, [Spinney, 2000]).

Research report

Throat-baring, a visible sign of submission, has been studied in mammals (e.g., dogs and wolves) and in reptiles (e.g., crocodilians). The prominence of our neck dimple as we face each other and speak has led to diverse cultural fashions for exhibiting, adorning or covering the throat.

See also *Adams-apple-jump*.

Neckwear

Body adornment

An item of clothing or jewelry worn to conceal or reveal the frailty of the neck (see *Neck dimple*). In reveal mode, one may accent its masculine thickness (i.e., strength) or feminine thinness (gracility).

Usage

The human neck is comparatively slim and suggestive of vulnerability. Thus, a man may "widen" his neck with a button-up shirt collar and knotted tie. A long tie adds an eye-catching line to accent the vertically ascending height of the face, head and torso; see *High-stand display*). A shirt's right and left collar points juxtapose to show an arrow shape pointing upward, thereby drawing eyes upward to a man's face. A woman may conceal the frailty of her neck dimple with a choker or scarf to enhance authority and formality in business and military affairs. In courtship, men and women may wear collarless clothing to showcase the neck's visual gender appeal.

Anthropology

In battle, even shirtless men may cover their throats. The costume of the traditional African Masai warrior, for example – which consists of a red tunic worn over bared shoulders and arms – includes a layer of beaded necklaces to mask the neck's frailty. In more verbose combat venues of the corporate world, an executive's silk tie or MBA scarf plays a similar role.

Evolution

The earliest necktie-like garment may have been the neckband worn by Roman legionnaires. Later in the French Revolution, neckbands signified political stances: white for "conventional," black for "revolutionary." Later still, the 19th-century cravat survived to become a precursor of the modern tie. The latter then evolved as a means to show moods, occupations and allegiances – and to cover throats around the conference table.

Research report

On the streets of New York City, people are four times more likely to give money to panhandlers wearing ties than to those who are tieless (Molloy, 1988).

See also *Business suit*.

Neuroaesthetic sense

Aesthetic faculty

Of or pertaining to those parts of the human nervous system involved in the appreciation of pleasure, order, balance, beauty and good taste. Among noteworthy neurological regions and circuits that participate in aesthetic messaging are the limbic system, pleasure pathways, prefrontal cortex, vagus nerve (cranial X) and enteric brain.

Usage

The neuroaesthetic sense has nonverbal dimensions evident in art cues, taste cues and music) as well as verbal dimensions in literature, lyrics and poetry. It enables the artistic perception of artifacts, dance, narrated words and other forms of human communication.

History

The term "neuroaesthetic" was introduced in 1999 by neuroscientist Semir Zeki, who has studied the biological underpinnings of beauty, color and love.

See also *Object fancy*.

New car smell

Aroma cue

A generic name for dozens of scented consumer products designed to mimic the leather, rubber, plastic and vinyl aromas of a show-room-new motor vehicle interior.

Usage

We find the synthetic odor of new car smell pleasant because it contains chemical analogs of natural plant resins, animal esters and sexual steroids.

See also *Apocrine odor*, *Arpege®*.

Newgrange

Nonverbal narrative

A 5,200-year-old monumental Irish artifact whose messaging features encode information about life, light, space and time. Newgrange is a megalithic passage grave that contains hidden underground messages pertaining to life and death. The great size of Newgrange's reconstructed surface mound attracts thousands of visitors annually, who stand in awe of its looming presence and shrouded messages within (see *Loom*).

Usage

Newgrange was designed to showcase the first morning glow of winter-solstice sunshine. Perfectly aligned with the sunrise, amber rays of light shines through a stone roof box to brilliantly illuminate Newgrange's bouldered inner passage. For the comparatively few who get to see it in person, the brilliant light shining on cold rock may suggest life's renewal.

Monumental sign

Like pyramids, skyscrapers and the Great Wall of China, Newgrange is a colossal monument that encodes a plethora of nonverbal signs and symbols. Among the latter is the triskelion, a symbolic representation of infinity (see *Sign*, *Triskelion*).

Nicotine

In 1925, Old Gold® cigarettes appeared, with the slogan, "Not a cough in a carload". "With men in the Army, the Navy, the Marine Corps, and the Coast Guard, the favorite cigarette is Camel®" (Camel advertisement on back cover page of *Life* magazine, July 10, 1944).

Afferent (incoming) cue

A potent alkaloid drug ($C_{10}H_{14}N_2$) of the tobacco plant, ingested by hundreds of millions of men, women and children in products such as cigars, cigarettes and snuff (see *Consumer product*). The most widely addictive chemical substance used by *Homo sapiens*.

Usage

Nicotine "speaks" nonverbally to the brain as an incoming chemical cue. Currently, there is a worldwide epidemic of nicotine use.

Neuro-notes

Nicotine "mimics the neurotransmitter acetylcholine by acting at the acetylcholine site and stimulating the nerve cell dendrite" (Restak, 1995, 116). Nicotine leads to the release of pleasure-enhancing dopamine and morphine-like endorphins (see *Pleasure cue*).

See also *Coca-Cola®*.

Nonverbal brain

Neuro term

Those circuits, centers and modules of the central nervous system involved in sending, receiving and processing speechless signs. In right-handed individuals, modules of the right brain cerebral hemisphere, considered more nonverbal, holistic, visuospatial and intuitive than the verbal, analytic, sequential and rational left brain hemisphere (see *Human brain*, Right brain, left brain). Those ancient centers (e.g., nuclei) and paleocircuits of the nervous system that evolved in vertebrates – from the jawless fishes to early human beings – for communication before the advent of speech.

Usage

Just as the brain's newer speech centers (e.g., Broca's area) control language communication, earlier areas of the nonverbal brain control communication apart from words. Knowing their parts and wiring helps us decode nonverbal messages.

Evolution

Our nonverbal brain consists of six interrelated divisions, outlined in the following, which merged in an evolutionary process from ca 500-to-2 mya:

1 Aquatic brain and spinal cord

The oldest neural division, present in the jawless fishes, includes the spinal cord's interneuron pools and motor neuron pathways for tactile withdrawal and the rhythmic, oscillatory movements of swimming (and, much later, for walking).

2 Amphibian brain

With amphibians, the pontine reticular excitatory system becomes more elaborate. The pontine tegmentum's link to the spinal cord's anterior horn motor neurons and muscle spindles raised the body by exciting antigravity extensor muscles (see *Antigravity sign*).

1   The vestibulospinal pathway elaborated – from receptors in the inner ear via the vestibular nerve (cranial VIII) and via cerebellar fibers to the vestibular nucleus in the upper medulla – running the length of the spinal cord for body posture (i.e., basic stance) in relation to gravity.

2   The tectospinal tract evolved, consisting of the superior and inferior col-
     liculus and its links, via the brain stem, running to cervical cord interneu-
     rons, then to anterior horn motor neurons, then to spinal nerves and
     finally reaching muscle spindles for postural reflexes to sights and sounds.
3   The rubrospinal tract further evolved. Paleocircuits from the red nucleus
     of the midbrain running to thoracic cord interneurons, then to anterior
     horn motor neurons and finally to muscles and muscle spindles for pos-
     tural tone of the limbs' flexor muscles.

3 Reptilian brain

With reptiles,

the vestibuloreticulospinal system evolves to control axial and girdle muscles
for posture relative to positions of the head. The basal ganglia-ansa lenticularis
pathway reverberates links between the amygdala and basal ganglia via the ansa
lenticularis and lenticulate fasciculus to the midbrain tegmentum, red nucleus
and reticular system to spinal cord interneurons required for the high-stand
(see *High-stand display*).

4 Mammalian brain

With mammals,

A   the amygdalo-hypothalamic tract becomes more elaborate: the central amyg-
     dala's link to the hypothalamus, via the stria terminalis, provided wiring for
     defensive postures (see, e.g., *Broadside display*).
B   Hypothalamus-spinal cord pathways adapt as well: the hypothalamus' dorso-
     medial and ventromedial nuclei feed indirectly via the brain stem's reticular
     system and directly through fiberlinks to lower brain-stem and spinal-cord
     circuits to cord motor neurons for emotion cues (see, e.g., *Emotion*).
C   The septo-hypothalamo-midbrain continuum evolves: the medial forebrain
     bundle (from the olfactory forebrain and limbic system's septal nuclei) via the
     hypothalamus' lateral nuclei to midbrain-tegmentum brain-stem motor cent-
     ers, mediates emotions (see, e.g., *Fear*).
D   The cingulate gyrus facial circuit evolves: links run from the anterior cingulate
     cortex to the hippocampus, amygdala, hypothalamus and brain stem and finally
     to the vagus (cranial X) and facial (cranial VII) nerves which, respectively, con-
     trol the larynx and facial muscles required for vocalizing and moving the lips.

5 Primate brain

With primates,

A   The neocortex's corticospinal tract further evolves: the posterior parietal cor-
     tex linked to supplementary motor, premotor and primary motor cortices
     (with basal-ganglia feedback loops) via the corticospinal tract, to cervical and
     thoracic anterior-horn spinal interneurons and to motor neurons in control of

arm, hand and finger muscles for skilled movements of the precision grip (see *Hand*).

B Modules of the inferior temporal neocortex evolve to provide visual input to the occipital neocortex's parvocellular interblob system (V1 to V2 and V4), permitting recognition of complex shapes, and to the inferior temporal cortex permitting heightened responses to hands and the ability to recognize faces (see *Facial expression*).

6 Human brain

A The corticobulbar tract further evolves: corticobulbar pathways to the facial nerve (cranial VII) permitted intentional facial expressions (see, e.g., *Smile*).

B Broca's cranial pathways evolves: Broca's-area neocircuits via corticobulbar pathways to multiple cranial nerves permitted speech.

C And Broca's spinal pathways evolve: Broca's-area neocircuits via corticospinal pathways to cervical and thoracic spinal nerves permitted manual sign language and linguistic-like mime cues (see *Mime cue*).

See also *Nonverbal learning*.

Nonverbal dreaming

Sleep signals

Nonverbal communication occurs in the awake state but may continue into the sleep state as phantasmagoric dreams. Dreaming can involve any or all of the senses, including balance and pain, but rarely smell.

Usage

Of what use are dreams? Thinkers from Descartes to Freud have proposed ideas about dreams and dreaming. Research continues in the 21st century, but at present, there is no definitive answer.

Nonverbal nature of dreams

Millions of years older than speech, dreaming is still principally nonverbal. Research suggests that dreaming is widespread in vertebrates (animals with backbones) and invertebrates (those without) and may be ca. 500 million years old. Its deep neural roots and evolutionary conservation through time attest to the central role of dreams in sleep – a role, however, yet to be explained.

Rapid eye movement

Our most vivid and complex nonverbal dreams are audiovisual and take place in the rapid eye movement (REM) sleep stage, detectable in sideward eye movements visible beneath closed lids. Emotional sensations (e.g., of euphoria and fear), along with imaginary and memory-based visions (e.g., of faces and street scenes), tastes (strawberry shortcake), touch (caresses and hugs) and vestibular sensations (falling and flying), take place sequentially in a quasi-narrative order, from chronological beginning to end. When describing a dream in words, we may use temporal-order memory to follow the narrative.

Neural relay

That the sense of smell is virtually absent in dreamland echoes the role of our brain's thalamus in dreaming. The thalamus is a central switchboard that links incoming sensory information (excepting smell) to processing centers above. In non-REM sleep, the switchboard turns off, while in REM sleep, it activates to within waking levels as audio, cognitive, emotional, gustatory, tactile, vestibular and visual centers populate our dreams.

Sensory content

In their review of dreaming research, Fox and colleagues (2013) estimate that 100 percent of human dreams contain visual elements (see *Vision cue*), ca. 57 percent contain audio (see *Auditory cue*) and all other senses account for ca. 1 percent of content (see *Balance cue*, *Olfactory cue*, *Pain cue* and *Taste cue*). They estimate, further, that emotions populate ca. 70 to 75 percent of dreams (see *Emotion cue*), and bizarre or impossible dream elements populate between 32 and 71 percent.

Neuro-notes

In dreaming, the brain's afferent sensory channels shut down (see *Afferent cue*). In REM sleep, efferent channels shut down as well (see *Efferent cue*) and skeletal body movements cease: nonverbally, the body is silent. Audiovisual dreaming predates speech and involves diverse areas of the hindbrain, midbrain and forebrain. While the body movements and facial expressions we "see" in dreams, as well as the voice tones we "hear," may seem real, they are neurological phantoms, imaginary, elusive and easily forgotten.

Figure N.1 Nonverbal entertainment

Nonverbal entertainment

Amusement cues

To send or receive wordless messages that momentarily amuse or divert attention through pleasure (see *Pleasure cue*).

Usage

Nonverbal entertainment is the principal narrative of competitive sports – such as football, ice skating and soccer – based on the rhythmic, alternating steps of walking (see *Walk*). Athleticism displayed in body motions while moving to catch a passed ball, land a quadruple jump or kick a soccer goal gives pleasure to performers and spectators alike. In nonverbal celebrations, the athlete may raise both arms in triumph while fans loudly vocalize and applaud (see *Triumph display*).

Neuro-notes I

The pleasure of scoring and winning in sports is due to releases of dopamine mediated by the ventral striatum of the basal ganglia. The reward is both social and emotional (Bhanji and Delgado, 2014).

Neuro-notes II: mirror neurons

Watching a player score a goal stimulates mirror neurons and suggests that we, ourselves, had kicked the score. The fans' vicarious feeling of victory may be as strong as the athlete's pleasure after scoring. Upon seeing the scorer's triumph display, a fan's victorious pleasure may increase, as if he or she had performed it. Indeed, mirroring the kicker, some fans will triumphantly raise their own arms. The player's triumphant feeling may be heightened, as well, upon hearing the crowd applaud.

Nonverbal learning

Primate see, primate do

The act of gaining nonverbal knowledge and skills apart from language, speech or words. The extralinguistic transmission of cultural knowledge, practices and lore.

Usage

A great deal of knowledge – from using a computer to sailing a boat – may be gained by watching, imitating or practicing the body movements of someone who knows. In diverse "nonverbal apprenticeships," the only vocal input may be, "Watch me." (N.B.: English "apprentice" comes from the 7,000-year-old Indo-European root word *ghend-*, to grasp with the hands, seize, take.)

Fundamental knowledge

Through a panoply of unspoken messages from Nonverbal World, we gain fundamental knowledge and experience about the business of life and living. Today even the most technical knowledge may be transmitted through nonverbal apprenticeships, in which students watch and do rather than read a manual.

Nonverbal directions

In airports, train stations and theme parks and on the highway systems linking them, international graphic symbols – nonverbally in pictorial format – are used to show people where they are and where they need to go (see *Isotype*).

Practice

Some nonverbal learning involves the practice-makes-perfect principle of repetition, for example, of repeating a golf swing, baseball pitch or balance-beam routine. Repeated swinging, throwing and jumping target the cerebellum rather than speech areas of the cortex.

Shape

In Bali, dance teachers may grasp and physically mold a student's fingers to choreograph the proper hand shape (Bateson and Mead, 1942).

Show

Learning to sail a boat by reading a manual may be less efficient than watching an experienced sailor pilot his or her craft. Knowledge is most efficiently transmitted through a combination of verbal and nonverbal means that simultaneously engages both cerebral hemispheres of the human brain.

See also *Nonverbal brain* and *Education*.

Nonverbal learning disorder

Introduction

A frequently misdiagnosed state of anxiety, confusion and social withdrawal caused by inabilities to send and receive common gestures, facial expressions and body-language cues. Persons with nonverbal learning disorder (NLD) may misread everyday nonverbal signals, display awkward body movements and have difficulty associating visual signs in space and time.

Usage

Children with NLD rely on the concreteness of verbal speech and written words and may be unable to process the subtleties of nonverbal expression.

Research reports

There is evidence that social intelligence may be different from general intelligence (Humphrey, 1976). For example, people who have autistic spectrum disorder may present with lower social intelligence as compared to their academic intelligence (Klin et al, 2006). Using neuroimaging methods with individuals who present with Asperger syndrome or high-functioning autism, Baron-Cohen et al. (1999) found evidence for a "social brain," where social intelligence seemed independent of general intelligence.

See also *Autism, Body dysmorphic disorder*.

Figure N.2 Nonverbal memes

Nonverbal memes

Motion memories

A meme is a verbal or nonverbal unit of memory transmitted forward in time. On the nonverbal side, a meme may be a gesture a viewer sees and imitates. The imitated gesture may then be picked up and shared by a third person, and perhaps eventually by millions of additional people in the manner of a fashion, tradition, fad or virus (i.e., "goes viral"). Examples of nonverbal memes include the high-five (ca. 1977–79), low-five (ca. 1920s), stadium wave (ca. late 70s), fist-bump (ca. late 1800s, then 2008) and other gestures of elation and triumph in sports. Nonverbal memes may be short-lived, like the now nearly extinct low-five, or persist for generations, like the European cheek-kiss.

Usage

Nonverbal memes transmit information about relationships, feelings and moods. In sports, the high-five may be used to show elation when a favored team scores a goal. Seeing the score, an elated spectator may abruptly share the feeling with fans nearby who root for the same team. Upon seeing another's high-five, viewers may imitate the gesture and spread its popularity (see *Isopraxism*).

Nonverbal nomenclature

Kinesiology

Kinesiology is the scientific study of body movement. It provides a useful terminology for body motions used in both verbal and nonverbal communication. Kinesiological vocabulary is used throughout this Routledge Dictionary to describe the diverse movements and articulations of body parts.

Abduction and adduction

Abduction occurs when a body part moves away from another. In the arms-akimbo posture, outward-bowed elbows – in tandem with the upper arms' abducted position away from the torso – widen, expand and visually "enlarge" the upper body (see *Hands-on-hips*).

Adduction occurs when a body part moves toward another. In the shoulder-shrug display, elbows are bent (flexed) and held into the body (see *Shoulder-shrug*).

Anterior and posterior

Anterior refers to the body's front side. The face is on the anterior side of the head. Posterior refers to the body's back side. The shoulder-shrug gesture is managed by posterior upper-trapezius muscles of the back.

Dorsal and palmar

Regarding hands, dorsal refers to the superior or top surface. A hand's dorsal surface may be featured in the fist gesture (see *Fist*). Palmar refers to the hand's palm side (see *Palm-up*).

Dorsal and plantar

Regarding feet, dorsal refers to their superior or top surfaces. In footwear, women's shoes may expose more of the foot's dorsal surface than men's shoes. Plantar refers to a foot's inferior of bottom surface. In a military march, a foot's plantar surface sharply strikes the ground (see *Goose-step*).

Extension and flexion

Extension occurs when a body part straightens, as in an extended index finger's pointing gesture (see *Point*). Flexion occurs when body parts fold or curl, as in tightly flexed fingers of the fist gesture.

Lateral and medial

Lateral refers to a body part that is away from the midline position. Regarding the entire body's anterior (front), the midline bisects its right and left sides. In a right- or lefthand direction, the body may bend laterally away from midline (see *Angular distance, Bend-away*). Medial refers to a body part that is moved toward the midline. Fingertips are brought medially parallel to midline in a steeple gesture (see *Steeple*).

Pronation and supination

Regarding forelimbs, pronation occurs when a hand rotates downward as in a floor pushup. An example of a pronated hand gesture in the palm-down cue (see *Palm-down*). Supination occurs when a hand rotates upward, as in a pleading or begging position. An example of a supinated hand gesture is the palm-up cue.

See also *Kinesics*.

Nonverbal release

Principle

The idea that certain body movements and gestures (e.g., hand-behind-head) may be touched off automatically by strong emotions, feelings and moods (see *Hand-behind-head*).

Usage

Nonverbal release is neurologically wired in paleocircuits that govern vestibular reflexes, neck reflexes and flexion withdrawal. Nonverbal release is a reminder that much of our body-motion communication is emitted apart from consciousness.

Visibility in sports

Nonverbal release may be seen when a posture requires "optimal control" (Ghez, 1991b, 602). When a baseball player, for example, raises and hyperextends an arm's glove-hand to catch a ball, the other arm may unconsciously flex from release of the asymmetrical tonic next reflex (see *ATNR*).

See also *Nonverbal consciousness*.

Nonverbal trail blazers

Pioneering research

Though nonverbal communication has been used by humans at least since the origin of *Homo sapiens*, its scientific study has barely begun. The following researchers have played major roles in decoding nonverbal signs, signals and cues:

Charles Darwin

In *The Expression of the Emotions in Man and Animals* (1872), Darwin studied the biological basis and origins of human nonverbal communication (see, e.g., *Shoulder-shrug display*).

Ray Birdwhistell

In *An Introduction to Kinesics* (1952), Birdwhistell studied the relationship between verbal and nonverbal communication from a linguistic point of view (see *Kinesics*).

Edward T. Hall

In "A System for the Notation of Proxemic Behavior" (1963), Hall opened the nonverbal study of spatial signs, signals and cues (see *Proxemics*).

Michael Argyle and Janet Dean

In a pioneering article, "Eye-Contact, Distance and Affiliation" (1965), Argyle and Dean opened the study of nonverbal distance, gaze cues and emotional affiliation (see *Affilative cue*).

Adam Kendon

In "Some Functions of Gaze-Direction in Social Interaction" (1967), Kendon studied the role of nonverbal cues such as eye contact in interpersonal communication (see *Eye contact*).

Robert Sommer

In *Personal Space: The Behavioral Basis of Design* (1969), Sommer advanced Edward Hall's spatial concepts to architectural design (see *Artifact*, Monumental).

Paul Ekman and Wallace V. Friesen

In "Constants Across Cultures in the Face and Emotion" (1971), Ekman and Friesen studied universal human facial cues that express primary emotions such as anger, disgust and surprise (see *Facial expression*).

Albert Scheflen

In *Body Language and the Social Order* (1972), Scheflen expanded his study of the role of nonverbal communication in human society, and helped popularize the concept of "body language" (see *Body language*).

Robert Rosenthal

"Sex Differences in Accommodation in Nonverbal Communication" (Rosenthal and DePaulo, 1979) is Rosenthal's study of expectancy theory – that a person's nonverbal communication unwittingly scripts a recipient's behavior (see *Expectancy theory*).

D. Michael Stoddart

In *The Scented Ape: The Biology and Culture of Human Odour* (1990), Stoddart focused nonverbal attention on olfaction and smell (see *Aroma cue*).

Andrew H. Bass and B. Chagnaud

In "Shared Developmental and Evolutionary Origins of Neural Basis of Vocal-acoustic and Pectoral-gestural Signaling" (2012), Bass and Chagnaud identified the neural link between human vocal speech and manual gesture (see *Gesture*).

Nonverbal communication

Concept

The process of sending and receiving wordless messages by means of facial expressions, gaze, gestures, postures and tones of voice. Also included are grooming habits, body positioning in space and consumer product design (e.g., clothing cues, food products, artificial colors and tastes, engineered aromas, media images and computer-graphic displays).Nonverbal cues include all expressive signs, signals and cues – audio, visual, tactile, chemical, visceral and vestibular – used to send and receive messages apart from manual sign language and speech.

Usage

Each of us gives and responds to literally thousands of nonverbal messages daily in our personal and professional lives – and while commuting back and forth between the two. From morning's kiss to business suits and tense-mouth displays at the conference table, we react to wordless messages emotionally, often without knowing why. The boss' head-nod, the clerk's bow tie, the next-door neighbor's hairstyle – we notice the minutiae of nonverbal behavior because their details reveal both how we feel and relate to one another and who we think we are.

Evolution

Anthropologist Gregory Bateson has noted that our nonverbal communication is still evolving: "If . . . verbal language were in any sense an evolutionary replacement of communication by means of kinesics and paralanguage, we would expect the old, predominantly iconic systems to have undergone conspicuous decay. Clearly they have not. Rather, the kinesics of men have become richer and more complex, and paralanguage has blossomed side by side with the evolution of verbal language" (Bateson, 1968, 614).

Kinds of cues

Nonverbal signals may be learned, innate or mixed. Eye-wink, thumbs-up and military-salute gestures, for example, are clearly learned. Eye-blink, throat-clear and facial-flushing, on the other hand, are clearly inborn or innate. Laugh, cry, shoulder-shrug and most other body-language signals are "mixed," because they originate as innate actions, but cultural rules may later shape their timing, energy and use.

Nature-nurture

Researchers do not always agree on the nature-nurture issue. Like Charles Darwin, human biologists suppose that many body-motion signs are inborn. Like the founder of kinesics, Ray Birdwhistell, some cultural anthropologists propose that most – or even all – gestures are learned, while others combine the biological and cultural approaches. Research by psychologist Paul Ekman and colleagues has shown that the facial expressions of disgust, surprise and other primary emotions are universal across cultures.

Research note

An early scientific study of nonverbal communication was published in 1872 by Charles Darwin in his book *The Expression of the Emotions in Man and Animals*. Since the mid-1800s, thousands of research projects in archaeology, biology, cultural and physical anthropology, linguistics, primatology, psychology, psychiatry and zoology have been completed, establishing a generally recognized corpus of nonverbal cues. Discoveries in neuroscience funded during the 1990–2000 U.S. "Decade of the Brain" have provided a clearer picture of what the unspoken signs in this corpus actually mean. Because we now know how the brain processes nonverbal cues, nonverbal communication has come of age in the 21st century as a science to help us understand what it means to be human.

Neuro-notes

Nonverbal messages are so potent and compelling because they are processed in ancient brain centers located beneath newer areas used for speech (see *Verbal center*). From paleocircuits in the spinal cord, brain stem, basal ganglia and limbic system, many nonverbal cues are produced and received below the level of conscious awareness (see *Nonverbal brain*). They give our days the look and feel we remember long after words are forgotten.

See also *Verbal communication*.

Nonverbal surveillance

Introduction

"You can observe a lot by watching." – Lawrence Peter ("Yogi") Berra (Berra's 2008 book title; John Wiley & Sons)

Watching and listening

The act of observing the behavior and body language of persons or groups under suspicion. Systematic observations, openly made as well as covert, conducted in airports, at border crossings and in other public venues, often for reasons of national security.

Usage

With the threat of terrorism, nonverbal communication has come to play a vital role in the training of government, military and law-enforcement personnel. The ability to see danger signs in anomalous behaviors and time patterns, in intention cues, clothing cues, gaze patterns, voice tones and deception cues is essential to ensure public security.

Elevator scenario

Software has been developed to interpret nonverbal behaviors captured by television cameras as being either "normal" or "abnormal." Staying too long in an elevator, for example, would be classed as an abnormal time usage which would set off a remote alarm. Abnormal physical movement in the elevator – for example, a man assembling a mechanism or opening a suitcase on the floor – would also trigger an alarm.

Face monitoring

Facial recognition software enables cameras to recognize faces in airports, ports of entry, government buildings, casinos and stores. Artificial intelligence software may recognize facial expressions of emotion as well (see *Motion energy map*).

Together, then apart

Two or more individuals interacting as a cohesive group or unit who subsequently split up and act individually, each on his or her own agenda, and following his or her own pathways, may be considered an unusual behavior pattern. For example, people seen huddling together upon entering an airport terminal, who then enter ticket lines or screening checkpoints apart from colleagues, may be trying to disguise their affiliation as a group.

Visual monitoring

Unusual behavior may include the act of watching a check station, security door or food-delivery system at an airport, especially from areas not usually frequented by passengers, friends and family or airport staff.

Walking in line

Two men walking side by side together in an airport may be benign. But two men walking in line together (i.e., one following closely behind the other) may represent a single-minded mission in pursuit of unsavory goals. Border patrol officers have identified walking in line as an unwitting sign given by persons intending to cross the U.S. border illegally as a team.

Nonverbal World

Concept

A domain of ancient social, emotional and cognitive signs, established millions of years before the advent of speech. A sensory dimension apart from that which is defined by words. An often unconscious medium, between reflex and reason, governed by the oldest parts of our vertebrate brain (see *Nonverbal brain*).

Speechless

For millions of years, our forbearers lived in a nonverbal wilderness, devoid of spoken or manually signed language. Their skill at encoding and decoding speechless information is evident in our sentient existence today.

Good place

Nonverbal World is a landscape without language, billboards or signposts, a realm without writing or symbols of any kind. It is a place where information consists of colors, shapes, textures, aromas and natural sounds – untouched by narration. This is the unspoken world we seek on mountaintops and island retreats, the good place apart from words.

Usage

We reside today in a world of words but still make many of our most important decisions about life and living as if we had never left. We do not need words to define a kiss, decode a business suit or decipher new car smell; these depend on ancient signals from a wordless past. Even technical knowledge may be transmitted through nonverbal means, in which we watch and do rather than read a manual (see *Nonverbal learning*). We choose our vehicles, homes and mates essentially on nonverbal grounds and select wardrobes based on clothing's look and feel. Many scientists think in visual, spatial and physical images rather than using mathematical terms and words. (N.B.: That theoretical physicist Stephen Hawking [1942–2018] used an arboreal term to picture the cosmos – affirming that the universe could have different "branches" – is a tribute to his visually sensitive primate brain.)

Nose

Body part

A projecting part of the human face containing the nostrils and organs of smell.

Usage

The nose is one of the most defining features of human identity.

Anatomy

Located at the very center of our face, the nose is a rounded prominence of bone, gristle, fatty tissue and flesh. Unlike animal noses, its vertical, freestanding shape reinforces the height of our face and accents the stability of facial features.

Culture

In the Trobriand Islands, couples may gently bite noses while making love. Among Eskimos, Maoris and Polynesians, touching another's face or head with the tip of the nose is used as a friendly greeting.

Gender

The generally larger noses of men give an illusory appearance of "strength." Women's often smaller noses – which may be further reduced with makeup to keep from upstaging the lips and eyes – give an illusory appearance of "youth" by showing features of the infantile schema (see *Infantile schema*). (N.B.: In fashion-magazine ads, the feminine nose may "disappear" into the flatness of the face.)

Gestures

Many human gestures emanate from or begin with the nose. In his book *Bodytalk* (1994), British zoologist Desmond Morris lists over 40 entries for nose-involved cues, including "nose snub," "nose tap" and "nose thumb." Nose gestures are often demeaning, pejorative and negative, as they reference noxious odors and stench. One may use the classic Shanghai gesture – place the thumb pad (nail pointing downward) against the nose tip, spread (abduct) the fingers and point with an extended little finger – to silently scoff the world.

Imagery

That noses are key nonverbal features of the human face is reflected in two well known images – the 20,000 BP Birdman of Lascaux Cave, France, and the 1971 "P-Head" figure designed as the logo of the U.S. Public Broadcasting Service (PBS). The former, a Paleolithic image, depicts a human stick figure whose head-in-profile bears a nose-like bird beak. The latter P-Head image depicts an adult-male face with a large, definitely human nose, designed to connote an allegiance to "Everyman."

See also *Facial I.D.*

Nostril-flare

Figure N.3 Nostril-flare

Body movement

Enlargement of the nasal opening at the bottom of the nose.

Usage

Dilated nostrils work to increase the uptake of oxygen to the lungs.

Meanings

Nostril-flare is a polysemous non-verbal sign with many meanings, some of which are emotional. Dilation may indicate a breathing problem, such as asthma, influenza or pneumonia. To increase oxygen uptake, nostrils may flare during and after physical exercise. Due to interaction of the facial muscles, nostrils may flare when one smiles, laughs or cries. As the body mobilizes an emergency response (e.g., in anger or fear), nostrils may flare to increase oxygen uptake. Bodily arousal brought on by sexual attraction may show in flared nostrils.

Anatomy

Nostril dilation is achieved through contraction of the alar part of the nose's nasalis muscle, aided by depressor septi. These muscles are controlled by the emotionally responsive facial nerve (see *Special visceral nerve*).

See also *Nose*.

Nut substitute

Consumer product

An assortment of nonverbal aroma, taste and touch cues designed to satisfy the primate appetite for such hard-shelled fruit seeds as coconuts, mongongo nuts and palm nuts. A baked or deep-fried food product (e.g., cookies, crackers or Fritos®) designed to mimic the taste and crunchy texture of roasted nuts and seeds.

Usage

As primates, we are seemingly pre-adapted to enjoy the flavor and texture of nut substitutes. Throughout the Middle East, for example, crusty breads, pastries and candies are liberally sprinkled or covered with whole seeds for their flavor, texture and crunch. Wonton noodles, pappadoms, tortilla chips and Crackerjacks® – along with taro, yucca sweet-potato, beet, parsnip, carrot, rutabaga, celery root and sea-weed chips – are among the thousands of ethnic cuisines designed to satisfy our need for culinary snap, crackle and pop.

Existential crunch

That crispy snacks so delight us is because, as an existentialist philosopher might say, they represent an "authentic" form of existence which transcends the desire for softer "unreal" foods, such as Twinkies®.

Neuro-notes

Our back teeth and the forward two-thirds of our tongue receive incoming (afferent) crunch sensations from nut substitutes through branches of the facial nerve (cranial VII). Like flavor cues, texture cues are processed simultaneously on two levels: consciously in the cerebral cortex and unconsciously in the limbic system. As crunching registers in the forebrain, nut substitutes may provide a pleasurable snack-food experience.

See also *Existential crunch*.

Nutty taste

Flavor sign

The usually pleasant flavor of hard-shelled seeds – such as almonds, filberts and mongongo nuts – perceived by the sense of taste. A taste cue much esteemed by primates, emanating from the kernels of any of these.

Usage

We remind ourselves that we are primates when we add pecans to poultry stuffing, sliced almonds to frostings and walnuts to fruitcake. Peanuts are staples of Chinese, Thai and many other cuisines. In powder form, peanuts are oft-hidden ingredients in processed foods worldwide.

Chemical code

Food researchers cracked the code of nutty taste, which is signaled, in part, by 2,3-dimethylpyrazine, a flavor molecule found in roast beef (see *Meaty taste*). Peanuts have a green note – 2-propylpyrazine – as well, that is present in some roasted coffee beans (McGee, 1990).

See also *Nut substitute*.

O

Object fancy

Fight, tight

According to N. G. Blurton Jones (1967, 355), "Among three to five-year-old children in nursery schools, fights occur over property and little else." According to M. Marsel Mesulam (1992, 696), "in more severe forms [of the grasping reflex], any visual target will elicit manual reaching followed by tight grasping."

Emotion

The desire to pick up, handle and hold a material object, especially a consumer product of elegant design. The urge to touch, own, arrange, display, talk about or collect a manufactured human artifact (see *Collection*).

Usage

Products "speak" to us nonverbally as material gestures. Their design features – for example, the shine, shape and smoothness of a platinum bracelet – send compelling messages to capture our attention. That we respond to their appeal shows in the sheer number of artifacts we possess. Our personality may be caricatured by the object(s) we desire, for example, jewelry, boats, shoes and so on. We may hold treasured artifacts with two hands, in a gentle caressing embrace between the tactile pads of the thumbs and forefingers (see *Decision grip*). Forever beckoning from TV monitors, store shelves and catalogues, products gesture until we answer their call.

Neuro-notes

The "magnetic effect triggered by objects" originates with the innate grasping reflex (see *Grab*). Subsequently, it involves a balance between the parietal lobe's control of object fancy and the frontal lobe's "thoughtful detachment" from the material world of goods (Mesulam, 1992, 697). In patients with frontal lobe lesions, the mere sight of an artifact is "likely to elicit the automatic compulsion to use it," while lesions in the parietal network "promote an avoidance of the extrapersonal world" (Mesulam, 1992, 697).
  See also *Shopping, Talisman*.

Orienting reflex

Neuro term

An unlearned response in which animals alert to new features of their environment – to novel sensations, sights, sounds or smells in the nonverbal sense-surround.

Usage I

The orienting reflex (OR) is an innate, protective response designed to answer the question, "What's that?" The automatic OR provokes both cognitive and emotional concerns and also may trigger immobility (see *Freeze reaction*), when we are suddenly faced with a novel, unusual or potentially dangerous person, place or thing.

Usage II

The messaging features of consumer products may be designed to provoke the OR. Attention-grabbing signals from commercial broadcast messages may trigger the OR as well (see *Media*).

Reptiles

In reptiles, orienting involves a refocusing of the sense organs and freezing of the body's gross-motor movements. A slowed heart rate (bradycardia) has been observed as well, for example, in iguanas and in the death-feigning ritual of hognose snakes (see *Freeze reaction*).

Mammals

The reptilian orienting pattern is present in mammals, where it is usually followed by a more active (i.e., a non-reflexive, voluntary) attention phase and an arousal of emotion. That is, after the reptilian orienting reflex itself occurs, a mammal may voluntarily attend (i.e., look, listen and sniff the air), produce facial expressions and emit vocal mood-sign calls.

Anatomy I

In mammals and primates, a diagnostic set of nonverbal signs associated with the OR is mediated by the five cranial nerves that arise from the pharyngeal arches (i.e., from the primitive gill arches; see, for example, *Eyebrow-raise*, *Flashbulb eyes* and *Jaw-droop*). The trigeminal (cranial V, for chewing) and facial (cranial VII, for facial expressions) nerves link to (i.e., communicate with) the glossopharyngeal (cranial IX, for swallowing), vagus (cranial X, for vocalizing and communicating with the viscera) and accessory (cranial XI, for turning the head and shoulder-shrugging) nerves.

Anatomy II

In mammals and primates, the nucleus ambiguus (NA) mediates control of the pharynx, soft palate, larynx and esophagus (see *Adam's-apple-jump*, *Throat-clear*). Chemoreceptors enable the third pharyngeal arch's carotid body to sense CO_2 and O_2 levels. The accessory nerve (cranial XI) positions the neck, assisted by the vagus nerve (cranial X) (Porges, 1995).

Anatomy III

NA mediates control of the heart and vocal intonation. Its efferent fibers mediate feeding and breathing, as well as some body movements, emotions and forms of communication (e.g., growling; see *Special visceral nerve*). "The NA-vagus provides the vagal brake that mammals remove instantaneously to increase metabolic output to foster fight-or-flight behaviors. The NA-vagus provides motor pathways to shift the intonation of vocalizations (e.g., cry patterns) to express emotion and to communicate internal states in a social context" (Porges, 1995, 309).

Evolution

In orienting reptiles and mammals, according to Porges (1995), the control of bradycardia (slowed heart rate) by the dorsal motor nucleus of the vagus nerve (cranial X) may have evolved from an ancient vertebrate gustatory response. "Gustation is the primary method for identifying prey (including other appropriate food sources) and predators in aquatic environments" (Porges, 1995, 309) See *Aroma cue, Taste cue*).

See also *Startle reflex*.

P

Pain cue

Nonverbal sign

A visible muscle contraction of the face or body in response to unpleasant sensations of suffering due to physical injury, trauma or emotional distress.

Usage

Painful touches to the skin, for example, may excite the midbrain's reticular area enough to produce a visible response, such as a facial wince or frown. Since physical and psychic pain are closely related in the brain and nervous system, a casual touch from someone we dislike may produce the same response.

Anatomy

Pain may show in narrowed or closed eye openings, with raised cheeks as the eye-orbit muscles contract; eyebrow-lowering with wrinkling on the bridge of the nose as corrugator and associated muscles contract and a raised upper-lip with wrinkling at sides of the nose as levator muscles contract.

Chest pain

"A clenched fist to the centre of the sternum conveys the gripping quality of the pain (Levine's sign. . .) while a flat hand describes the sensation of crushing heaviness. . . . Tight band-like chest pain may be represented by a movement of the palmar surfaces of both hands laterally from the centre of the chest" (Edmondstone, 1995, 1660).

FACES pain scale

Introduced as a nonverbal rating for use in U.S. children in 1981, The 0-to-10 scale utilizes simple line drawings of faces ranging from "No Hurt" (0: eyebrow-raise, wide-open eyes and zygomatic smile) to "Hurts Worst" (10: lateral eyebrow-lower, medial eyebrow-raise [grief]; partially closed, lidded eyes; tears [cry] and frown). The FACES Scale has been successfully decoded for cross-cultural use by African-American, Caucasian, Chinese, Hispanic, Japanese and Thai children.

Neuro-notes: Mirror neurons

"Pain neurons" in the brain's cingulate cortex fire when dermal tissue is stuck by a needle. They also fire when we see someone else take a needle stick. "Thus, for these kinds of neurons, [also] known as mirror neurons, there is no boundary between the self and the other" (McGill University Web tutorial on the brain
[http://thebrain.mcgill.ca/flash/i/i_12/i_12_cr/i_12_cr_con/i_12_cr_con. htm], accessed Dec. 28, 2012).
See also *Zygomatic smile*, Smiley face.

Paisley

Art cue

A bilateral, teardrop-shaped design element, of Persian origin, popularized in the 1960s by media icons such as the Beatles (see *Media*).

Usage

Paisley prints may be used to decorate women's gowns, blouses and shawls, and men's neckties, jacket linings and robes. The artful richness of paisley may appear in the clothing of royalty (see *Clothing cue*).

Design features

Paisley designs are highly expressive, both individually and when grouped in symmetrical or random patterns. Rhythmically repeated dots and cilia-like vibrissae lining the teardrop's contoured frame attract notice and breathe "life" into the paisley cell. Like organelles in living cells, paisley cells may contain miniature subunits – some symbolic – of hearts, butterflies, whorls, circles and daisies. Often displayed in groups, paisley design units appear to be kinetically in motion, as if interacting, chasing and swimming together.

History

The iconic paisley shape originated in ancient Persia, where it may have symbolized life and eternity (see Sign, *Triskelion*).

Media

Paisley design was further popularized – and its psychedelic messages highlighted – in 1960s magazine, newspaper and televised images of the Beatles.

Paramecium parallel

Some have noticed paisley's resemblance to the ciliated shape of an animated genus of single-celled creatures known as *Paramecium*. In 2019, a new design appeared in the U.S. called Paramecium Paisley, currently used in textiles, wall paper and gift wrap.

See also *Art cue*, Form constants.

Paleocircuit

Neuro term

A preconfigured pathway or network of nerve cells in the forebrain, brain stem or spinal cord utilized in nonverbal communication. A pre-established neural program, of great age, for sending or receiving nonverbal signs. An ancient neural "platform" for bodily expression, configured millions of years before the advent of cortical circuits for speech.

Usage

Paleocircuits are modules and passageways preserved in living nervous tissue, much as fossils have solidified no-longer-living tissues into lifeless stone. Tracing the paleocircuits of nonverbal signs helps us unravel their origin, evolution and meaning.

Anatomy

Paleocircuits channel the electrochemical impulses required for muscles to contract, as, for example, visible signs of happiness or sadness, in the nonverbal present. As "living fossils," paleocircuits preserve information about gestures from the nonverbal past as well (see *Information*).

Evolution

In the aquatic brain and spinal cord, for example, ancient networks of motor neurons and interneurons evolved to control the body movements of our oldest animal ancestors, the jawless fishes. From these neuronal micropaths, instructions reached local muscle groups to move individual body parts. From the very beginning of vertebrate life, microscopic systems of spinal interneurons stood between motor neurons and sense receptors, affecting the input and outflow of nonverbal signs. Thus, it was established early on that the spinal cord should be more than a passive pipeline to carry sensory messages to the brain and motor signals back to the body. Like the brain itself, our spinal cord is replete with paleocircuits which have "minds of their own" (e.g., for managing tactile withdrawal, and the oscillating, rhythmic movements of walking; see *Walk*).

Figure P.1 Palm-up

Palm-up

Gesture

A speaking or listening gesture made with the fingers extended and the hand(s) rotated to an upward (or supinated) position. A gesture made with the opened palm raised to an appealing, imploring, "begging" or affiliative position (see *Affiliative cue*).

Usage

Uplifted palms suggest a vulnerable or nonaggressive pose that appeals to listeners as allies rather than as rivals or foes. Throughout the world, palm-up cues reflect moods of congeniality, humility and uncertainty. Palm-up gestures contrast with palm-down cues, which are more domineering and assertive-like in tone (see *Palm-down*). Accompanied by "palm shows," our ideas, opinions and remarks may seem patronizing or conciliatory rather than aggressive or "pointed." Held out to an opponent across a conference table, the palm-up cue may, like an olive branch, enlist support as an emblem of peace.

Anatomy

As Darwin (1872) noted, palm-up signs are part of a shoulder-shrug posture involving the entire body. Lifting a shoulder stretches trapezius and levator scapulae muscles of the neck, tilting the head toward the shoulders' high side. Head-tilt-side, meanwhile, excites muscle-spindle receptors in the neck – stimulating a posture designed to stabilize the head relative to the body and the pull of gravity – released by the asymmetrical tonic neck reflex or ATNR. In the shoulder shrug, the fingers on the neck's tilted side automatically extend as the hand rotates to a raised position, producing the palm-up cue. Rotation is due to contraction of the forearm's supinator muscle, stimulated by the sixth cervical nerve through the brachial plexus. The upper arm's prominent biceps muscle flexes the elbow joint and brings it closer into the body's side (i.e., adducts the arm at the elbow). Aiding supinator, biceps assists in rotating the palm to its uplifted position.

Observations

A sales representative appeals to her boss with a palm-up cue: "Do you really want me to fly out to Cleveland tomorrow?" A teenager asks to borrow his mother's car, using a raised palm to plead: "Please, Mom?" In Ghana, a tribal woman gestures with lifted palms after hearing that her husband favors polygamy: "What can we women do?" she asks hopelessly. In the boardroom, a CEO appeals to his senior staff with a palm-up gesture and implores, "I need your help." Palm-up speaking gestures are used by Ongka, a native Kawelka (Papuan language) speaker, in the 1974 documentary film Ongka's Big Moka: The Kawelka of Papua New Guinea.

Research reports

The first scientific study of palm-up gestures was conducted by Charles Darwin (1872), who saw them as signs derived from a larger shoulder-shrug display. The open-palm-up hand-shrug is a sign of helpless uncertainty and confusion (Ekman and Friesen, 1968). In chimpanzees, palm-up signs are used to beg for food, to invite bodily contact and to seek support during a conflict: "We call the gesture with the extended arm and open palm 'holding out a hand.' It is the most common hand gesture in the colony" (de Waal, 1982, 34–36). Palm-up cues are used to ask "who," "what," "when," "why," "where" and "how" questions in diverse sign languages of the deaf from Papua New Guinea to Manhattan, New York.

Neuro-notes I

Upraised palms are gestural byproducts of an ancestral crouch display, a protective vertebrate posture designed to be defensive rather than offensive. Neural roots of palm-up cues thus reach back further in time than palms themselves – at least 500 mya – to protective paleocircuits for flexion withdrawal built into the aquatic brain and spinal cord. These circuits reflexively bend the ancestral body wall, neck, arms and legs away from danger, while palms and forearms rotate upward through the action of primeval neck reflexes (see *Paleocircuit*).

Neuro-notes II

Note that our palm-up rotations tend to be one-handed when stimulated by turning our head sideward and when tilting it left or right – but two-handed when our neck is bent forward or backward (Kandel, 1991). We do not ordinarily make conscious choices about the gesture, because we are too busy talking to notice or care. The emotions responsible for palms-up are located above the spinal cord in defensive areas of our forebrain's limbic system (notably the amygdala), passing through basal ganglia and brain-stem links to the cord below. Thus, our emotional brain unwittingly touches off flexor-withdrawal gestures designed to protect us from real and imagined harm, in jungles as well as corporate boardrooms. That we do not deliberately gesture with palm-up cues places them among our most trustworthy signs.

Neuro-notes III

Mirror neurons: Mirror neurons provide brain circuitry that enables us – intuitively – to decode and understand the meaning of palm-up cues. When we see a palm-up hand gesture, mirror neurons set up a motor template, a prototype or blueprint in our own brain, that allows us to read the cue. Through links to the limbic system, there are also mirror neurons to help us decode its emotional nuances and meanings. We are seemingly wired to interpret the palm-up actions of others as if we ourselves had enacted them.

See also *Mime cue*.

Parade

Semiotic symphony

Any of several mostly nonverbal venues in which one group of humans walks and rides past – and sometimes flies above – another group of usually stationary, seated viewers. Through a moving narrative of aroma, auditory, color, taste, touch and vision cues, festive events such as the Rose Parade in Pasadena, California, pleasantly overload the human nervous system. Displays of uniformed marching soldiers, rolling tanks and guided missiles – designed to encode might rather than mirth – may be less pleasing to the senses.

Usage

Parades are used around the world to commemorate special events, such as the Chinese New Year, Christmas and St. Patrick's Day. Marched gatherings may be used to proclaim group resolve, togetherness and unity, as in gay-pride parades. Military parades may be used nonverbally to proclaim and reinforce political control (see *Goose-step*).

Hand-waving

In pleasant parades, those in the moving group may wave their hands and smile at those in the seated, stationary group, who respond by waving and smiling back. Unable to converse in words across parade-ground distances, communication may be wholly nonverbal. In military parades, smiling and waving may be withheld.

Color

In the American Rose Parade, brilliantly colored floats and multi-hued costumes beckon for attention and positive emotional response. In North-Korean-style military marches, drab shades dominate and negative emotions reign.

Neuro-note

Mirror neurons enable seated spectators to feel as if they, themselves, were variously walking, riding, dancing, smiling, waving and twirling batons in the parade (see *Baton*). Nonverbally, an effective parade become a moveable feast for the senses – a wholly embodied semiotic experience.

See also *Costume*.

Paralanguage

Paralanguage is a term which encompasses vocal activity, vocal qualities and vocal sounds used to convey nonverbal messages. It includes vocalizations (such as "ahh," "uh-huh," whistling and hissing), intensity, rhythm control, dialect, hesitations, pitch, tempo, pauses, timbre, resonance, modulation, and voice intonation.

It is argued that paralanguage is very relevant to contexts involving sarcasm, irony and humor (Plazewski and Allen, 1985, 148). The study of paralanguage is called paralinguistics. Facial paralanguage has received considerable attention (for example, see Chovil, 1991), given the connection between facial movements and speech (e.g. lips, cheeks, tongue and pharynx).

Parallel process model of nonverbal communication

Automatic and controlled processes

This model (Patterson, 1995) endeavors to integrate both the social behavioral and the social judgment components of human communication. It provided for the sending and receiving of nonverbal messages within automatic and controlled processes. As such, it represented "the dynamic relationship between the goal-driven sending and receiving sides of nonverbal communication and the fluctuating role of automatic and controlled processes in the pursuit of goals" (Patterson, 2019, 116).

Encode and decode

This model frames the encoding and decoding processes of nonverbal communication into one system (Patterson, 2019). The key determinants identified within this model are biological, cultural, gender based and personality based. Biological determinants are included, as evolutionary pressures can affect patterns of communication. Cultural determinants include how nonverbal communication may differ across cultures. Gender-based determinants are identified, as societal norms and genetic hardwiring can affect gender nonverbal communication. Personality is identified as individual differences that can affect communication styles.

Critiques

It has been argued that the parallel process model is deficient in "adequately representing a dyadic-level analysis" and in providing a framework which specifies the "broader environmental contexts" for nonverbal interactions (Patterson, 2019, 116).

Percent nonverbal

Oft-cited

An often cited statistic in the communication-studies field is that of U.S. psychologist Albert Mehrabian, claiming that nonverbal expression accounts for 93 percent of human communication. His claim is popularly known as the "7%-38%-55% Rule."

Usage

Mehrabian's 93 percent figure is frequently cited in classrooms, seminars and published works on nonverbal communication. Though not often an academic issue, the proportion of human communication that is nonverbal is a popular "frequently asked question" or FAQ (see *Nonverbal communication*, FAQ).

Reliability

In two 1960s academic studies – with questionable assumptions and research designs – Mehrabian and colleagues used small samples of female college students' emotional judgments of words, voice tones and facial expressions. Subjects were asked to judge each of the three as being "positive" or "negative" in tone. From their responses, it was concluded that words themselves played a 7 percent role in the judgments. Nonverbal voice tones played a 38 percent and facial expressions a 55 percent role in the emotional judgment, thus summing to the 93-percent figure. Reliability for the 93 percent figure remains questionable.

Persuasiveness

Nonverbal factors

Factors such as attractiveness, credibility and power are intricately woven into literature which examines persuasion. As Burgoon et al. (2016, 343) observe, in addition to factors such as power, "nonverbal communication also plays an instrumental role in the persuasion process." Nonverbal behaviors such as kinesic/proxemic immediacy, kinesic relaxation and "vocal pleasantness" have been connected with persuasiveness (Burgoon et al., 1990, 140). Within this realm, Burgoon et al. (1990) also found that vocal and facial "pleasantness" and facial expressiveness are associated with perceptions of competence. More positive attitudes towards a proposal ensue when the communicators' nonverbal behaviors such as leaning forward, approaching, smiling, eye contact and nodding reveal interest. The corollaries to these behaviors, such as poor eye contact, signal disinterest and disengagement (Burgoon and Dillman, 1995). Research by Gunnery and Hall (2014) found that people who can deliberately produce a Duchene smile are "more persuasive."
See *Smiling*.

Persuasion and dominance

Burgoon et al. (2002, 462) observe that "behavioural signs of attractiveness and dominance might increase persuasiveness." Interpersonal dominance and "portraits" of socially skilled people have been shown to be connected with persuasiveness. Dominant communicators evoke perceptions of credibility (Burgoon et al., 1990). For example, "they make direct eye contact, have rapid loud delivery, use facial expressiveness, and use few adapters, all of which serve to engender the perception of credibility and to increase compliance" (Burgoon et al., 2002, 454).

Affiliation and expressiveness

Eye contact, is often used to infer the trustworthiness of the speaker, most specially when in conjunction with other nonverbal behaviors which indicate affiliation and expressiveness. Bettinghaus and Cody (1994) advise that perceptions of trustworthiness can be established when the speaker employs behaviors associated with affiliation such as maintaining eye contact, smiling and nodding frequently, using the arms and hands in an open manner.

Anxiety vs. relaxation

Speakers who are perceived to be relaxed and poised have been found to be more persuasive (Andersen and Bowman, 1999; Burgoon et al., 1998).

Verbal fluency

A study by a team led by Burgoon in 1990 found that verbal fluency is a strong predictor of persuasiveness. Additionally, "higher speech rate and volume" (Mehrabian, 1972, 71) have been attributed to persuasiveness. In short, people are fluent when they know what they are talking about (Eggert, 2010). During the process of conversation, the manner in which speaker and listener adapt to each other is also relevant to persuasiveness (Burgoon et al., 2016). See *Interaction adaptation theory*.

Meta-cognition: behaviors and their assumed effect

Meta-cognition has been shown to have an effect in terms of nonverbal communication and persuasiveness. Research by van Kleef et al. (2015) showed that people have more positive attitudes to a topic which is negatively "framed" (e.g., removing bobsleighing from the Olympics) if the topic's source has a sad rather than happy facial expression. Equally, if a topic is introduced in a positive frame (e.g., introducing kite surfing at the Olympics) with a happy (rather than sad face) the participants reported a positive attitude.

Guyer et al. (2019) also point out that when it comes to the persuasive value of nonverbal behaviors, it is not always accurate to assume a direct connection between a particular nonverbal behavior and the typically assumed effect. For example, while there is significant research evidence to indicate that smiling can have a positive emotional value ("validity" – Guyer et al, 2019, 226) and accordingly, have an associated positive persuasive effect, it cannot be assumed that this is always the case. For example, smiling is typically associated with positive emotions, and when people communicate with a smiling speaker (as opposed to a frowning speaker), they tend to create more positive thoughts about the message being delivered (Burgoon et al., 1990; Ottati et al., 1997). However, smiling may also occur within contexts of disdain and embarrassment. In these cases, it cannot be assumed that a smile promotes a positive perception in these contexts.

See also *Gesture, Attractiveness*.

Pharyngeal arch

Evolution

A column of tissue in the throat (or pharynx) of the human embryo that separates the primitive visceral pouches or "gill" slits. Originally, tissues used by the Silurian jawless fishes as part of their feeding and breathing apparatus.

Usage

Many facial expressions derive from muscles and nerves of the pharyngeal arches, which were programmed to constrict in response to potentially harmful chemical signs detected in seawater. Today, paleocircuits consisting of special visceral nerves mediate displays of emotion by causing branchiomeric muscles between the head and body to contract.

Picture writing

Culture and semiotics

Any of several worldwide proto-writing systems used to depict objects, actions and narratives iconically in linear sequences of nonverbal pictographs. Pictographic traditions – both proto-writings and true pictographic scripts – rest on semiotic principles that have deep roots in human perception and cognition. The representational signs often depict an object, such as a human head, by framing it with a line. The gestalt cognitive property of the enclosing linear frame, in tandem with the brain's perceptual sensitivity to edges, confers upon the simple line a pan-culturally expressive potency. The drawn line indeed may be a cultural universal. Not only do line-based pictographs underlie Near Eastern cuneiform, Egyptian hieroglyphic and Chinese writing systems, but the line is the most critical component in less well-developed, nonlinguistic "picture writings" that show a worldwide distribution (e.g., Native North America, Central America, Crete, Aboriginal Australia, Russia, Siberia and Tibet).

See also *Isotype*.

Pigeon toes

Posture

When sitting down or standing, our feet may splay outward in "military oblique," align in a parallel position or "pigeon toe," with toes angling inward. The latter toe-in posture may be due to a clinical abnormality of tibial torsion, a chronic condition due to misalignment of the tibia with the upper leg bone or femur. However, as a component of – and a nonverbal sign derived from – the shoulder-shrug display, a pigeon-toed posture may reveal social-emotional stances of submissiveness, shyness and reserve.

See also *Palm-up*.

Figure P.2 Point

Point

Gesture

Extending an index finger (or less frequently, other body parts such as the lips) to indicate the presence or location of objects, features or forces. Stiffening a forefinger to direct attention to people, places or things. A stabbing motion of the index finger, as given in anger.

Usage

Pointing has two distinctive usages, one emotional (as in anger) and the other cognitive (as in pointing to show mom a butterfly on the wing). We may point with the second digit to turn another person's attention to something we, ourselves, see, hear or smell.

Referential point

Because it refers to the outside world, the referential point is a high-level, language-like gesture. In babies, the referential point first appears at ca. 12 months of age, in tandem with the first use of words. Prior to the appearance of speech, pointing is a reassuring indicator of an infant's probable language ability. While animals such as honeybees, for example, can refer to environmental features, only humans point them out with fingers.

Angry point

At close quarters, pointing at another human being is almost universally considered an aggressive, hostile or unfriendly act. Because it focuses so much attention upon a recipient, close-quarters pointing is frowned upon throughout the world.

Anatomy

We may extend all four fingers (the thumb has its own extensor muscles) in a coordinated way by contracting the forearm's extensor digitorum muscle. Our index finger, however, has an extra forearm muscle (extensor indicis), which enhances the neural control of its muscular ability to point.

U.S. politics I

On January 26, 1998, President William Jefferson Clinton pointed his index finger aggressively at the American people and stated, "I did not have sexual relations with that woman, Miss Lewinsky."

U.S. politics II

In his November 7, 2018, press conference in the East Room of the White House – after the midterm elections returned Democratic power to the U.S. House of

Representatives – a visibly upset Donald Trump used aggressive, pronated, palm-down, hyperextended index-finger-pointing gestures to direct anger toward press members who asked questions he did not wish to hear or answer. CNN's Jim Acosta received the lion's share of Trump's angry-finger cues.

Word origin

Point originates from the ancient Indo-European root, *peuk-* ("to prick"); derivatives include pugilism, punctuate and puncture.

Point-light

Biological motion

Distinctive bodily movements of animals in activities such as running, crawling and leaping. "Point-light" reveals that we may decode bodily actions from a relatively small number of physical prompts. Our ability to decode animate actions, such as walking, from minimal point-light cues is likely due to mirror neurons.

Light spots

Pioneered by Swedish researcher Gunnar Johansson in the 1970s, point-light methodology has enabled study of biological motion in human activities such as walking, throwing and dancing. Researchers attach as few as 12 small "light spots" to the body, one each attached to the head, shoulders (at the widest points), elbows, hands, pelvic girdle (at the midpoint), knees and feet. As the body moves, the lighted points – and only the lighted points – are filmed.

Nonverbal significance

From animated movements of the attached spots alone (all other bodily features are invisible), viewers are able to identify a point-light subject's gender, physical activity (such as climbing stairs) and even emotions.

See also *Animal sign*.

Posture

Nonverbal sign

A physical bearing, pose or stance of the body or its parts – for example, a crouched posture. A fixed, stationary body position as opposed to a fluid movement.

Usage

When sustained (i.e., held longer than ca. 2 seconds), a body movement such as a bowed head may be considered a posture. Though duration varies, postures may be more expressive of attitudes, feelings and moods than gestures and other brief motions of the body.

Research reports

An early experimental study (James, 1932) identified four postural categories: (1) forward lean ("attentiveness"), (2) drawing back or turning away ("negative," "refusing"), (3) expansion ("proud," "conceited," "arrogant") and (4) forward-leaning trunk, bowed head, drooping shoulders, and sunken chest ("depressed," "downcast," "dejected") (Mehrabian, 1972, 19). Frieda Fromm-Reichman (1950) inferred feelings from observing and imitating the postures of psychiatric patients (Mehrabian, 1972, 17). Albert Mehrabian proposed two primary postural dimensions: immediacy and relaxation (Richmond et al., 1991, 63).

See also *Angular distance, Body wall*.

Power grip

Tight clasp

Introduced by British anthropologist John R. Napier in 1956, the power grip is a manner of grasping an object tightly, in a usually closed fist, between the palm and fingers (see *Fist, Grab*). To clutch, hold or seize a bat, branch, club or other object firmly with the hand.

Usage

Holding objects such as a steering wheel, post, handrail or other object tightly may be curiously pleasurable, perhaps as a holdover from our primate past and penchant for climbing trees; see *Primate brain*). Thus, power-grip sports such as baseball, cricket, tennis and golf are popular today (see *Branch substitute, Golf*).

Neuro-notes

In grasping a golf club, bat, billy club or tennis racket, sensory feedback to the motor cortex may unconsciously tighten one's grip. Stimulated by grasping, pressure-sensitive tactile receptors may cause further excitement and contraction of muscles to unwittingly increase a grip's tightness.

See also *Precision grip*.

Primate brain

Evolution

Collectively, those specialized areas of the human brain that evolved during the primate adaptation to diurnal (daylight) living and to a life in trees. Specifically, those modules of forebrain that process color, eye-hand coordination, facial recognition, grasping and 3D navigation by sight.

Usage

With the primate brain, nonverbal communication takes a dizzying turn toward complexity. Many signs (see, e.g., *Color cue, Eye contact, Eyebrow-raise, Facial expression* and *Precision grip*) depend on its neural circuitry. The primate brain, which developed from modules and paleocircuits of the mammalian brain, began its arboreal evolution ca. 65 mya in the Paleocene.

Hand signals I

With agile digits designed for climbing, our primate ancestors extended their forelimbs to reach for and grasp insects, fruits and berries. Through advances in motor, premotor, supplementary and association areas of the neocortex, manual dexterity led to the use of leaves, sticks, bones and stones as tools (see *Artifact*).

Hand signals II

The primate brain enabled voluntary movements of the hands and arms to achieve goals beyond locomotion (see *Walking*) and standing on all fours. Sophisticated motor-control centers permitted new movements, such as reaching, grasping and grooming with the fingertips. Later, these body movements would be used as gestures.

Eye signs

By ca. 35-to-40 mya in the earliest apes, the primate brain dedicated distinct modules of visual cortex to the precise coordination of hand-and-eye movements and the recognition of faces (see *Facial recognition*). In the living apes, dedicated nerve cells of the lower temporal lobe respond to hands and faces exclusively (Kandel et al., 1991).

Climbing cues

Visual learning is the hallmark of the primate brain. Foraging in trees, using sight rather than scent to find colorful fruits and berries went hand in hand with remembering where and what to pick and eat. Unlike birds, which can fly directly to food spotted in trees, primates chart a clever route through labyrinthine vines, limbs and leaves. They navigate from point A to point B by decoding branch ways from many angles.

In their 3D world, primates became skilled arboreal navigators. Today's monkeys, for example, have sharp color vision, depth perception and enhanced memory to recall the location of edibles scattered among forking branches and twisting vines.

Neuro-notes

A novel feature of the primate brain is its ability to grasp deliberately – that is, to grasp on purpose – through the corticospinal tract, thus bypassing older brain-stem circuits altogether. This more advanced nerve tract, which began its evolution in the mammalian brain, elaborated in the primate brain. The corticospinal tract adds precision and voluntary control to our grasping gestures.

See also *Human brain*.

Figure P.3 Probing point

Probing point

Nonverbal insight

An opportunity to examine an unverbalized, hidden, undisclosed or withheld belief, mood or opinion as revealed by nonverbal cues.

Usage

A probing point – signified, for example, by a lip-purse, shoulder-shrug or throat-clear – may appear when a word or phrase in the stream of dialogue "touches a nerve." The probing point presents a strategic opportunity to search beneath words. Questions may be specifically designed to target those unvoiced agendas or attitudes or hidden uncertainties marked by body-language cues.

Unwitting cue

Produced unconsciously, autonomic (see, e.g., *Fight-or-flight*), reflexive (see, e.g., *ATNR*) and visceral ("gut reactive") signs (such as the *Adam's-apple jump*, *Gaze-down*, *Hand-behind-head* and *Tense-mouth*) reliably reflect unstated emotions.

See also *Deception cue*.

Procession

Likeminded journey

Nonverbally, an organized, usually linear walkabout in which participants act alike, dress alike and think alike – as they solemnly proceed toward a common destination in space-time, often a political headquarters or religious shrine.

Usage

A procession may be used as a moveable nonverbal narrative to reinforce the power and strength of a belief, conviction or idea.

Neuro-notes

Gatherings may be biologically pleasurable (see *Pleasure cue*). Humans are intensely sociable beings for whom face-to-face interaction in corroborees, pilgrimages and processions, may stimulate the brain's reward circuitry, including its ventral striatum. Nonverbal processions may bond likeminded participants ("like" as evidenced by same behaviors, similar clothing (see *Costume*) and shared destinations) through the reptilian principle of "same behavior" (see *Isopraxism*). Thanks to the limbic mirror system, those who proceed together to distant religious shrines may experience a pleasurable "brain coupling."

See also *Parade*.

Profile of Nonverbal Sensitivity

Developed by Robert Rosenthal et al. (1979), this is a multi-channel test containing 220 auditory and visual segments presented in a 45-minute video tape. Each segment is a 2-second, emotionally rich scene portrayed by a white American woman. Examples of scenes include "admiring a baby" and "criticising someone for being late." The test assesses abilities to recognize affective or attitudinal states.

The Profile of Nonverbal Sensitivity (PONS) test has been praised as a "highly successful test of nonverbal sensitivity with clearly demonstrated predictive validity" (Banziger et al., 2011, 202). However, the PONS test can be time consuming to administer and has been critiqued for its reliance on a "lone sender" and the use of "posed" rather than genuine emotions (Riggio, 2006, 82).

Mini-PONS

This test, developed by Banziger et al. (2011) is a shortened version of the PONS) consisting of 64 items which provides for a swifter screening of emotion recognition.

Proxemics

Spatial signs, signals and cues

According to its founder, American anthropologist Edward T. Hall (1914–2009), proxemics is the study of humankind's "perception and use of space" (Hall, 1966, 83).

Usage

Like facial expressions, gestures and postures, space "speaks." The prime directive of proxemic space is that we may not come and go everywhere as we please. There are cultural rules and biological boundaries everywhere.

Body space I

Scientific research on how we communicate nonverbally in private and public spaces began with studies of animal behavior (ethology) and territoriality in the 19th and early 20th centuries. In 1959, Hall popularized spatial research on human beings – calling it proxemics – in his classic book, *The Silent Language*.

Body space II

Hall identified four bodily distances – intimate (0 to 18 inches), personal-casual (1.5 to 4 feet), social-consultive (4 to 10 feet) and public (10 feet and beyond) – as key points in human spacing behavior.

Hall noted, too, that different cultures set distinctive norms for closeness in, for example, speaking, business and courting, and that standing too close or too far away may lead to misunderstandings and even culture shock. People in Arabic-speaking countries stand physically closer to listeners, for example, than do native English speakers from Britain or North America. In cross-cultural settings, the latter may consider the former standing "too close" for comfort – while the former may sense that the foreigner is standing an "unfriendly" distance away.

Culture

It has been shown that there are variations in conversational distance according to your culture. For example, infants reared in different cultures learn different rules about interaction spaces. In Japan, mothers spend a lot of time with their infants by comparison to, say, American mothers. Indeed, in Japan, one may "hand-prow" (i.e., face the palm-edge of one hand vertically forward in front of the nose), and bow the head slightly, to apologize for crossing between two people or intruding into another's space to move through a crowded room. "The hand acts like the prow of a ship cutting through water" (Morris, 1994, 115).

In some cultures, mother, father and infant sleep in the same room (e.g., Japan), and in other cultures, they sleep in separate rooms (e.g., the United Kingdom), while in others, the infant sleeps in the mother's arms at night (e.g., Kenya). This has an effect on the children and their preconceptions of what are comfortable and uncomfortable interaction distances. In those cultures where the infant and mother/family are in close proximity, there is a tendency towards interaction at closer distances.

Some research shows that there are differences in interaction distances among children according to race. For example, in 1985, Halberstadt found that on entering elementary school, black children were more inclined to speak at closer interaction distances than white children. However, this tendency had almost vanished by the time they reached fifth grade. There may also be differences in interaction distances according to class. For example, in 1974, Scherer also found that middle-class children maintained greater conversational distances from each other. On the other hand, lower-class children, by comparison, maintained shorter conversational distances

Robotics

Researchers in artificial intelligence may include proxemics norms in the design of robotic interactions with human users (see *Artificial intelligence*).

Neuro-note

Violations of proxemic norms may register in the limbic system's amygdala.

Proxemics and territories

Typically, the human world is divided into four kinds of territory.

The primary territory is one which is "owned" by the individual, for example, a home or a bedroom. There are also primary possessions such as a watch or handbag. Humans have an inbuilt need for a primary territory. Some research suggests that those who have appropriate primary space have better levels of adaptation. In Japan, where there can be considerable overcrowding in the home, a study of Japanese women by Omata in 1996 found that those who had few private spaces of their own in the home showed poorer levels of adaptation than those who did.

Secondary territory is not as central to the human as primary territories. An example of these kinds of territories are places where people tend to go regularly, such as the local pub or the same seat on a train. One of the fascinating pieces of work in this area involved a study by Gress and Heft in 1998 where they gradually increased the number of students who were forced to share a room. As the number increased, so too did the territorial behavior of the occupants! In particular, they created barriers and arranged the room in certain ways which prohibited interaction. Earlier work on the crowding of students by Sinha and Mukherjee (1996) found that where students are in crowded conditions, such as sharing a room, they actually come to need larger personal space and begin to dislike sharing even more than would be expected.

The third type of territory is known as public territory. This is the kind of space that is available to all humans and has a public domain, for example: park benches, telephone booths and car park spaces. Public spaces typically have clear rules about their occupancy. Such rules are signaled by markers. Examples of markers include library books on desks, jackets on seats, towels on a pool deck-chair.

Finally, there is a type of territorial space which involves perceptions of others. It is often termed interaction territory. This is a space that individuals create around themselves. For example, two teachers having an "after-school chat" in the school car park will cause people to "walk around" them.

Proxemics and personality

Personal space involves the zone within which a functioning human feels comfortable. Dosey and Meisels (1969) argue that each individual's needs in this regard rise from a deep-felt human need to "self-protect." Personal space needs have been shown to have connections with personality type. For example, (Hayduk, 1983) found that violent offenders need more personal space than other individuals. They also seek more space behind them than in front of them, which contrasts with other individuals, who typically need more personal space in front. Argyle (1988, 178) makes the point that proximity is "decoded in terms of personality qualities." He points out that Type A personalities, who can be people who are very driven, time conscious and competitive and also includes introverts, highly anxious people and violent offenders, need to have larger personal space than others (Argyle, 1988). Introverts and anxiety-prone individuals tend to stand further away than extroverts. On the other hand, people who have a high concept of themselves, have affiliative needs, are high on interdependence, are self-directed or are low on authoritarianism tend to stand closer than others. Even preschool children are perceptive of how close we stand to each other (King, 1966). Interestingly, individuals who require more personal space have been shown to perform less well in recall and information processing tasks when they are placed in situations with a "high social density" (Sinha et al., 1999).

People also stand closer to those they like (Mehrabian, 1972). In particular, within contexts of flirtation, closing the interaction distance with an intended romantic partner is a signal of interest (Shotland and Craig, 1988). Indeed, people make a host of calculations about another person's personality based on distances of interaction (Patterson, 1968). Research on interview situations shows that where people choose closer distances when interacting, they are often seen as being warmer, liking one another more and being more empathic and more understanding. In an intriguing study which examined the dynamics of interviews, Patterson and Sechrest (1970) found that those interviewees who came closest to the interviewers were judged as friendly, extroverted, aggressive and dominant.

Spatial behaviors also influence perceptions of dominance. Greater distances are chosen between persons of unequal status. Like the dominant monkeys in troop of baboons, the higher the status of the individual, the more space they are afforded.

While moving closer to another person who is talking can signal interest and liking, there are constraints on such movements. Typically, when another individual who is not an intimate contact "invades" someone's space, people start to feel a little uncomfortable at c. 70 cm, moderately so at c. 50 cm inches and very uncomfortable at under c 30 cm (one foot). People with large personal space needs will have even lower tolerance of these space invasions (Hayduk, 1983, 1981).

See also *Angular distance*.

Pupil size

Emotion cue

The round, dark pupil in the middle of our eye may vary in size from ca. 2 to 8 mm depending on light level. As light goes up, pupils reflexively constrict; as light dims, pupils reflexively dilate. In the 1960s Eckhard Hess (1916–1986), a German-born American psychologist, discovered that pupil size also responds to emotions (see *Emotion*).

Usage

Regarding emotion, pupil size may be used to gauge psychological arousal. Anger, excitement and fear, for example, may cause pupils to enlarge. Hess noted that pupils dilate when presented with attractive stimuli and shrink with unattractive or disliked stimuli. Moreover, Hess found that people with enlarged pupils are judged more attractive than those with smaller ones.

Social cue

Studies of the brain show that the amygdala response to others' pupil size in a nonconscious way (Amemiya and Ohtomo, 2012). Lovers may look in a prolonged way into each other's eyes to unconsciously assess pupil size as an involuntary cue of love feelings (Morris, 1985).

Neuro-notes

Pupil dilator and constrictor muscles of the iris are mediated by the oculomotor nerve (Cranial III), which has both a sensory and visceral component. The dilator is composed of radial fibers and the sphincter of concentric fibers (Breithaupt, 2015). Both are smooth muscles that respond to autonomic control (see *Fight-or-flight, Rest-and-digest*).

Rest-and-digest nerve fibers activate the pupillary sphincter muscles of the irises to constrict the pupils. Fight-or-flight nerve fibers from the superior cervical ganglion activate dilator muscles to expand the diameter of the pupils. The latter muscles link to the brain's emotional hypothalamus (see *Hypothalamus*).

See also *Eye-roll*.

Q

Quad

Architectural sign

Nonverbally, a quad (short for the English word "quadrangle") is a monumental arrangement of buildings enclosing a usually rectangular, cultivated, often grassy empty space with long-seated benches and walkways (see *Neo-savannah grassland*).

Usage

Peristyle quads – perimeter-column-defining courtyards – have been used since ancient Greek and Roman times and continue to be used as design elements on university campuses and in government, religious and royal architecture. As 90-degree angles are rare in the natural world, quads may send an implicit message of separation from nature.

Paleo-semantics

Ironically, the architectural meaning of a quad is to reconnect human beings – daily ensconced in a constructed, indoor world of walled compartments and cubicles – with fellow species members in a natural outdoor environment, resembling the primordial flatlands of Eastern Africa from whence their kind evolved ca. 2 mya.
See also *Walk*.

Quaff

Pleasure cue

To display enhanced enjoyment of an alcoholic beverage – often a wide-mouth mug or schooner of Guinness®, beer or ale – by conspicuously gulping and guzzling its frothy contents for all to see. A quaffer's lips may overflow, requiring eye-catching wipes with a napkin or back of a hand.

Usage

Nonverbally, one may quaff to draw fellow pub goers into camaraderie of drinking together through the principle of isopraxism ("monkey see, monkey do"; see also *Chameleon effect*).

Queue wait

Proxemic delay

Nonverbally, the often uncomfortable act of waiting behind another person, similarly waiting in line, for food, goods or services.

Usage

For safety and ease of travel, animals from ants to elephants may walk long distances single file in orderly lines. Similarly, human beings often walk single file on hiking trails, sidewalks and parade grounds (see *Parade, Procession*).

Waiting lines

Unlike generally pleasant linear walking, human beings may find linear waiting in queues at bank windows, check-out counters and service desks unpleasant. Patrons may uncomfortably face away from nearby patrons in line (see *Angular distance*), avoid mutual gaze (see *Eye contact*) and wear neutral, socially discouraging facial expressions (see *Blank face*). The proxemics of waiting may be that strangers are simply too close for comfort (see *Stranger anxiety*). Ca. 75 percent of British respondents, for example, felt that coming within touching distance of another's clothing in a checkout line was "too close" (Tensator Ltd. N.D.). Fewer than 3 percent of British shoppers talk to others in line (Tensator Ltd. N.D.).

Crowding

Of particular distaste to many humans is the specter of crowding into waiting lines. When "queue jumping" occurs – though 92 percent of British respondents consider the behavior "very annoying," it has been estimated that ca. 67 percent of patrons will refrain from verbally challenging crowders (Tensator Ltd. N.D.). U.S. patrons may respond nonverbally with frowns (see *Eyebrow-lower*) tense lips (see *Lip-compression*) and with unfriendly vocalizations (see *Groan, Tsk* [as per anecdotal observations by David Givens]).

See also *Waiting time*.

R

Figure R.1 Rapport

Rapport

Relationship

A pleasant feeling of mutual trust, affinity and friendship established through verbal and nonverbal means.

Usage

Rapport may show in such nonverbal cues as reduced angular distance, direct body alignment, mutual eye contact, palm-up gestures, affirmative head-nodding, shared laughter and the use of "same behaviors" (i.e., in the chameleon effect; see *Isopraxism*). Research by Lakin and Chartrand (2003, 334) suggests that "behavioral mimicry may be part of a person's repertoire of behaviors, used nonconsciously, when there is a desire to create rapport."

Courtship

We may use nonverbal cues sent and received in courtship to establish rapport in business to please customers, solicit clients and woo colleagues to our point of view (see *Love signal*).

Salesmanship

"Your nonverbal strategy . . . is not to mirror the prospect's stiff, closed posture but to lead him into more relaxed, open postures by your example" (Delmar, 1984, 43–44).

Word origin

English "rapport" derives from Old French ("to bring back") via Latin ("to carry"), from the 7,000-year-old Proto-Indo-European root word *per-*, "fellow traveler" (Soukhanov, 1993). Nonverbally, traveling together may enhance rapport through the reptilian principle of isopraxism (see *Walk*).

Research reports

1   "We can observe how in human beings conversation is practiced as a bond-forming ritual. In such conversations hardly any factual information is passed on, as they consist largely of extremely banal, constantly repeated statements concerning such matters as the weather" (Eibl-Eibesfeldt, 1971, 151).
2   "More smiling, facial pleasantness, head nods, frequent and open gestures, and eyebrow raises have the same effects as more gaze: They accompany a desire for intimacy" (Burgoon et al., 1989, 322).
3   Some research suggests a "natural ecological" basis to rapport. Work by Grahe and Bernieri (1999, 253) found that within thin slice observations of behavior, people "with access to nonverbal, visual information were the most accurate perceivers of dyadic rapport." The ability to make these accurate perceptions within such short windows of observation suggest the role of "implicit theories" of rapport and natural ecology.

Antonym: *Fight-or-flight*. See also *Affiliative cue*, *Immediacy*.

Raspy voice

Voice quality

A manner of calling, singing or speaking in a low-pitched, grating or rasping tone of voice. A vocal register that contrasts with the normal modal, and the high-pitched falsetto, voice. Also known as "vocal fry," the raspy voice may add a degree of "forcefulness" and is used by many pop singers today.

Young women

Linguists note a steady increase in use of the raspy voice by young women since the 1960s. The lower-pitched voice may enable parity with deeper-voiced men with whom, increasingly since the 1960s, they compete in the workplace.

Anatomy

A raspy voice is produced by creaky, popping or rattling vibrations of the constricted, partially closed laryngeal glottis (see *Tone of voice*). "Antonym: see *Falsetto*."

Reproductive force

Nonverbal genesis

Arguably, the "reproductive force" could be considered the fifth fundamental force of nature, after the strong, weak, electromagnetic and gravitational forces of physics. The reproductive force appeared ca. 3.7 bya with RNA and later DNA in the origin of life on Earth.

Usage

A significant portion of human nonverbal communication was – and continues to be – in service to the reproductive force.

Reproduction

RNA and DNA molecules encode information (via codons) about how to reproduce themselves. Selfishly enforced, guided and shaped by primordial messaging molecules, self-replication became the prime directive – the summum bonum or "greatest good" – of life and living, pursued for its own sake and solely on its own behalf. The reproductive force remains a potent motivator in humans today in their overall demeanor, goals, clothing, automobiles, music, media, art, religion, hairdos, shoes and prom dresses and diverse additional nonverbal signs, signals and cues.

Prom dresses

In service to the reproductive force, clothing cues encoded in American prom dresses evolved in the early 20th century to broadcast information about physical presence ("I am here"), gender ("I am female") and reproductive fitness for purposes of courtship. Worldwide, the reproductive force is similarly celebrated in diverse coming-of-age ceremonies as teenagers reach reproductive age. Japanese women may don kimonos; young women from Ghana may wear colorful beads and body paint and Tamil women from Sri Lanka may display with heavy makeup, eye-catching jewelry and saris.

Cells

Living RNA and DNA molecules are environmentally fragile. Early on, life found a way to compartmentalize itself protectively in cells. Before RNA, the chemical structure of water (H_2O), and of fatty-acid, particles – and their electromagnetically attracting forces – combined to form membranous proto-cells.

Magic bubbles

Bubbles form between gasses and liquids due to the electromagnetic forces of particle adhesion and cohesion. Biofilms are adhesive conglomerates of micro-organism particles within a slimy, extracellular matrix. Composed of lipid bilayers, cell membranes surround and contain the contents of cells and mediate the chemical information they send and receive from other cells and the outer world (see *Information*).

Hosts

Over billions of years, cells combined to form living organisms, from bacteria to human beings. Living plants and animals serve as hosts for the DNA they contain and strive imperatively to pass this DNA forward in time to successive hosts. While hosts eventually wear out and need to be replaced, the genetic information they pass ahead is arguably immortal.On a micro level, the reproductive force expresses itself nonverbally – within and between body cells – through diverse messaging molecules. Some have likened this incredibly complex cellular communication to language. From the macro view, the reproductive force infuses the body language, voice tones and spatial behaviors that hosts use in service to courtship.

See also *Courtship*.

Reproductive imagery

Sexual signage

A male or female sexual trait as depicted in a drawing, etching, painting, photograph, video or sculpted figurine. A significant proportion of human imagery is in service to the reproductive force. Nonverbally, sexual signage in advertising, magazines and motion pictures is a constant reminder of the reproductive imperative: to perpetuate the human species.

Prehistory I

The earliest sexual illustrations were realistic and abstract renderings of female and male sexual organs painted on Upper Paleolithic cave walls in western Europe between 34,000 and 12,000 years ago. The most common themes depicted on Paleolithic cave walls were food and sex, in that order.

Prehistory II

Dating to ca. 25,000 years ago, female Venus figurines with exaggerated breasts, buttocks and tummies have been found across Europe from Spain to Russia. The figurines had less to "say" about beauty than fertility.

Media

In U.S. college bookstores of the 1990s, the number one, two and three best-selling magazines, respectively, were *Cosmopolitan*, *Glamour* and *Vogue*, read by young women seeking to enhance their sex appeal. Americans view thousands of sexually suggestive scenes a year on TV.

See also *Barbie doll*.

Reptilian brain

Evolution

Collectively, those parts of the human brain that developed during the reptilian adaptation to life on land. Of particular interest are modules of the forebrain which evolved to enable reptilian body movements, mating rituals and signature (i.e., self-assertion) displays.

Usage I

Many common gestures, postures and nonverbal routines (expressive, e.g., of dominance, submission and territoriality) elaborated ca. 280 mya in modules of the reptilian brain. The latter itself evolved from modules and paleocircuits of the amphibian brain.

Usage II

In the house of the reptile, it makes a difference whether one crouches or stands tall. Flexing the limbs to look small and submissive, or extending them to push-up and seem more dominant, is a reptilian ploy used by human beings today (see *High-stand display*). Size displays as encoded, for example, in boots, business suits and hands-on-hips postures, have deep, neural roots in the reptilian forebrain, specifically in rounded masses of grey matter called basal ganglia.

Reptilian ritual

In Nonverbal World, the meaning of persistence (e.g., repeated attempts to dominate) and repetition (e.g., of aggressive head-nods or shakes of a fist) are found in underlying reptilian-inspired rituals controlled by the habit-prone basal ganglia, identified as the "protoreptilian brain" or R-complex by Paul D. MacLean (1990).

Reptilian routine

According to MacLean (1990), our nonverbal ruts start in the R-complex, which accounts for many unquestioned, ritualistic and recurring patterns in our daily life's master routine. Countless office rituals such as the morning coffee huddle, the routinized lunch break and afternoon trip to the restroom are performed in a set manner throughout the workdays of our lives.

Prehistory

As reptiles adapted entirely to life on land, terrestrial legs grew longer and stronger than those of aquatic-buoyed amphibian ancestors. In the reptilian spinal cord and brain stem, antigravity reflexes worked to straighten limbs through extensor muscle contractions that lifted the body higher off the ground. Advances in the forebrain's basal ganglia enabled reptiles to walk more confidently than amphibians – and to raise and lower their bodies and broadsides in status displays.

See also *Mammalian brain*.

Rest-and-digest

Relaxation response

A pleasant feeling of calmness and well-being experienced as heart rate slows, smooth muscles contract and glands secrete while the body digests its food.

Usage

Many involuntary nonverbal signs (e.g., contracted pupils; moistened eyes, glistening brought on by stimulation of the lacrimal glands; slowed breathing rate and watery mouth, due to secretions of the salivary glands, accompanied by increased swallowing) – along with signs of relaxation (e.g., warm, dry palms, forward or backward-lean and satiation [feeling "full"]) are evident in the rest-and-digest response.

Observations

Rest-and-digest-related cues – affiliative signals such as body alignment, eye contact, "digestive" vocalizations ("hmm," "ooh," "um"), head-nods and smiling are often visible in business-luncheon meetings (see *Lunch*). Courting couples may eat together to relax, relate and respond in rest-and-digest mode. In a restaurant, contractions of the urinary bladder prompted by rest-and-digest circuits may cause frequent trips to the restroom.

Evolution

Rest-and-digest is an ancient parasympathetic response pattern which, in the aquatic brain, slowed heart rate and reduced ventricular force to conserve energy and prepare a fish to digest its meal.

Neuro-note

Rest-and-digest is controlled by the brain's hypothalamus. "Antonym: see *Fight or flight*."

Rhythmic repetition

Reflex-like cue

Rhythmic repetition is a key ingredient in many nonverbal signs, signals and cues. It includes repeated, stereotyped body movements that may become automatic over time. The rhythmic-repetition maxim may be encoded in architecture, art, biology, clothing, dance, music and diverse additional nonverbal domains.

Usage

In the architectural domain, a gazebo exemplifies how rhythmic repetition may be used (see *Gazebo*). Nonverbally, the harmonic repetition of its design features – of its columns, cupolas and horizontal trim – serve to unify the gazebo's structure, add narrative flow and simulate a sense of motion.

Neuro-notes

In biology, rhythmic repetition dates to ca. 500 mya in vertebrate spinal-cord, brain-stem and cortical-motor areas (Ghez, 1991b). "Once initiated, the sequence of relatively stereotyped movements may continue almost automatically in reflex-like fashion" (Ghez, 1991b, 534). Neurologically, rhythmic repetition may stimulate a sense of movement.

See also *Dance*.

Rings of Venus

Gender cues

One-to-four horizontally indented, epidermal lines (or flexures) visible on the front (ventral) surface of female neck skin.

Usage

Though early-onset neck lines may appear in teenage girls, Venus rings are usually decoded as signs of aging. Faint to more obvious neck rings may also be read as gender signs, distinguishing women from men.

Anatomy

A woman's gracile neck and thinner neck skin may reveal contractions of the platysma muscle, visible as horizontal flexure lines in epidermal skin. Platysma is controlled by the emotionally responsive facial nerve (cranial VII; see *Special visceral nerve*).

Art cue

Faint neck rings are visible above the suprasternal notch (or "neck dimple") of the ca. 100 BC classic armless Greek sculpture Venus de Milo, for which Venus rings are named.

See also *Neck dimple*.

Ritualization

Conceptual hypothesis

The zoological concept of ritualization was introduced by Austrian ethologist Konrad Lorenz in his 1963 book *On Aggression*. Ritualization is an evolutionary process through which a behavior or series of behaviors become communicative signs. It is hypothetical in that zoologists are unable to observe changes over the expansive time periods required for ritualization to occur.

Usage

Ritualized nonverbal signs often derive from body motions that encode intentions. An intention movement is a preparatory and incomplete step in a series leading to a behavioral act, such as canine biting. Prior to a dog bite, the canine may raise and retract its upper lip to keep from biting itself. Through a gradual process of ritualization, the lifted-lip snarl-face itself becomes a communicative sign that biting is imminent and a likely next step. The snarl-face evolves as a ritualized warning to a human of fellow dog, and actual biting need not occur (see *Bite*).

The human smile may be a ritualized primate play-face (see *Zygomatic smile*).

See *Intention cue*.

S

Figure S.1 Sadness

Sadness

Emotion

An unpleasant visceral feeling of sorrow, unhappiness, depression, loss or gloom.

There is agreement that the facial expression of sadness is universally recognized.

Evolution

Sadness is a mammalian feeling that stems from grief associated with maternal-infant separation; discomfort in losing a battle for dominance or loss of a parent, companion or mate (see *Mammalian brain*).

Primatology

Our close primate relatives may experience grief, discomfort and loss. "Gradually, over several years, he [a chimpanzee who lost his mother at age 3] developed abnormal behavior, consisting of social isolation, unusual posturing, rocking, an increase in self-grooming, and a habit of pulling out hairs and chewing them."

Anatomy

In acute sadness, muscles of the throat constrict, salivary glands release viscous fluid, repeated swallowing movements may take place, eyes may close tightly and lacrimal glands release tears.

Display of sadness

In a meta-analysis study of facial expressions (Nelson and Russell, 2013), sadness was ranked as the third most recognizable facial expression (after happiness and surprise) and before anger, disgust and fear. Displays of sadness involve the brows (raising the brow, lowering the brow), the lips (lowering the corner of the lips) and in some cases raising the chin (Ekman, 1994). Work by Namba et al. (2017) identified additional facial actions such as the dimpler, the lip tightener, the lip presser and the lip suck. Displays of sadness cause increases in heart rate and skin temperature (Levenson, 1992). Vocal expression is also connected with the recognition of sadness (Hawk et al., 2009).

It is important to note that as an emotion, sadness may not necessarily present as singular to the emotion of sadness. For example, disappointment is a combination of sadness and surprise.

Culture and gender

Women are more likely than men to facially express sadness (Blier and Blier-Wilson, 1989). Such displays do have cultural parameters. In those cultures which have a strong "masculine" archetype for men, it expected they will display fewer signs of sadness than women. For example, crying during a film. The United States is regarded as a moderately masculine culture. Countries along the coastal regions of the Pacific such as Chile and Peru are regarded as feminine cultures. Moreover, women are more adept than men at recognizing vocal expressions of sadness (Vasconcelos et al., 2017).

Neuro-notes

Each of the four cranial nerves for chewing (V); moving the lips, crying and salivating (VII) and sighing and swallowing (IX and X) originally played a gut-reactive, visceral role (see *Special visceral nerve*) related to the gastrointestinal tract. The sick "gut feeling" we associate with sadness is mediated by the enteric nervous system, located in the stomach, intestines and colon (see *Enteric brain*).

Antonym: *Happiness*. See also *Sad sign*.

Figure S.2 Sad sign

Sad sign

Emotion cue

Any of several nonverbal indications of grief, lamentation or loss (see *Sadness*).

Usage

As incoming (afferent) cues, sad signs reveal a sender's unhappy state of mind. As outgoing (efferent) cues, they may be used to elicit sympathy from viewers.

Bow, flex and slump

Sadness may show (1) in bowing postures of the body wall; (2) in the cry face and lip-pout; (3) in a downward gaze; (4) in slumped, flexed-forward postures of the shoulders and (5) in audible sighs.

Empathy

Our emotional ability to feel what others feel is enabled by facial expressions and mirror neurons. Seeing someone's frown or sad eyes, for example, may elicit sadness and sympathetic frowns in onlookers. As neurologist Marco Iacoboni notes, "The neural activity in the limbic system triggered by these signals from mirror neurons allows us to feel the emotions associated with the observed facial expressions – the happiness associated with a smile, the sadness associated with a frown" (Iacoboni, 2008, 112).

Expressions

Facial signs may include (1) frowning eyebrows (corrugator supercilii, occipitofrontalis and orbicularis oculi muscles contract), (2) frowning mouth (depressor anguli oris), (3) pouted or compressed lips (orbicularis oris) and (4) depression and eversion of the lower lip (depressor labii inferioris), as the facial features constrict – as if to seal off contact with the outside world.

Research reports

Signs of sadness may include drooping eyelids; flaccid muscles; hanging head; contracted chest; lowered lips, cheeks and jaw ("all sink downwards from their own weight"); downward-drawn mouth corners; raised inner ends of the eyebrows (i.e., contraction of "grief muscles") and remaining motionless and passive (Darwin, 1872, 176–177). Sadness shows most clearly in the eye area (Ekman et al., 1971).

Auditory cues

Sadness may be heard in nonverbal groans and sighs. The sound of music, too, may connote or suggest sadness. The mournful clarinet, oboe, viola and violin notes of Austrian composer Franz Schubert (1797–1828), for example, are often mournful and suggestive of death and dying; Schubert is thought to have suffered from depression (see *Sadness*). Schubert's haunting String Quartet No. 14 ("Death and the Maiden") is a poetic case in point.

See also *Happy sign*.

Figure S.3 Sarcasm

Sarcasm

Biting voice tone

An often aggressive or passive-aggressive manner of speaking, using a sharp, staccato voice with greater-than-normal intensity, elongated vowel sounds, slowed tempo, nasalized timbre and heavily stressed articulations (see *Tone of voice*). A sarcastic voice may be accompanied by facial signs of anger, annoyance, disgust and/or disliking (see subsequently, Sarcastic facial signs); inappropriate smiles and exaggerated expressions of emotion.

Usage

A congratulatory verbal phrase, such as, in English, "Great job!," may be reversed nonverbally if spoken in a sarcastic tone of voice (meaning "Poor job!"). American teenagers may use nonsense words such as "Duh!" sarcastically in nonverbal taunts to challenge parental authority.

Word origin

English "sarcasm" derives from ancient Greek *sarkazein*, to tear flesh or bite the lip (see *Bite*). Dangerous cutting, slicing and teeth are implied.

Negative expressions often accompany vocal sarcasm. These include eye-rolls (see *Eyes*), sneers (see *Lip-retraction*) and tightened lips (see *Lip-compression*).

See also *Disgust*.

Figure S.4 Saving face

Saving face

Shame avoidance

Any of several verbal or nonverbal means of helping oneself and others avoid negative feelings of embarrassment, humiliation or dishonor. Nonverbally, those audible or visible mannerisms given to enhance, improve or maintain one's self-respect (see *Auditory cue*, *Vision cue*).

Chinese origin

The English phrase "saving face" evolved from Chinese notions of preserving a positive public image.

Losing face

Nonverbally, the antonym of saving a face is losing it, with a consequent emotional feeling of shame. English "face" is used metaphorically once again, as the visage it labels is a major source of emotional communication. A sad face, for example, may be lowered (tilted ventrally, forward; see *Bow*) to reduce the visibility of its features. In embarrassment, one may cover the face with a hand or both hands or turn it away to one side (see *Cut-off*), losing visibility in the process and becoming "faceless."

See also *Shame*.

Self-touch

Tactile sign

The act of establishing physical contact with one's own clothing or body parts (esp. hands to face; see *Homunculus*). The act of stimulating one's own tactile receptors for pressure, vibration, heat, cold, smoothness and pain.

Usage

Like a lie-detector (or polygraph) test, self-touch cues reflect the arousal level of our sympathetic nervous system's fight-or-flight response. We may unconsciously touch our body when emotion runs high to comfort, relieve or release stress. Lips are favorite places for fingertips to land and deliver reassuring body contact.

Self-stimulating behaviors such as (1) holding an arm or wrist; (2) massaging a hand and (3) scratching, rubbing or pinching the skin increase with anxiety and may signal deception, disagreement, fear or uncertainty.

Self-touching can be associated with situational anxiety or stress (Cheek and Buss, 1981). Other speculations and hypotheses about self-touching include the possibility that we rub ourselves to provide self-assurance. Covering one's eyes can be associated with shame or guilt. Self-grooming, such as straightening your hair or fixing your tie can indicate concern for one's self-presentation (Knapp and Hall, 2002, 286). Self-touching has also been associated with mental concentration (Heaven and McBrayer, 2000).

Categories

Desmond Morris (1971) categorized "self-touches" into four categories: shielding, cleaning actions, specialized actions and self-intimacy actions.

1   Shielding actions are undertaken to reduce information coming in or going out through the senses. For example, putting one's hand over one's mouth.
2   Cleaning actions include hair grooming or straightening clothes – a kind of preening.
3   Specialized actions are used to convey specific messages. For example, we may cup our ear to show we cannot hear someone speaking.
4   Self-intimacy actions, which are essentially comforting actions. Such actions unconsciously represent comforting touches by someone else. Examples of these kinds of actions include holding one's hands, folding the arms and crossing the legs.

Adaptors

Self-touches sometimes fall into the category of "adaptors." According to Burgoon and associates, "Because they are designed to help the individual adapt to stresses or needs, adaptors are habits that usually are not intended to communicate a message" (Burgoon et al., 1989, 45). Nonetheless, they add, adaptors can be "quite informative" about one's internal state.

Scratching

Ekman and Friesen (1972) argue that scratching is related to one's hostility or suspicion of another person. Theoretically, what is happening here is that picking and scratching actions are manifestations of aggression.

Culture

Diverse cultural gestures involve self-touching. In Spain, holding a single long hair between the thumb and forefinger and lifting it vertically above the head, is a sign of "frustration." "This female gesture is a symbolic way of 'tearing your hair out' when feeling intensely frustrated" (Morris, 1994, 102).

Ethology

"They are called displacement activities because it was at one time thought that they are triggered by 'nervous energy' overflowing (displaced) from the strongly aroused motivational systems" (Brannigan and Humphries, 1969, 408).

Media

Hollywood stars once seemed robotic – stiff, wooden and "unreal" – until method actors Marlin Brando and James Dean brought natural, self-touch cues to the screen. Brando clasped his neck as he groped for words in The Wild One (1954). Dean's hand-behind-head gesture in Giant (1956) humanized the actor, as the squirm cue revealed vulnerability. Earlier, in The Big Sleep (1946), Humphrey Bogart blazed a trail by fingering the right earlobe with his right hand several times while pondering deep thoughts.

Primatology

"The more intense the anxiety or conflict situation, the more vigorous the scratching becomes. It typically occurred when the chimpanzees are worried or frightened by my presence or that of a high-ranking chimpanzee" (Lawick-Goodall, 1968, 329 [also recorded in gorillas, baboons, Patas monkeys and humans "under similar circumstances"]).

Power

High-powered individuals are less likely to engage in self-touching, while lower-powered individuals engage in "more frequent" self-touching (Carney et al., 2005, 116).

Neuro-notes

Apparently trivial self-touch gestures help us calm our nerves. Physical contact with a body part stimulates tactile nerve endings and refocuses orienting attention inward, away from stressful events "out there." Self-touch works on the physiological principle of acupressure massage or shiatsu. Massaging the right hand, for example, takes attention from the left, and vice versa. Catching the thumb in a drawer, we may vigorously rub its nerve endings to compete with the brain's awareness of pain. Since the forebrain's thalamus cannot process all incoming signals at once, self-touch reduces anxiety as it blocks pain.

Research reports

1   Earlobe-pulling, arm-scratching and rubbing a worry stone have been classed as adaptors: "residuals of coping behaviors that were learned very early in life" (Ekman and Friesen, 1969b, 62).
2   Rubbing the face is a reaction to spatial invasion (Sommer, 1969).
3   Automanipulation is a sign of "fearfulness" in children (McGrew, 1972).
4   "Body-focused hand movements are arguably one of the most common types of nonverbal behavior produced by humans" (Kenner, 1993, 274).
5   Self-touching, such as touching the face (the doctor touching their own face) has been shown to promote feelings of immediacy (warmth) in doctor-patient interactions (Harrigan, 1985).
6   "Tactile stimulation may also serve a calming or reassuring function when it is self-directed" (Goodall, 1986, 125).
7   In public speaking, the most common touch may be finger-to-hand (Kenner, 1993).

8   "Unconscious face-touching gestures indicate disbelief in what is being said by the companion" (Morris, 1994, 31). Because the listener feels a mental conflict in voicing his disagreement, he performs "a minor act of self-comfort" (Morris, 1994, 31).

9   Self-clasping gestures (along with upper-body rocking for comfort [see *Balance cue*]) are signs given by Romanian children raised in orphanages of the 1980s-90s (Blakeslee, 1995a, 1995b).

See also *Lip-touch*.

Shame

Origins and evolution

By the age of 7 months, most babies can display the emotion of shame (Izard, 1978). There are some who argue that human shame has origins in ancient non-verbal submissive behavior by humans where the open expression of submission indicated self-awareness of "inappropriate behaviour." Such awareness was important for the group, indicating that the individual can be trusted by virtue of their awareness of the inappropriate behavior (Fessler et al, 2007). In their research on shame, Tracy and Matsumoto (2008) argue that those behavioral expressions associated with shame are likely to be innate and as such support an evolutionary basis for its expression, with shame (and pride) being regarded as "affective mechanisms of promoting and inhibiting social status" (Tracy and Matsumoto, 2008, 11660).

Emotion cue

A usually unpleasant feeling of disgrace, embarrassment, guilt, humility or withdrawal that may be accompanied by some or all of the following nonverbal signs: cut-off, gaze aversion, hand-behind-head, eyebrow-lower, narrowed chest, slumped shoulders, shoulder-droop, shoulder-shrug, verbal pauses, vocal fillers and vocal groans.

Usage

Apologetic shame cues may be used to show remorse, sadness or sorrow and to solicit forgiveness.

Shellfish taste

Flavor cue

The usually pleasant aroma and taste of cooked arthropods, including shrimp, lobster and crab. A flavor enhanced by umami (Konosu et al., 1987; see *Glutamate*) that "speaks" to the tongue as "meat" (see *Meaty taste*).

Usage

Many have a powerful craving for the cooked muscle tissue of shellfish, insects, spiders and grubs. The appetite is deeply rooted in our primate past as insectivores.

Evolution I

The earliest-known Paleocene primate (*Purgatorius* sp.) ate insects, which belong to the biological phylum (Arthropoda) of lobsters and shrimp. Primates have been heavy insect eaters throughout their 65-million-year history, and lemurs, lorises and tarsiers (the least evolved of the living primates) eat mainly insects today. The evolutionary raw bar is open for our closest primate relatives, as well. Chimpanzees enjoy termites, and lowland gorillas snack on ants.

Evolution II

Our love of arthropod flesh reaches further back in time than primates, however. The saga began ca. 450 mya in Ordovician seas, when the giant lobster *Pterygotus* dined on then-soft-headed vertebrates. For 100 million years, shellfish ate vertebrates, until the latter's bony brain case formed in the late Devonian period. (N.B.: Our hardened skull may have originated, in part, as a defense against giant lobsters.) The evolutionary table then turned, as harder-headed amphibians pursued arthropods and ate them instead.

Anthropology

Theaters in parts of Mexico sell fried leaf-cutter ants as a crunchy snack food (see *Existential crunch*). Fried ants taste like bacon, according to members of the New York Entomological Society, who sampled ants and exotic insects at their 100th anniversary banquet in 1992. Roasted kurrajong grubs from Australia resemble lean sausages, they discovered, and fried mealworms taste like honey-roasted nuts.

See also *Nutty taste*.

Shopping

Hunting and gathering

The usually pleasurable act of wandering through stores in search of products and services (see *Consumer product*).

Usage

Shopping is a uniquely human activity with prehistoric roots in hunting and gathering, primate roots in foraging and neonatal roots in the grasping reflex (see *Object fancy*).

Evolution

Wild primates make daily foraging trips in search of food to consume and seemingly enjoy the quest. Chimpanzees use color vision to browse for nuts, fruits and berries. By ca. 2 mya, early human forebears spent less time hunting than foraging, gathering and scavenging – in family groups – for whatever they could find. The landscape itself was their mall.

Today

We spend a great deal of social time collectively browsing for apparel, colorful artifacts and edibles in superstores and shopping malls (see *Artifact*). The shopping quest is emotionally rewarding whether we actually buy or not.

See also *Golf*.

Shoulders

Body parts

Paired, jointed organs that connect arms to the torso. Prominently rounded as well as angular parts of the external anatomy that give the torso its squared-off silhouette. Very visible body parts often singled out for nonverbal display in movements and clothing (see *Arm-show, Business suit*).

Usage

The flexibility and visibility of human shoulders and the fact that they are moved by emotionally sensitive, branchiomeric or "gut reactive" muscles render them highly expressive as signs (see *Shoulder-shrug*). Their size and angular silhouette when squared may bespeak dominance (see *Broadside display*).

Anatomy

The bones of our shoulder girdle consist of a pair of flattened shoulder blades (scapulas), each connected to a bracing collar bone (clavicle). The sides of the bony girdle sit upon our rib cage not unlike shoulder pads. Unattached to any bones but the clavicles, the scapulas glide up and down, move back and forth and rotate about our back and spine. Only the clavicles' attachments to the breastbone stabilize their motion.

Neuro-note

Nonverbally, upper trapezius is highly significant because it is emotionally sensitive and innervated by special visceral nerves.

Figure S.5 Shoulder-shrug

See also *Shoulder-shrug, Shoulder-shrug display, Dominance*.

Shoulder-shrug

Gesture

To lift, raise or flex-forward one or both shoulders in response to another person's statement, question or physical presence or to one's own inner thoughts, feelings and moods. One of several constituents of the larger shoulder-shrug display.

Usage I

The shoulder-shrug is a likely universal sign of resignation, uncertainty and submissiveness. Shrug cues may modify, counteract or contradict verbal remarks. With the statement, "Yes, I'm sure," for example, a lifted shoulder may suggest, "I'm not so sure." A shrug may reveal misleading, ambiguous or uncertain areas in dialogue and oral testimony and thus provide a probing point, that is, an opportunity to examine an unverbalized belief or opinion (see *Probing point*).

Usage II

The shrug bears an interesting relationship to the English word, "just," as in, "I don't know why I took the money – I just took it." In this sense, "just" conveys a feeling of powerlessness and uncertainty as to motive. The word also connotes "merely," as in "just a scratch" (Soukhanov, 1992, 979). These diminutive aspects of the word resonate with the cringing, crouched aspect of the shoulder-shrug cue (see below, Origin).

Anatomy

Trapezius and levator scapulae muscles lift the shoulder blades (scapulas). Trapezius (assisted by pectoralis major, minor, and serratus anterior) medially rotates (i.e., ventrally flexes) the shoulders as well.

Origin

The shrug gesture originates from an ancient, protective crouch pattern innervated by paleocircuits designed for flexion withdrawal. The shoulder-shrug complex was originally identified by Charles Darwin in 1872. The earliest mention of a shrug cue may come from observations of the Greek orator, Demosthenes (384–322 BC): "He removed the distortion of features which accompanied his utterance by watching the movements of his countenance in a mirror; and a naked sword was suspended over his left shoulder while he was declaiming in private, to prevent its rising above the level of the right [in what likely was a sign of uncertainty or diffidence]" (Peck, 1898).

Outer space

On July 11, 1996, while orbiting in the Russian spacecraft, Mir, U.S. astronaut Shannon Lucid shrugged her shoulders, tilted her head, and gestured with her palm up as she answered questions about her 6-week delay in returning to Earth. "You know," she told NBC's Today Show, "that's life."

U.S. politics

On September 9, 1998, in Orlando, Florida, President Bill Clinton shrugged his shoulders and gazed down at a public apology as he said, "I've done my best to be your friend. But I also let you down, and I let my family down, and I let this country down" (*Washington Post*, September 10, 1998).

Neuro-notes

As a branchiomeric muscle, upper trapezius is emotionally responsive (i.e., "gut reactive"; see *Pharyngeal arch*), and hard to control by conscious means. Upper trapezius is innervated by the accessory nerve (cranial XI), a special visceral nerve that also feeds into the voice box (or larynx). Thus, shoulder-shrugs and vocal whines may be given at the same time.

See also *Shoulder, Shoulder-shrug display, Shoulder wear*.

Shoulder-shrug display

Global body movement

Identified by Charles Darwin in1872, an interrelated set of 13 body motions, from the head to the toes, used worldwide to show helplessness, resignation and uncertainty.

Usage

Individually or in combination, signs from the shoulder-shrug display (e.g., head-tilt-side, shoulder-shrug and pigeon-toes) may suggest feelings of resignation, powerlessness and submission. In courtship and rapport, the cues show harmlessness and friendly intent, thus inviting physical approach and affiliation (see *Affiliative cue*).

Constituents

The shoulder-shrug display involves the entire body in a visual crouch. As described by Darwin (1872), the display consists of the following:

1 raised shoulders (elevated; trapezius and/or levator scapulae muscles contracted),
2 head-tilt sideward (lateral flexion),
3 elbows bent and held into the body (flexed and adducted),
4 upraised palms (forearms supinated; see *Palm-up*),
5 palm-show (wrist extended),
6 open hand (digits extended),
7 fingers spread (abducted),
8 eyebrows raised (frontalis contracted; see *Eyebrow-raise*), and
9 mouth opened (digastric and suprahyoid contracted; see *Jaw-droop*).
   A century later,
10 pouted lips (mentalis contracted; see *Lip-pout*),
11 "knock-knee" position (tibial torsion),
12 bending forward at the waist (flexion, slight bowing; see *Bow*), and
13 "pigeon-toe" position (toes angled in) were added to the display (Givens, 1977).

Origin

The shoulder-shrug display incorporates defensive crouching movements from the protective tactile withdrawal reflex (*Flexion withdrawal*).

Neuro-notes

Socioemotional stimuli for shrug-display cues involve the forebrain's amygdala (LeDoux, 1995, 1996) and basal ganglia (MacLean, 1990). Submissive feelings find expression in coordinated muscle contractions designed to bend, flex and rotate parts of the axial and appendicular skeleton, to "shrink" the body and show a harmless "lower" profile.
   See also *Shoulder, Shoulder wear*.

Shout

Auditory cue

An overloud vocalization that attracts attention through its volume.

Usage

A shouted verbal phrase may be used as a command (e.g., "Stop!"), salutation ("Hi!") or warning ("Look out!"). A loud call ("Hey!") may be used to communicate at a distance. Shouting is often accompanied by exaggerated arm-and-hand gestures.

Illusory "size"

Big-seeming auditory cues (e.g., deep or loud cries) suggest – and may substitute for – physical size itself (see *Loom*). Like the bullfrog's croaking sound, a deep human voice may suggest greater size, authority and strength. Interestingly, Dunn et al. (2015) found a trade-off between vocal investment and testes size in howler monkeys. Monkeys with louder shouts have smaller testes.

Neuro-notes

A shout attracts attention by triggering the auditory startle (see *Startle reflex*). The brain's inferior colliculi receive auditory cues from the lateral lemniscus (see *Amphibian brain*) and control such auditory reflexes as flinching in response, for example, to a karate master's yell. Postural reflexes to loud sounds are triggered by the inferior colliculi through brain-stem-cervical cord interneurons to anterior horn motor neurons that link to spinal nerves in charge of muscle spindles.

See also *Growl*.

Sign

Communication

From Latin signum ("identifying mark"), something that "suggests the presence or existence of a fact, condition, or quality" (Soukhanov, 1992, 1678). In philosophy, as defined by Charles S. Peirce, "a sign stands for something else" (Flew, 1979, 327). For example, the hand is a sign of humanity. The general term for anything that communicates, transmits or carries information (see *Information*).

Usage I

Sign is the most generic label for a nonverbal unit of expression, such as a gesture. While in a technical sense their meanings differ, sign, signal and cue often may be used interchangeably.

Usage II

It is useful to distinguish at the outset between a sign vehicle: the material carrier or physical substratum of a sign, the tangible "sign stuff" (i.e., its actual stone, clay, metal, glass, paper or concrete substance) and a sign form: the pattern or arrangement of lines, scratches, punctures, meanders and shapes, which can appear on varied vehicles. The sign form of ancient Scandinavian runes, for example, comprises the runic characters themselves. Runic sign vehicles, on the other hand, consist variously of stone, wood and paper materials (Givens, 1982).

Symbol

Signs may be symbolic. A symbol such as the American flag is, "Something that represents something else by association, resemblance, or convention, especially a material object used to represent something invisible" (Soukhanov, 1992, 1817). Symbolic signs may have an arbitrary (i.e., non-iconic or un-obvious) connection to that which they represent, and therefore must be learned. According to Peirce, "Man is a symbol" (Young, 1978, 9).

Triskelion

One of the oldest human sign artifacts is the 5,000-year-old Neolithic triskel-ion, a graphic signal consisting of three juxtaposed whorls. Three may be the most symbolic of numbers, suggesting strength, stability and synergy. The spirals themselves pleasantly suggest balance, harmony, order, proportion, rhythm and symmetry. The single continuous line that forms the tri-spiral suggests "infinity," as conveyed by later signs such as the Möbius strip and the figure-eight symbol of infinity.

See also *Message*.

Signal

Communication

From Latin signalis ("sign"), an "indicator, such as a gesture or colored light, that serves as a means of communication" (Soukhanov, 1992, 1678). In biology, "any behavior that conveys information from one individual to another, regardless of whether it serves other functions as well" (Wilson, 1975, 595). Any type of sign used to inform as to what may happen next (e.g., a hand-behind-head gesture may signal that a listener is likely to argue).

Chinese lanterns

The color, glow, placement and shape of a Chinese paper lantern signals good luck, birth, death, long life, marriage, sickness and other symbolic messages in neighborhood alleys of Beijing, Hong Kong and Shanghai. A plump, bright red lantern (deng) betokens good luck; its roundness recalls the rounded shape of yuan (money). The vitality and energy of redness also signal a birth or marriage (see *Colors decoded*). A blue lantern, in contrast, signals sickness by suggesting energy in decline. Two white lanterns signal death and mourning in a household.

Emergency signaling

The three critical features of emergency signals, according to the 336th Training Group's Survival School at Fairchild Air Force Base in Spokane, Washington, US, are size, contrast and movement. According to a Survival School expert there, "We don't have a few ribbons tied up to attract attention, we have a big space blanket hanging from the trees to move in the breeze and reflect light in contrast with the dark green forest" (*Spokesman-Review*, February 7, 2010, C11).

See also *Cue*.

Sign language

Hand signals

Verbal and nonverbal signals emitted by fingers, hands and arms addressed to a receiver's sense of vision (see *Vision cue*). Hand signals may include "coded gestures" which form part of a formal system of signals, which actually constitute a real lan-guage. "The special feature of this category is that the individual units are valueless without reference to the other units in the code" (Morris, 1977, 34–35)

Usage

Sign language may be used to send diverse verbal and nonverbal messages and blends of each. One may greet or beckon with a waving hand, tell a story in American Sign Language (ASL) or officiate a football game with hand signals. Verbal and linguistic-like messages may be sent by users of Irish, Plains-Indian and Australian Aborigine sign languages.

Aboriginal sign language

The meaning of Australian sign has much to do with substituting manual signs for words at times when the latter are taboo, as during initiation ceremonies and periods of mourning. They are also used when silence is called for, as in hunting, and when physical distance precludes hearing. A fully or partially extended index finger may be used as a visual pronoun to point at oneself ("I," "me") or others ("you," "you all").

Irish Sign Language

Now ca. 200 years old and shaped by British Sign Language and French Sign Language, Irish Sign Language (ISL) was created by and for deaf people. It bears little grammatical resemblance to spoken English or Irish. The pronouns "I," "me" and "you" may be signed with a partially or fully extended index finger aimed at the self ("me") or other ("you"). There is less digit or arm extension in the briefer sign-language point than is found in the longer-lasting, index-finger-point used as a speaking gesture (see *Point*).

Plains sign language

Native North American tribes devised manual sign systems enabling members to communicate with speakers of mutually unintelligible languages. The systems include both grammatical, iconic, linguistic and symbolic hand shapes and movements. In pointing to another person ("you"), for example, Na-Dene speakers may aim, adduct (hold together) and extend the index and middle fingers, symbolically, to refer to combined female and male aspects of the person to whom one points. To point at oneself, speakers may use an extended thumb to symbolize one's sacredness, just as they thumb-point at babies (considered sacred) and sacred medicine bags. To point to animals in a distant field, speakers may adduct and extend all four fingers, palm down, to symbolize Earth. To greet a friend, a Na-Dene speaker may point to the left or heart-side of the chest with an extended thumb, followed by the palm-down, four-finger gesture extended horizontally away from the body. The sign's sweeping, physical extension symbolically extends one's own sacredness outward to the friend and world at large.

Neuro-notes

We respond to hand signs and gestures with an extreme alertness because specialized nerve cells in the lower temporal lobe respond exclusively to hand positions and shapes.

See also *Language*.

Figure S.6 Signature

Signature

Name sign

A usually hand-written, cursive string of alphabetical signs expressive of one's legal and personal identity. Signatures stand at the curious intersection of our verbal and nonverbal worlds.

Usage

Signatures may be used variously to sign autographs, baseball cards, certificates, checks, contracts, credit cards, documents, letters, loyalty oaths, pledges and tax returns.

Penmanship

"The art, skill, style or manner of handwriting: calligraphy" (Soukhanov, 1992, 1339). The ability to sign one's name is an incredibly high neurological skill that involves a uniquely human hand grip (see *Precision grip*). One's signature combines both verbal and nonverbal traits.

Verbal or nonverbal?

Just as a word may be verbal, while its paralinguistic expression may be nonverbal (see *Tone of voice*), a written signature combines both forms of communication in the same sign. In this respect, signatures are like type fonts. While a printed word is verbal, the selected typeface may be nonverbal. Consider, for example, Times New Roman, Bradley Hand and Herculanum typefaces. The use of serifs in the former does not affect a word's meaning yet expresses a nonverbal style. The appearance of one's written signature, as well, may be indicative of age, education, emotion, gender, health and nationality.

Personality

Arguably, signatures may reflect personality. A classic case in is the ornate, larger-than-life signature of John Hancock (1737–1793) on the U.S. Declaration of Independence (1776). Many decode the bold signature as a nonverbal sign of egotism.

In biology, calling attention to oneself – announcing "I am here" – is a widespread message encoded in diverse nonverbal "signature displays," such as the lizard's head-bob, the lion's roar and the gorilla's chest-pound (see *Chest-beat*). Instead of written cursive, had all of the Declaration signatories been printed in Helvetica – the least nonverbal of modern fonts – Hancock's signature would have been verbal but, nonverbally, devoid of its "signature."

See also *Bauhaus*, Helvetica.

Silence

Not heard

Nonverbally, the condition or quality of being difficult or impossible to hear, as in walking stealthily, swallowing a cry, curtailing bodily noises and refraining from speech. Synonyms include secretive (see *Deception cue*), reserved (see *Submission*) and tightlipped (which, in English, implies a conscious decision to withhold information; see *Lip-compression*).

Usage

Animals from reptiles to human beings have devised ingenious ways to be silent in order to avoid detection.

Media I

Dead air: "An unintended interruption in a broadcast during which there is no sound" (Soukhanov, 1992, 478).

Media II

"Silence Speaks Volumes" – Title of August 27, 2001 editorial in *USA Today* (p. 14A) criticizing Rep. Gary Condit's tight-lipped refusal to discuss his relationship with Washington, D.C., intern Chandra Levy in connection with her mysterious disappearance. "Asked why Condit shouldn't step down from his seat on the House Intelligence Committee because of the risk of blackmail, [his attorney] Abbe Lowel argued that Condit has 'shown his ability to hold information.'"

Pregnant pause

While giving a brief report at a conference table, speaking points may be dramatized by inserting a brief silent pause immediately after their delivery. In a lengthier report, silent pauses may be used to separate main sections of the presentation; listeners feel refreshed by silence and pay renewed attention to vocalizations delivered afterward (see *Orienting reflex*).

Right to silence

Though its origin is unclear, the right to remain silent is a widespread legal principle that exempts suspects from answering questions posed by police. Nations may differ as to whether jurors are permitted to interpret the silence as a valid sign of guilt.

Silence is golden

That silence may often be pleasant is affirmed by the proverbial English phrase, "silence is golden." The phrase is often used in contrast to speech, which at times may be emotionally unpleasant, as in noise pollution.

See also *Invisibility*.

Singing

Musical sign

Nonverbal vocalizations, spoken words and manual gestures set to the emotional and highly evocative harmony, melody, rhythm and timbre of music.

Emotional range

Human song may express the entirety of felt emotion: agreement, anger, certainty, control, disagreement, disgust, disliking, embarrassment, fear, happiness, hate, interest, liking, love, sadness, shame, surprise and uncertainty.

Usage

Around the world, music is both vocal (e.g., chanting, humming and singing) and gestural (manual, e.g., clapping, finger-snapping, and playing varied musical instruments with the hands).

Evolution

Beginning with the use of speech ca. 200,000 years ago, the human voice became increasingly melodic, harmonious and oratorical. The rationale for vocal softness and melody most certainly involved serenading in courtship (see subsequently, Serenades). As it became more verbally linguistic, human courtship signaling likely favored vocal tenderness over harshness. The former voice quality is contact inviting, while the latter promotes distance.

Vocal music

Unlike the wooden or metal tubes of a pipe organ, the human windpipe is pliable and protean in its ability to change shape. Encased in cartilage, the vibrating vocal folds produce sounds modified by elastic, membranous tissues and supple ligaments, further modified within mobile, mucus-lined pharyngeal, nasal and oral chambers of the head. The musicality of human voices is processed in the planum temporale, a cortical auditory area found only in great apes and *Homo*.

Prosody

Linguists call the quasi-musical qualities of human speech "prosody." English prosody comes from Greek prosoidia, "song sung to music" or "accent." Linguistic prosody includes accentuation, phrasing, rhythm, stress and the tonal qualities of speech. On the nonverbal side, prosody includes the duration, muscular tension and rhythm of hand movements that accompany words. Vocal and gestural prosody play important roles in the production and perception of human communication. Through them, we detect emotions such as happiness, sadness, anger, fear and uncertainty in utterance and body movement.

Duets

In a duet, two singers join in song and feel an emotional closeness though the principle of isopraxism or "same behavior." Singing in tandem doubles the force of a comical, romantic or tragic performance. Among great love duets in opera are those of "Liebesnacht," "La Boheme" and "Andrea Chenier."

Fight songs

Football, rugby and soccer fans may erupt in song to show allegiance and exhort their teams to win. Just as they sit together and wear the same team colors, fans may simultaneously sing the same words to bond as a force to be reckoned with. Famous fight songs include "Eye of the Tiger," "We Will Rock You" and "Na Na Hey Hey Kiss Him Goodbye."

Serenades

In classic form, a serenade is an evening song sung to attract a lover in courtship. Its nonverbal traits include musical voice tones and palm-up gestures reached out to the listening loved one. A famous version is Luciano Pavarotti's operatic rendition of "Serenade," delivered with exquisite vocal melody and lyrical motions of his fingers and hands.

Voice and gesture

That vocal (laryngeal) and gestural (pectoral) articulations are both important in singing may be explained, in part, by the fact that muscles in charge of the human larynx and pectoral girdle evolved from hypobranchial muscles that originally opened the mouths and gill openings of ancient fishes. Paleocircuits that mediate our laryngeal and pectoral movements are connected in the posterior hindbrain and anterior spinal cord (Bass and Chagnaud, 2012).

Vocal and pectoral vibrations

Human singing has incredibly ancient vertebrate roots, which may explain why song is such a compelling nonverbal venue today. The sonic properties of vocalizing and pectoral vibration were recruited ca. 420 mya (Early Silurian, or earlier) for social signaling in a watery world. The sounds were basically "assertion displays" used to announce physical presence, attract mates and repel rivals.

See also *Dance, Tone of voice, Whistle*.

Slow motion

Chronemic cue

A sequence of audio or visual behaviors performed or recorded in slower-than-normal speed.

Usage

Slow motion may be used to call attention to or dramatize nonverbal units in the stream of behavior (see *Action unit*). Electronically recorded auditory cues, body movements, facial expressions and gestures may be played back in slower-than-normal time for purposes of teaching, transcription, research and dramatization.

Transcription

Slow motion enables greater accuracy in recording nonverbal behavior via available alpha-numeric notation systems and coding schemes (see, e.g., *FACS*).

Dramatization

Viewed in slow motion, facial expressions, gestures and body movements may appear more visually dramatic than when viewed in real time. Body movements given and received in spoken conversations, for example, appear more serious and dramatic when slowed to below-normal speed. In particular, behavioral synchrony and stimulus-response relationships evident in the behavioral stream may stand out.

Media

In televised sports such as American football, competitive gymnastics and ice skating, some body movements may be blurred in real time. In the latter sport, for example, a twirled quadruple jump is difficult to see unless played back at slower-than-normal speed. Movie directors may use slow motion as a dramatic device to call attention to or enhance selected behavioral scenes. Cinematic contrast between real and slowed time may bring notice through a viewer's orienting reflex.

See also *Fast motion*.

Smile

Emotion cue

Any of several displays of upwardly lifted lip corners, ranging from intentional (wan or unenthused) to spontaneous (zygomatic or enthused) grins (see *Zygomatic smile*).

Usage

The human smile may be used to encode a variety of emotions, feelings and moods from happiness to sarcasm to despair (see *Sadness*). While the smile is likely a cultural universal, its magnitude, meaning and use may be subject to societal shaping.

Physical shape

The iconic emoticon for smiling (a symmetrically open upward curve) is precisely opposite to that for frowning (a symmetrically open downward curve). While the visual opposition resembles Charles Darwin's (1872) "principle of antithesis," neither facial expression is "unserviceable." Indeed, both derive from digestive facial-muscle contractions (see *Enteric brain*). The upward-curved shape may be a ritualized version of digestive pleasure (see *Pleasure cue*) and the downward curve one of revulsion (see *Disgust*).

Antonym: *Frown*. See also *Ritualization*.

Research reports

1   Infants begin smiling as early as 3 months old (Wörmann et al., 2014). Believe it or not, a smile can be perceived from a distance of 300 feet; the length of a football field (Blum, 1998, 34).
2   Much of the research suggests that smiling is a "universal signal of honesty." As such, it functions as a type of social glue (Centorrino et al., 2015). However, it is important to note that within the context of smiling as a social glue, it can be "faked" due to the ease with which humans can produce smiles (Me´hu and Dunbar, 2008).

3   It has been shown that smiling increases attractiveness (Reis et al., 1990).

4   A large number of studies show that people who smile are perceived as happier (Otta et al., 1994) and more attractive (Hess et al., 2002).

5   Smiles with a slow start (ranging between 0.5 and 0.75 seconds), shorter apex and a slow offset are judged as more genuine (Krumhuber and Kappas, 2005; Schmidt et al., 2003).

6   A number of studies suggest that there are differences between genders in the manner in which smiles are used. For women, it has been found that smiling can have an interactional foundation, while for men, it is more of an emotional expression (LaFrance and Mayo, 1979). Women tend to smile more than men (LaFrance et al., 2003), and there is a greater expectation for them to do so (Brody and Hall, 2008). Research by Krumhuber et al. (2007) indicates that women are better than men at distinguishing smiles.

7   While Ekman (2001, 2003) described 18 types of smiles (and suggested there might be as many as 50 types), typically, smiling is described within three main domains (Niedenthal et al., 2010):

    a   Enjoyment smiles occur in times when the human (and some primates) experience pleasure or success.

    b   Affiliative smiles involve the communication of positive social intentions.

    c   Dominance smiles have to do with status and control. They can include smiles which could be described as "proud," or "critical" or "scheming."

8   Within the discourse on smiling, the work of Duchenne de Boulogne has received much attention and has spawned numerous other studies. In fact, a smile entitled the "Duchenne smile" has been named in honor of this Frenchman. Frank and Ekman (1993) argue that the "Duchenne smile" is a true indicator of enjoyment, involving muscle activation around the eye corners. This argument is grounded in the belief that the felt smile cannot be "faked" because of the muscle activation around the eyes. The primary reason cited for this "felt" smile centers on the difficulty in controlling the orbicularis oculi muscles at the corner of the eyes. It is important to note that research by Schneider and Josephs (1991) showed that Duchenne smiles can arise as the result of a negative experience (such as losing a game).

9   When compared to spontaneous smiles, it has been found that posed smiles are longer in duration (Schmidt et al., 2006). Indeed, the belief that Duchenne smiles are "spontaneous" and accordingly cannot be fabricated has been questioned in more recent times (Schmidt et al., 2006). Recent research indicates that people can deliberately mobilize the muscles used in the creation of a Duchenne smile (Gosselin et al., 2010). A "sizeable minority" of people can do this and are more persuasive as a result (Gunnery and Hall, 2014, 181).

Sneaker

Footwear

A casual sports shoe made with a usually colorful canvas or nylon upper, and a soft, thick sole of rubber, latex or vinyl.

Usage I

Since they cover our very expressive feet (see *Foot*), we are choosy about the brands, insignia and styles of the sneakers we wear (see *Messaging feature*). Encoding nonverbal signs of gender, presence and personality, sneakers may, like hair cues and hats, communicate "who we are."

Usage II

Sneakers are rarely seen beneath conference tables because they do not support the power metaphor of suits (see *Business suit*), and their thick, cushioning soles may suggest "awkwardness." Soles greater than one-eighth inch thick can project a clumsy appearance, suggestive of less coordination, grace and savoir-faire than thinner, more elegant leather soles of Italian or British design. Nonverbally, sole thickness is equivalent to the visual contrast between mittens and kid gloves.

Media

Sneakers were popularized by James Dean in Guys and Dolls (1955) and by Elvis Presley's teen cohort in Jailhouse Rock (1957). In the 1950s, sneakers broke the formality of corporate leather shoes to express a kinder, gentler world for feet and the lifestyle for which they stand.

See also *Boot*, *Men's shoes*, *Women's shoes*.

Social distancing

Introduction

Just how incredibly sociable human beings are – both verbally and nonverbally – was dramatized in 2020 when national governments advised that, due to the world coronavirus pandemic, people should avoid close physical contact and remain sheltered in their homes for months at a time.

Public health

Social distancing is a public health practice with the objective of preventing sick individuals from coming in close physical contact with healthy individuals. Such practice aims to reduce disease transmission. Governments can introduce measures which include distancing from others by approximately 2 meters, closing public gatherings, closing schools and banning all public gatherings unless essential. The World Health Organization (WHO) suggested that "physical distancing" was a better term to describe practices associated with "social distancing" during the 2020 Covid-19 pandemic. With respect to the Covid-19 pandemic (2020), the Centers for Disease Control and Prevention (CDC) defined social distancing as "remaining out of congregate settings, avoiding mass gatherings, and maintaining distance (approximately 6 feet or 2 meters) from others when possible."

Historical context

Social distancing of 2 meters from another individual was ordered by almost all governments of countries which experienced high volumes of the Covid-19 outbreak in 2020. However, while the scale of governments' reactions to the Covid outbreak and the corresponding imposition of social distancing was unheralded in 2020, the actual practice of social distancing is not new. For centuries, social distancing was commonplace for those who came into contact with people from leper colonies and lazarettos. Similarly, during the 1916 New York City polio epidemic, the 1918 flu pandemic (also known as the Spanish flu) and the severe acute respiratory syndrome (SARS) outbreak of 2003, social distancing was commonplace.

Touch and social distancing

In 2020, the CDC outlined that people may experience emotions such as fear and anxiety with respect to Covid-19. Such fears and anxieties are grounded in actual fears of contracting the disease and associated worries about its effects. From the perspective of social distancing, there may also be other deleterious effects associated with Covid-19. The practice of social distancing imposes severe restrictions on touch, which, as one of the first human senses to develop, is elementary to human welfare.

Social facilitation effect

The presence of others

This effect involves the influence of others on performance. Some of the discourse on the social facilitation effect argues that human performance is enhanced by the presence of others (Harkins and Szymanski, 1987). Other arguments point out that the presence of others can have both a positive and negative influence on performance. Within the latter perspective, social facilitation is said to occur when there is an increase or decrease in behavior caused by the presence of another human being (Guerin, 1993). For example, Zajonc (1965) in a meta-analysis of a range of studies, argues that the presence of others improves simple or well-known tasks, while it can weaken performance on complex tasks. Later, Bond and Titus (1983) undertook a meta-analysis of 241 studies and derived similar findings. They argue that the presence of others "increases the speed of simple task performance and decreases the speed of complex task performance," while the presence of others impairs "complex performance accuracy" (Bond and Titus, 1983, 265).

Special visceral nerve

Neuro term

A nerve linked to a facial, jaw, neck, shoulder or throat muscle that once played a role in eating or breathing. A cranial nerve whose original role in digestion and respiration renders it emotionally responsive today.

Usage

Special visceral nerves mediate those "gut reactive" signs of emotion we unconsciously emit through facial expressions, throat-clears, head-tilts and shoulder-shrugs. Nonverbally, these nerves are indeed "special" because the muscle contractions they mediate are less easily (i.e., voluntarily) controlled than those of the skeletal muscles (which are innervated by *somatic* nerves).

Evolution

Associated with the pharyngeal arches, special visceral nerves control the branchio-meric muscles that once constricted or dilated the "gill" pouches of the ancient alimentary canal.

Anatomy I

Special visceral nerves include efferent fibers of (1) the *trigeminal nerve* (cranial V, for biting and chewing), (2) the *facial nerve* (cranial VII, for facial expression), (3) the *glossopharyngeal nerve* (cranial IX, for swallowing), (4) the *vagus nerve* (cranial X, for tone of voice) and (5) the *accessory nerve* (cranial XI, for head-shaking and the shoulder-shrug).

Anatomy II

The paleocircuits of visceral nerves – which originally mediated the muscles for *opening* (dilating) or *closing* (constricting) parts of the primitive "gill" apparatus in eating and breathing – are today linked to the limbic system.

Emotional signs, pains and twitches

Special visceral efferent nerves control our facial expressions, cause many of our neck pains and trigger the occasional twitches we feel in our mammalian-inspired platysma muscle.

　　See also *Disgust*.

Speech

Spoken language

A verbal means of communicating emotions, perceptions and thoughts through vocal articulations (see *Word*). The organization of systems of sound into language, which has enabled *Homo sapiens* to transcend the limits of individual memory and to store vast amounts of knowledge (see *Information*).

Usage I

Speech (and manual sign language, e.g., ASL) has become an indispensable means for sharing ideas, observations and feelings and for conversing about the past, present and future. Speech so engages the brain in self-conscious deliberation, however, that we often overlook our place in Nonverbal World.

Usage II

"Earth's inhabitants speak some 6,000 different languages" (Raloff, 1995).

Anatomy

To speak, we produce complex sequences of body movements and articulations not unlike the coordinated motions of gesture. Evolutionary recent speech-production areas of the neocortex, basal ganglia, and cerebellum enable us to talk (see *Verbal center*), while additional evolutionary-recent areas of the neocortex give heightened sensitivity to voice sounds (see *Auditory cue*) and visible positions of the fingers, hands, lips and tongue.

Evolution I

Spoken language is considered to be between 200,000 (Lieberman, 1991) and 2 million years old (Gibson, 1993). The likely precursor of speech is sign language (see *Language origin*). Our ability to converse using manual signs and to manufacture stone tools (see *Artifact*) evolved in tandem on eastern Africa's savannah plains. Signing may not have evolved without artifacts, nor artifacts without signs. Anthropologists agree that some form of communication was needed to pass knowledge about tool design from one generation to the next (see *Nonverbal learning*).

Evolution II

Handling, seeing, making and carrying stone implements stimulated the creation of conceptual categories, available for word labels, which came in handy, for example, for teaching the young. Through an intimate relationship with tools and artifacts, human beings became information-sharing primates of the highest order.

Evolution III

Preadaptations for vocal speech included dexterity of the human tongue for "food tossing" (see *Language origin*).

Speaking gestures I

In speech, hand gestures may aid memory and thought. According to the American psychologist Susan Goldin-Meadow, gestures make thinking easier, as they enlist spatial and other nonverbal areas of the brain. Information processing improves when gestures and words are congruent.

Speaking gestures II

Both gestures and speech are physical articulations enabled by neuromuscular movements of specific bony and cartilaginous body parts. Beginning ca. 500 mya in the ancient chordate spinal cord and hindbrain – in a shared caudal hindbrain, rh8-upper-spinal compartment – circuits for vocal-laryngeal and gestural-pectoral communication provide neural linkage between voiced words and forelimb cues (Bass and Chagnaud, 2012).

See also *Speech errors*.

Speech errors

Vocal cues

Mistakes in verbal fluency, including repetition, stuttering, mispronounced words, incomplete clauses and throat-clearing (see *Throat-clear*).

Usage

An increased frequency of speech errors may indicate anger, anxiety or stress (Mehrabian, 1974, 89; see *Emotion*).

Hem and haw

Hem: "A short cough or clearing of the throat made especially to gain attention, warn another, hide embarrassment, or fill a pause in speech" (Soukhanov, 1992, 841). Haw: "An utterance used by a speaker who is fumbling for words" (Soukhanov, 1992, 829).

Research reports

Speech hesitations tend to occur at the beginnings of clauses, usually after the first word (Boomer, 1965). "George Mahl of Yale University has found that errors become more frequent as the speaker's discomfort or anxiety increases" (Mehrabian, 1974, 89). Some research on lie detection suggests that cognitive load may cause speech errors (De Paulo et al., 2003).

Neuro-notes

Emotion from the limbic system carries to the larynx and pharynx through "gut reactive" nerves (see *Special visceral nerve*). Anxiety may divert mental concentration.

See also *Adam's-apple jump*, *Deception cue*.

Spitting

Polysemous action

The usually male act of forcefully ejecting fluid from the mouth. Among primates, humans are the only members who regularly spit.

Meanings

Few human acts have as many meanings as spitting. A lone farmer in a field may spit freely, but the same behavior on a busy sidewalk may evoke disgust in passersby. While the former may be solely a physical action, the latter is a nonverbal sign. For many observers, spitting is a sign of poor education.

Usage

Spitting may be used to express anger, to deter evil (e.g., an evil eye), to insure good luck and to guard against illness. Among men, repeated spitting may be a territory-proclaiming gesture. Young boys may imitate their elders to seem more "mature."

Literature

As Frazer (1890, 229) wrote in *The Golden Bough*, "In the Sandwich Islands chiefs were attended by a confidential servant bearing a portable spittoon, and the deposit was carefully buried every morning to keep it away from sorcerers. On the Slave Coast of Africa, for the same reason, whenever a king or chief expectorates, the saliva is scrupulously gathered up and hidden or buried."

Media

In the 1948 movie Key Largo, actress Lauren Bacall angrily spat on actor Edward G. Robinson's face.

SPOT program

Nonverbal surveillance

In 2003 the U.S. Transportation Security Administration (TSA) implemented its Screening Passengers by Observation Techniques (SPOT) program. TSA airport officers were trained to observe a set of 94 mostly nonverbal behaviors – for example, Adam's-apple-jump, blushing and excessive sweating – that may be indicative of anxiety, stress, deception or evil intent. Passengers exhibiting such suspicious behaviors may be subjected to a physical patdown and additional verbal screening.

Usage

TSA began training agents for the SPOT program in 2006. Though controversial, thousands of TSA personnel have undergone SPOT training, and the program continues to the present day. In usage, U.S. SPOT is similar to the intensive verbal and nonverbal methods employed in Israel, for example, at Tel Aviv's Ben Gurion airport.

Nonverbal criteria

According to the U.S. Government Accountability Office (GAO), many of SPOT's nonverbal indicators were derived from anthropologist David Givens' Nonverbal Dictionary (May 20, 2010; www.gao.gov/new.items/d10763.pdf; accessed May 21, 2010).

Application

BDOs (behavior detection officers) are trained to observe each passenger for a continuous 30 seconds and may or may not engage in casual conversation. Whenever the observer displays cues related to deception or criminal intent it adds a point to a type of checklist. When a particular numerical threshold is reached, the subject is deemed suspicious. If he/she continues displaying more cues and reaches a second threshold, officers approach for additional questioning and search of the person and his/her property. If the suspect still displays behavior worthy of mistrust, BDO leads the suspect to a LEO (law enforcement officer) for further investigation.

See also *Nonverbal surveillance*.

Figure S.7 Startle reflex

Startle reflex

Neuro term

A sudden, involuntary movement made in response to a touch, an unexpected motion or a loud noise. A set of automatic protective movements designed to withdraw the body and its parts from harm.

Usage

Many defensive postures and submissive gestures (e.g., diverse movements of the shoulder-shrug display) derive from paleocircuits of the mammalian startle. Its status as a reflex explains why people in every culture blink and grimace; flex the neck, elbows, trunk and knees and elevate the shoulders when feeling physically, emotionally or socially threatened (Andermann and Andermann, 1992).

Media

Eccentric twisting, plunging, blinking and flexing spasms made from 1989–98 by Seinfeld TV character Cosmo Kramer are typical of people with an *exaggerated* startle response. Increasing – in frequency and strength (amplitude) – with anxiety and fatigue, the startle underlies such culturally recognized "startle syndromes" as Indonesian *latah*, Japanese *imu* and Lapland's *Lapp panic* (Joseph and Saint-Hilaire, 1992, 487–488).

Research reports

The startle reflex is related to the Moro or "clamping" reflex of young primates, which includes arm, leg and spinal-column extension movements; head bowing and crying (McGraw, 1943, 19). Present in the human fetus after 30 weeks, the startle is predominantly a flexor reflex, possibly rooted in the primitive orienting response (Joseph and Saint-Hilaire, 1992, 487).

Neuro-notes

Sudden movements, looming objects or bright lights may trigger midbrain optic centers to automatically turn our faces and eyes toward what could be dangerous – before the forebrain knows on a conscious level that danger exists. The midbrain's auditory lobes, meanwhile, are reflexively attuned to changes in sound. Located just below the optic-center lobes, these pea-sized areas control our auditory startle. Picked up by the cochlear nucleus, a scream received by the auditory lobes triggers the amygdala and circuits of the reticulospinal tract to activate the startle. Thus, for example, recoiling from a karate yell is a primal response prompted by paleocircuits of the amphibian brain.

See also *Flexion withdrawal*.

Statue signs

Frozen gestures

Any of several small, life-size or monumental iconic bronze, concrete, plaster, stone (e.g., granite, jade, marble) or wooden – usually freestanding – sculptures depicting upright, seated or reclining human bodies. The arrangement, position and varied shapes of a statue's sign features may encode nonverbal narratives about cognition, emotion states and social bonds.

Usage

Statues may be used to commemorate important moments in time, memorialize military victories or celebrate religious figures (as in Marian shrines). Monumental statues may be used by autocrats to suggest overwhelming political power (see *Loom*).

Cognitive cues

Originally called The Poet (1880) Rodin's The Thinker depicts a solitary, seated muscular man painfully contemplating the fate of humanity, as portrayed in his own Gates of Hell sculpture cast through the lens of Dante's *Divine Comedy*, for which it stands. In his own words, Rodin identified the man's visible agony in "compressed lips" (see *Lip-compression*), "distended nostrils" (see *Nostril-flare*) and "knitted brow" (see *Eyebrow lower*). The statue's oppositionally twisted upper and lower body (see *Contrapposto stance*), flexed and adducted self-touching signs and strongly contracted muscle tone visible in arms, back and legs reveal his mental anguish. The sculpture shows strong stimulation of the Thinker's lips – with his bare knuckles – as a tactile means of coping with mental anguish through physical stimulation (see *Self-touch*). Nonverbally, Rodin's statue also could be entitled The Worrier.

Emotional states

In nonverbal contrast to The Thinker, Michelangelo's marble Pieta (1499) depicts a seated young woman, Mary, holding a recumbent male figure, Jesus, shortly after his tortured death by crucifixion. There is no visible agony in either face (see *Blank face*), nor in Mary's relaxed posture or Jesus' supine position in her lap. It was Michelangelo's artistic intent to show an emotional tone of acceptance and comfort in Jesus' accomplishments on Earth – and return to Heaven – rather than revealing sadness or pain upon his death.

Social bonds

Finally, in Rodin's Burghers of Calais (1889), a group of six men stand bonding in an historical scene depicting a likely group execution. Faces are anguished, clenched and frowning (see *Lip-compression, Frown*). Arms drop flaccidly in defeat to knee level; eyes gaze down in despair (see *Gaze-down*). One man lifts a hand upward, as if gesturing in speech (see *Gesture*); another implores with lowered arms and upturned palms of the deferential shoulder-shrug (see *Shoulder-shrug display*).

See also *Art cue*.

Steeple

Gesture

A position in which the tactile pads of the fingertips of one hand gently touch their counterparts on the other.

Usage

Identified by the American anthropologist Ray L. Birdwhistell, the steeple often reflects precise thought patterns. It may be used while listening, speaking or thinking; to entertain a provocative or novel idea or to contemplate a creative solution to a problem at hand. Steepling is typically associated with the portrayal of confidence (Borg, 2008).

Parallel palms

A common variant of steepling is the widespread parallel-palms gesture. In parallel palms, the open hands are held facing – that is, parallel to – one another as they are raised and lowered together, in tandem, in beating or chopping motions to strengthen a verbal point. As demonstrative speaking gestures, parallel palms are commonly seen in the courtroom as lawyers seek to manifest or prove an oral argument. Parallel palms are used by politicians to present arguments they believe are cogent and valid. Thus, parallel palms is an "exploded" version of the steeple cue, in which a speaker's opened hands are extended and energetically shaken at listeners to suggest emotional conviction about the thought's validity. (N.B.: Since the hands are held midway between the palm-down and palm-up positions, parallel palms may suggest the physical act of grasping, holding or seizing a mental concept.)

The raised steeple

The raised steeple occurs when the two palms are placed together and the fingertips touch gently together. In this position, the elbows are resting on the table. Pease and Pease (2004) comment that when we place the steeple in front of our faces, it gives us a God-like appearance.

Lowered steeple

The lowered steeple occurs when the palms and fingertips are touching. In this scenario, the elbows are not propping the steeple; they are resting on something (e.g., a table). This type of formation is regarded as giving messages of self-assuredness but also cooperation (Borg, 2008). Pease and Pease (2004) argue that it can often be found in scenarios where a superior and subordinate are interacting, with the superior using the steeple and perhaps also pointing.

Business

Steeple gestures may be used above a conference table to show that one is listening thoughtfully to a colleague's ideas commentary.

World politics

Sir Winston Churchill and Mikhail Gorbachev used steeple gestures to signal self-confidence. Regarding Gorbachev, the American physician and psychology professor Elisa Shipon-Blum writes, "He steeples in Moscow. He steeples in Washington. He steeples when he listens. He steeples when he talks. He steeples high. He steeples low. He even steeples when he smiles" (Blum, 1998, 3–14).

Research note

Fingers steeple, a widespread gesture, means "I am thinking" (Morris, 1994, 65).

Neuro-notes I

Steepling arose from brain modules in control of the precision grip, a position of the hands used ca. 2.6 mya when ancestors opposed their digits to make stone tools. Controlled in part by highly evolved areas of the parietal lobe (see *Human brain*), precision gestures bear a close relationship to tool-making itself – that is, to the sequentially ordered hand movements used to chip flakes from a core of stone. Today, steepling reflects higher-order thought processes, as dexterous brain modules for tool-making shift into gear for problem-solving, planning and design.

Neuro-notes II

The brain's supplementary motor area (SMA) helps organize the voluntary finger movements of the steeple cue.
    See also *Mime cue.*

Figure S.8 Submission

Submission

Status sign

The act of acknowledging, complying with or surrendering to the power or will of another.

Usage

Nonverbally, submission may show in a variety of signs that include bowing, facial flushing, downward gazing and giving-way.

Research reports

Submissive or flight elements include evade (sharp head or shoulder movements away from another), chin in (tucked strongly into chest), mouth corners back, lip licks, lower lip out, lower lip tremble, lips in and swallow (Grant, 1969, 528–530). Submissive acts in young children include cry, scream, rapid flight, cringe, hand cover, flinch, withdraw and request cessation (Strayer and Strayer, 1980).

Courtship

By disclaiming aggression, submissive cues may show that one is "approachable" (see *Love signal*).

Evolution

Submission originated from an ancient biological tendency to flee from danger (see *Fight-or-flight*). Nonverbal signs (e.g., crouching postures and diminutive size displays) evolved to mimic the visual act of escape – of increased physical separation between bodies, which then seem "smaller" through the optical illusion of distance.

Transexuality

The loss of male hormones "made me more retiring, more ready to be led, more passive" (Morris, 1974, 152).
    See also *Dominance.*

Sunglasses

Shade signs

Eyewear designed to protect the eyes from excessive glare, reflected light and sunshine. Also known as dark glasses – and colloquially as "shades" – sunglasses may protect against unwanted gaze monitoring (see *Eye contact*). A mask-like fashion statement, sunglasses may suggest a sense of aloofness, mystery, opacity, secrecy and reticence to interact (see *Invisibility*).

Usage

The earliest known sunglasses, of Caribou Inuit origin from Canada's Nunavet Territory, were worn ca. 2,000 years ago to prevent snow blindness. Subsequently, modern sunglasses were used by motion-picture personalities in Hollywood as protection from glaring studio lights and by surfers to protect against rays of California sun.

Markedness

In linguistic parlance, some words are "normal" while others are "marked." A case in point is the English "verbal," which is simple, and the marked word, "nonverbal," made more complex by adding the prefix. In being "unusual," the marked form may attract more attention than the simpler form. Nonverbally, since sunglasses "mark" the face, they may attract more attention than the face alone.

Media

Among the world's most famous celebrity sunglasses were designed by Oliver Goldsmith for the British actress Audrey Hepburn's (1929–1993) role in the 1961 movie Breakfast at Tiffany's. Called Manhattans®, the abnormally large, rounded frames gave her shaded eyes a beguiling look of alert, wide-eyed innocence. Through the principle of nonverbal imitation (see *Isopraxism*), sunglasses spread rapidly in the 20th century as they were featured in print, motion-picture and video-media scenes.

See also *Glasses, Mask*.

Suspender

Pants hanger

A usually elastic strap buttoned or clipped to the backside of one's trousers, looped over a shoulder and attached to the front.

Usage

By themselves or in tandem with belts, suspenders are used to hold up one's pants. Prominently situated upon the body, like hats and neckties, suspenders may make strong fashion statements (see *Hat, Neckwear*). Typically, the strap is looped over the ipsilateral shoulder, maintaining a clear vertical line, nevertheless, it can be attached at the back at the opposite sagittal side creating an "X" in the scapula of the user (but never in the front).

Evolution

Suspenders made of ribbon originated as undergarments in 18th-century France. Like underwear, they were not meant to be viewed in public. Modern suspenders called "braces" appeared in Britain in the 1820s as a means of holding one's pants high above the waistband as dictated by British fashion of the day. As time passed and pants were worn lower on the waist, belts gradually replaced suspenders. Today, suspenders have a worldwide distribution and may be worn for utilitarian purposes, for example, by workmen and farmers, or by high-end dressers to make dapper fashion statements.

Fashion

Unlike belts, which can go unnoticed when covered by shirts or tops, suspenders may make strong statements about one's lifestyle and worldview. The most generic message is a signature statement announcing, "I am here." Suspenders may also signal one's calling in life, as in "I am a hipster" or "I farm the land."

Media

Suspenders have been featured in movies and on television by such celebrities as Ben Affleck, Drew Barrymore, Matt Damon, Ellen DeGeneres, Leonardo DiCaprio, Larry King and Beyoncé (see *Isopraxism*).

Sexual attraction

That suspenders originated as undergarments, to be hidden beneath outerwear, renders them sexually attractive today. They are often colorful and designed to be noticed (see *Love signals I*). Moreover, as bold lines that descend from the shoulders to the pelvic area, suspenders draw attention downward to a wearer's pants and hip.

Swagger-walk

Broadside display

A slight or moderate exaggeration in the side-to-side movements of walking (see *Walk*). A usually masculine style of upper-body strutting. A visual means of filling up space and occupying a greater expanse of personal territory (see *High-stand display*).

Usage

In greetings, a man may use the swagger-walk while approaching another man to suggest dominance and project strength. The swagger-walk is not generally used to approach women. In a culturally elaborated version, men may drag one foot and limp from side-to-side in a "pimp strut." The swagger-walk may be seen as men enter taverns or bars to show "attitude" before engaging in courtship.

Primatology

Our close primate relatives, the great apes, may show dominance by straightening and holding their arms away from the body as they swagger-walk from side to side.

Transgender

The noted Welsh transgender woman Jan Morris commented on male swagger from her male and female points of view: "I never mind the swagger of young men. It is their right to swank, and I know the sensation!" (Morris, 1974, 83).

Media

The best-known swagger-walk belonged to American actor John ("Duke") Wayne (1907–1979), seen in such movie classics as Rio Bravo (1959), The Alamo (1960) and The Green Berets (1968).

Personality

There is some correlation between gait style and aggression. For instance, "When walking, the body naturally rotates a little; as an individual step forward with their left foot, the left side of the pelvis will move forward with the leg and the left shoulder will move back and the right shoulder forward to maintain balance. Put simply, an aggressive walk is one where this rotation is exaggerated" (Satchell et al., 2017, 42–43).

See also *Goose-step, Stomp.*

Sweaty palms

Emotion cue

The excretion of eccrine-gland moisture onto the palmar surfaces of the hands in response to anxiety, stress or fear.

Usage

Sweaty palms may be detected while shaking hands. It is reputed that former U.S. FBI director J. Edgar Hoover would not hire candidates whose handshakes were moist and cold.

Research reports

Cannon's "emergency reaction" involves redistribution of blood from the skin and viscera to the muscles and brain (Cannon, 1929; see *Fight-or-flight*). A college student's galvanic skin response (GSR) is greatest when he or she is approached frontally by a member of the opposite sex (McBride et al., 1965; see *Stranger anxiety*).

Neuro-notes

Like other body-movement cues, sweating requires a movement of body parts to deliver its watery substance to the skin's surface. Myoepithelial cells, which contain smooth-visceral-muscle-like organs, contract to squeeze the sweaty fluid through thin ducts in the skin. Myoepithelial "muscles" are innervated by sympathetic nerve fibers; the muscle-like organs also contract in response to adrenaline.

See also *Apocrine odor, Facial flushing.*

Systems Model of nonverbal communication

Dynamic interplay

The Systems Model, which focuses on face-to-face nonverbal exchanges, endeavors to explain the "dynamic interplay" between individual, dyadic and environmental processes in nonverbal communication (Patterson, 2019, 111). In so doing, the model takes account of the perceptual, cognitive, emotional, motivational and social ecological factors at play within the unique context of an interaction. The model builds on previous models and theories of nonverbal interaction by taking into account the role of culture, biology, gender, personality, the dominance of automatic processes, the relevance of controlled processes, the importance of unconscious and conscious goals, social judgment processes and parallel behavior processes.

Perceptions of behavior and appearance

With these various factors and processes as foundational, the Systems Model focuses on the perception of the behaviors and appearance by both the receiver and sender. Outcomes from this interaction are also influenced by what the receiver and sender "bring to the interaction" (see previously) and by the environment in which the interaction takes place. Patterson (2019) also argues that the model could be applied to studies of interactions between humans and social robots.

T

Table-slap

Gesture

A palm-down cue in which a tabletop or another level surface is struck with a percussive clap of an open hand.

Usage

The table-slap may be used to accent a key speaking point; object to another speaker's statement; demonstrate an emotion, for example, anger or mirth and call attention to one's physical presence.

Observations

In the workplace, table-slaps may be visible at meetings around a conference table. In offices with cubicles, senior staff may table-slap the dividers of junior staff members at will, but the latter may not slap a supervisor's partition, railing or office door. Striking a subordinate's cubicle partition, the table-slap may signal "I am here," "I have something to say" and suggest that "I am more important than you." Example: Hearing his boss' slap, a senior executive in range establishes eye contact and slaps a nearby surface to answer the call. Each subsequently averts gaze, approaches the other with a swagger-walk and leans on a junior staff member's partition to chat before returning to private offices a short distance away.

Primatology

Slapping the ground with an open hand is a gesture directed by adult or young adult baboons to other baboons in the wild (Hall and DeVore, 1972).

Research reports

Slamming an open hand on a tabletop is called a baton, a nonverbal sign used to emphasize a speaking point (Ekman and Friesen, 1969b). The pound gesture is a sharp blow by one hand against the other immobile hand or against an object (Brannigan and Humphries, 1969). Slap ground is an aggressive gesture in langurs (Dolhinow, 1972) and savannah baboons (Hall and DeVore, 1972). "The animal [a chimpanzee] raises one or both hands forward or to the sides and hits the ground or an inanimate object with a flat palm" (Berdecio and Nash, 1981, 30). "In this study the gesture always appeared to function as an attention getting device. In general, instances performed with the alert face served as play invitations" (Berdecio and Nash, 1981, 30). Palm-down ground-slapping is a threat gesture in chimpanzees (Goodall, 1990) and in bonobos (de Waal and Lanting, 1997).

See also *Palm-down*.

Talisman

Object charm

A usually handheld artifact or natural object believed to have protective or other magical powers. Common examples include amulets, four-leaf clovers, lucky horseshoes and rabbits' feet.

Usage

A talisman may be carried, hung from a rearview mirror or attached to a living-room wall to bring good luck and protection or to ward off evil (see *Evil eye*).

Word origin

A talisman is "An object marked with magic signs and believed to confer on its bearer supernatural powers or protection" (Soukhanov, 1992, 1831). The English word derives from the 7,000-year-old Indo-European root *kwel-*, derivatives of which include "pain," "penalty" and "punish."

Messaging features

Through their messaging features, talismans "speak" to us as gestures. A talisman may include words, symbols and other brief communications crafted into its design. Meaningful marks, lines, shapes, textures, colors and decorations may be added to transmit information apart from the object's material functionality, durability or strength.

Neuro-notes

Nonverbally, a lucky horseshoe or rabbit's foot has a great deal to "say." In the former talisman, the weight of iron sensed by Golgi tendon organs, muscle spindles and Pacirian corpuscles add psychological reality, importance and gravitas. Iron has long been considered a natural repellent of evil forces. A horseshoe's curvilinear, open-ended shape registers in the visual system as a container in which to store or distribute its magical contents. In the rabbit's foot, sensory neurons in the fingers and palm, known as mechanoreceptors, respond to the pleasurable softness and protectiveness of fur.

See also *Object fancy*.

Tear apart

Rip sign

The usually bimanual act of forcefully separating a length of cloth or piece of paper into smaller, torn sections. Often done in anger or disgust, ripping connotes a sense of finality and relief (see *Emotion*).

Usage

Physically tearing apart a book, contract, note or personal letter may psychologically "remove" the ripper from the document's author and written contents.

U.S. politics

On February 4, 2020, House of Representatives Speaker Nancy Pelosi methodically tore up her copies of President Donald Trump's State of the Union speech.

Media

Televised images of Speaker Pelosi's nonverbal, ripping hands may have drawn more commentary, pro and con, than the president's speech itself. That her deliberate tearing had been decided beforehand is indicated by the prearrangement of pages into four neatly separated stacks. During applause at the end of his presidential address, Speaker Pelosi – moving from her left to right (see *Chirality*) – picked up each stack and firmly tore it in half, breadthwise. After four dramatic rippings, Pelosi gathered together pieces of the destroyed document and summarily dropped them on the tabletop, as refuse.

Verbal responses

"I thought it was a terrible thing when she ripped up the speech,' Trump, 73, told reporters on Friday" (Dibble, 2020). "'So it was, in my view, a manifesto of mistruths, falsehoods, blatantly really dangerous to the well-being of the American people if they believed what he said,' Speaker Pelosi said Thursday" (Stoddart, 2020).

Neuro-notes

Ripping paper involves both deliberation and precision (see *Precision grip*). In the context of strong emotion, tearing apart another's written words may be cathartic as a substitute for tearing apart the writer (see *Anger, Disgust, Intention cue*). Tearing fabric and paper may be curiously pleasurable to tactile-vibration sensors (see *Touch cue*).

See also *Gesture, Hands*.

Figure T.1 Tense-mouth

Tense-mouth

Facial expression

A gesture produced by compressing, in-rolling and narrowing the lips to a thin line. A position of the mouth in which the lips are visibly tightened and pressed together through contraction of the lip and jaw muscles.

Usage

Lips are among the most emotionally expressive human features. Lip and jaw tension may reflect anxious feelings, nervousness and emotional concerns. Thus, a tense-mouth may precisely mark the onset of a mood shift, novel thought or sudden change of heart.

Meaning

The tense-mouth has been observed as a sign of anger, frustration and threat, determination, sympathy and cognitive processes while pondering, thinking or feeling uncertain. The face may show obvious muscular tension with the lips held tightly together or less noticeable tension with the lips parted and slightly tightened.

U.S. politics

The lips of a chronically angry, anxious or intense person may "freeze" in a permanently tight-lipped expression, as shown, for example, in 1960s photos of former FBI director J. Edgar Hoover. The tense-mouth is visible in AP photos of President William Jefferson Clinton, sitting in the Map Room of the White House on August 17, 1998, minutes before making a televised statement to the American people: "Indeed, I did have a relationship with Ms. Lewinsky that was not appropriate."

See also *Bite, Lip-pout.*

Thin slicing

Video footage

Thin slicing involves the presentation of short excerpts of nonverbal stimuli from a stream of behavior. Thin slices are often used in research, with the nonverbal stimuli being presented for varying lengths of time. It can involve video footage of several minutes or still images for less than a second (Matsumoto et al., 2000).

First impressions

Thin slicing is also used in connection with research on first impressions. Here "thin slicing" refers to people's tendency to form first impressions of others based on "thin slices" of information (Ambady and Rosenthal, 1993). Interestingly, a number of studies have shown that these first "thin slice" impressions, which have a strong nonverbal component, can be accurate (Ambady et al., 1999; Babad et al., 2003; Kammrath et al., 2007).

Test of Nonverbal Cue Knowledge

Explicit knowledge of nonverbal cues

The Test of Nonverbal Cue Knowledge (TONCK) is a pencil-and-paper test designed by Rosip and Hall (2004) which measures explicit knowledge of nonverbal cues and meanings. The test contains 81 items. The participant marks each of these items either true or false. Examples of items include:

- Widening of the eyelids while speaking signifies emphasis on what was said (True).

- People are likely to engage in self-touching when thinking (processing information) (True).
- People are more likely to touch themselves while telling the truth than when lying (False).

Reliability and predictive abilities

The test was found to be "reliable and to have predictive ability" (Rosip and Hall, 2004, 267). In various studies using the TONCK, the researchers (Rosip and Hall, 2004) found trends across the data indicating that knowledge of nonverbal cues is a significant predictor of one's accuracy in nonverbal decoding. Also, these studies found that knowledge of nonverbal cues has a gender factor, with women scoring higher than men. The authors do point out that "the explicit knowledge that is revealed on the TONCK is still only a modest indicator of how good a person will be when judging actual nonverbal cues" (Rosip and Hall, 2004, 278).

Thumbs up signal

The "thumbs up" signal is used to indicate approval. As you would expect, the thumbs up signal also conveys confidence (Borg, 2008). Sometimes, it can be quite subtle. Think of the late John F. Kennedy and his tendency to have a thumb (or two) sticking out of his pocket. Some commentators note that this was no accident (Borg, 2008).

Tickle

Touch cue

Tickle is a tingling, tactile sensation, considered both pleasant and unpleasant, which may result in laughter, smiling and involuntary twitching movements of the head, limbs and torso.

Usage

The two tickle types are knismesis (a light tickle which may or may not produce laughter) and gargalesis (a heavy tickle that may produce the laugh response).

Neuro-notes

Tickle and itch sensations are produced through mild stimulation of group C unmyelinated nerve-fiber endings for pain. Heavy tickling of one's own body does not lead to laughter. Imaging studies suggest that the brain's cerebellum anticipates the tickling movements and thus unconsciously nullifies the element of surprise. Still, the reason human beings laugh while being tickled remains largely unknown.
    See also *Pain cue*.

Time

Time line

The placement of nonverbal signs, signals and cues in temporal order. The time line may be absolute or relative. In the absolute sense, two hand signals – for example, palm-down and palm-up – may be recorded in terms of standard clock time: seconds, minutes and hours or fractions thereof. In the relative sense, nonverbal signs may be seen as preceding, co-occurring or following one another in time.

Usage

Both absolute and relative time lines have been used in observational studies of nonverbal communication.

Chronemics

In the 1970s, Radford University communication professor Thomas J. Bruneau introduced "chronemics" as the study of time and tempo in human communication.
　　See also *Proxemics*.

Tongue-show

Introduction

"Don't bother me now!" – "[Research] at the University of Western Australia identified the [slightly] protruded tongue as a particularly effective cue for this message" (Burgoon et al., 1989, 411).

Facial expression

A momentary protrusion of the tongue between the lips. A gesture of the tongue found in gorillas and other primates, in children and in all ethnic groups studied.

Usage I

The tongue-show is a likely universal mood sign of unspoken disagreement, disbelief, disliking, displeasure or uncertainty. It can modify, counteract or contradict a verbal remark. Following the statement, "Yes, I agree," for example, a protruded tongue may suggest, "I do not agree." Tongue-shows can reveal misleading, ambiguous or uncertain areas in dialogue, public statements and oral testimony and thus may signal probing points – unresolved verbal issues to be further analyzed and explored (see *Probing point*).

Research reports

The tongue-show has been studied in both gorillas and human beings as a negative sign of aversiveness and social stress (Smith et al., 1974). A gorilla pushed from its favorite sitting place, for example, or a man entering a roomful of strangers may unwittingly show the tongue in "displeasure." Staring, striking or scolding another primate may release a tongue protrusion, which has been decoded as a fragment of the emotion cue for disgust (Smith et al., 1974). Tongue between lips is a defensive sign children may use when approaching strange adults (Stern and Bender, 1974).

E-commentary

"About body language acts, in police interrogations I have many times observed the tongue-showing cue just before the defendant would confess." – Marco Pacori (12/17/00 9:53:16 AM Pacific Standard Time)

Neuro-notes

Subcortical: The tongue-show reflects negative emotions of the amygdala acting through brain-stem paleocircuits of the hypoglossal nerve (cranial XII). Stimulation of the amygdala can produce unwitting tongue movements associated with eating and the sense of smell (Guyton, 1996, 758–759). Cortical: That we often tongue-show while performing tasks that involve precise manual dexterity – such as when threading a needle – may reflect the neural linkage between human tool-making and speech (see *Word*).

Top hat

High-standing headgear

In the western world, an often formal, imposing, usually masculine item of headgear with a flat, circular top (or crown) and precipitous vertical sidewalls that descend to a narrow, horizontal brim. Top hats may be made of leather, silk or wool and are normally black (see *Colors decoded*, Black).

Usage

Today, top hats may be worn on solemn occasions (e.g., funerals and inaugurations), ceremonial gatherings (weddings) and yearly on February 2 (Groundhog Day). Yesterday's top hats were originally worn by upper- and middle-class members to connote superiority over lower-class folk (giving rise to the English phrase, "high hat"). At the beginning of the 20th century, top hats were worn by men from all social classes and became signature features in the uniforms of chimneysweeps.

Evolution

Top hats originated from earlier capotain designs and swiftly replaced the trisome headgear worn by men of the 1700s, often including pirates. The first silk top hat appeared in England in 1793.

Looming effect

By exaggerating a man's standing height, top hats conferred a nonverbal power advantage in social status (see *High-stand display*, *Loom*).

U.S. presidential politics

The last American president to wear an inaugural top hat was John F. Kennedy (1917–1963), on January 20, 1961.

Look-alikes

The sudden, widespread adoption of top hats is a prime example of the nonverbal principle of imitation (see *Isopraxism*).
   See also *Hat*.

The Touch Experiences and Attitudes Questionnaire

Designed by Trotter et al. (2018), this questionnaire is a self-report instrument which examines attitude and experiences of social and affective touches. As a wide selection of research cites the value of human touch (Trotter et al., 2018), the questionnaire is of value in a range of disciplines such as medicine, psychiatry and psychology. The questionnaire originally contained 117 items and following analysis and was reduced to 57 items. The questionnaire is underpinned by components related to touch associated with family and friends, current intimate touch, childhood touch, attitude to unfamiliar touch, attitude to self-care and attitude to intimate touch. Examples of items include:

I dislike people being very physically
   affectionate towards me
I have to know someone quite well
   to enjoy a hug from them
I find it natural to greet my friends
   and family with a kiss on the cheek

Touch cue

Haptics

Nonverbal specialists may refer to touch cues as "haptics." "Of or relating to the sense of touch; tactile" (Soukhanov, 1992, 822). Haptics comes from the Greek word *haptikos*, "to touch."

Anatomy

Figure T.2 Touch cue

The outer covering of skin is our body's largest "part." Skin makes up ca. 15 percent of body weight (ca. 23 lbs.) and occupies some 21 square feet of surface area (Wallace et al., 1983). Pain and protopathic touch cues are received via free nerve endings in the skin and hair follicles. More specialized nerve endings have evolved for finer, epicritic touch and temperature discrimination. Mechanoreceptors (including Pacinian corpuscles, Merkel's disks and Meissner's corpuscles) sense pressure, stretching and indenting the skin. Thermoreceptors (Krause end bulbs for cold and organs of Ruffini for heat) are sensitive to changes in temperature.

Tactile signal

Afferent: An incoming sign received through physical contact with a body part (e.g., a hand or lip), causing it to feel (see *Homunculus*). Efferent: A sign of physical contact (e.g., of pressure, temperature or vibration) delivered to a body part (see, e.g., *Kiss*).

Usage I

Touch cues are powerfully "real." If "seeing is believing," touching is knowing – that is, knowing "for sure." Touch cues are used worldwide to show emotion in settings of childcare, comforting and courtship and to establish personal rapport. They are one of the most primitive forms of communication. Touch is one of the earliest and most basic forms of stimulation the human experiences, beginning in the womb. It has primal origins, and, as Sachs (1988, 28) observes: "Touch, in short, is the core of sentience, the foundation for communication with the world around us and probably the single sense that is as old as life itself."

Usage II

Self-touching is often seen in anxious or tense settings, as a form of consolation by means of self-stimulation (see subsequently, Usage IV).

Examining touch

Touch is typically examined within the following parameters: (1) intensity – for example Was it aggressive? Was it hard? Was it a soft touch?; (2) number of body parts (e.g., fingertips and limbs in affectionate touching); (3) length – the time length of the touch, for example, duration of holding hands while walking; (4) nature – for example, static touch versus stroking touch, self-care versus intimate touch; (5) frequency – the actual number of touches that occur; (6) location – the place where the person is touched, for example, hand and (7) instrument of touch – that is, was an object used (e.g., a hair brush), or was it part of the human body (e.g., a finger?).

Classifications of touch

Burgoon et al. (2016), following an examination of a variety of studies on the function of touch, provide valuable classifications as follows:

1 *Instrumental Touch*. For example, helping a child put on their shoes.
2 *Socially Polite Touches*. For example, a handshake.
3 *Affectionate Touches*. For example, hugging.
4 *Comforting Touch*. For example, a pat on the back.
5 *Appreciative and Congratulatory Touch*. For example, children giving each other a high five.
6 *Sexual Touch*. For example, French kissing and the touching of private body parts.
7 *Playful Touch*. For example, tickling.
8 *Control Touch*. For example, patting someone on the shoulder and saying "look at that!."
9 *Negative Affect Touches*. For example, pulling or pushing another. Less common examples include punching, kicking or beating someone up.
10 *Hybrid Touches*. These are touches which combine the aforementioned variations of touch. For example, the act of cradling a crying child while applying a bandage to a grazed knee involves both instrumental and affectionate touches.

Evolution

The most primitive, specialized tactile-sense organ in vertebrates is the neuromast, a fluid-filled pit in the skin of today's fishes, which picks up vibrations, heat, electrical and perhaps chemical signals in surrounding water. Each neuromast contains a hair cell, which, when moved by water currents generated, for example, by a nearby fish, stimulates a sensory nerve. Through the neuromast, the current becomes a nonverbal sign of another fish's presence.

Touch and romance

Touch is an important component of intimate relationships (Jakubiak and Feeney, 2016; Heslin and Boss, 1980). In this regard, touch is significant because it can release oxytocin and endorphins (Uvnäs-Moberg et al., 2015) and dopamine (Keltner, 2009). It is an important feature of relationships. In the early stages of romantic relationships, it is more probable that men will initiate touch; however, in marriages, it is more probable that women will initiate touching (Willis and Dodds, 1998).

Touch and gender

Men are more inclined to perceive touch in a more sexual way than women (Hanzal et al., 2008). Generally, in comparing men to women, "women engage in touching more than men and are touched more than men" (Burgoon and Bacue, 2003).

Touch and human development

The importance of touch for the physical and biological wellbeing of infants and their later development in social and psychological spheres is well recognized (Richmond and McCroskey, 2000a). Indeed, a study by Adler and Towne in 1996 found that despite being well cared for in terms of bodily needs, institutionalized babies had slower rates of thriving and had higher mortality rates than the norm. They attributed the inability of these babies to thrive to not being lifted, fondled or cuddled as frequently as babies in non-institutional settings (Hargie and Dickson, 2004). Research by Gerhart (2004) and Perry (2002) found that in the first year and a half of life, toddlers who received inadequate tactile stimulation had underdeveloped brain pathways used for the processing of social and emotional information.

Touch and healing

Knapp and Hall (2006, 277) observe that throughout history, "wondrous healings" have occurred, with "interpersonal touch" being a key contributing factor to such healing (Knapp and Hall, 2006, 277). For example, Jesus is credited with healing many by touch. Massage therapy sessions have been shown to have beneficial effects on blood pressure, heart rate and anxiety (Moyer et al, 2004).

Space

When U.S. Apollo 11 pilot Michael Collins flew above the Moon, he felt he could "almost reach out and touch it" (Collins, 1988, 5).

Neuro-notes I

"In primitive brains, subcortical and extrathalamic sensory structures were crucial to sensory processing. Comparable structures continue to be important in the advanced brains of modern mammals, even though the role of the cerebral cortex and thalamus in sensory processing has expanded enormously" (Willis, 1998b, 109).

Neuro-notes II: mirror neurons

The sight of someone being touched may activate mirror neurons in the observer's parietal somatic sensory cortex (Keysers and Fadiga, 2008).

See also *Aroma cue, Emotion cue, Touch experiences and attitude questionnaire.*

Tree sign

Arbor signal

A message emitted by the bark, branches, crown, leaves and/or trunk of a perennial woody plant.

Usage

People of all ages find something elementary and comforting in trees, which have long been symbols of transcendental beliefs among traditional folk, such as the Druids. Taking the world as a whole, the custom of climbing trees is still widespread, especially among those young enough to mend after a fall. (N.B.: The phone number of Tree Climbers International, a voluntary association of human beings dedicated to arboreal climbing, is 404/659-TREE.)

Word origin

The English word "tree" comes from the ancient Indo-European root *deru-*, derivatives of which include "endure," "trust" and "truth."

Anthropology

An arboreal theme is rooted in human perception, language and thought. Trees and tree-climbing have become psychic planks in the mind's evolutionary platform not only of Druids but modern folk as well. Bark and limbs still appeal to hands, and even now a human's primate eyes may seek shelter and safety overhead in branches and boughs. Thus influenced and inspired, Claude Monet (1840–1926) painted willows, while poets have celebrated oaks and municipal governments have lined their city streets with sycamores, maples and elms.

Culture

In the British Isles, knuckle-touch-wood – rapping the knuckles on a wooden surface – offers "protection." "This is an ancient superstitious practice dating back to the days of tree-worship, when it was the custom to touch the sacred oak to placate the powerful Tree Spirits. The roots of the mighty oak were thought to descend into the underworld" (Morris, 1994, 151).

Media

To focus world attention on the plight of redwood trees, American activist Julia Hill lived in an ancient redwood named "Luna" for 738 days, beginning on December 10, 1997. Explaining the significance of her bold gesture and months of survival on a wooden platform 180' above terra firma in northern California's Humboldt County, Hill invoked the nonverbal medium of touch: "'They [the redwoods] touched me unlike any malls, cars, make-up and [sic] magazines,' said Hill, who brought the audience to laughter by simulating the first time she hugged a redwood. 'It was a spiritual level that no cathedral, church or money could touch in me' (Tran, 2000).

Sacred trees

Nonverbally, the often great size of trees may be a factor in their worship (see *Loom*).

Important in the sacredness of trees, as well, is a spatial concept of being at the center (see *Proxemics*): "The tree cult is most clearly present in Ireland where there was a special term for the sacred tree, *bile*. Each tribe had a sacred tree, or grove of trees, probably at an inauguration site near the centre of the tribal territory" (Eliade, 1959).

See also *Branch substitute*; *Colors decoded*, Green; *Power grip*.

Trigeminal taste

"Taste" cue

The trigeminal sense is a third chemical sensor, working alongside smell and taste. Trigeminal (cranial V) nerve endings in the tongue and oral cavity sense, for example, pungent chemicals given off by such "hot" spices as red chili pepper (capsaicin), black pepper (piperine), mustards and horseradish (isothiocyanates) and onions (diallyl sulfide). They also respond to "cool" spices, such as mint (menthol) and to the chemical "bite" or "sharpness" of ethyl alcohol in tequila and rum.

Irritant

In each of these cases, trigeminal nerves respond to chemical irritants rather than to gustatory taste cues sensed by the facial nerve (cranial VII). Trigeminal taste is an important ingredient in many – perhaps in most – of the world's cuisines. (N.B.: Though babies initially experience aversive reactions to pungency in food, by adulthood many have acquired a seemingly indispensable need for trigeminal stimulation at mealtime.)

Nonverbal warning signs

Trigeminal taste evolved as a pain warning system, to protect the tongue and oral cavity from potentially dangerous or toxic substances. Many plants – notably those used as spices – have evolved efferent "pain" messages to discourage organisms such as snails, insects and mammals from eating their leaves, stems, fruit and seeds (see *Secondary product*). Why humans crave trigeminal stimulation in foods, beverages and oral-care products such as minty mouthwashes, toothpicks and toothpastes is as yet unknown. It has been suggested that the capsaicin in chili peppers works to release opioid substances which address the brain as pleasure cues. Perhaps, too, we like the thrill of culinary danger (see *Herbs and spices*).

See *Taste cue*.

Triumph display

Victory stance

A widespread, usually involuntary – and possibly universal – posture adopted shortly after kicking a goal, scoring a point or winning a game.

Usage

Triumph displays are used at diverse sporting events, from chess matches to soccer games, to proclaim victory after a win. The associated felt emotion is one of sudden joy, jubilation or happiness at winning.

Anatomy

In the triumph display one or both arms may be fully extended and lifted above the shoulder(s). Pronated hands may be open or fisted. One may stand or remain seated, and be silent or emit an exhilarated vocal cheer.

Nonverbal celebration

Triumph displays are ephemeral interjections given in the emotional heat of winning moments in time. The display may be evoked unconsciously by the brain's basal ganglia (see Neuro–notes, subsequently).

Neuro–notes

In spectator sports, triumph displays are contagious and may be performed simultaneously by thousands of like-minded fans (see *Isopraxism*). Collective cheering leads to emotional bonding and the release of oxytocin, while defeating a foe may release serotonin and dopamine to boost energy and release excited extension movements of the arms.

The display's arm extension involves paleocircuits of the basal ganglia and small networks of spinal-cord interneurons in charge of the muscle stretch reflex. These mini-networks mediate antigravity responses (see *Antigravity sign*), that is, muscular contractions that automatically extend our limbs to keep us standing upright without our consciously deciding to do so.

See also *Hand-clap, High-stand display*.

Trunk

Introduction

When discussing "trunk," the terms body and torso are often used interchangeably. The trunk refers to the central core part of the human body. It does not include the limbs or neck which protrude from the trunk. It includes the shoulders, back, abdomen and all the major organs of the body with the exception of the brain.

Examination of trunk movements typically fall into the two main categories of "trunk lean" and "trunk orientation."

Trunk lean

Trunk lean examines the degree to which the trunk makes an angle with a vertical line drawn from the mid-line of the head and chest to the mid-line of the hips. It is measured as erect, forward leaning or backward leaning. Trunk movements are also examined as a measure of "swivel." Here the degree to which the shoulders are turned so that one shoulder is in front of the hips and the other shoulder is behind the hips is examined.

Trunk orientation

Trunk orientation examines the degree to which the trunk is oriented to another individual. Typically, orientation is "scored" from 0 to 90 degrees, with 0 degrees representing direct orientation to another individual and 90 degrees representing a scenario where the trunk is turned perpendicularly to the other individual.

Tsk

Auditory cue

A voiceless dental click produced when the tongue tip lifts from the alveolar ridge of the palate to produce an audible clicking sound. The resulting "tsk" (American English) or "tut" (British English) may be heard in diverse societies as a nonverbal sign of emotional anger, annoyance, disapproval or sorrow. In a small number of traditional societies in southern Africa, dental clicks are used linguistically as consonants, as phonemic components of words.

Usage

Nonverbally, a tsk or series of tsks may be used as emotional signs of annoyance, confusion (Mexico), disapproval (Britain, United States) or grief; as logical signs of negation (Arabic, Hebrew) or affirmation (some Arabic tongues) and as attention-soliciting cues to animals (e.g., dogs, horses), young children and babies.

See also *Gasp*.

U

Ululation

Auditory trill

A protracted nonverbal, high-pitched vocal wailing or wavering sound modified by rapid, oscillating, side-to-side or up-and-down movements of the tongue. Ululations encode strong emotions – such as anger, happiness or sadness – and are most often given by women, rarely by men. Ululation is a usually group response that has been likened, in biology, to the contagious group-gobbling of turkeys (Soukhanov, 1993; see *Isopraxism*).

Usage

As celebratory or mourning calls, ululations may be used as nonverbal interjections at birth ceremonies, dances, funerals, graduations and weddings in areas of Africa, India, the Middle East and southern Europe. The oldest historical evidence for this practice dates to ancient Egypt and Greece. Prehistoric evidence is unknown, but since humans are primates – for whom vocal calling is common – the biological roots of ululation may reach back millions of years before the advent of vocal speech.

Neuro-note

The highly dexterous primate tongue evolved to manage food processing and avoid injury by the teeth. Its acrobatic movements are controlled by the hypoglossal nerve (Cranial XII).

See also *Falsetto*.

Uncertainty

Emotion

A cognitive feeling of indecision, misgiving or doubt.

Usage

Uncertainty may show in involuntary sideward eye movements called CLEMS; self-touching gestures; frowns; hand-behind-head cues; side-to-side head-shakes; head-tilt-side; lip-pout, lip-purse and tense-mouth; palm-up gestures and shoulder-shrugs. Fragmentary components of these nonverbal signs (e.g., a slightly lifted left shoulder) may reveal uncertainty as well.

Evolution

Feelings of uncertainty demonstrate a link between emotional and cognitive (or "thinking") modules of the brain.

Pervasive uncertainty

A current of free-floating uncertainty is often detectable in a spoken conversation's behavioral stream. Nonverbally, this may be evident in the frequency of a speaker's inadvertent shoulder-shrugs. Verbal uncertainty may be present as well in the use of such English hedge words as "someday," "somehow" and "something" and in phrases such as "maybe so," "sort of" and "kind of" (see *Kinda sorta*). In linguistics, a hedge word or phrase may signal a speaker's confidence in an assertion's truth. As the French philosopher René Descartes (1596–1650) noted, certainty must be supplemented by indubitability (Flew, 1979, 59).

Research reports

Signs of "perplexed reflection" include the frown (contraction of the corrugator "muscle of reflection"); down-cast eyes; touching the forehead, mouth or chin and beard-pulling (Darwin, 1872, 220–226). "In states of perplexity men will rub their chins with their hand, or tug at the lobes of their ears, or rub their forehead or cheeks or back of the neck. Women have very different gestures in such states. They will either put a finger on their lower front teeth with the mouth slightly open or pose a finger under the chin" (Montagu, 1971, 208). "The huu of puzzlement, surprise, or slight anxiety is directed toward such things as small snakes, unknown creature rustlings, dead animals, and the like. This sound is made even when a chimpanzee is alone" (Goodall, 1986, 131).

Neuro-notes I

An uncertain feeling is a secondary emotion mediated by the emotional limbic system (esp. the amygdala and anterior cingulate gyrus) and linked to cognitive thought processes via circuitry in prefrontal, sensory and association modules of the cerebral cortex (Damasio, 1994).

Neuro-notes II

Not everyone considers uncertainty an emotion, as Jerome Kagan (2007) does. An argument in favor is emotional uncertainty's involvement in the shoulder-shrug display. Like the muscles that activate facial expressions, upper trapezius activates our shrugs via links to emotional brain modules through special visceral efferent, rather than by somatic, nerves.

Neuro-notes III

In human beings free-floating uncertainty about one's fate in life – that is, existential doubt – begins in the anterior cingulate cortex (ACC). Through links to the amygdala, hypothalamus and pituitary and adrenal glands, the ACC triggers a sympathetic-nervous system response and release of cortisol (a stress hormone) into the bloodstream – and thence back into the brain.

See also *Human brain*.

V

Vehicular grille

Introduction

"Not long ago I started detecting what seemed like facial expressions while look-ing at cars and I thought I was going nuts" (E-Commentary: G.L.-C., CPNet.com (3/15/00 8:50:48 AM Pacific Standard Time).

Messaging feature

A nose- or mouth-shaped grating of metal or vinyl, used as a decoration at the front of an automobile, truck or bus. The "face" of a motor vehicle, unwittingly designed to show attitude.

Usage

The modern grille expresses a vehicle's personality by mimicking features of the face, esp. the lips, nose and teeth. Windshields and headlights may participate as illusory "eyes." Grilles suggest a variety of facial mood signs – from the friendly smile to the emotional tense-mouth – as they beckon for deference, demeanor and respect on the road.

Evolution

Through a process of consumer product selection, automobile front-ends today resemble faces. Originally, in the Ford family, for example, the 1903 Model A had neither a grille nor a vertical front end, but from 1908–1927, the Model T had a vertical front end with a framed radiator as a "proto-grille." In 1928, the Model A had a shapely, contoured radiator, like that of the early Lincoln, which suggested a vertically ascending nose. In 1932, the high-brow Lincoln's V-type radiator was clearly nose-like from the front view.

Recent history

In the 1940s, grille design shifted from noses to mouths. A case in point is Mercury's aggressive, tooth-showing grille of 1946, which resembled an angry bulldog poised to bite. After 1946, mouth motifs predominated, and subsequent nose shapes inad-vertently damaged sales of less expensive cars. Edsel's ill-fated "horse-collar" grille of 1958, for example, modeled after Packard's vertical center grille, doomed it to extinction. And yet nasal illusions helped sales of "aristocratic" vehicles such as the Jaguar and Mercedes-Benz, which "looked down their noses" at lesser automobiles (see *Head-tilt-back*). In 1955, the Mercury Montclair featured a redesigned bumper grille housing what looked like free-standing teeth and thick, horizontal projections that resembled tusks. From 1955–57, the Ford Thunderbird featured "tusks" as well and a mouth-like grille poised, seemingly, to shout, "Hey!" In 1963, the Mercury

Breezeway added tusk-like dual headlights to its grille configuration. In 1966, the Mercury Comet Cyclone's tense-mouth grille appeared toothless and without tusks, but non-functional hood scoops compensated for its defanged look by adding "muscle" (i.e., engine power) to the car. In the same year, the Mercury Cougar's front end featured a bumper that curled up on the outer extremities and an insouciant grille resembling the silent-bared teeth face of monkeys and apes (Van Hooff, 1967)

Neuro-notes

Links between biting, chewing, showing fangs, anger and fear have been found in the anterior hypothalamus "in a region of converging nerve fibres involved in angry and defensive behaviour" (MacLean, 1973, 16). Like faces, grilles are decoded in the anterior inferotemporal cortex, while their familiarity registers in the superior temporal polysensory area (Young and Yamane, 1992, 1327). The emotional impact of grilles registers in the amygdala.

See also *Vehicular stripe*.

Vehicular stripe

Introduction

"It was an effort to make the car look longer and lower."

Messaging feature

A horizontal pinstripe, painted by hand or mechanical means, running the length of a motor vehicle just below the windows. Any of several thin, linear markings of chrome stripping or vinyl, or stamped as embossments or indentations, running along the sides of an automobile or truck body.

Usage

Vehicular stripes decorate virtually all U.S. automobiles produced since 1927. Through a nonverbal optical illusion, horizontal stripes suggest that cars are both "longer" and "lower" to the ground. Horizontal stripes also may suggest greater "speed."

Neuro-notes

The human eye is highly stimulated by edges, lines and linear details (perhaps from a primate fascination with branches and trees). Just as the linear necktie (see *Neckwear*) creates an illusion of greater verticality and physically imposing height (see *High-stand display*), the automobile pinstripe creates an illusory vision of length and speed. This is because one layer of our primary visual cortex contains specialized orientation-selective neurons which respond only to vertical or horizontal lines or to linear angles between the two.

See also *Vehicular grille*.

Velvet

Tactile-visual-verbal cue

A delightfully soft, colorful fabric – esteemed by royalty since ca. 2,000 years ago in Egypt and subsequently in China and Turkey – that continues to delight the senses today. Woven in a variety of fibers from cotton to wool, the softest velvets are made of silk.

Usage

Velvet is used worldwide in clothing (see *Clothing cue*), drapery and tapestries.

Nightly stars

Among the most popular of all velvet tapestries are those of the classic painting, The Starry Night (1889) by Vincent van Gogh (1853–1890). As a nonverbal composition, velvet versions of "Starry Night" deliciously engage our senses of balance (see *Balance cue*), color (*color cue*) and touch (*touch cu*E). In a triumphant sensory symphony, velvet Starry Night hits the brain with a hallucinogenic rush (see *Art cue*, Form constants).

Verbal velvet

English "velvet" derives from Latin *villus*, "shaggy hair" (see *Hair cue*). The word has been extended from fabric to music (e.g., Bobby Vinton's 1963 dance rendition of "Blue Velvet"; see *Dance*), demeanor ("suave"), food ("velvety texture") and vocal tone (Mel Tormé [1925–1999] "The Velvet Fog"; see *Tone of voice*).

See also *Glitter, Paisley, Verbalized nonverbal*.

Verbal communication

Concept

The process of sending and receiving word-based messages by means of manual sign language and voice (see *Speech, Word*). Also included are written texts – writings – using alphabetic, diagrammatic, ideographic, numeric, pictographic and syllabic signs to convey messages (see *Information*). As concepts, though "verbal" and "nonverbal" contrast, they are not logical opposites; both may be intimately linked, and boundaries between the two often overlap.

Usage

Verbal communication is used to record, share, store and transmit information about, for example, environmental conditions, events, feelings, ideas, locations, measurements, objects and relationships in space and time.

Punctuation

In writing systems, punctuation marks may be both verbal and nonverbal. English ellipses, for example (. . .), may be used to suggest a nonlinguistic pause between linguistic signs. English exclamation points (!!) may be used to suggest an emotional commitment or overloud tone of voice. The precise boundaries between verbal and nonverbal signs are not always clear.

Language origin

Anthropologists estimate that human language originated between ca. 200,000 (Lieberman, 1991) and 2 million (Gibson, 1993) years ago. Linguistic communication likely evolved from diverse forms of nonverbal communication commencing with electromagnetic transmissions of information and ending with the protean design of the human larynx. Fifteen nonverbal steps leading to speech have been proposed, including acrobatic tongue movements, dexterous lips and binocular vision. "Today's verbal communication reflects the earlier medium's role in (1) self-assertion, (2) species recognition, (3) genetic reproduction, (4) emotional expression and (5) attention to objects (Givens, 2020).

See also *Nonverbal communication*.

Figure V.1 Verbalized nonverbal

Verbalized nonverbal

Verbal sign

A written or spoken word or phrase with the same meaning as the nonverbal sign it labels.

Usage

Verbalized nonverbals are used in writing and speaking to mimic the actions of visual nonverbal signs.

Red flag

An example of a verbalized nonverbal is the English phrase, "red flag." The nonverbal referent of a spoken red-flag phrase includes the usually rectangular, reddened cloth waved, or emplaced, as a visual warning sign to onlookers of impending danger. The flag's flapping movement and vivid hue attract notice to such issues as high fire danger or a riptide. Early red flags include the ca. 1300 crimson warning streamers of Norman ships, flown as warnings to possible enemies.

Verbalization

Not only does a colloquial "red flag" refer to the material scarlet cloth but also may signal an impending danger in the economic, medical or legal sense. The "red flag laws" enforced in several U.S. states are cases in point. These laws enable states to temporarily seize the firearms of likely dangerous people.

See also *Color cue*, Red.

Verbal pause

Nonverbal sign

In face-to-face settings, a momentary break in speech dialogue often brought on by a difficult or challenging question.

Usage

As a significant deviation from baseline speaking behavior (see *Baseline demeanor*), a verbal pause may be used as an opportunity to examine an unverbalized – that is, a hidden, undisclosed or withheld – belief, mood or opinion (see *Probing point*).

Emotion cues

Verbal pauses may show that strong, sudden-onset emotions – such as anger (displeasure), fear (stage fright), shame (embarrassment) and uncertainty (bewilderment, confusion) – are likely interfering with rational thought. Such aroused feelings may "give pause" and lead speakers to become temporarily speechless.

Neuro-notes

Right-brain-hemispheric emotions may be sufficiently aroused to transiently shut down left-brain speech centers, such as Broca's area.

See also *Vocal filler*.

Vision cues

Visual signals

Incoming signs received through the eyes, causing the brain to see. Outgoing signs produced by the reflection of light from physical objects (e.g., automobile grilles, clothing and footwear) or body parts (e.g., the hands in waving and the eyelids in blinking).

Evolution

Our higher-primate (anthropoid) ancestors ca. 35–40 mya had an enlarged visual cortex at the back of the head on the occipital lobe with which to process color vision and depth. Today, the anthropoid's is the most complex visual cortex on earth, with anatomically separate areas for analyzing form, coordinating hand-and-eye movements and recognizing faces. A few nerve cells in the lower temporal lobe are so narrowly specialized that they respond only to hands and faces.

Neuroanatomy I

Light reflected from objects and body parts casts tiny images on the eye's nerve-sensitive retina. From here, electrochemical impulses cable through the optic nerve to a visual area at the back of the neocortex called V1. V1 neurons respond to linear details and to wavelengths of color (see *Color cue*).

Neuroanatomy II

A second visual area, V2 (in front of V1), enhances our image of linear and color aspects of objects and bodily features. Additional processing takes place in V3 (recognition of form and movement), V4 (additional color recognition) and V5 (movement) (Restak, 1994). Apart from our awareness, these modular areas of neocortex unify and give nonverbal meaning to our vision of objects and body parts.

Neuroanatomy III

In the primate brain, modules of the inferior temporal neocortex evolved to provide visual input to the occipital neocortex's parvocellular interblob system (V1 to V2 and V4), permitting recognition of complex shapes, and to the inferior temporal cortex, permitting heightened responses to hand gestures and the ability to recognize faces and facial expressions.

Neuro-notes

The inferior temporal cortex receives information fed forward through a series of sensory and association areas, beginning with the retina's relay in the occipital lobe. The temporal cortex itself has become a remarkably specialized part of the nonverbal brain. Some of its cells respond, for example, only to frontal or profile views of the face, while others fire only when facial expressions appear (Kandel, 1991, 459). Familiarity registers in the superior temporal polysensory area (Young and Yamane, 1992, 1327).

See also *Eyes*.

Vocal filler

Filled pause

A voiced word (e.g., "well . . .") or nonword sound ("um . . .") inserted into an otherwise fluent stream of verbal speech. English "well" is often used to preface a vocal response to questions; versions of the "well" vocalization are in widespread use around the world (e.g., Irish Gaelic *bhoil*, Italian *allora* and Norwegian *vel*).

Usage

Vocal fillers may be read as nonverbal signs of agreement (e.g., "mmm"), disagreement ("huh-uh"), interjection ("eee") or uncertainty ("ah" or "uh"). Fillers also may be used to maintain speaking turns while thinking or mentally searching for words.

Speech rate

People typically speak at an average speech rate of between 125 and 175 words per minute. This contrasts with the average rate of words produced cognitively, which is between 400 and 800 words per minute. In some instances, this gap may be filled with silences, speech dysfluencies or filled pauses.

Silent pauses

Silent pauses (when nothing is said) represent thinking time, allowing for speaker to plan the words and sentence clauses to come. Spontaneous speech usually has a rhythm which incorporates these clauses. We alternate between fluent and hesitant phases. So how do we interpret these pauses?

Filled pauses

These occur when some form of phonation is inserted to fill the pause. Examples include "er," "um," "mmm" and "uh." While some who coach people in the art of rhetoric argue that filled pauses (with, for example, utterances such as "um" or "er") detract from the persuasive nature of speech (Deese, 1984), there is significant evidence to indicate that the use of "ers" and "ums" in speech does not indicate poor speaker competence about the topic in question (Schachter et al., 1991). Rather, the use of "ers" and "ums" has been found to increase as the topic becomes more abstract and complex (Reynolds and Paivio, 1968; Christenfeld, 1994) and as the speaker engages with a wider vocabulary (Schachter et al., 1991). When one considers the number and frequency of "filled pauses," Christenfeld (1995) found that too many filled pauses produced negative evaluations from the listener.

Gender

On a gender level, some research has found that found that "filled pauses" figure more prominently in the speech patterns of men rather than women (Hall, 1984).

Neuro-note

Some vocal fillers may show that Broca's area has momentarily shut down, as in aphasia (see *Verbal center*, Broca's area).

See also *Verbal pause*.

Voice (tone)

Voice quality

The manner in which a verbal statement is presented, for example, its breathiness, hoarseness, loudness, rhythm or pitch. Those paralinguistic qualities of speaking and vocalizing not usually included in the study of languages and linguistics (see subsequently, Research reports).

Figure V.2 Voice tone

Usage

Tone of voice may reflect psychological arousal, feelings and mood (see *Emotion*). It may also carry social information, as in a sarcastic, superior or submissive manner of speaking.

The voice and emotion

The human voice provides significant social information about the speaker's emotional state (Banse and Scherer, 1996) and their social intentions (Mitchell and Ross, 2013). The human makes inferences about other individuals' emotions based on how their voice sounds (e.g., Pell and Skorup, 2008). The ability to decode information and expressions of emotion from the voice has been found to improve with age, until mid-adolescence. By this age, adult-like skills are evident (Allgood and Heaton, 2015; Zupan, 2015). However, some recent work which examines the "social brain network" in adolescence suggests that emotional processes may continue to be fine-tuned into adulthood (Kilford et al., 2016). It may come as a surprise, but "it is still debated whether the voice conveys discrete emotions to listeners" (Juslin et al., 2018). Inconsistent findings from research on emotion and particular voice cues have made it difficult for researchers to "attach" particular vocal expressions or characteristics to particular emotions (Cowie et al., 2001; Frick, 1985; Juslin and Laukka, 2003; Murray and Arnott, 1993; Scherer, 1986).

Vocal intonation and pitch

Pitch has to do with the number of vocal vibrations of the vocal folds. These vibrations are dependent on the length and thickness of the vocal cords. The vibrations are also affected by the tightening and relaxation of the muscles surrounding the vocal chords. This explains why women generally have higher voices than men do – they have shorter vocal cords. The sound of your voice changes as the rate of the vibrations varies. As the number of vibrations per second increases, so does the pitch, meaning the voice would sound higher. Faster rates form higher voices (higher pitches), while slower rates produce deeper voices, or lower pitches. To illustrate this, think of situations where people become frightened or excited. The muscles around the voice box (or larynx) unconsciously contract, putting strain on the vocal cords, making the pitch higher.

Aprosodia

Like aphasia (the dominant, left-brain hemisphere's inability to articulate or comprehend speech), aprosodia is an inability to articulate or comprehend emotional voice tones. Aprosodia is due to damage in the right-brain's temporal-lobe language areas. Patients with aprosodia may miss the affective (or "feeling") content of speech. Persons with damage to the right frontal lobe may speak in a flat or monotone voice devoid of normal inflection.

Non-linguistic sounds

Many of the sounds humans produce in everyday life are non-linguistic (Provine, 2012a, 2012b). Indeed, for humans, the use of language involves older neural networks which produce non-linguistic vocalizations (Ackermann et al., 2014). For example, congenitally deaf (Scheiner et al., 2006) infants make sounds like typical infants (e.g., laughing). Evidence from evolutionary history suggests that human vocalizing abilities may "have been essentially in place 400,000 years ago" (Patel and Scherer, 2013, 167). There is a view that primitive vocalizations involved "affect bursts" of language which had a means for affective and social communication. Patel and Scherer (2013, 168) argue that "this implies that the phylogenetically recent, highly cognitive mode of speech communication has been grafted upon a phylogenetically old vocal call system mainly used for affective and social signalling."

Dominance

According to "communication accommodation" researchers, people may unconsciously adapt to each other's voice tones. When two people converse, the person whose deeper, low-toned voice changes the least may be perceived by both parties as having the more dominant social status.

Universality

Though subject to cultural modification and shaping, a significant number of voice qualities may be universal across human cultures.

1   Around the world, for example, adults may use higher-pitched voices to speak to infants and young children. The softer pitch is innately "friendly" and suggests a nonaggressive, non-hostile pose.
2   With each other, men and women may use higher-pitched voices in greetings to show harmlessness and invite emotional closeness (see *Courtship*).
3   In many languages, speakers use rising intonations to ask questions. The higher vocal register may appease a request for information – possibly an imposition – and is often accompanied by diffident palm-up gestures and submissive shoulder-shrugs (see *Shoulder-shrug display*; for neurological links between tone of voice and these body movements, see *Special visceral nerve*).
4   The human brain is programmed to respond with specific emotions to certain specific vocal sounds (see, e.g., *Cry*, Infancy; *Music*, Neuro-notes I; *Startle reflex*, Neuro-notes).

Ritual

Human beings may use emotion-evoking nonvocal sounds in their ceremonies, rites and rituals. In Japan, for example, the rhythmic clacking of cherry wood clappers (*hyoshigi*) is used to begin traditional sumo contests. The rhythmic sound appeals emotionally to the right-brain cerebral hemisphere rather than logically to the left (see *Human brain*, Right brain, left brain).

Politics

1   "Would Martin Luther King's 'dream' [speech] have captured the imagination of white and black Americans alike had he pronounced his vision in a squeaking soprano? Doubtful" (Blum, 1998, 3–8).
2   Dunbar and Bernhold (2019, 269) observe that "people perceive male politicians with lower-pitched voices as more dominant, attractive, trustworthy, intelligent, and honest, as well as less likely to be involved in a government scandal."

See also *Kinesics*, *Throat-clear*.

Vroom-vroom

Announcement of presence

A loud roaring noise emitted by a motor vehicle as it accelerates or as a driver pumps the gas.

Usage

Nonverbal vrooming noises are often used by young men to attract attention to themselves in service to courtship (see *Reproductive force*).

Media

A popular recorded version of vrooming by The Shangri-Las singing group became a number-one U.S. hit in 1964. "Leader of the Pack" featured rhythmically repeated motorcycle-engine revving sounds to accent the song's instrumentation and words (see *Music*).

Emotional valence

That we perceive a vrooming sound as being either pleasant or unpleasant is due, in part, to the evolutionary nature of sound. Since the latter sensation evolved from the tactile sense, it may connote a sense of being touched, an often intimately personal sensation.

Semantics

The essential meaning of vroom-vroom is "I am here; notice me!" Like its more pleasant biological cousin, birdsong, noisy vrooming sounds may simultaneously attract potential mates and challenge rivals.

Neuro-notes

The deep growling, guttural sound of vrooming may be sensed as anger by the emotional brain (see *Amygdala*). Its loudness elicits a looming response that makes the vehicle and its driver seem "larger." Its sudden onset may trigger the brain's auditory startle response (see *Startle reflex*).

See also *Auditory cue*.

W

Waiting time

Introduction

According to the American anthropologist Edward Hall, "Time talks" (1973, 2). "Until the early 1300s, the length of an hour in London could vary from 38 minutes to 82 minutes. It wasn't because they had lousy clocks in the Middle Ages. They just had a different attitude toward the passage of that mysterious thing called time" (Suplee, 1994, H1).

Chronemic cue

The number of seconds, minutes, hours, days or weeks spent between a scheduled appointment and a meeting with a business associate, medical professional, program administrator or friend. Emotionally, the longer one is made to wait, the angrier he or she may become.

Usage

Waiting time varies across cultures. Appointments with business executives or government officials in Latin America, for example, may require longer wait times than are customary for U.S. workers. The different cultural norms for time spent waiting may trigger anger and disliking and may damage rapport. (N.B.: Waiting time may be less for attractive, liked or high-status individuals.)

Cultural differences

"In northern Europe, the people are exact and precise about time, much like Americans on the East Coast. The northern Germans and Swiss are particularly punctual" (Vargas, 1986, 127). "In South America, most people know no other way of living and never explain or apologize [for being late]. To my [U.S.] upper Midwest sensitivity, their lack of respect for clock time is almost unbelievable" (Vargas, 1986, 127).

Media

"In Italy . . . television stations make no effort to begin their programs on the hour or half hour. One program is run until finished, and a new one begins with no concern for clock times or schedules" (Vargas, 1986, 127).

Time messages

In the West, time is thought to be non-spatial, linear, continuous and irreversible and to have a past, a present and a future. In nonverbal studies, time is included in what researchers call chronemics, the role of time in human communication.

Time sense

Along with balance, hearing, sight, smell, taste and touch, human beings have a highly developed sense of time. So time oriented has our species become that we may define distance in chronometric terms. By international agreement, "the meter is defined as the distance light travels in 1/299,792,458 of a second" (Itano and Ramsey, 1993, 64).

Research reports

According to Hall (1959), as a nonverbal sign, waiting time in the United States has eight levels of duration: immediate, very short, short, neutral, long, very long, terribly long and forever.

See also *Proxemics*.

Figure W.1 Walk

Walk

Body movement

To travel by taking steps with the legs and feet, at a pace slower than jogging, sprinting or running.

Usage

Walking underlies some key nonverbal signs. While we walk on hind limbs to commute from point A to B, the manner and style of one's gait (e.g., marching, mincing or swaggering) telegraphs information about status, feelings and moods. Our bipedal walk's two-point rhythm provides the neurological foundation for music's syncopated beat, and for the oscillating movements of dance.

Anthropology

A bipedal stride enabled human ancestors to cover great distances on African grasslands ca. 3 mya. Survival required that they stay continually on the move (Devine, 1985). The earliest physical evidence for human-style walking dates back 3.5 mya to the tracks of three upright ancients, probably australopithecines, who strolled across a bed of fresh volcanic ash one day on the East-African savannah in what is now Laetoli, Tanzania. The footprints are nearly identical to those of modern humans, only smaller.

Kinematic movement

One way of examining walking styles involves an examination of the kinematic features of walking. This involves an examination of "the centre of movement."

A person's center of movement can be determined from examining the relation between the swing of the hips and shoulders. It is a reference point around which all bodily movements have geometric relations. For example, males have a lower centre of movement as compared with females (Cutting and Kozlowski, 1977).

Point-light displays

Point-light displays provide a lighted "picture" of the moving human corpus (they do not include extraneous points such as hair). Using such displays, a number of researches have been able to show considerable reliability in people's abilities to judge age and dominance and to identify both themselves and friends (Stevenage et al., 1999; Montepare and Zebrowitz-McArthur, 1988; Runeson and Frykholm, 1983).

Age of body overgeneralization effect

The age of body overgeneralization effect occurs when people's impressions of others are influenced by age-related gait and body structures. For example, research by Montepare and Zebrowitz-McArthur (1988) which examined young adults who dragged their feet and had a slower walking speed (a gait similar to a 70-year-old) were perceived as less powerful when compared to the more energetic walk of their peers. Indeed, this research found that "young adults with youthful gaits were perceived as more powerful and happier than peers with older gaits, irrespective of their masculine gait qualities, sex, and perceived age" (Montepare and Zebrowitz-McArthur, 1988, 547).

Media I

"I am in the moment, living the experience, when I am walking" – Joy Jones ("Meaningful Steps," *Washington Post*, p. D5, September 11, 1992).

Media II

The scariest movie monsters walk upright like human beings. Their resemblance to people renders them even more terrible than ordinary land (i.e., quadrupedal), air and sea monsters. Bipedal dinosaurs (e.g., *Velociraptor* and *Tyrannosaurus* in the 1993 movie Jurassic Park), insectoids (Aliens, 1996) and primates (King Kong, 1933) resonate with horrific images of the looming, upright human form.

Neuro-notes I

The natural rhythm of our upright, bipedal gait is coordinated by the same spinal paleocircuits that programmed the oscillatory swimming motions of the early fishes (Grillner, 1996).

Neuro-notes II

Impulses to go on walkabout are coordinated by oscillatory circuits of the spinal cord, by excitatory centers of the amphibian brain and by basal ganglia of the reptilian brain.

Research reports

1   Gait changes with age. Toddlers have a different gait to adults by virtue of the wider stance and shorter steps (Connor et al., 1978). Adults also walk faster and have longer step length as compared to toddlers (Cowgill et al., 2010). On the other hand, compared with younger adults, older adults take shorter steps and have a slower gait, with less arm swing and more forward lean (Murray et al., 1969).

2   Sometimes people make extrapolations about emotions based on gait. For example, a strong walk with long strides is sometimes attributed to anger. A happy emotion can be inferred from a gait with a fast pace and bouncy steps (Montepare et al., 1987). Satchell et al. (2017), found connections between personality traits and their manifestation in people's gait, specifically in relation to walking speed and the degree of upper and lower body movement.

3   Research also suggests that certain individuals can exhibit vulnerability through their gait and that these cues are particularly relevant for potential victims of interpersonal crimes (Book et al., 2013; Stevens, 1994; Wheeler et al., 2009). Research by Blaskovits and Bennell in 2019 found that observers were agreed on the walk of 'easy targets' and these 'easy targets' for victimization tended to exhibit vulnerable gait cues. Specifically, they found that individuals who "exhibited long or short strides, a lateral, diagonal, or up/down shift movement, a gestural walk, unilateral arm/leg movements, and lifted foot movements, tend to be perceived as those most vulnerable to experience future victimization" (Blaskovits and Bennell, 2019, 330)

4   Stevenage et al. (1999) suggest that the human gait is a marker of personal identity and that the human perceptual system is finely tuned to appraising this gait.

5   Deliberate attempts to deceive an observer by changing one's walk (for example, faking a limp) have been shown to be difficult to do. In "faking" some of the body movements, the human will not be able to create all of the kinematic details of the real and proper actions in order to convince the perceiver that the "fake gait" is real (Runeson and Frykholm, 1983).

See also *Arm-swing*, *Goose-step*, *Swagger-walk*.

Walk the dog

Tail gait

A daily ritual in which a nonverbal canine and very verbal primate stroll together on a usually flat surface, such as a road, sidewalk or lawn (see *Neo-savannah grassland*). While the canine pays attention to chemical signals on tree trunks and fire hydrants (see *Aroma cue*), the primate may watch the canine's tail for signs of emotion and mood.

Usage

Dog walks are nonverbal colloquies between man and beast. They are used for rapport-building and exercise. Both species walk to explore landscapes in and around the residents' shared home base. While humans visually scan the landscape, dogs sniff and smell. Both walkers alert to fundamentally different environmental features (see *Orienting reflex*).

Pedestrian petition

A dog may bark, bring a leash or face the front door to request a walk. A human may respond verbally – "Go for a walk?" – in an excited voice with rising pitch. The dog may paw at the door and make eye contact to confirm the request, and the walk begins. Such "conversation" precedes a walk, and the nonverbal colloquy continues on route.

Tail talk

As they stroll, the tailless primate may decode the canine's tail movements and positions as signs. A tail curled downward between the legs indicates fear. A dog's lateral tail-wag (through contractions of the sacrococcygeus ventralis muscle) suggests a positive "happy" state. Tail talk is mediated by limbic-system fiber links to the pelvic floor (Holstege, 2016).

See also *Animal sign.*

Figure W.2 Wan smile

Wan smile

Grim grin

A feeble smirk modified by facial and bodily signs of regret or unhappiness (see *Sadness*).

Usage

A wan smile may be used to show that one is hoping to rise above a misfortune, reversal or setback. "Manage a wan smile" is a frequently used phrase in English literature, as in the 2010 historical novel *The Scarlet Contessa*: "Despite the horror of the preceding day, I managed a wan grin"(Kalogridis, 2019).

Verbal

English "wan" (suggestive of paleness, weariness or unhappiness) derives from Old English *wann* (dark, gloomy; Soukhanov, 1992). Many spoken languages have phrases pointing to weak smiles, as in Spanish *sonreír con poco entusiasmo*, "to smile with little enthusiasm."

Laconic smile

A wan smile may also be laconic, as in brief, short-lived or terse (see *chronemics*). Some wan grins may be wry as well, that is, annoyed, displeased or disgusted (see *Disgust*).

See also *Zygomatic smile.*

Wedding dress

Clothing cue

A bridal gown designed to showcase feminine nonverbal signs and draw attention to the wearer in a marriage ceremony. An expressive garment, often of ample fabric, whose color may be of emotional, social or symbolic significance. A usually dramatic display of fertility in service to the reproductive force.

Usage

A wedding dress is used to visually announce that its wearer is about to change – or has changed – her social status from single to married. For younger wearers, the dress may also be read as a change from child to adult status. Wedding gowns may be preceded by ceremonial, coming-of-age clothing, such as the American prom dress, whose messaging features closely mirror those of matrimonial gowns.

Messaging features

Wedding gowns may be designed to highlight physical contrasts between female and male bodily features. A gown may suggestively reveal a woman's gracile neck; curvilinear shoulders and thinner arms, wrists and waist. Sleeveless gowns bare shoulders, while puffy sleeves suggest a diffident shrug (see *Shoulder-shrug*). Excessive fabric may encode a surreal message of "floating" and of a larger-than-life presence (see *Loom*). A wedding dress may be symbolically color coded.

Red

In China, Japan and other Eastern countries, wedding dresses may be bright red to attract attention and symbolize good luck.

White

In Canada, Ireland and the United States, wedding gowns may be white to suggest purity and wealth. White was widely emulated in the West after England's Queen Victoria wore white at her wedding in 1840 (see *Isopraxism*).

Plaid

Native American brides of California's Yurok tribe wore white (to symbolize the east), blue (south), yellow or orange (west) and black (north) to suggest an emotional connection to Earth.

See also *Love signal*, *Reproductive force*.

Whisper

Voiceless chatter

An often intimate, breathy manner of speaking with little or no auditory vibration of the larynx (see *Speech*). Whisper chat is often addressed in very close proximity to one of a listener's ears (see *Ear*).

Universality

Based on the large number of languages that have a freestanding word for "whisper" (e.g., Hungarian suttogas, Japanese sasayaku and Spanish susurro), whispering is a widespread behavior. That some languages, such as Navajo, may not have a whisper word suggests that whispering is not universal. According to the Summer Institute of Linguistics (SIL), all human languages have at least one voiceless consonant (in English, e.g., "p," "s" and "t"), which suggests that the ability to speak without vocalizing is a phonological universal.

Nonverbal qualities

Though a hushed mode of verbal speech, whisper talk exhibits an assortment of nonverbal traits. Whispering may take place in Edward Hall's "intimate zone" (see *Proxemics*), close to another's body, head and shoulders. As those nearby are excluded, whisper senders and receivers may bond as secret sharers. A whisper may take place with an open hand cupped beside the whisperer's face for added privacy. Given the physical closeness of a whisper huddle, mutual eye-contact and speaking gestures may be minimal or absent (see *Gesture, Eye-contact*). At close quarters, the listener will feel the warmth and smell the ambient aroma of a speaker's breath (see *Aroma cue*).

Manual whispering

Users of manual sign languages (e.g., ASL and ISL) may "whisper" to another by making their hand signs smaller or by reducing their visibility (e.g., dropping signs below the waist; see *Sign language*).

Nonverbal Antonym: *Shout*.

Whistle

Auditory cue

Any of several nonverbal, usually high-pitched, pure tones used to send messages designed to attract attention, emit warnings and musically entertain. A whistled sound may be produced by an artifact such as a fabricated reed, a consumer product such as a police whistle or by human lips in a pucker whistle. When they encode intonation patterns of human speech, whistles may emit verbal messages (see *Whistled languages*).

Usage

Nonverbal whistles may be used variously to announce, beckon, caution, flirt, greet and warn of danger. Verbal whistling may be used to communicate linguistic information in the manner of speech. Some airport security systems (e.g., Screening of Passenger by Observational Techniques) label whistling as an indicator of stress (Denault et al., 2019).

Artifact

Whistles have been fashioned from gourds, shells and wood since prehistoric times. The semantic messages sent by the first whistles are unknown, but surely a generic "I am here" message was among the earliest to be sent and received.

Consumer products

Mass-produced whistles are available for purchase today as consumer products. Among the first commercial items was the police or "pea" whistle, marketed to Scotland Yard in 1884. The whistle's enclosed tiny round ball gave an alternating, trilled sound effect to its high-pitched tone, adding both loudness and "authority" ("I repeat: Hear me!") to the emitted call. A whistle's trill commands attention and is, like the Alpine yodel, audible over great distances. The sound cuts through ambient environmental background noise like a siren.

Whistled languages

Introduction

Human lip – "pucker" – whistles may be used melodically as music to carry a tune. The most popular whistled tune may be Bing Crosby's 1942 birdlike rendition of "White Christmas." Whistled speech is found in more than 30 of the world's languages (Meyer, 2008). Their signals encode the vocal words of the spoken language. A number of whistle languages have evolved in Africa (e.g., Yoruba), the Americas (esp. Mexico), Asia (Hmong) and Europe (La Gomera) to carry melodic intonations of speech across gorges, rain forests, rivers and other distances over which spoken conversation is not possible face to face.

Communication

There are some strong overlaps between spoken and whistled language. Research shows, for example, that among proficient whistlers, those areas of the brain which are activated during spoken language are also active in whistling, showing similarities in how the brain processes this kind of information (Carreiras et al., 2005).

Women's shoes

Clothing cue

A feminine style of footwear marked with messaging features designed to contrast with those of men's shoes (see, e.g., *High heel*).

Usage

In expressive style, women's shoes may reveal, conceal or mask the feminine foot (see *Feet*).

Baring

Women's revealing shoes bare the toes, heel, ankle and (or) top of the foot (i.e., the instep). Revealing shoes call attention to a woman's usually thinner bones, smaller joints and more delicate Achilles tendons. Examples include 1920s low-cut pumps, with straps buttoned or buckled across the instep; 1930s high heels with ankle straps and peep-toes and pointed, stiletto heels of the 1950s and 60s (which may also reveal toe cleavage, i.e., the hollow between the big toe and second digit).

Binding

Concealing shoes cover, yet do not hide, the feet. Rather, they enhance the foot's feminine silhouette, contour and shape. A concealing shoe's laces and close, binding fit may transmit a suggestive, erotic message of tight containment. Types of concealing shoes include ankle-high buttoned boots of the 1900s; 1970s mid-calf boots, cut close to the leg and tight, patent-leather, ankle-high shoes worn by pop singers of the 1980s.

Masking

Revealing and concealing shoes proclaim femininity, individuality and sexual allure. In contrast, the lady's masking shoe covers the foot but suggests little about sexuality, individuality or mood. Indeed, because they are visually quiet, masking shoes downplay personality by discouraging its notice. Worn with socks, "sensible" shoes tend to be boxy, sturdy, squared-off and somewhat masculine in appearance.

Personality

Women's shoes may display more "personality" than men's. Many styles, for example, are given personal names, such as the Nordstrom® line's "Angelique," "Gretta" and "Bree." See also *Leg wear* and *Men's shoes*.

Word

Verbal signal

An articulated sound or sounds uttered to convey information, express emotion, suggest ideas or opinions or greet a person, place or thing (see *Speech*). In manual sign language, an articulated body movement or movements used to communicate as in speech. In writing, an alphabetical, ideographic, pictographic or symbolic version of a verbal sound or body motion that may be variously stored through inscriptions carved in stone, characters on paper or images saved on computers.

Usage I

Words have diverse uses as labels for objects (e.g., "walnut"), directions ("west") and activities ("walk"). Some words (e.g., "the") have linguistic uses rather than referential or conceptional meanings. Words are spoken, signed or written in the sequential order governed by cultural rules, syntax and grammar.

Usage II

A great deal of our verbiage is about artifacts (e.g., Big Macs®, blue jeans and shoes), that is, about items in the ever-growing stockpile of material goods we possess or dream of owning. The partnership between consumer products and words may be as ancient as Oldowan stone tools and the likely labels our ancestors may have used to articulate knowledge of their design. Echoing prehistory, artifacts and brand names form a natural partnership in the mind – and in the media – today.

Anthropology

"To know the 'true name' of a thing was thought to be a source of power over it in many traditions" (Deacon, 1997, 321).

Authors' note

When asked about the irony of using words to study nonverbal communication, we answer that words help raise nonverbal issues to a conscious awareness. (N.B.: As Joseph Conrad prefaced in *The Nigger of the "Narcissus"*: it is "by the power of the written word, to make you hear, to make you feel – it is, before all, to make you see").

Gesture origin

"We take the view that language is based in gesture – that is, bodily movement to which human beings attach meaning" (Armstrong et al., 1995, 3). (Authors' note: Words themselves are produced by articulated body movements of the vocal tract.)

Literary criticism

"The very act of naming something is an attempt both to define it and possess it" (Cohen, 1993, 3).

Media

In the beginning was the "Pause," which became the "Real Thing" (see *Coca-Cola®*). 1929: "The Pause that Refreshes." 1961: "Things go Better with Coke." 1969: "It's the Real Thing." 1982: "Coke is it!" 1993: "Always the Real Thing." 1995: According to a Gallup Organization poll, over 60 percent of the Chinese population say they have heard the brand name Coca-Cola®.

Neuro-notes

At the level of neurons, saying, signing or writing a word is not unlike striking flakes from a pebble core to make a stone tool. In right-handed people, all four activities involve premotor and motor areas on the left side of the forebrain (which controls the right side of the body). Older regions of forebrain (see *Basal ganglia* and *Reptilian brain*) underlie tool making and the ability to speak. Through general coordination of motor control, the substantia nigra of the midbrain is part of the speech process as well. The hindbrain's neocerebellum, too, plays a role in coordinating the voluntary movements of our very verbal digits and very vocal tongue. Thus, neural templates for tools and words are shared on many levels of the brain (see *Language origin*).

See also *Language origin*, *Verbal center*.

X

X-ray

Micro wave

An electromagnetic, wave-like particle of light – an energized photon. Photons are at the very root of human communication, verbal and nonverbal.

Usage

Invisible to the naked eye, x-rays and other photons are ubiquitous and provide a basis for information storage and transmission (see *Information*). Photons transmit sunlight and electric light and power the world's myriad microwave ovens.

I am here

The first information was sent and received by fundamental subatomic particles ca. 13.8 bya. Specifically, electrons communicated with individual electrons by means of an emitted photon, warning each other, for example, to avoid collision by changing course (Krauss, 2017). The essential meaning was "I am here." It was established early on that electrons should send and receive such photon warning messages. This extremely early proto-signaling set the stage for later communication in the lives and languages of *Homo*.

Information carrier

Princeton University researchers "have built a device in which a single electron can pass its quantum information to a particle of light. The particle of light, or photon, can then act as a messenger to carry the information to other electrons" (Zandonella, 2016).

Electromagnetic force

"The force carrier for the electromagnetic force is the photon. Photons, which are commonly called light waves, and referred to as gamma rays, X-rays, visible light, radio waves, and other names depending on their energy" (Duke University Physics Education Project [phy.duke.edu/~kolena/modern/forces.html, accessed May 27, 2018).

X-rays, photons and nonverbal communication

X-rays were discovered by Wilhelm Roentgen (1845–1923) in 1895. Ten years later, in 1905, Albert Einstein (1879–1955) discovered the photon. For the field of nonverbal communication, the implications of these and other discoveries pertaining to electromagnetism cannot be overstated. The electromagnetic force provides both the template for, and the major channel of, our nonverbal signs, signals and cues. The human brain, nervous system and sensory organs are all electromagnetically activated, designed and motivated. The classic poem about the human body – "I Sing the Body Electric" – by American transcendentalist Walt Whitman (1819–1892) is aptly titled, indeed.

See also *Reproductive force*.

Xenophobe

Unalike dislike

One who displays an emotional distaste or disliking for those features of dress, facial appearance, gesture, mannerisms, music, paralanguage, skin color and other nonverbal signs that differ significantly from one's own cultural background and racial heritage.

Biological roots

Nonverbal xenophobia is widespread among humans in today's world. Our racism and prejudicial feelings appear to be biologically rooted in preferences for genetic similarity over diversity (see subsequently, Neuro-notes).

Neuro-notes

Nonverbally, vertebrates – including human beings – find qualities of "sameness" safer than differences, and the latter may be perceived as being somehow threatening or "unsafe." People from predominantly light-skinned societies, for example, may have an aversive reaction to darker-skinned individuals, and vice versa (see *Aversive cue*). Significant nonverbal differences may register in the brain's fear center (see *Amygdala*) and may stimulate emotional anger or fright (see *Fight-or-flight*). There is ample evidence to suggest that the "love" neurohormone, oxytocin, may mitigate xenophobia.

See also *Love signal*.

Xylophone

Tree tune

A percussive instrument with usually hardwood vertical bars that may be sequentially struck with mallets to produce musical notes (see *Music*).

Usage

Today, xylophones and allied instruments are used worldwide in a variety of venues, from calypso to jazz to orchestral symphony. The nonverbal sounds they produce are generally pleasing to the human ear (see *Auditory cue*).

Prehistory

The oldest xylophones likely originated in Africa and/or Asia, but since early wood and bamboo bars may not have survived in the archaeological record, the origin remains unclear.

Stone age precursors

Inspiration for xylophones may have been the "rock music" of earlier, more durable lithophones. Enjoying a worldwide prehistoric distribution, the usually cylindrical large stones may be struck with antler, bone, stone or wooden mallets to produce pleasant musical notes. Among the oldest U.S. lithophones yet discovered include a sample of 22 weighty specimens from southern Colorado's San Luis Valley, dated to 6,000 B.P. The lithic evidence suggests that our ancestors had a high nonverbal aptitude for the sound of music.

Y

Figure Y.1 Yawn

Yawn

Sign

An involuntary deep breath due to sleepiness, fatigue, boredom or emotional conflict. A socially contagious gaping behavior, often difficult to suppress. Yawning involves the wide opening and stretching of the jaws to make a deep inhalation of air and thence the exhalation of air, which is shorter in duration. Under the control of neurotransmitters and neuropeptides, yawning may include the movement of facial muscles (e.g., tightened cheek muscles); open mouth; the closing or squinting of the eyes; arm extension or flexion; tearing; head tilting; salivation; the opening of the Eustachian tubes of the ear and cardiovascular, neuromuscular and respiratory acts.

Usage

Yawning is "a response to and facilitator of change in behavioural or physiological state. The change may be in sleepiness, arousal, aggression, brain temperature, or some yet unrecognized conditions" (Provine, 2012b, 37). Yawns typically last for approximately 6 seconds, but they can also be much shorter (e.g., 4 seconds).

1   Yawning can be triggered by boredom, hunger, drowsiness, arousal and certain emotional conditions. It has also been connected to some neurological diseases and drug abuse (Muchnik et al., 2003). It is also prevalent at times before and after sleeping.
2   Yawning may also occur in tense business meetings as a sign of mild anxiety, disagreement or uncertainty. When an otherwise alert listener yawns in response to a controversial suggestion or idea, the yawn may signal a probing point, an opportunity to explore or clarify unvoiced objections or concerns.
3   Often when people yawn, they cover the mouth. It is thought that this practice has spiritual origins, where people covered the mouth to prevent spirits (e.g., the soul) escaping and also to prevent spirits entering (Walusinski, 2004).
4   In young adults between the ages of 17 and 35 years, the daily average number of yawns is 8.7 (Baenninger, 1997). Interestingly, there are fewer yawns among the elderly (over 75 years of age) (Zilli et al., 2008). At later ages, both in the

young and old, the number of yawns increases in the early morning, and again in the evening before sleeping time (Provine and Fischer, 1989; Baenninger, 1997; Zilli et al., 2008).

Neuro-notes

Yawning is a reflexive, highly contagious act. Babies born without a brain above the midbrain (anencephalic infants) can still yawn and stretch. As yawning is evidenced in both prenatal and new-born baby development, it is argued that such behavior indicates an evolutionary basis to the act (Provine, 2012b). "Yawning is evidence that beneath our veneer of culture, rationality, and language, ancient, unconscious processes influence our lives" (Provine, 2012b, 27). Indeed, beyond the human world, yawning is found in a wide range of species, including most mammals, birds and fish.

Stimuli associated, for example, with tiredness, the sight of others yawning or social stress, pass (1) from higher brain centers (2) to respiratory centers in the brain-stem's medulla and then (3) to somatic motor nuclei of the trigeminal (cranial V) and facial (cranial VII) nerves. Excitement of motor fibers in the facial nerve and in the trigeminal's mandibular branch opens the mouth widely and stimulates activity in the phrenic (cervical 3, 4 and 5) nerves to the diaphragm and intercostal (thoracic 1–12) nerves to the external intercostal muscles, causing a deep inspiration followed by deep exhalation.

Contagious yawns

Yawns have been shown to be contagious, with people being twice as likely to yawn (55 percent) while observing others yawn (Provine, 2010).

See also *Cry*.

Z

Zebra stripes

Emblem enigmas

Often sinuous, alternating bands of black-and-white fur marking the bodies of three wild species of African horses (*Equus* sp). Like human dermatoglyphs (see *Fingerprint*), zebra stripe patterns are unique to each individual. Several communicative functions have been proposed, but each remains controversial.

Usage

Proposed uses include camouflage (see *Invisibility*), motion dazzle, parasite deterrence, species recognition and thermoregulation.

Camouflage

On the open-grassland savannah, bold stripes may increase visibility. In dense foliage, meanwhile, edge-cutting stripes may visually interrupt a zebra's bodily silhouette and outline. In densely packed zebra herds, the multiplicity of stripes may confuse and suggest an organism far too large for predators to attack (see *Loom*).

Motion dazzle

In rapid motion, stripes make it harder to judge a zebra's speed, distance and direction of movement. Known as "motion dazzle," the visual principle may account for the popularity of striped rugby shirts (see *Clothing cue*).

Parasitic insects

Though horseflies and tsetse flies will approach zebras, they may be deterred from landing by the visual stripes.

Species recognition

Nonverbally, zebra stripes likely play a courtship role in recognizing that prospective mates are alike and members of the same species (see *Isopraxism*).

See also *Animal sign*.

Zeitgeist archetypes

Nonverbal patterns through space-time

"Zeitgeist" is a German word labeling broad societal outlooks, spirits, fads and overall tastes of the times. Artwork is a dominant zeitgeist, for example, in the 15th- and 16th-century European Renaissance. Nonverbally, zeitgeist may be used to label important evolutionary developments that broadly influence and shape our nonverbal communication. So critically basic are these game-changing paradigm shifts that we call them zeitgeist archetypes.

Archetype

English "archetype" derives from Greek *arkhe* (primitive) and *tupos* (model). A non-verbal archetype is a prototypical pattern of wordless behavior and thought that dwells in unconscious recesses of our nervous system and brain. Nonverbal archetypes evident, for example, in the biology of color vision, physiology of grasping hands and primatology of facial expression continue to motivate human feelings and behavior apart from consciousness today. Among the world's important non-verbal archetypes are the following:

Messaging molecules (3.7 bya)

Molecular communication began ca. 3.7 bya with blue-green algae and contin-ues to this day in diverse organs of the human body. Our bodily organs, includ-ing the brain and nervous system, communicate information via electromagnetic signals.

Zeitgeist: Messaging molecules provide the background electromagnetic infra-structure required for all nonverbal communication. The underpinning neural framework is entirely out of conscious awareness unless something, for example, a stomach ache, should signal malfunction (see *Enteric brain*).

Sexual signaling (2 bya)

The archetype of sexual signaling began ca. 2 bya with bacteria and continues to this day in human beings. Humans send and receive sexually meaningful nonverbal signs through virtually every sensorimotor channel. Daily sexual signaling occupies a significant bandwidth in our nonverbal communication (see *Love signal, Reproduc-tive force*).

Zeitgeist: The Austrian neurologist Sigmund Freud (1856–1939) was correct in asserting that Eros and sexual instincts are dominant themes in human life. Sexual-ity strongly influences, informs and shapes our fundamental human feelings and *weltanschauung* (world view).

Sound and gesture (500 mya)

It was established ca. 500 mya that vertebrate vocalizations and pectoral ges-tures should be linked in the stream of nonverbal communication. Researchers recently found a physiological connection between aural and gestural channels in a shared compartment of the hindbrain and upper spinal cord (see *Hands*, Neuro-notes IV).

Zeitgeist: Vocal-pectoral signs proclaim identity and personal presence: viz., that "I am here." We proclaim our own existence with the sound of our voice (see *Audi-tory cue*), our speaking gestures (see *Speech*) and with salutary waves of our hands.

Primate color vision (65 mya)

Color-vision is an archetype that reemerged ca. 65 mya in primates and broadly continues to this day in human beings. While mammals have rather poor color vision, the advent of primates in the Paleocene Epoch rendered the world brilliantly colorful again (see *Color cue*). Today colors play a central role in our daily nonverbal routine in the clothes we wear (see *Clothing cue*), the stores we frequent (see *Shopping*) and the homes in which we live (see *Interior design*).

Zeitgeist: Chromatic vision informs "color fancy." We love color, and each of us may have a favorite hue, frequently blue. Color for the French artist Claude Monet (1840–1926) was his greatest emotional obsession and joy. And for the Swiss-born painter Paul Klee (1879–1940), color was "everything."

Binocular sight (65 mya)

The archetype of 3D binocular sight emerged ca. 65 mya in primates and continues to this day in human beings. A stereoscopic view makes objects more visibly and psychologically "real." Binocular vision is highly adapted in arboreal, tree-climbing primates (see *Eyes*). Seeing branches, berries and insects from two angles at once provides a greater depth of field than does monocular vision and enables greater "object integrity." Seen in the round, physical objects stand out and have a clearer, sharper image, a visually more objective presence. Binocular vision facilitates the manufacture of implements from natural materials such as stones, bones and horn. Additionally, 3D vision enhances the perception of distance and makes hand and arm gestures easier to see.

Zeitgeist: Nonverbally, greater depth perception leads to enhanced spatial communication in *Homo* (see *Proxemics*).

Grasping hands (65 mya)

The archetype of grasping hands emerged ca. 65 mya in primates and continues to this day in human beings. Unlike animals with flippers, hooves or paws, primates have skilled prehensile hands that can hold, explore and manipulate objects. Complex sensorimotor areas of the brain enable grasping hands to craft artifacts and tools from materials they can hold (see *Hand*). In tandem with binocular vision, holding a physical item makes it seem psychologically interesting and more objectively "real." Grasping hands enable chimpanzees and humans to assemble and use diverse tools and material artifacts (see *Consumer product*).

Zeitgeist: Grasping hands enable reaching out to others. They also afford a potent means of manipulation for feeling in control.

Facial expressions (35–40 mya)

Our higher-primate (anthropoid) ancestors had an enlarged visual cortex at the back of the head on the occipital lobe with which to process color vision and enhanced depth of field. Today the anthropoid's is the most complex visual cortex on earth, with anatomically separate areas for analyzing form, coordinating hand-and-eye movements and recognizing faces (see *Facial recognition*).

Zeitgeist: Faces, facial identity and facial cues have become key components of our nonverbal communication. The face is the most photographed of all body parts.

Tool-making (2.6 mya)

As a nonverbal archetype, tool-making is a paradigm shift of great magnitude for the human species. The English word "artifact" comes from Latin *arte* ("by skill") and *factum* ("made"; via the ancient Indo-European root *dhe-*, "to set," "put," derivatives of which include deed, did and do; skill "by hand" is implied). The earliest known artifacts come from Africa. At numerous sites from that continent, sharply flaked stone tools have been found dating back ca. 2.6 million years before present.

Zeitgeist: Modern tools such as cranes, drills and tractors have led to unprecedented human control over the environment. With control has come a dubious feeling that human beings are more powerful than nature.

Language (2 mya)

Like tool-making, signed and spoken language represents a major paradigm shift in human communication. Rather than arising spontaneously, however, as a self-contained system in itself, verbal language gradually evolved from preexisting patterns of nonverbal communication. Nonverbal messaging preceded linguistic expression by roughly 3 billion years. The former not only came before but also established the patterns and standards of linguistic communication through body movement, gesture and vocalization (see *Speech*, *Word*).

Zeitgeist: Among its diverse social benefits, from storytelling to information storage to psychoanalysis, language has enabled us to reflect on the origin, evolution and meaning of human nonverbal communication. By assigning words to actions, the latter may be raised to conscious awareness for deliberation and inquiry.

Art (1.6 mya)

The aesthetic-arts archetype involves aromatic, auditory, tactile, taste, vestibular and visual signs designed by human beings to affect the nonverbal sense of beauty. Arrangements, combinations, contrasts, rhythms and sequences of signs have been designed in emotional languages to bespeak elegance, grace, intensity, refinement and truth. The earliest evidence for human aesthetics may be the thousands of ca. 1.6-million-year-old fist-sized hand-axes that bear a standardized, symmetrical, leaf-shaped design and were chipped in East Africa by forebears of *Homo*. Known as Acheulean bifaces, these artifacts exhibit a beautiful symmetry and aesthetic form. A likely artistic concern with form may have exceeded functional needs.

Zeitgeist: At least 1.6 million years old, the artistic sense is a major paradigm shift in human nonverbal archetypes. Today an aesthetic sensitivity pervades our lives and permeates communication apart from words.

Architecture (1/2 mya)

Early architecture represents a major paradigm shift in human proxemic and spatial communication. The earliest physical evidence for permanent sheltering is the 490,000-year-old Terra Amata Shelter in France, consisting of post-hole arrangements suggesting multiple large homes and a settled community life. Before settling, ancient humans were nomadic. Early sheltered communities evolved into villages, cities, roads, bridges and civilization, each of which has dramatically influenced how we communicate verbally (see *Verbal communication*) and apart from words (see *Nonverbal communication*) through space-time.

Zeitgeist: With the architectural comes a sense of permanence, along with settlement patterns that "speak" nonverbally to our aesthetic, emotional and social senses. The Two Towers (Dui Torre: Asinelli and Garisenda), for example, are remnants of ca. 180 looming towers built between the 12th and 13th centuries within the ring-walled city of Bologna, Italy. The Two Towers were constructed as nonverbal indices of familial wealth and political power. Medieval Bologna resembled, on a smaller scale, what New York's Manhattan looks like today. Trump Tower, for example, is a remnant of the Middle-Ages notion that "big is better" (see *Loom*). An iconic U.S. 20th-century looming monument is the 1,046'-high, 77-floor, brick-and-steel Chrysler Building in East Side Manhattan, New York, completed in 1930. Readable signs include hubcaps, fenders, radiator caps and hood ornaments attached to the exterior as nonverbal suggestions of automobiles; eagle-gargoyle figures suggestive of flight and upward-pointing triangles crowned with vertical, stainless-steel needles to suggest otherworldly height and power.

Clothing (200,000 years ago)

Nonverbally, human clothing represents a key paradigm shift in how we present ourselves to one another, emotionally and socially, in everyday life (see *Clothing cue*). Full-body dress originated in Africa or Eurasia to protect the body and keep it warm. The first clothes were made of prepared animal hides. Stone scraping tools from Neanderthal sites in Europe provide indirect evidence for hide preparation, suggesting that cold-weather clothing could be at least 200,000 years old. The earliest domesticated sheep, from Zawi Chemi Shanidar, Iraq, suggest that wool clothing originated ca. 10,500 years ago. Unwoven skirts and shawls made of flounces of tufted wool or flax were worn by the ancient Sumerians 5,000 years ago. More recently, the invention of the flying shuttle (1733), the spinning jenny (1764) and the 19th-century power-loom made cotton fabrics available in ever-greater quantities (see *Consumer products*). Mass-produced clothing first appeared in 1851 with the invention of the sewing machine and increased in production with the use of synthetic fibers. As the adornment medium became subject to greater control, the diversity and number of nonverbal clothing cues burgeoned.

Zeitgeist: Clothing is dramatically expressive and has been fodder for fashion and fads from its first appearance as a fur substitute millennia ago. Nonverbal fashion statements may be closely noted, appreciated and imitated (see *Attire, Body adornment* and *Isopraxism*).

Zipper

Audio-visual fashion cue

Patented in the U.S. in 1851, the zipper has two rows of interlocking teeth that may be locked or unlocked by means of a slider held by the fingertips' tactile pads (see *Hands*). English "zipper" is an onomatopoetic word that mimics the product's "zip" sound (see *Word*).

Usage

Functionally designed for fabric as a closure device, zippers later evolved to make decorative fashion statements in luggage, handbags and clothing (see *Messaging feature*). Visually in clothing, zippers may be used to attract attention to specific bodily areas and body parts. Audibly in products, a zipper calls attention to itself with a pleasingly distinctive zip sound (see *Auditory cue*). The generic nonverbal message of a zipper is about self-assertion: viz., that "I am here," often in service to courtship (see *Love signals*).

Display vs. conceal

Zippers may be conspicuously attached at the front of a woman's top or inconspicuously hidden as a zipper fly in Levis® jeans (see *Invisibility*). In the former garment, the slider may be attached to a gleaming, suggestive pull-ring that seems to say, "Pull down here" (see *Reproductive force*).

Zipper cues

Zippers are often displayed as artwork in fashion and art museums, including the Museum of Modern Art (MoMA) in New York City (see *Art cue*). A conspicuously zippered Prada® backpack has been displayed at the MoMA, for example, as has the Schott Perfecto® black-leather motorcycle jacket, with its descending and centrally placed main zipper accompanied by three matching silver pocket zippers, diagonally placed at insouciant slants. The jacket's nonverbal message is clear: "See me – I am here!" Meanwhile, with its single horizontal zipper and six slanted counterparts, the asymmetrical little black dress (LBD) by Alexander Wang (the Sunburst® zipper dress) sends the same eye-catching, rhythmically repeated message: "See me."

See also *Button*.

Zombie mime

Death signals

The act of imitating the body movements, facial expressions and gestures of fictional "dead" people, reanimated to "life" and known as zombies (see *Mime cue*).

Usage

Zombie mime is a theatrical performance used to cope with and parody the reality of death and dying. Nonverbally, by acting as if mortality may be reversed, humans reassure themselves that life may never actually end.

Body movements

Zombie actors display slower-than-normal movements (see *Slow motion*), suggesting diminished neural control.

Facial expressions

Faces may be devoid of emotional expression (see *Blank face*). Little to no eye contact may be exchanged, either with fellow zombies or with the living victims they relentlessly pursue. The "undead" look more dead than alive.

Gestures

Few hand and arm gestures are given, and voices are speechless, save for audible moans (see *Groan*). Zombie actors have little to say as they harass the living. Their morbid body movements speak for themselves.

Walking

The bipedal gait of zombies has been likened to the gait of mechanical automatons. Slowed feet alternately shuffle forward with no visible "spring" in the step (see *Walk*).

Media

In the classic U.S. horror film, Night of the Living Dead (1968, 1990), the disheveled zombie look was popularized and zombie mime appeared in additional motion pictures, TV shows, Halloween costumes, zombie parties and comic books. The central nonverbal narrative of zombie media is that life is inevitably subject to the assaults of death.

Word origin

The English word "zombie" has West African roots that eventually spread elsewhere, for example, to Brazil and Haiti. Semantically, zombies are soulless corpses reanimated by witchcraft and supernatural means. Recently, the word has been extended as a label for persons who are unaware of and unresponsive to their surroundings. The potent alcoholic Zombie drink is so named for producing these psychological effects (see *Word*).

Myth or reality?

While zombies are mythical creatures, the nonverbal movements and postures of zombie mime are real.

See also *Talisman*.

Zygomatic smile

Facial expression

A true smile of happiness, gladness or joy. An expression in which the corners of the mouth curve upward, and the outer corners of the eyes crinkle into crow's-feet.

Origin I

In the last half of the 20th century, it was received wisdom that the human smile derived from the primate fear grin. In the latter expression, the lip corners pull sideward and upward to reveal the teeth in fearful settings. In chimpanzees, for example, the theory was that by grimacing with a fear grin, a chimp would show appeasement, harmlessness and a mood of "friendliness." The submissive grin, used to show "I am afraid," came to suggest that "I am harmless – and therefore friendly – as well" (Morris, 1994). The link between smiling and humor, love and joy was not explained.

Origin II

In the early 21st century, an alternative view of smile evolution emerged. Instead of the fear grin, the primate play face is now thought to underlie human smiling. In contexts of "rough and tumble" play, for example, chimpanzees grin, emit laugh-like vocalizations and use hand-and-arm reaching, grasping and tickling gestures.

The combination of laryngeal vocalizations and pectoral-limb gestures may be central to the play-face-origin hypothesis. In chordates, circuits for vocal-laryngeal and pectoral-movement communication link in a caudal hindbrain, rh8-upper-spinal-cord compartment (Bass and Chagnaud, 2013). This neurological linkage explains why hand gestures and vocalizations are intimately coupled in primate play.

Vocalization cues and grooming gestures are controlled by the cingulate gyrus – the evolutionary new wing of the mammalian brain. The cingulate gyrus is the most recent part of the primate limbic system and is responsible for grooming, maternal caring, play and audiovocal signals. Through an evolutionary process of ritualization, the play-face grin itself (apart from vocalizations and gestures) became a stand-alone sign of friendly intentions.

Usage

Though we may show a polite grin or camera smile at will, the zygomatic or heartfelt smile is hard to produce on demand. While the former cue may be consciously manipulated (and is subject to deception), the latter is controlled by emotion. Thus, the zygomatic smile is a more accurate reflection of mood.

Anatomy

Lip corners curl upward through contraction of zygomaticus muscles; crow's-feet show when the zygomaticus muscles are strongly contracted, and/or when orbicularis oculi muscles contract. In the polite (i.e., intentional, weak or "false") smile, lip corners stretch sideward through contraction of risorius muscles, with little upward curl and no visible crow's-feet.

Malicious smile

People with antisocial personality disorders may smile while inflicting or thinking about inflicting harm on others. In popular culture, perhaps the strongest example of a malicious smile is that of actor Jack Nicholson in his role as Jack Torrance in the 1980 film The Shining. Possessed by ghosts, Jack pushed his face – baring the evil smile – through a smashed bathroom door and said, "Here's Johnny!" Nicholson's dramatically evil smile reveals a blend of emotions, including disgust (curled upper lip), anger (bared lower teeth, as in readiness to bite; lowered eyebrows) and perverse joy (strongly contracted zygomaticus muscles).

Supermarket mandatory smile

In the late 1990s, Safeway, then the second-largest supermarket chain in the United States, instructed its store employees to smile and greet customers with direct eye contact. In 1998, USA Today ("Safeway's Mandatory Smiles Pose Danger, Workers Say") reported that 12 female employees had filed grievances over the chain's smile-and-eye-contact policy after numerous male customers reportedly had propositioned them for dates. Commenting on the grievances, a Safeway official stated, "We don't see it [the males' sexual overtures] as a direct result of our initiative."

Smiley face

The yellow "smiley face," a popular graphic symbol designed by commercial artist Harvey Ball in the early 1960s, has become a universal sign of happiness. Its color is associated with the brightness of the sun (see *Color cue*). According to son Charlie Ball, Harvey "understood the power of it (the smiley face) and was enormously proud of it [even though others, rather than Ball, profited financially from the design]. He left this world with no apologies and no regrets, happy to have this as his legacy" (Woo, 2001, A6).

Neuro-notes I

The zygomatic smile is controlled "from the anterior cingulate region, from other limbic cortices (in the medial temporal lobe), and from the basal ganglia" (Damasio, 1994, 140–141). "We cannot mimic easily what the anterior cingulate can achieve effortlessly" (Damasio, 1994, 141–142).

Neuro-notes II

Mirror neurons: Mirror neurons play a role in decoding the smile: "Baby smiles, the parent smiles in response. Two minutes later, baby smiles again, the parent smiles again. Thanks to the imitative behavior of the parent, the baby's brain can associate the motor plan necessary to smile and the sight of the smiling face. Therefore – presto! Mirror neurons for a smiling face are born" (Iacoboni, 2008, 133–134). "When I see you smiling, my mirror neurons for smiling fire up, too, initiating a cascade of neural activity that evokes the feeling we typically associate with a smile. I don't need to make any inference on what you are feeling, I experience immediately and effortlessly (in a milder form, of course) what you are experiencing ["The Mirror Neuron Revolution: Explaining What Makes Humans Social," July 1, 2008 interview with Jonah Lehrer in Scientific American]."

References

Ackerman, B. P., Abe, J. A., and Izard, C. E. (1998). *Differential Emotions Theory and Emotional Development Mindful of Modularity.* In Mascolo, M. F., and Griffin, S. (Eds.), *What Develops in Emotional Development?* New York: Plenum Press, pp 85–106.

Ackermann, H., Hage, S. R., and Ziegler, W. (2014). Brain mechanisms of acoustic communication in humans and nonhuman primates: An evolutionary perspective. *Behavioral and Brain Sciences*, 37(6), pp 529–546.

Adams, R., and Nelson, A. (2016). Eye behavior and gaze. In Matsumoto, D., Hwang, H., and Frank, M. (Eds.), *APA Handbook of Nonverbal Communication*, 1st ed. Washington: American Psychological Association, pp 335–362.

Adelmann, P. K., and Zajonc, R. B. (1989). Facial efference and the experience of emotion. *Annual Review of Psychology*, 40, pp 249–280.

Adler, R., and Towne, N. (1996). *Looking Out, Looking in*, 8th ed. Fort Worth, TX: Harcourt Brace.

Afifi, T., and Denes, A. (2013). Feedback processes and physiological responding. In Manusov, V., and Patterson, M. L. (Eds.), *The Sage Handbook of Nonverbal Communication.* Thousand Oaks, CA: Sage, pp 481–500.

Aktas, G., and Ogce, F. (2005). Dance as a therapy for cancer prevention. *Asian Pacific Journal of Cancer Prevention*, 6, pp 408–411.

Alibali, M. W., and Goldin-Meadow, S. (1993). Gesture-speech mismatch and mechanism of learning. What the hands reveal about a child's state of mind. *Cognitive Psychology*, 25(4), pp 468–523.

Alibali, M. W., Heath, D., and Myers, H. (2001). Effects of visibility between speaker and listener on gesture production: Some gestures are meant to be seen. *Journal of Memory and Language* (44), pp 169–188.

Allgood, R., and Heaton, P. (2015). Developmental change and cross-domain links in vocal and musical emotion recognition performance in childhood. *British Journal of Developmental Psychology*, 33, pp 398–403.

Almaney, A. J., and Alwan, A. J. (1982). *Communicating with the Arabs: A Handbook for the Business Executive.* Prospect Heights, IL: Waveland Press.

Alpert, P. T. (2011). The health benefits of dance. *Home Health Care Management and Practice*, 23(2), pp 155–157.

Altemus, M., Deuster, E. G., Carter, C. S., and Gold, P. (1995). Suppression of hypothalamicpituitary-adrenal axis responses to stress in lactating women. *Journal of Clinical Endocrinology and Metabolism*, 80, pp 2954–2959.

Altmann, S. (1967). The structure of primate communication. In Altmann, S. (Ed.), *Social Communication Among Primates.* Chicago: University of Chicago Press, pp 325–362.

Amato, I. (1992). In search of the human touch. *Science*, 258 (November 27), pp 1436–437.

Ambady, N., Hallahan, M., and Conner, B. (1999). Accuracy of judgments of sexual orientation from thin slices of behaviour. *Journal of Personality and Social Psychology*, 77, pp 538–547.

Ambady, N., Hallanan, M., and Rosenthal, R. (1995). On judging and being judged accurately in zero acquaintance situations. *Journal of Personality and Social Psychology*, 69, pp 518–529.

Ambady, N., and Rosenthal, R. (1993). Half a minute: Predicting teacher evaluations from thin slices of nonverbal behaviour and physical attractiveness. *Journal of Personality and Social Psychology*, 64, pp 431–441.

Ambady, N., and Weisbuch, M. (2010). Nonverbal behaviour. In Fiske, S. T., Gilbert, D. T., and Lindzey, S. (Eds.), *Handbook of Social Psychology*, vol. 1. Hoboken, NJ: John Wiley and Sons, pp 464–497.

Amemiya, S., and Ohtomo, K. (2012). Effect of the observed pupil size on the amygdala of the beholders. *Social Cognitive and Affective Neuroscience*, 7(3), 332–341.

American Psychiatric Association. (2000). *Diagnostic and Statistical Manual of Mental Disorders – DSM-IV-TR*. Washington: American Psychiatric Association.

Andermann, F., and Andermann, E. (1992). Startle epilepsy. In Joseph, A. B., and Young, R. R. (Eds.), *Movement Disorders in Neurology and Neuropsychiatry*. Cambridge, MA: Blackwell Scientific Publications, pp 498–500.

Andersen, P. A. (1985). Nonverbal immediacy in interpersonal communication. In Siegman, A. W., and Feldstein, S. (Eds.), *Multichannel Integrations of Nonverbal Behavior*. Hillsdale, NJ: Lawrence Erlbaum Associates, pp 1–36.

Andersen, P. A. (1998). The cognitive valence theory of intimate communication. In Palmer, M. T., and Barnett, G. A. (Eds.), *Progress in Communication Sciences Vol XIV*. Westport: Praeger Publishing, pp 39–72.

Andersen, P. A. (2008). *Nonverbal Communication: Forms and Functions*, 2nd ed. Long Grove, IL: Waveland Press.

Andersen, J. F., Andersen, P. A., and Jensen, A. D. (1979). The measurement of nonverbal immediacy. *Applied Communication Research*, 7, pp 153–180.

Andersen, P. A., and Andersen, J. F. (1982). Nonverbal immediacy in instruction. In Barker, L. (Ed.), *Communication in the Classroom*. Englewood Cliff, NJ: Prentice-Hall, pp 98–120.

Andersen, P. A., and Andersen, J. F. (1984). The exchange of nonverbal intimacy: A critical review of dyadic models. *Journal of Nonverbal Behavior*, 8(4), pp 327–349.

Andersen, P. A., and Andersen, J. F. (2004). Measurements of perceived nonverbal immediacy. In Manusov, V. L. (Eds.), *The Sourcebook of Nonverbal Measures: Going Beyond Words*. London: Taylor and Francis, pp 113–126.

Andersen, P. A., and Bowman, L. L. (1999). Positions of power: Nonverbal influence in organizational communication. In Guerrero, L. K., DeVito, J. A., and Hecht, M. L. (Eds.), *The Nonverbal Communication Reader: Classic and Contemporary Readings*. Waveland, IL: Prospect Heights, pp 317–334.

Anderson, J. L., Crawford, C. B., Nadeau, J., and Lindberg, T. (1992). Was the duchess of Windsor right? A cross-cultural review of the socioecology of ideals of female body shape. *Ethology and Sociobiology*, 13, pp 197–227.

Andrew, R. J. (1965). The origins of facial expression. *Scientific American* (213), pp 88–94.

Anikin, A., Bååth, R., and Persson, T. (2018). Human non-linguistic vocal repertoire: Call types and their meaning. *Journal of Nonverbal Behaviour*, 42, pp 53–80.

Anonymous. (2001). After 5 months, shuttle crew ready to return home. Spokesman Review (AP, August 8), p A7.

Archer, D., and Costanzo, M. (1988). The Interpersonal Perception Task. Berkeley, CA: University of California Extension Media Centre.

Archer, D., Costanzo, M., and Akert, R. (2001). The interpersonal perception task (IPT): Alternative approaches to problems of theory and design. In Hall, J. A., and Bernieri, F. J. (Eds.), *Interpersonal Sensitivity: Theory and Measurement*. Mahwah, NJ: Lawrence Erlbaum Associates, pp 161–182.

Archer, D., Iritani, B., Kimes, D. D., and Barrios, M. (1983). Face-ism: Five studies of sex differences in facial prominence. *Journal of Personality and Social Psychology*, 45(4), pp 725–735.

Argiolas, A., and Melis, M. R. (1998). The neuropharmacology of yawning. *European Journal of Pharmacology*, 343(1), pp 1–16.

Argyle, M. (1972). *The Psychology of Interpersonal Behaviour*, 2nd ed. London: Penguin.

Argyle, M. (1988). *Bodily Communication Second Edition*. London: Methuen.

Argyle, M. (1994). *The Psychology of Interpersonal Behaviour*. London: Penguin.

Argyle, M., and Dean, J. (1965). Eye-contact, distance and affiliation. *Sociometry*, 28, pp 289–304.

Armstrong, D. F., Stokoe, W. C., and Wilcox, S. E. (1995). *Gesture and the Nature of Language*. New York: Cambridge University Press.

Armstrong, E. (1986). Enlarged limbic structures in the human brain: The anterior thalamus and medial mammillary body. *Brain Research*, 362(2), pp 394–397.

Arnold, A. J., and Winkielman, P. (2020). The mimicry among us: Intra- and inter-personal mechanisms of spontaneous mimicry. *Journal of Nonverbal Behaviour* (44), pp 195–212.

Aune, R. K., Levine, T. R., Ching, P. U., and Yoshimoto, J. M. (1993). The influence of perceived source reward value on attributions of deception. *Communication Research Reports*, 10, pp 15–27.

Auyeung, B., Lombardo, M. V., Heinrichs, M., Chakrabarti, B., Sule, A., Deakin, J. B., Bethlehem, R. A., Dickens, L., Mooney, N., Sipple, J. A., Thiemann, P., Baron-Cohen, S. (2015). Oxytocin increases eye contact during a real-time, naturalistic social interaction in males with and without autism. *Translation Psychiatry*, 5(2) (February 10), p e507. doi: 10.1038/tp.2014.146. PMID: 25668435; PMCID: PMC4445747.

Axel, R. (1995). The molecular logic of smell. *Scientific American*, 273(4), pp 154–159.

Babad, E., Avni-Babad, D., and Rosenthal, R. (2003). 'Teachers' brief nonverbal behaviours in defined instructional situations can predict students' evaluations. *Journal of Educational Psychology*, (86) pp 120–125.

Bachorowski, J. A., and Owren, M. J. (2001). Not all laughs are alike: Voiced but not unvoiced laughter readily elicits positive affect. *Psychological Science*, 12(3), pp 252–257.

Baenninger, R. (1997). On yawning and its functions. *Psychonomic Bulletin & Review*, 4, pp 198–207.

Bailenson, J. N., and Yee, N. (2007). Virtual interpersonal touch and digital chameleons. *Journal of Nonverbal Behavior*, 31, pp 225–242.

Bailenson, J. N., Yee, N., Brave, S., Merget, D., and Koslow, D. (2007). Virtual interpersonal touch: Expressing and recognizing emotions through haptic devices. *Human-Computer Interaction*, 22, pp 325–353.

Ball, V. (1965). The aesthetics of colour: A review of fifty years of experimentation. *Journal of Aesthetics and Art Criticisms*, 23, pp 441–452.

Banse, R., and Scherer, K. R. (1996). Acoustic profiles in vocal emotion expression. *Journal of Personality and Social Psychology*, 70, pp 614–636.

Banziger, T., and Scherer, K. R. (2010). Introducing the Geneva multimodal emotion portrayal (GEMEP) corpus. In Scherer, K. R., Bänziger, T., and Roesch, E. B. (Eds.), *Blueprint for Affective Computing: A Sourcebook*. Oxford: Oxford Press, pp 271–294.

Banziger, T., Scherer, K. R., Hall, J. A., and Robert Rosenthal, R. (2011). Introducing the MiniPONS: A short multichannel version of the profile of nonverbal sensitivity (PONS) *Journal of Nonverbal Behaviour*, 35, pp 189–204.

Barak, A., Patkin, J., and Dell, D. M. (1982). Effects of certain counselor behaviors on perceived expertness and attractiveness. *Journal of Counseling Psychology*, 29, pp 261–267.

Barakat, R. (1973). Arabic gestures. *Journal of Popular Culture*, 6, pp 749–787.

Barber, E. W. (1994). *Women's Work: The First 20,000 Years*. New York: W. W. Norton and Co.

Baron-Cohen, S., Ring, H. A., Wheelwright, S., Bullmore, E. T., Brammer, M. J., Simmons, A., and Williams, S. R. (1999). Social intelligence in the normal and autistic brain: An fMRI study. *European Journal of Neuroscience*, 11, pp 1891–1898.

Bass, A. H., and Chagnaud, B. (2012). Shared developmental and evolutionary origins of neural basis of vocal-acoustic and pectoral-gestural signaling. *Proceedings of the National Academy of Sciences*, 109 (*USA*) (November 11, 2013).

Bateson, G. (1968). Redundancy and coding. In Sebeok, T. A. (Ed.), *Animal Communication*. Bloomington: Indiana University Press, pp 614–626.

Bateson, G., and Mead, M. (1942). *Balinese Culture: A Photographic Analysis*. New York: New York Academy of Sciences.

Bavelas, J. B. (1994). Gesture as part of speech: Methodological implications. *Research on Language and Social Interaction*, 27, pp 201–221.

Bavelas, J. B., and Chovil, N. (1997). Faces in dialogue. In Russell, J. A., and Fernandez-Dols, J. M. (Eds.), *The Psychology of Facial Expression*. Cambridge: Cambridge University Press.

Bavelas, J. B., and Chovil, N. (2000). Visible acts of meaning: An integrated message model of language in face-to-face dialogue. *Journal of Language and Social Psychology*, 19, pp 163–194.

Bavelas, J. B., and Chovil, N. (2006). Hand gestures and facial displays as part of language use in face-to-face dialogue. In Manusov, V., and Patterson, M. L. (Eds.), *The Sage Handbook of Nonverbal Communication*. Thousand Oaks, CA: Sage, pp 97–115.

Bavelas, J. B., Coates, L., and Johnson, T. (2000). Listeners as co-narrators. *Journal of Personality and Social Psychology*, 79, pp 941–952.

Beattie, G. (2004). *Visible Thought, the New Psychology of Body Language*. London: Routledge.

Beattie, G., and Shovelton, H. (1999a). Do iconic hand gestures really contribute anything to the semantic information conveyed by speech? An experimental investigation. *Semiotica*, 123, pp 1–30.

Beattie, G., and Shovelton, H. (1999b). Mapping the range of information contained in the iconic hand gestures that accompany spontaneous speech. *Journal of Language and Social Psychology*, 18, pp 438–462.

Beattie, G., and Shovelton, H. (2001). An experimental investigation of the role of different types of iconic gesture in communication: A semantic feature approach. *Gesture*, 1, pp 129–149.

Beattie, G., and Shovelton, H. (2002). An experimental investigation of some properties of individual iconic gestures that mediate their communicative power. *British Journal of Psychology*, 93, pp 179–192.

Beattie, G., Webster, K., and Ross, J. (2010). The fixation and processing of the iconic gestures that accompany talk. *Journal of Language and Social Psychology*, 29, pp 194–213.

Beaver, J. D., Mogg, K., and Bradley, B. P. (2005). Emotional conditioning to masked stimuli and modulation of visuospatial attention. *Emotion*, 5(1), 67–79.

Behrens, F., and Kret, M. E. (2019). The interplay between face-to-face contact and feedback on cooperation during real-life interactions. *Journal of Nonverbal Behaviour*, 43, pp 513–528.

Berdecio, S., and Nash, L. T. (1981). *Chimpanzee Visual Communication: Facial, Gestural and Postural Expressive Movement in Young, Captive Chimpanzees* (*Pan troglodytes*, Arizona State University, Anthropological Research Papers No. 26).

Bernhold, Q. S., and Giles, H. (2020). Vocal accommodation and mimicry. *Journal of Nonverbal Behaviour*, 44, pp 41–62.

Bernieri, F. J., and Gillis, J. S. (2001). Judging rapport: Employing Brunswik's lens model to study interpersonal sensitivity. In Hall, J. A., and Bernieri, F. J. (Eds.), *Interpersonal Sensitivity: Theory and Measurement*. Mahwah, NJ: Lawrence Erlbaum Associates, pp 67–88.

Bernieri, F. J., and Rosenthal, R. (1991). Coordinated movement in human interaction. In Feldman, R. S., and Rime, B. (Eds.), *Fundamentals of Nonverbal Behaviour*. New York: Cambridge University Press, pp 401–432.

Berry, D. S., and McArthur, L. Z. (1985). Some components and consequences of a baby-face. *Journal of Personality and Social Psychology*, 48, pp 312–323.

Berscheid, E., and Walster, E. H. (1974). Physical attractiveness. In Berkowitz, L. (Ed.), *Advances in Experimental Social Psychology*, vol 7. New York: Academic Press.

Bettinghaus, E. P., and Cody, M. J. (1994). *Persuasive Communication*, 5th ed. Fort Worth, TX: Harcourt Brace.

Bhanji, J. P., and Delgado, M. R. (2014). The social brain and reward: Social information processing in the human striatum. *Wiley Interdisciplinary Review of Cognitive Science*, 5(1), pp 61–73.

Bilous, F. R., and Krauss, R. M. (1988). Dominance and accommodation in the conversational behaviours of same- and mixed-gender dyads. *Language and Communication*, 8, pp 183–194.

Birdwhistell, R. (1952). *An Introduction to Kinesics*. Louisville: University of Louisville.

Birdwhistell, R. (1970). *Kinesics and Context*. Philadelphia: University of Pennsylvania.

Blakeslee, S. (1995a). In brain's early growth, timetable may be crucial. *New York Times, Science Times* (August 29), pp C1–C3.

Blakeslee, S. (1995b). How a bad beginning can affect the brain. *New York Times* (August 31), p. C1, C6.

Blaskovits, B., and Bennell, C. (2019). Are we revealing hidden aspects of our personality when we walk? *Journal of Nonverbal Behaviour*, 43, pp 329–356.

Blass, E. M. (1992). The ontogeny of motivation: Opioid bases of energy conservation and lasting affective change in rat and human infants. *Current Directions in Psychological Science* (August), pp 116–120.

Blier, M. J., and Blier-Wilson, L. A. (1989). Gender differences in sex-rated emotional expressiveness. *Sex Roles*, 21, pp 287–295.

Blum, D. (1998). Face it. *Psychology Today*, 5(31), pp 32–40.

Blurton, J. (1967). An ethological study of some aspects of social behaviour of children in nursery school. In Morris, D. (Ed.), *Primate Ethology*. Chicago: Aldine, pp 347–368.

Boecker, H., Sprenger, T., Spilker, M. E., et al. (2008). The runner's high: Opioidergic mechanisms in the human brain. *Cerebral Cortex*, 18, pp 2523–2531.

Boker, S. M., Cohn, J. F., Theobold, B., Matthews, I., Brick, T. R., and Spies, J. R. (2009). Effects of damping head movement and facial expression in dyadic conversation using real-time facial expression tracking and synthesized avatars. *In Philosophical Transactions of the Royal Society*, 364(1535), pp 3485–3495.

Bond, C. F., and DePaulo, B. M. (2006). Accuracy of deception judgments. *Personality and Social Psychology Review*, 10(3), pp 214–234.

Bond, C. F., and Titus, L. J. (1983). Social facilitation: A meta-analysis of 241 studies. *Psychological Bulletin*, 94(2), pp 265–292.

Book, A., Costello, K., and Camilleri, J. A. (2013). Psychopathy and victim selection: The use of gait as a cue to vulnerability. *Journal of Interpersonal Violence*, 28(11), pp 2368–2383.

Boomer, D. S. (1965). Hesitation and grammatical encoding. *Language and Speech*, 8, pp 148–158.

Borg, J. (2008). *Body Language*. London: Pearson.

Bornstein, M. H., and Arterberry, M. E. (2003). Recognition, discrimination and categorization of smiling by 5-month-old infants. *Developmental Science* (6), pp 585–599.

Bouissac, P. (1973). *La Mesure des Gestes: Prolegomenes à la Semiotique Gestuelle* (Approaches to Semiotics, Paperback Series, vol. 3). The Hague: Mouton.

Brannigan, C., and Humphries, H. (1969). I see what you mean. *New Scientist*, 42, pp 406–408.

Breed, G. (1971). *Nonverbal Behaviour and Teaching Effectiveness. Final Report*. Vermillion: South Dakota University. (ERIC ED 182).

Breithaupt, J. (2015). *Physics in Context for Cambridge International AS and A Level*. Oxford: Oxford University Press-Children.

Broaders, S., Cook, S. W., Mitchell, Z., and Goldin-Meadow, S. (2007). Making children gesture reveals implicit knowledge and leads to learning. *Journal of Experimental Psychology: General*, 136(4), pp 539–550.

Brody, L., and Hall, J. (2008). Gender and emotion in context. In Lewis, M., Haviland-Jones, J., and Barrett, L. F. (Eds.), *Handbook of Emotions*. New York: Guilford Press, pp 395–408.

Brooks, R., and Meltzoff, A. N. (2005). The development of gaze following and its relation to language. *Developmental Science*, 8, pp 535–543.

Bryant, G. A., and Aktipis, C. A. (2014). The animal nature of spontaneous human laughter. *Evolution and Human Behavior*, 35(4), pp 327–335.

Buck, R. (1976). A test of nonverbal receiving ability: Preliminary studies. *Human Communication Research*, 2, pp 162–171.

Buck, R. (1980). Nonverbal behaviour and the theory of emotion: The facial feedback hypothesis. *Journal of Personality and Social Psychology*, 38, 811–824.

Buck, R., Powers, S. R., and Hull, K. S. (2017). Measuring emotional and cognitive empathy using dynamic, naturalistic, and spontaneous emotion displays. *Emotion* (1), pp 1–17.

Buck, R., Renfro, S., and Sheehan, M. (2005). *CARAT-05: A New Version of the Communication of Affect Receiving Ability Test* (Unpublished paper, Department of Communication Sciences, University of Connecticut).

Bull, R., and Rumsey, N. (1988). *The Social Psychology of Facial Appearance*. New York: Springer.

Burgoon, J. K. (1994). Nonverbal signals. In Knapp, M. L., and Miller, G. R. (Eds.), *Handbook of Interpersonal Communication*, 2nd ed. Thousand Oaks, CA: Sage, pp 229–285.

Burgoon, J. K. (2005). The future of motivated deception detection. In Kalbfleisch, P. (Ed.), *Communication Yearbook*, vol. 29. Mahwah, NJ: Lawrence Erlbaum Associates, pp 49–95.

Burgoon, J. K. (2018). Micro expressions are not the best way to catch a liar. *Frontiers in Psychology*, 9.

Burgoon, J. K., and Bacue, A. (2003). Nonverbal communication skills. In Burleson, B. R., and Greene, J. O. (Eds.), *Handbook of Communication and Social Interaction Skills*. Mahwah, NJ: Lawrence Erlbaum Associates, pp 179–219.

Burgoon, J. K., Birk, T., and Pfau, M. (1990). Nonverbal behaviours, persuasion and credibility. *Human Communication Research*, 17, 140–169.

Burgoon, J. K., Buller, D. B., Hale, J. L., and deTruck, M. (1984). Relational messages associated with nonverbal behaviours. *Human Communication Research*, 10, pp 351–378.

Burgoon, J. K., Buller, D. B., and Woodall, W. G. (1989). *Nonverbal Communication: The Unspoken Dialogue*. New York: Harper and Row.

Burgoon, J. K., and Dillman, L. (1995). Gender, immediacy, and nonverbal communication. In Kalbfleisch, P. J., and Cody, M. J. (Eds.), *Gender, Power, and Communication in Human Relationships*. Hillsdale, NJ: Lawrence Erlbaum Associates, pp 63–82.

Burgoon, J. K., and Dunbar, N. (2000). An interactionist perspective on dominance-submission: Interpersonal dominance as a dynamically situationally contingent social skill. *Communication Monographs*, 67, pp 96–121.

Burgoon, J. K., Dunbar, N. E., and Segrin, C. (2002). Nonverbal influence. In Dillard, J. P. (Eds.), *Persuasion Handbook: Developments in Theory and Practice*. New York: Sage.

Burgoon, J. K., Floyd, K., and Guerrero, L. K. (2010a). Nonverbal communication theories of interpersonal adaptation. In Berger, C., Roloff, M. E., and Ewoldsen, D. R. (Eds.), *The New Sage Handbook of Communication Science*. London: Sage, pp 93–110.

Burgoon, J. K., Guerrero, L. K., and Floyd, K. (2010b). *Nonverbal Communication*. Boston: Allyn and Bacon.

Burgoon, J. K., Guerrrero, L. K., and Floyd, K. (2016). *Nonverbal Communication*. New York: Routledge.

Burgoon, J. K., and Hobbler, G. (2002). Nonverbal signals. In Knapp, M. L., and Daly, J. (Eds.), *Handbook of Interpersonal Communication*. Thousand Oaks, CA: Sage, pp 240–299.

Burgoon, J. K., Johnson, M. L., and Koch, P. T. (1998). The nature and measurement of interpersonal dominance. *Communication Monographs*, 65, pp 308–335.

Burgoon, J. K., and Koper, R. (1984). Nonverbal and relational communication associated with reticence. *Human Communication Research*, 10, pp 601–626.

Burgoon, J. K., and Le Poire, B. A. (1999). Nonverbal cues and interpersonal judgments: Participant and observer perceptions of intimacy, dominance, composure, and formality. *Communication Monographs*, 66, pp 105–124.

Burgoon, J. K., Stern, L. A., and Dillman, L. (1995). *Interpersonal Adaptation: Dyadic Interaction Patterns*. New York: Cambridge University Press.

Buss, D. M. (1994). *The Evolution of Desire: Strategies of Mate Selection*. New York: Basic Books.

Butterworth, B., and Hadar, U. (1989). Gesture, speech, and computational stages: A reply to McNeill. *Psychological Review*, 96, pp 168–174.

Calvert, G. A., Bullmore, E. T., Brammer, M. J., Campbell, R., Williams, S. C. R., McGuire, P. K., Woodruff, P. W. R., Iversen, S. D., and David, A. S. (1997). Activation of auditory cortex during silent lipreading. *Science*, 276 (April 25), pp 593–596.

Cameron, C., Oskamp, S., and Sparks, W. (1978). Courtship American style: Newspaper advertisements. *The Family Coordinator*, 26, pp 27–30.

Camras, L. A., Sullivan, J., and Michel, G. (1993). Do infants express discrete emotions? Adult judgements of facial, vocal and body actions. *Journal of Nonverbal Behaviour*, 17(3), pp 171–186.

Camurri, A., Lagerlof, I., and Volpe, G. (2003). Recognizing emotion from dance movement: Comparison of spectator recognition and automated techniques. *International Journal of Human-Computer Studies*, 59, pp 213–225.

Camurri, A., Mazzarino, B., Ricchetti, M., Timmers, R., and Volpe, G. (2004). Multimodal analysis of expressive gesture in music and dance performances. In Camurri, A., and Volpe, G. (Eds.), *Gesture-Based Communication in Human-Computer Interaction*. Berlin Springer, pp 357–358.

Cannon, W. B. (1929). *Bodily Changes in Pain, Hunger, Fear, and Rage*, vol. 2. New York: Appleton.

Cannon, W. B. (1942). 'Voodoo' Death. *American Anthropologist*, 44, pp 169–181.

Cappella, J. N. (1993). The facial feedback hypothesis in human interaction: Review and speculation. *Journal of Language and Social Psychology*, 12, pp 13–29.

Capella, J. N., and Greene, J. O. (1982). A discrepancy-arousal explanation of mutual influence in expressive behaviour for adult and infant-adult interaction. *Communication Monographs*, 49, pp 89–114.

Carlson, J. M. (2016). Facilitated orienting underlies fearful face-enhanced gaze cueing of spatial location. *Cogent Psychology*, 3(1).

Carney, D. R., Hall, J. A., and LeBeau, L. S. (2005). Beliefs about the nonverbal expression of social power. *Journal of Nonverbal Behavior*, 29(2), pp 105–123.

Carreiras, M., Lopez, J., Rivero, F., and Corina, D. (2005). Neural processing of a whistled language. *Nature*, 433, pp 31–32.

Carrera-Levillain, P., and Fernandez-Dols, J. (1994). Neutral faces in context: Their emotional meaning and their function. *Journal of Nonverbal Behavior*, 18, pp 281–299.

Carrere, S., Buehlman, K. T., Gottman, J. M., Coan, J. A., and Ruckstuhl, L. (2000). Predicting marital stability and divorce in newlywed couples. *Journal of Family Psychology*, 14(1), pp 42–58.

Centorrino, S., Djemai, E., Hopfensitz, A., Milinski, M., and Seabright, P. (2015). Honest signalling in trust interactions: Smiles rated as genuine induce trust and signal higher earnings opportunities. *Evolution and Human Behavior*, 36, pp 8–16.

Chaikin, A. (1978). Students' reactions to teachers' physical attractiveness and nonverbal behavior: Two exploratory studies. *Psychology in the Schools*, 15(4), pp 588–595.

Chakrabarti, M. (2019). *The Rise of Deepfakes: Things Are Not What They Appear to Be.* Boston: WBUR.org (June 19).

Chaplin, W. F., Phillips, J. B., Brown, J. D., Clanton, N. R., and Stein, J. L. (2000). Handshaking, gender, personality, and first impressions. *Journal of Personality and Social Psychology*, 79(1), pp 110–117.

Chartrand, T. L., and Bargh, J. A. (1999). The chameleon effect: The perception-behavior link and social interaction. *Journal of Personality and Social Psychology*, 76, pp 893–910.

Chawla, P., and Krauss, R. (1994). Gesture and speech in spontaneous and rehearsed narratives. *Journal of Experimental Social Psychology*, 30, pp 580–601.

Cheek, J. M., and Buss, A. H. (1981). Shyness and sociability. *Journal of Personality and Social Psychology*, 41, pp 330–339.

Chelminski, R. (1999). Secret soldier. *Reader's Digest* (April; excerpt of Chelminski's book *Secret soldier*), pp 200–201.

Chevalier-Skolnikoff, S. (1973). Facial expression of emotion in nonhuman primates. In Ekman, P. (Eds.), *Darwin and Facial Expression*. New York: Academic Press, pp 11–89.

Chovil, N. (1991). Social determinants of facial displays. *Journal of Nonverbal Behaviour*, 15, pp 141–154.

Christenfeld, N. J. S. (1994). Options and urns. *Journal of Language and Social Psychology*, 13, 192–199.

Christenfeld, N. J. S. (1995). Does it hurt to say um? *Journal of Nonverbal Behaviour*, 19, pp 171–186.

Christensen, J., Cela-Conde, C. J., and Antoni Gomila, A. (2017). Not all about sex: Neural and biobehavioral functions of human dance. *Annals New York Academy of Science*, pp 8–32. New York Academy of Sciences.

Church, R., Ayman-Nolley, S., and Mahootian, S. (2004). The role of gesture in bilingual education: Does gesture enhance learning? *International Journal of Bilingual Education and Bilingualism*, 7, pp 303–319.

Cialdini, R. (2001). *Influence: Science and Practice*. Boston: Allyn and Bacon.

Clark, H. H. (1996). *Using Language*. Cambridge: Cambridge University Press.

Clark, H. H., and Krych, M. A. (2004). Speaking while monitoring addressees for understanding. *Journal of Memory and Language*, 50, pp 62–81.

Cohan, C. L., Booth, A., and Granger, D. A. (2003). Gender moderates the relationship between testosterone and marital interaction. *Journal of Family Psychology*, 17, pp 29–40.

Cohen, A. (1977). The communicative functions of hand illustrators. *Journal of Communication*, 27, pp 54–63.

Cohen, R. (1993). Thy name, in vain. *Washington Post Magazine* (February 14), p 3.

Coker, D. A., and Burgoon, J. K. (1987). The nature of conversational involvement and nonverbal encoding patterns. *Human Communication Research*, 13, pp 463–494.

Collins, M. (1988). *Liftoff: The Story of America's Adventure in Space*. New York: Grove Press.

Colonnesi, C., Stams, G. J., Koster, I., and Noom, M. (2010). The relationship between pointing and language development: A meta-analysis. *Developmental Review*, 30, pp 352–366.

Congdon, E. L., Novack, M. A., Brooks, N., Hemani-Lopez, N., O'Keefe, L., and Goldin Meadow, S. (2017). Better together: Simultaneous presentation of speech and gesture in math instruction supports generalization and retention. *Learning and Instruction*, 50(6), pp 65–74.

Conn, C., and Silverman, I. (Eds.). (1991). *What Counts: The Complete Harper's Index*. New York: Henry Holt and Co.

Connor, F. P., Williamson, G. G., and Siepp, J. M. (1978). *Program Guide for Infants and Toddlers with Neuromotor and Other Developmental Disabilities*. New York: Teachers College Press.

Cook, S. W., and Goldin-Meadow, S. (2006). The role of gesture in learning: Do children use their hands to change their minds? *Journal of Cognition and Development*, 7(2), pp 211–232.

Costanzo, M., and Archer, D. (1989). Interpreting the expressive behaviour of others: The interpersonal perception task. *Journal of Nonverbal Behavior*, 13, pp 225–245.

Costanzo, M., and Archer, D. (1993). The Interpersonal Perception Task-15. Berkeley, CA: University of California Extension Media Centre.

Cowgill, L. W., Warrener, A., Pontzer, H., and Ocobock, C. (2010). Waddling and toddling: The biomechanical effects of an immature gait. *American Journal of Physical Anthropology*, 143, pp 52–61.

Cowie, R., Douglas-Cowie, E., Tsapatsoulis, N., Votsis, G., Kollias, S., Fellenz, W., et al. (2001). Emotion recognition in human–computer interaction. *IEEE Signal Processing Magazine*, 18, pp 32–80.

Crivelli, C., and Fridlund, A. J. (2019). Inside-out: From basic emotions theory to the behavioral ecology view. *Journal of Nonverbal Behavior*, 43, pp 161–194.

Cunningham, M. R. (1986). Measuring the physical in physical attractiveness: Quasi-experiments on the sociobiology of female facial beauty. *Journal of Personality and Social Psychology*, 50, pp 925–935.

Cunningham, M. R., Barbee, A. R., and Pike, C. L. (1990). What do women want? Facial-metric assessment of multiple motives in the perception of male facial physical attractiveness. *Journal of Personality and Social Psychology*, 59, pp 61–72.

Cunningham, M. R., Roberts, A. R., Barbee, A. P., Druen, P. B., and Wu, C.-H. (1995). "Their ideas of beauty are, on the whole, the same as ours": Consistency and variability in the cross-cultural perception of female physical attractiveness. *Journal of Personality and Social Psychology*, 68(2), pp 261–279.

Cutting, J. E., and Kozlowski, L. T. (1977). Recognizing friends by their walk: Gait perception without familiar cues. *Bulletin of the Psychonomic Society*, 9, pp 353–356.

Dael, N., Mortillaro, M., and Scherer, K. R. (2012). The body action and posture coding system (BAP): Development and reliability. Journal of Nonverbal Behaviour (36), pp 97–121.

Damasio, A. R. (1994). *Descartes' Error: Emotion, Reason and the Human Brain*. New York: D. G. Putnam and Sons.

Daniel, M., Martin, A. D., and Carter, J. (1992). Opiate receptor blockade by naltrexone and mood state after acute physical activity. *British Journal of Sports Medicine*, 26, pp 111–115.

Darwin, C. (1872). *The Expression of the Emotions in Man and Animals*, 3rd ed. New York: Oxford University Press, 1998.

Datta, P. (2014). Self-concept and vision impairment: A review. *British Journal of Visual Impairment*, 32(3), pp 200–210.

Davidoff, J. (1991). *Cognition Through Color*. Cambridge, MA: MIT Press.

Davis, R. L., Wiggins, M. N., Mercado, C. C., and Sullivan, P. S. (2007). Defining the core competency of professionalism based on the patient's perception. *Clinical and Experimental Ophthalmology*, 35, pp 51–54.

De Gennaro, L., and Violani, C. (1988). Reflective lateral eye movements: Individual styles, cognitive and lateralisation effects. *Neuropsychologia*, 26, pp 727–736.

de Meijer, M. (1989). The contribution of general features of body movement to the attribution of emotions. *Journal of Nonverbal Behavior*, 13(4), pp 247–268.

De Paulo, B. M., Kirkendol, S. E., Tang, J., and O Brien, T. P. (1988). The motivational impairment effect in the communication of deception: Replications and extensions. *Journal of Nonverbal Behaviour*, 12(3) pp 177–202.

de Waal, F. (1982). *Chimpanzee Politics*. London: Jonathan Cape.

de Waal, F. (1989a). *Chimpanzee Politics*. Baltimore, MD: Johns Hopkins.

de Waal, F. (1989b). *Peacemaking Among Primates*. Cambridge, MA: Harvard University Press.

de Waal, F., and Lanting, F. (1997). *Bonobo: The Forgotten Ape*. Berkeley: University of California Press.

Deacon, T. W. (1997). *The Symbolic Species: The Co-Evolution of Language and the Brain*. New York: W. W. Norton and Co.

Deese, J. (1984). *Thought into Speech: The Psychology of Language*. Englewood Cliffs, NJ: Prentice Hall.

Delmar, K. (1984). *Winning Moves: The Body Language of Selling*. New York: Random House.

Denault, V., Plusquellec, P., Jupe, L. M., St-Yves, M., Dunbar, N. E., Hartwig, M., Sporer, S. L., Rioux-Turcotte, J., Jarry, J., Walsh, D., Otgaar, H., Viziteu, A., Talwar, V., Keatley, D. A., Blandón-Gitlin, I., Townson, C., Deslauriers-Varin, N., Lilienfeld, S. O., Patterson, M. L., and van Koppen, P. J. (2019). The analysis of nonverbal communication: The dangers of pseudoscience in security and justice contexts. *Anuario de Psicología Jurídica*, 30, pp 1–12.

DePaulo, B. M., and Kirkendol, S. E. (1988). The motivational impairment effect in the communication of deception. In Yuille, J. (Ed.), *Credibility Assessment*. Belgium: Kluwer Academic Publishers, pp 50–69.

DePaulo, B. M., Lindsay, J. J., Malone, B. E., Muhlenbruck, L., Charlton, K., and Cooper, H. (2003). Cues to deception. *Psychological Bulletin*, 129(1), pp 74–118.

Devine, J. (1985). The versatility of human locomotion. *American Anthropologist*, 87, pp 550–570.

Dibble, M. (2020). Trump: Pelosi 'broke the law' by ripping up State of the Union speech. *Washington Examiner* (February 7). www.washingtonexaminer.com (accessed February 7, 2020).

Dijk, C., Fischer, A. H., Morina, N., Van Eeuwijk, C., and Van Kleef, G. (2018). Effects of social anxiety on emotional mimicry and contagion: Feeling negative, but smiling politely. *Journal of Nonverbal Behaviour*, 42(1) pp 81–99.

Dimberg, U., and Soderkvist, S. (2011). The voluntary facial action technique: A method to test the facial feedback hypothesis. *Journal of Nonverbal Behavior*, 35, pp 17–33.

Dimberg, U., Thunberg, M., and Elmehed, K. (2000). Unconscious facial reactions to emotional facial expressions. *Psychological Science*, 11, pp 86–89.

Dimberg, U., Thunberg, M., and Grunedal, S. (2002). Facial reactions to emotional stimuli: Automatically controlled emotional responses. *Cognition and Emotion*, 16, 449–471.

Dion, K. K. (1986). Stereotyping based on physical attractiveness: Issues and conceptual perspectives. In Herman, C. P., Zanna, M. P., and Higgins, E. T. (Eds.), *Physical Appearance, Stigma, and Social Behavior: The Ontario Symposium*, vol. 3. Hillsdale, NJ: Lawrence Erlbaum Associates, pp 7–21.

Dion, K. K., Berscheid, E., and Walster, E. (1972). What is beautiful is good. *Journal of Personality and Social Psychology*, 24, pp 285–290.

Dittmann, A. (1972). The body movement-speech rhythm relationship as a cue to speech encoding. In Seigman, A., and Pope, B. (Eds.), *Studies in Dyadic Communication*. New York: Pergamon Press, pp 135–152.

Dittrich, W. H., Troscianko, T., Lea, S. E. G., and Morgan, D. (1996). Perception of emotion from dynamic point-light displays represented in dance. *Perception*, 25(6), pp 727–738.

Doherty, W. (1997). The emotional contagion scale: A measure of individual differences. *Journal of Nonverbal Behavior*, 21(2), pp 131–154.

Dolcos, S., Sung, K., Argo, J. J., Flor-Henry, S., and Dolcos, F. (2012). The power of a handshake: Neural correlates of evaluative judgments in observed social interactions. *Journal of Cognitive Neuroscience*, 24(12), pp 2292–2305.

Dolhinow, P. (1972). *Primate Patterns*. San Francisco: Holt, Rinehart, and Winston.

Dosey, M., and Meisels, M. (1969). Personal space and self-protection. *Journal of Personality and Social Psychology*, 11, p 97.

Dovidio, J. F., Ellyson, S. L., Keating, C. F., Heltman, K., and Brown, C. (1988). The relationship of social power to visual displays of dominance between men and women. *Journal of Personality and Social Psychology*, 54, pp 233–242.

Dovidio, J. F., Hebl, M., Richeson, J. A., and Shelton, J. N. (2006). Nonverbal communication, race, and intergroup interaction. In Manusov, V., and Patterson, M. L. (Eds.), *The Sage Handbook of Nonverbal Communication*. Thousand Oaks, CA: Sage, pp 481–500.

Driscoll, J. (1969). *The Effects of a Teacher's Eye Contact, Gestures and Voice Intonation on Student Retention of Factual Material* (Unpublished doctoral dissertation, University of Southern Mississippi, University MICROFILMS International, Ann Arbor, MI, No. 7905119).

Dunbar, N., and Bernhold, Q. (2019). Interpersonal power and nonverbal communication. In Agnew, C., and Harman, J. (Eds.), *Power in Close Relationships*. Cambridge: Cambridge University Press, pp 261–278.

Duncan, S. (1975). On the structure of speaker-auditor interaction during speaking turns. *Language in Society*, 2, pp 161–180.

Dundes, A. (1992). *The Evil Eye: A Casebook*. Madison: University of Wisconsin Press. https://uwpress.wisc.edu/books/0291.htm (accessed February 20, 2020).

Dunn, J. C., Halenar, L. B., Davies, T. G., Cristobal-Azkarate, J., Reby, D., and Sykes, D. (2015). Evolutionary trade-off between vocal tract and testes dimensions in howler monkeys. *Current Biology*, 25(21), pp 2839–2844.

Duran, J. I., Reisenzein, R., and Fernandez-Dols, J.-M. (2017). Coherence between emotions and facial expressions. In Fernandez-Dols, J.-M., and Russell, J. A. (Eds.), *The Science of Facial Expression*. New York: Oxford University Press, pp 107–129.

Dyett, L. (1992) *Lear's magazine*, November, pp 95.

Edmondstone, W. M. (1995). Cardiac chest pain: Does body language help the diagnosis? *British Medical Journal* (311), pp 1660–1661.

Eggert, M. (2010). *Brilliant Body Language*. London: Pearson.

Eibl-Eibesfeldt, I. (1970). *Ethology: The Biology of Behavior*. San Francisco: Holt, Rinehart, and Winston.

Eibl-Eibesfeldt, I. (1971). Transcultural patterns of ritualized contact behavior. In Esser, A. H. (Eds.), *Behavior and Environment*. Boston, MA: Springer.

Eibl-Eibesfeldt, I. (1973). The expressive behaviour of the deaf-and-blind-born. In von Cranach, M., and Vine, I. (Eds.), *Social Communication and Movement. European Monographs in Social Psychology*, vol. 4. New York: Academic Press, pp 163–194.

Eibl-Eibesfeldt, I. (1989). *Ethology: The Biology of Behavior*. New York: Holt, Rinehart and Winston.

Eibl-Eibesfeldt, I. (2007). *Human Ethology*. London: Taylor and Francis.

Eisenberger, N. I., and Lieberman, M. D. (2004). Why rejection hurts: A common neural alarm system for physical and social pain. *Trends Cognitive Science*, 8(7), pp 294–300.

Ekman, P. (1977). Facial Expression. Ch. 4. In Siegman, A., and Feldstein, S. (Eds.), *Nonverbal Behavior and Communication*. Mahwah, NJ: Lawrence Erlbaum Association, pp 97–116.

Ekman, P. (1993). Facial expression and emotion. *American Psychologist*, 48, pp 384–392.

Ekman, P. (1994). Strong evidence for universals in facial expression: A reply to Russell's mistaken critique. *Psychological Bulletin*, 115, pp 268–287.

Ekman, P. (1998). Commentaries. In Darwin, C. (Eds.), *The Expression of Emotion in Man and Animals*, 3rd ed. New York: Oxford University press.

Ekman, P. (1999). Basic emotions. In Power, T. D. T. (Ed.), *The Handbook of Cognition and Emotion*. Sussex: Wiley, pp 45–60.

Ekman, P. (2001). *Telling Lies: Clues to Deceit in the Marketplace, Politics, and Marriage*. New York: W. W. Norton and Co.

Ekman, P. (2003). *Emotions Revealed: Recognizing Faces and Feelings to Improve Communication and Emotional Life*. New York: Henry Holt.

Ekman, P., and Friesen, W. V. (1968). Nonverbal behavior in psychotherapy research. In Shlien, J. (Ed.), *Research in Psychotherapy*. Washington, DC: American Psychological Association, pp 179–216.

Ekman, P., and Friesen, W. V. (1969a). Nonverbal leakage and clues to deception. *Psychiatry*, 32(1), 88–106.

Ekman, P., and Friesen, W. V. (1969b). The repertoire of nonverbal behavior: Categories, origins, usage, and coding. *Semiotica*, 1, pp 49–98.

Ekman, P., and Friesen, W. V. (1971). Constants across cultures in the face and emotion. *Journal of Personality and Social Psychology*, 17, pp 124–129.

Ekman, P., and Friesen, W. V. (1972). Hand movements. *Journal of Communication*, 22, pp 353–374.

Ekman, P., and Friesen, W. V. (1975). *Unmasking the Face: A Guide to Recognizing Emotions from Facial Clues*. Englewood Cliffs, NJ: Prentice-Hall.

Ekman, P., and Friesen, W. V. (1976). *Pictures of Facial Affect*. Palo Alto, CA: Consulting Psychologists Press.

Ekman, P., and Friesen, W. V. (1978). *Facial Action Coding System: A Technique for the Measurement of Facial Movement*. Palo Alto, CA: Consulting Psychologists Press.

Ekman, P., Friesen, W. V., and Hager, J. C. (2002). *Facial Action Coding System*. Salt Lake City, UT: Research Nexus, Network Research Information.

Ekman, P., Friesen, W. V., and Tomkins, S. S. (1971). Facial affect scoring technique: A first validity study. *Semiotica*, 3, pp 37–58.

Ekman, P., Levenson, R. W., and Friesen, W. V. (1983). Autonomic nervous system activity distinguishes among emotions. *Science*, 22, pp 1208–1210.

Ekman, P., Sorenson, E. R., and Friesen, W. V. (1969). Pan-cultural elements in the facial display of emotions. *Science*, 164, pp 86–88.

Elam, K. K., Carlson, J. M., DiLalla, L. F., and Reinke, K. S. (2010). Emotional faces capture spatial attention in 5-year-old children. *Evolutionary Psychology*, 8(4), pp 754–767.

Elfenbein, H. A., and Ambady, N. (2003). When familiarity breeds accuracy: Cultural exposure and facial emotion recognition. *Journal of Personality and Social Psychology*, 85, pp 276–290.

Eliade, M. (1959). *The Sacred and the Profane: The Nature of Religion*. London: Harcourt Brace Jovanovich.

Emmers, T. M., and Dindia, K. (1995). The effect of relational stage and intimacy on touch: An extension of Guerrero and Andersen. *Personality and Relationship* (2), pp 225–236.

Escombe, A. R., Moore, D., Gilman, R., Navincopa, M., Ticona, E., Mitchell, B., Noakes, C., Sheen, P., Ramirez, R., Quino, W., Gonzalez, A., Friedland, J., and Evans, C. (2009). Upper room ultraviolet light and negative air ionization to prevent tuberculosis transmission. *PLoS Medicine*, 6(3).

Eysenck, H. J. (1981). Aesthetic preferences and individual differences. In O'Hare, D. (Ed.), *Psychology and the Arts*. Atlantic Highlands, NJ: Humanities Press, pp 76–101.

Farroni, T., Csibra, G., Simion, F., and Johnson, M. H. (2002). Eye contact detection in humans from birth. *Proceedings of the National Academy of Sciences*, 99, pp 9602–9605.

Farroni, T., Csibra, G., Simion, F., and Johnson, M. H. (2020). Eye contact detection in humans from birth. *Proceedings of the National Academy of Sciences*, 99(14), pp 9602–9605, 2002. Web. 09 October 2020.

Fehr, B. J., and Exline, R. V. (1987). Social visual interaction: A conceptual and literature review. In Siegman, A. W., and Feldstein, S. (Eds.), *Nonverbal Behavior and Communication*. Hillsdale, NJ: Lawrence Erlbaum Associates, pp 225–326.

Feingold, A. (1992). Good-looking people are not what we think. *Psychological Bulletin*, 111(2), pp 304–341.

Feldman, R. S., and Rime, B. (1991). *Fundamentals of Nonverbal Behaviour*. New York: Cambridge University Press.

Fernández-Dols, J. (2013). Nonverbal communication: Origin, adaptation, and functionality. In Hall, J., and Knapp, M. (Ed.), *Nonverbal Communication*, 1st ed. Germany: de Gruyter Mouton, pp 69–92.

Fessler, D. M. T., Tracy, J. L., Robins, R. W., and Tangney, J. P. (2007). In Tracy, J. L., Robins, R. W., and Tangney, J. P. (Eds.), *The Self – Conscious Emotions: Theory and Research*. New York: Guilford, pp 174–193.

Field, T. (2001). *Touch*. Cambridge, MA: MIT Press.

Fink, B., Neave, N., Manning, J. T., and Grammer, K. (2006). Facial symmetry and judgments of attractiveness, health and personality. *Personality and Individual Differences*, 41(3), pp 491–499.

Flack, W. F., Laird, J. D., and Cavallaro, L. A. (1999). Separate and combined effects of facial expressions and bodily postures on emotional feelings. *European Journal of Social Psychology*, 29, pp 203–217.

Flew, A. (1979). *A Dictionary of Philosophy*. New York: St. Martin's Press.

Flom, R., Lee, K., and Muir, D. (2007). *Gaze-Following: Its Development and Significance*. Mahwah, NJ: Lawrence Erlbaum Associates.

Floyd, K. (2006a). An evolutionary approach to understanding nonverbal communication. In Manusov, V., and Patterson, M. L. (Eds.), *The Sage Handbook of Nonverbal Communication*. Thousand Oaks, CA: Sage, pp 481–500.

Floyd, K. (2006b). *Communicating Affection: Interpersonal Behavior and Social Context.* Cambridge: Cambridge University Press.

Fogassi, L., and Ferrari, P. F. (2007). Mirror neurons and the evolution of embodied language. *Current Directions in Psychological Science*, 16(3), pp 136–141.

Fogel, A., Messinger, D. S., Dickson, K. L., and Hsu, H. (1999). Posture and gaze in early mother-infant communication: Synchronization of developmental trajectories. *Developmental Science*, 2, pp 325–332.

Forgas, J. P. (1998). On being happy and mistaken: Mood effects on the fundamental attribution error. *Journal of Personality and Social Psychology*, 75, pp 318–331.

Fox, K. C., Nijeboer, S., Solomonova, E., Domhoff, G. W., and Christoff, K. (2013). Dreaming as mind wandering: Evidence from functional neuroimaging and first-person content reports. *Frontiers in Human Neuroscience*, 7, p 412.

Frank, M. G., and Ekman, P. (1993). Not all smiles are created equal: The differences between enjoyment and non-enjoyment smiles. *Humor*, 6, pp 9–26.

Frazer, J. G. (1890). *The Golden Bough.* London: MacMillan.

Freitas-magalhães, A. (2018). *Facial Action Coding System 3.0: Manual of Scientific Codification of the Human Face.* Porto: FEELab Science Books.

Frick, R. W. (1985). Communicating emotion: The role of prosodic features. *Psychological Bulletin*, 97, pp 412–429.

Fridlund, A. J. (1991). Evolution and facial action in reflex, social motive, and paralanguage. *Biological Psychology*, 32(1), pp 3–100.

Fridlund, A. J., and Russell, J. (2006). The function of facial expressions. In Manusov, V., and Patterson, M. L. (Eds.), *The Sage Handbook of Nonverbal Communication.* Thousand Oaks, CA: Sage, pp 299–321.

Friedman, H., Prince, L., Riggio, R., and DiMatteo, M. (1980). Understanding and assessing nonverbal expressiveness: The affective communication test. *Journal of Personality and Social Psychology*, 39(2), pp 333–351.

Frieling, H. (1957). *Psychologische Raumgestaltung und Farhdynamik (Psychological Room Design and Color Dynamic).* Gottingen: Musterschmidt Verlag.

Friesen, W. V., and Ekman, P. (1984). *EMFACS-7: Emotional Facial Action Coding System* (Unpublished manuscript, University of California, San Francisco, CA).

Fromm-Reichman, F. (1950). *Psychoanalysis and Psychotherapy.* Chicago: University of Chicago Press.

Furlow, B. F., Armijo-Prewitt, T., Gangestad, S. W., and Thornhill, R. (1997). Fluctuating asymmetry and psychometric intelligence. *Proceedings of the Royal Society of London, Series B*, 264, pp 823–829.

Gaffney, M. (2011). *Flourishing: How to Achieve a Deeper Sense of Well-Being, Meaning and Purpose – When Facing Adversity.* Dublin: Penguin.

Galati, D., Scherer, K. R., and Ricci-Bitti, P. E. (1997). Voluntary facial expressions of emotion: Comparing congenitally blind with normally sighted encoders. *Journal of Personality and Social Psychology*, 73, pp 1363–1379.

Galati, D., Sini, B., Schmidt, S., and Tnti, C. (2003). Spontaneous facial expressions in congenitally blind and sighted children aged 8–11. *Journal of Visual Impairment and Blindness*, 97, pp 418–428.

Galen, B. R., and Underwood, M. K. (1997). A developmental investigation of social aggression among children. *Developmental Psychology*, 33(4), pp 589–600.

Gangestad, S. W., and Thornhill, R. (1997). Human sexual selection and developmental stability. In Simpson, J. A., and Kenrick, D. T. (Eds.), *Evolutionary Personality and Social Psychology.* Hillsdale, NJ: Lawrence Erlbaum Associates, pp 169–195.

Gerhart, S. (2004). *Why Love Matters: How Affection Shapes a Baby's Brain*. New York: Brunner-Routledge.

Geschwind, N. (1979). Specializations of the human brain. In Llinas, R. R. (Ed.), *The Workings of the Brain: Development, Memory, and Perception – Readings from Scientific American Magazine, 1976–1987*. New York: W. H. Freeman and Co., pp 105–120, 1990.

Ghez, C. (1991a). Posture. In Kandel, E. R., Schwartz, J. H., and Jessell, T. M. L. (Eds.), *Principles of Neural Science*, 3rd ed. Norwalk, CT: Appleton and Lange, pp 596–607.

Ghez, C. (1991b). Voluntary movement. Ch. 40. In Kandel, E. R., Schwartz, J. H., and Jessell, T. M. (Eds.), *Principles of Neural Science*, 3rd ed. Norwalk, CT: Appleton and Lange, pp 609–625.

Gibbons, A. (1997). Tracing the identity of the first toolmakers. *Science*, 276 (April 4), p 32.

Gibson, K. R. (1993). Overlapping neural control of language, gesture and tool-use. In Gibson, K. R., and Ingold, T. (Eds.), *Tools, Language and Cognition in Human Evolution*. Cambridge: Cambridge University Press, Part III Introduction, pp 187–192.

Givens, D. B. (1977). Shoulder shrugging: A densely communicative expressive behavior. *Semiotica*, 19, pp 13–28.

Givens, D. B. (1978a). The nonverbal basis of attraction: Flirtation, courtship, and seduction. *Psychiatry*, 41, pp 346–359.

Givens, D. B. (1978b). Social expressivity during the first year of life. *Sign Language Studies*, 20, pp 251–274.

Givens, D. B. (1978c). Greeting a stranger: Some commonly used nonverbal signals of aversiveness. *Semiotica*, 22, pp 351–367.

Givens, D. B. (1982). From here to eternity: Communicating with the distant future. *In Et Cetera*, 39(2), pp 159–179.

Givens, D. B. (1983). *Love Signals*. New York: Crown Publishing.

Givens, D. B. (2002). *The Language of Hands* (Unpublished report sponsored by Unilever Vaseline Research).

Givens, D. B. (2005). *Love Signals: A Practical Field Guide to the Body Language of Courtship*. New York: St. Martin's Press.

Givens, D. B. (2008). *Crime Signals: How to Spot a Criminal Before You Become a Victim*. New York: St. Martin's Press.

Givens, D. B. (2015). Measuring gestures. In Kosti, A., and Chadee, D. (Eds.), *The Social Psychology of Nonverbal Communication*. London: Palgrave Macmillan, pp 66–91.

Givens, D. B. (2016). Reading palm-up signs: Neurosemiotic overview of a common hand gesture." *Semiotica*, 2016(210), pp 235–250.

Givens, D. B. (2020). Nonverbal steps to the origin of language. Ch. 6. In Sternberg, R. J., and Kostic, A. (Eds.), *Social Intelligence and Nonverbal Communication*. London: Palgrave Macmillan, pp 163–189.

Givhan, R. D. (1995). Suede by popular opinion. *Washington Post* (November 29), pp Cl, C2.

Glenberg, A. M. (1997). What memory is for. *Behavioral and Brain Sciences*, 20, pp 1–55.

Glenberg, A. M. (2008). Toward the integration of bodily states, language, and action. In Semin, G. R., and Smith, E. R. (Eds.), *Embodied Grounding: Social, Cognitive, Affective, and Neuroscientific Approaches*. Cambridge: Cambridge University Press, pp 43–70.

Godøy, R. (2010). Gestural affordances of musical sound. In Godøy, R., and Leman, M. (Eds.), *Musical Gestures: Sound, Movement, and Meaning*. New York: Routledge, pp 103–125.

Goffman, E. (1959). *The Presentation of Self in Everyday Life*. New York: Doubleday.

Goffman, E. (1963). *Behavior in Public Places*. New York: The Free Press.

Goffman, E. (1967). *Interaction Ritual*. Chicago: Aldine.

Goldin-Meadow, S. (2004). Gesture's role in the learning process. *Theory into Practice*, 43(4), pp 314–321.

Goldin-Meadow, S., Kim, S., and Singer, M. (1999). What the adult's hands tell the student's mind about math. *Journal of Educational Psychology*, 91, pp 720–730.

Goldin-Meadow, S., Wein, D., and Chang, C. (1992). Assessing knowledge through gesture: Using children's hands to read their minds. *Cognition and Instruction*, 9, pp 201–219.

Goleman, D. (1996). *Emotional Intelligence, Why It Can Matter More Than IQ*. London: Bloomsbury.

Gonzales, A. L., and Hancock, J. T. (2008). Identity shift in computer-mediated environments. *Media Psychology*, 11, pp 167–118.

Goodall, J. (1986). *The Chimpanzees of Gombe: Patterns of Behavior*. Cambridge: Belknap Press of Harvard University.

Goodall, J. (1990). *Through a Window: My Thirty Years with the Chimpanzees of Gombe*. Boston: Houghton Mifflin Company.

Gorham, J., and Zakahi, W. R. A. (1990). Comparison of teacher and student perceptions of immediacy and learning: Monitoring process and product. *Communication Education*, 39(4), pp 354–368.

Gorham, W. I., Cohen, S. H., and Morris, T. L. (1999). Fashion in the classroom III: Effects of instructor attire and immediacy in natural classroom interactions. *Communications Quarterly*, 47(3), pp 281–299.

Gosling, S. D., Augustine, A. A., Vazire, S., Holtzman, N., and Gaddis, S. (2011). Manifestations of personality in online social networks: Self-reported Facebook-related behaviors and observable profile information. *Cyberpsychology, Behavior, and Social Networks*, 14, pp 483–448.

Gosselin, P., Perron, M., and Beaupré, M. (2010). The voluntary control of facial action units in adults. *Emotion*, 10, pp 266–271.

Gračanin, A., Bylsma, L. M., and Vingerhoets, A. J. J. M. (2018). Why only humans shed emotional tears. *Evolutionary and Cultural Perspectives. Human Nature*, 29, pp 104–133.

Grahe, J. E., Bernieri, F. J. (1999). The importance of nonverbal cues in judging rapport. *Journal of Nonverbal Behavior*, 23, pp 253–269.

Grant, E. (1969). Human facial expressions. *Man*, 4, pp 525–536.

Gray, H. (1995). *Gray's Anatomy*, 15th ed. New York: Churchill Livingstone.

Grayson, B., and Stein, M. I. (1981). Attracting assault: Victims' nonverbal cues. *Journal of Communication*, 31, pp 68–75.

Greenfeld, K. T. (2001). Blind to failure. *Time* (June 18), pp 52–57, 60, 62–63.

Gress, J., and Heft, H. (1998). Do territorial actions attenuate the effects of high density? A filed study. In Sanford, J., and Connell, B. (Eds.), *People, Places and Public Policy*. Edmond, OK: Environmental Design and Research Association.

Grillner, S. (1996). Neural networks for vertebrate locomotion. *Scientific American* (January), pp 64–69.

Guerin, B. (1983). Social facilitation and social monitoring: A test of three models. *British Journal of Social Psychology*, 22, 203–214.

Guerin, B. (1993). *Social Facilitation*. Cambridge: Cambridge University Press.

Guerrero, L. K. (1997). Nonverbal involvement across interactions with same-sex friends, opposite-sex friends, and romantic partners: Consistency or change? *Journal of Social and Personal Relationships*, 14, pp 31–58.

Guerrero, L. K. (2005). Observer ratings of nonverbal involvement and immediacy. In Manusov, V. (Ed.), *The Sourcebook of Nonverbal Measures*. Mahwah, NJ: Lawrence Erlbaum Associates, pp 221–235.

Guerrero, L. K., and Andersen, P. A. (1991). The waxing and waning or relational intimacy: Touch as a function of relational stage, gender and touch avoidance. *Journal of Social and Personal Relationships*, 8, pp 147–165.

Guerrero, L. K., and Andersen, P. A. (1994). Patterns of matching and initiation: Touch behavior and touch avoidance across relational stages. *Journal of Nonverbal Behavior*, 18, pp 137–154.

Guerrero, L. K., Andersen, P. A., and Afifi, W. A. (2007). *Close Encounters: Communication in Relationships*, 2nd ed. Thousand Oaks, CA: Sage.

Guillon, Q., Hadjikhani, N., Baduel, S., and Rogé, B. (2014). Visual social attention in autism spectrum disorder: Insights from eye tracking studies. *Neuroscience and Biobehavioral Reviews*, 42, pp 279–297.

Gunnery, S. D., and Hall, J. A. (2014). The Duchenne smile and persuasiveness. *Journal of Nonverbal Behavior*, 38, pp 181–194.

Gunnery, S. D., Hall, J. A., and Ruben, M. A. (2013). The deliberate Duchenne smile: Individual differences in expressive control. *Journal of Nonverbal Behavior*, 37, pp 29–41.

Güntürkün, O. (2003). Human behaviour: Adult persistence of head-turning asymmetry. *Nature*, 421, p 711.

Gur, R. C., Packer, I. K., Hungerbuhler, J. P., Reivich, M., Obrist, W. D., Amarnek, W. S., and Sackeim, H. A. (1980). Differences in the distribution of gray and white matter in human cerebral hemispheres. *Science*, 207, pp 1226–1228.

Gur, R. E. (1975). Conjugate lateral eye movements as an index of hemispheric activation. *Journal of Personality and Social Psychology*, 31, pp 751–757.

Guyer, J. J., Briñol, P., Petty, R. E., and Horcajo, J. (2019). Nonverbal behavior of persuasive sources: A multiple process analysis. *Journal of Nonverbal Behavior*, 43, pp 203–231.

Guyton, A. C. (1996). *Textbook of Medical Physiology*, 9th ed. Philadelphia: W. B. Saunders.

Haberstadt, A. L. (2015). Recent advances in the neuropharmacology of serotonergic hallucinogens. *Behavioural Brain Research*, 277, pp 99–120.

Hadar, U., Burstein, A., Krauss, R., and Soroker, N. (1998). Ideational gestures and speech in brain-damaged subjects. *Language and Cognitive Processes*, 13, pp 59–76.

Hadar, U., Steiner, T. J., and Rose, F. C. (1985). Head movement during listening turns in conversation. *Journal of Nonverbal Behaviour*, 9, pp 214–228.

Hageman, P. (1995). Gait characteristics of healthy elderly: A literature review. *Issues on Aging* 18, pp 2–14.

Hagendoom, I. (2011). *Dance, Aesthetics and the Brain*. https://pure.uvt.nl/ws/portalfiles/portal/10278840/Hagendoorn_dance_23_03_2012.pdf (accessed March 4, 2020).

Hager, J. C., and Ekman, P. (1997). The asymmetry of facial actions is inconsistent with models of hemispheric specialization. In Ekman, P., and Rosenberg, E. (Eds.), *What the Face Reveals*. New York: Oxford University Press, pp 40–62.

Haggard, E. A., and Isaacs, K. S. (1966). Micromomentary facial expressions as indicators of ego mechanisms in psychotherapy. In *Methods of Research in Psychotherapy. The Century Psychology Series*. Boston, MA: Springer.

Halberstadt, A. G. (1985). Race, socioeconomic status and nonverbal behaviour. In Siegman, A. W., and Feldstein, S. (Eds.), *Multichannel Integrations of Nonverbal Behaviour*. Hillsdale, NJ: Lawrence Erlbaum Associates.

Hall, E. (1959). *The Silent Language*. Garden City, NY: Doubleday.

Hall, E. (1966). *The Hidden Dimension*. New York: Doubleday.

Hall, E. T. (1963). A system for the notation of proxemic behavior. *American Anthropologist*, 65, pp 1003–1026.

Hall, E. T. (1973). *The Silent Language*. New York: Anchor Books.

Hall, J., and Knapp, M. (2013). *Nonverbal Communication*. Boston: De Gruyter, Inc., ProQuest.

Hall, J. A. (1984). *Nonverbal Sex Differences: Communication Accuracy and Expressive Style*. Baltimore: John Hopkins University Press.

Hall, J. A., Andrzejewski, S. A., and Yopchick, J. E. (2009). Psychosocial correlates of interpersonal sensitivity: A meta-analysis. *Journal Nonverbal Behaviour*, 33, pp 149–180.

Hall, J. A., Coats, E., and Smith LeBeau, L. (2005). Nonverbal social relations: A meta – analysis. *Psychological Bulletin*, 131, pp 898–924.

Hall, J. A., Rosip, J. C., Smith LeBeau, L., Horgan, T. G., and Carter, J. D. (2006). Attributing the sources of accuracy in unequal-power dyadic communication: Who is better and why? *Journal of Experimental Social Psychology*, 42, pp 18–27.

Hall, K., and DeVore, I. (1972). Baboon social behavior. In Dolhinow, P. (Ed.), *Primate Patterns*. San Francisco: Holt, Rinehart, and Winston, pp 125–180.

Hall, P. M., and Hall, D. A. S. (1983). The handshake as interaction. *Semiotica*, 45(3–4), pp 249–264.

Halpern, A. R., and Zatorre, R. J. (1999). When that tune runs through your head: A pet investigation of auditory imagery for familiar melodies. *Cerebral Cortex*, 9, pp 697–704.

Han, W., Tellez, L. A., Perkins, M. H., Perez, I. O., Qu, T., Ferreira, J., Quinn, D., Liu, Z. W., Gao, X. B., Kaelberer, M. M., Bohorquez, D. V., Shammah-Lagnado, S. J., de Lartigue, G., and de Araujo, I. E. (2018). A neural circuit for gut-induced reward. *Cell*, 175, pp 665–678.

Hanzal, A., Segrin, C., and Dorros, S. M. (2008). The role of marital status and age on men's and women's reactions to touch from relational partner. *Journal of Nonverbal Behavior*, 32, 21–35.

Hargie, O., and Dickson, D. (2004). *Skilled Interpersonal Communication: Research, Theory and Practice*. London: Routledge.

Harkins, S., and Szymanksi, K. (1987). Social facilitation and social loafing: New wine in old bottles. In Hendrick, C. (Ed.), *Review of Personality and Social Psychology*, vol. 9. Beverly Hills, CA: Sage.

Harnad, S. (1972). Creativity, lateral saccades and the nondominant hemisphere. *In Perceptual and Motor Skills*, 34, pp 653–654.

Harrigan, J. A. (1985). Self-touching as an indicator of underlying affect and language processes. *Social Science and Medicine*, 29, pp 1161–1168.

Harris, M. B., James, J., Chavez, J., Fuller, M. L., Kent, S., Massanari, C., Moore, C., and Walsh, F. (1983). Clothing: Communication, compliance and choice. *Journal of Applied Social Psychology*, 13, pp 88–97.

Hass, H. (1970). *The Human Animal*. New York: G. P. Putnam's Sons.

Hatfield, E., Cacioppo, J. T., and Rapson, R. L. (1992). *Emotional Contagion*. New York: Cambridge University Press.

Hatfield, E., and Sprecher, S. (1986). *Mirror, Mirror . . . The Importance of Looks in Everyday Life*. Albany: State University of New York Press.

Hatfield, R., Rapson, R., and Yen-Chi, L. L. (2009). Emotional contagion and empathy. In Decety, J., and Ickes, W. (Eds.), *The Social Neuroscience of Empathy*. Bradford, MA: Institute of Technology, pp 19–31.

Hawk, S. T., van Kleef, G. A., Fischer, A. H., and van der Schalk, J. (2009). "Worth a thousand words": Absolute and relative decoding of nonlinguistic affect vocalizations. *Emotion*, 9(3), pp 293–305.

Hayduk, L. A. (1981). The permeability of personal space. *Canadian Journal of Behavioural Science*, 13, pp 274–287.

Hayduk, L. A. (1983). Personal space: Where we stand now. *Psychological Bulletin*, 94, pp 293–335.

Heaven, L., and McBrayer, D. (2000). External motivators of self-touching behaviour. *Perceptual and Motor Skills*, 90, pp 338–342.

Hellstrom, A., and Tekle, J. (1994). Person perception through facial photographs – effects of glasses, hair and beards on judgements of occupation and personality traits. *European Journal of Social Psychology*, 4, pp 693–705.

Hennenlotter, A., Dresel, C., Castrop, F., Ceballos Baumann, A. O., Wohlschläger, A. M., and Haslinger, B. (2009). The link between facial feedback and neural activity within central circuitries of emotion – new insights from botulinum toxin–induced denervation of frown muscles. *Cerebral Cortex*, 19, pp 537–542.

Hersey, G. L. (2009). *Falling in Love with Statues: Artificial Humans from Pygmalion to the Present*. Chicago: University of Chicago Press.

Heslin, R., and Boss, D. (1980). Nonverbal intimacy in airport arrival and departure. *Personality and Social Psychology Bulletin*, 6(2), pp 248–225.

Hess, E. H. (1975). The role of pupil size in communication. *Scientific American*, 233, pp 110–119.

Hess, E. H., and Polt, J. M. (1960). Pupil size as related to interest value of visual stimuli. *Science*, 132, pp 349–350.

Hess, U., Adams, R. B., and Kleck, R. E. (2005). Who may frown and who should smile? Dominance, affiliation, and the display of anger and happiness. *Cognition and Emotion*, 19, pp 515–536.

Hess, U., Beaupre´, M., and Cheung, N. (2002). To whom and why – cultural differences and similarities in the function of smiles. In Millicent, A. (Ed.), *The Smile: Forms, Functions, and Consequences*. New York: The Edwin Mellen Press, pp 187–216.

Hess, U., and Fischer, A. (2013). Emotional mimicry as social regulation. *Personality and Social Psychology Review*, 17(2), pp 142–157.

Hess, U., Kappas, A., McHugo, G. J., Kleck, R. E., and Lanzetta, J. T. (1989). An analysis of the encoding and decoding of spontaneous and posed smiles: The use of facial electromyography. *Journal of Nonverbal Behavior*, 13, pp 121–137.

Heyman, T. (1992). *In an Average Lifetime*. New York: Ballantine Books.

Hill, E. M., Nocks, E. S., and Gardner, L. (1987). Physical attractiveness: Manipulation by physique and status displays. *Ethology and Sociobiology*, 8, pp 143–154.

Hinde, R. A. (1970). *Animal Behaviour*, 2nd ed. New York: McGraw-Hill.

Holland, E., Wolf, E. B., Looser, C., and Cuddy, A. (2016). Visual attention to powerful postures: People avert their gaze from nonverbal dominance displays. *Journal of Experimental Social Psychology*, 68, pp 60–67.

Holler, J., Shovelton, H., and Beattie, G. (2009). Do iconic hand gestures really contribute to the communication of semantic information in a face-to-face context? *Journal of Nonverbal Behavior*, 33, pp 73–88.

Holstege, G. (2016). How the emotional motor system controls the pelvic organs. *Sexual Medicine Review*, 4(4), pp 303–328.

Hostetter, A. (2011). When do gestures communicate? A meta-analysis. *Psychological Bulletin*, 137, pp 297–315.

Huazhong Ning, Tony X. Han, Yuxiao Hu, Zhenqiu Zhang, Yun Fu, and Thomas S. Huang. (2006). *A Realtime Shrug Detector* (IEEE International Conference on Automatic Face and Gesture Recognition (FG 2006), pp 505–510).

Humphrey, N. K. (1976). The social function of intellect. In Bateson, P., and Hinde, R. (Eds.), *Growing Points in Ethology*. Cambridge: Cambridge University Press.

Iacoboni, M. (2008). *Mirroring People*. New York: Farrar, Straus and Giroux.

Iacoboni, M. (2009). Imitation, empathy, and mirror neurons. *Annual Review of Psychology*, 60, pp 653–670.

Ickes, W., Tooke, W., Stinson, L., Lau Baker, V., and Bissonnette, V. (1988). Naturalistic social cognition: Intersubjectivity in same sex dyads. *Journal of Nonverbal Behaviour*, 12(1), pp 58–82.

Igualada, A. L., Esteve-Gibert, N., and Prieto, P. (2017). Beat gestures improve word recall in 3- to 5-year-old children. *Journal of Experimental Child Psychology*, 156, pp 99–112.

Illingworth, R. S. (1951). Sleep problems in the first three years. *BMJ: British Medical Journal*, 1, 722–728. http://dx.doi.org/10.1136/bmj.1.4709.722.

Itano, W. M., and Ramsey, N. F. (1993). Accurate measurement of time. *Scientific American* (July), pp 56–65.

Ito, K., Masuda, T., and Li, L. M. W. (2013). Agency and facial emotion judgment in context. *Personality and Social Psychology Bulletin*, 39(6), pp 763–776.

Iverson, J., and Goldin-Meadow, S. (1997). What's communication got to do with it? Gesture in children blind from birth. *Developmental Psychology*, 33, pp 453–467.

Iverson, J., and Goldin-Meadow, S. (1998). Why people gesture when they speak. *Nature*, 396.

Iverson, J., and Goldin-Meadow, S. (2005). Gesture paves the way for language development. *Psychological Science*, 16, pp 367–371.

Iverson, J. M., Tencer, H. T., Lany, J., and Goldin-Meadow, S. (2000). The relation between gesture and speech in congenitally blind and sighted language learners. *Journal of Nonverbal Behavior*, 24, pp 105–130.

Izard, C. E. (1971). *The Face of Emotion*. New York: Appleton-Century-Crofts.

Izard, C. E. (1978). Emotions as motivations: An evolutionary-developmental perspective. In Dienstbier, R. A. (Ed.), *Nebraska Symposium on Motivation*, vol. 25. Lincoln: University of Nebraska Press, pp 163–200.

Izard, C. E. (1994). Innate and universal facial expressions: Evidence from developmental and cross-cultural research. *Psychological Bulletin*, 115, pp 288–299.

Izard, C. E., and Malatesta, C. (1987). Perspectives on emotional development: Differential emotions theory of early emotional development. In Osofsky, J. D. (Ed.), *Handbook of Infant Development*. New York: Wiley, pp 494–554.

Jackson, D. (1999). Hot dogs are us. *Smithsonian* (June), pp 104–110, 112.

Jakubiak, B. K., and Feeney, B. C. (2016). Keep in touch: The effects of imagined touch support on stress and exploration. *Journal of Experimental Social Psychology*, 65, pp 59–67.

James, W. (1932). A study of the expression of bodily posture. *Journal of General Psychology*, 7, pp 405–437.

Jankowski, G. F., and Fuchs, D. C. (1995). *Television Today and Tomorrow*. New York: Oxford University Press.

Jansen, A. S. P., Van Nguyen, X., Karpitskiy, V., Mettenleiter, T. C., and Loewy, A. D. (1995). Central command neurons of the sympathetic nervous system: Basis of the fight-or-flight response. *Science* (270), pp 644–646.

Janssen, D., Schöllhorn, W. I., Lubienetzki, J., et al. (2008). Recognition of emotions in gait patterns by means of artificial neural nets. *Journal of Nonverbal Behaviour*, 32, pp 79–92.

Jasienska, G., Lipson, S. F., Ellison, P. T., Thune, I., and Ziomkiewicz, A. (2006). Symmetrical women have higher potential fertility. *Evolution and Human Behavior*, 27, pp 390–400.

Jerison, H. J. (1976). Paleoneurology and the evolution of mind. In Llinas, R. R. (Ed.), *The Workings of the Brain: Development, Memory, and Perception – Readings from Scientific American Magazine, 1976–1987*. New York: W. H. Freeman and Co., pp 3–16, 1990.

Johnson, K. J., and Tassinary, L. G. (2005). Perceiving sex directly and indirectly: Meaning in motion and morphology. *Psychological Science*, 16, pp 890–897.

Johnston, L., Hudson, S. M., Richardson, M. J., Gunns, R. E., and Garner, M. (2004). Changing kinematics as a means of reducing vulnerability to physical attack. *Journal of Applied Social Psychology*, 34, pp 514–537.

Jones, A. L., and Kramer, R. S. S. (2015). Facial cosmetics have little effect on attractiveness judgments compared with identity. *Perception*, 44, pp 79–86.

Jones, B. C., DeBruine, L. M., Main, J. C., Little, A. C., Welling, L. L., Feinberg, D. R., et al. (2010). Facial cues of dominance modulate the short-term gaze-cuing effect in human observers. *Proceedings of the Royal Society B*, 277, pp 617–624.

Jones, D., and Hill, K. (1993). Criteria of facial attractiveness in five populations. *Human Nature*, 4, pp 271–296.

Jones, N., Kearins, J., and Watson, J. (1987). The human tongue show and observers' willingness to interact: Replication and extensions. *Psychological Reports*, 60(3), pp 759–764.

Joseph, A. B., and Saint-Hilaire, M. (1992). Startle syndromes. Ch. 64. In Joseph, A. B., and Young, R. R. (Eds.), *Movement Disorders in Neurology and Neuropsychiatry*. Cambridge, MA: Blackwell Scientific Publications, pp 487–492.

Juslin, P. N., and Laukka, P. (2003). Communication of emotions in vocal expression and music performance: Different channels, same code? *Psychological Bulletin*, 129, pp 770–814.

Juslin, P. N., and Laukka, P. (2017). *The Truly Intense Vocal Affect Collection (TIVAC): Presentation and Validation* (Manuscript submitted for publication).

Juslin, P. N., Laukka, P., and Banzinger, T. (2018). The mirror to our soul? Comparisons of spontaneous and posed vocal expression of emotion. *Journal of Nonverbal Behaviour*, 42, pp 1–40.

Juslin, P. N., and Scherer, K. R. (2005). Vocal expression of affect. In Harrigan, J. A., Rosenthal, R., and Scherer, K. R. (Eds.), *Series in Affective Science. The New Handbook of Methods in Nonverbal Behavior Research*. Oxford: Oxford University Press, pp 65–135.

Kagan, J. (2007). *What Is Emotion? History, Measures, and Meanings*. Washington: Yale University Press.

Kahneman, D., and Beatty, J. (1966). Pupil diameter and load on memory. *Science*, 154(3756), pp 1583–1585.

Kaiser, S. B. (1997). *The Social Psychology of Clothing: Symbolic Appearances in Context*, 3rd ed. New York: Fairfield Publications.

Kalma, A. (1992). Gazing in triads: A powerful signal in floor apportionment. *British Journal of Social Psychology*, 31, pp 21–39.

Kalogridis, J. (2019). *The Scarlett Contessa: A Novel of the Italian Renaissance*. New York: St. Martin's Press.

Kammrath, L. K., Ames, D. R., and Scholar, A. A. (2007). Keeping up impressions: Inferential rules for impression change across the Big Five. *Journal of Experimental Social Psychology*, 43, pp 450–457.

Kandel, E. R. (1991). Perception of motion, depth, and form. In Kandel, E. R., Schwartz, J. H., and Jessell, T. M. (Eds.), *Principles of Neural Science*, 3rd ed. Norwalk, CT: Appleton and Lange, pp 440–466.

Kandel, E. R., and Jessell, T. M. (1991). Touch. In Kandel, E. R., Schwartz, J. H., and Jessell, T. M. (Eds.), *Principles of Neural Science*, 3rd ed. Norwalk, CT: Appleton and Lange, pp 367–384.

Kandel, E. R., Schwartz, J. H., and Jessell, T. M. (1991). *Principles of Neural Science*, 3rd ed. Norwalk, CT: Appleton & Lange, pp 440–466.

Kantowitz, B. H., and Sorkin, R. D. (1983). *Human Factors*. New York: John Wiley and Sons.

Karg, M., Kühnlenz, K., and Buss, M. (2010). Recognition of affect based on gait patterns. *Systems, Man, and Cybernetics, Part B: Cybernetics, IEEE Transactions*, 40(4), pp 1050–1061.

Karni, A., Rey-Hipolito, C., Jezzard, P., Adams, M., Turner, R., and Ungerleider, L. G. (1998). The acquisition of skilled motor performance: Fast and slow experience-driven changes in primary motor and cortex. *Proceedings of the National Academy of Sciences*, 95(3) (February 3), pp 861–868.

Karson, C. N. (1992). Oculomotor disorders in schizophrenia. In Joseph, A. B., and Young, R. R. (Eds.), *Movement Disorders in Neurology and Neuropsychiatry*. Cambridge, MA, Blackwell Scientific Pubs., pp 414–421.

Katsumi, Y., Suhkyung, K., Sung, K., and Dolcos, F. (2017). When nonverbal greetings "make it or break it": The role of ethnicity and gender in the effect of handshake on social appraisals. *Journal of Nonverbal Behaviour*, 41(4), pp 345–365.

Keillor, J. M., Barrett, A. M., Crucian, G. P., Kortenkamp, S., and Heilman, K. M. (2002). Emotional experience and perception in the absence of facial feedback. *Journal of the International Neuropsychological Society*, 8(1), pp 130–135.

Kelly, J. P., and Dodd, J. (1991). Anatomical organization of the nervous system. In Kandel, E. R., Schwartz, J. H., and Jessell, T. M. (Eds.), *Principles of Neural Science*, 3rd ed. Norwalk, CT: Appleton and Lange, pp 273–282.

Kelly, S., and Goldsmith, L. (2004). Gesture and right hemisphere involvement in evaluating lecture material. *Gesture*, 4, pp 25–42.

Keltner, D. (1995). Signs of appeasement: Evidence for the distinct displays of embarrassment, amusement, and shame. *Journal of Personality and Social Psychology*, 68(3), pp 441–454.

Keltner, D. (2009). *Born to Be Good: The Science of a Meaningful Life*. New York: W. W. Norton and Co.

Keltner, D., and Bonanno, G. A. (1997). A study of laughter and dissociation: Distinct correlates of laughter and smiling during bereavement. *Journal of Personality and Social Psychology*, 73(4), pp 687–702.

Keltner, D., and Buswell, B. N. (1997). Embarrassment: Its distinct form and appeasement functions. *Psychological Bulletin*, 122, pp 250–270.

Keltner, D., and Lerner, J. (2010). Emotion. In Fiske, S. T., Giblert, D. T., and Lindzey, G. (Eds.), *Handbook of Social Psychology*, vol. 1. Hoboken, NJ: Wiley, pp 317–342.

Keltner, D., Sauter, D., Tracy, J., et al. (2019b). Emotional expression: Advances in basic emotion theory. *Journal of Nonverbal Behaviour*, 43, pp 133–160.

Keltner, D., Tracy, J. L., Sauter, D., et al. (2019a). What basic emotion theory really says for the twenty-first century study of emotion. *Journal of Nonverbal Behaviour*, 43, pp 195–201.

Kendon, A. (1967). Some functions of gaze direction in social interaction. *Acta Psychologica*, 26, pp 22–63.

Kenner, A. N. (1993). A cross-cultural study of body-focused hand movements. *Journal of Nonverbal Behaviour*, 17, pp 263–279.

Kent, G. C., Jr. (1969). *Comparative Anatomy of the Vertebrates*, 2nd ed. Saint Louis: C. V. Mosby Co.

Key, M. R. (1975). *Paralanguage and Kinesics (Nonverbal Communication)*. New York: Scarecrow Press.

Keysers, C., and Fadiga, L. (2008). The mirror neuron system: New frontiers. *Social Neuroscience*, 3, pp 193–198.

Keysers, C., Wicker, B., Gazzola, V., Anton, J. L., Fogassi, L., and Gallese, V. (2004). A touching sight: SII/PV activation during the observation and experience of touch. *Neuron*, 42, pp 335–346.

Kilford, E. J., Garrett, E., and Blakemore, S. J. (2016). The development of social cognition in adolescence: An integrated perspective. *Neuroscience and Biobehavioral Reviews*, 70, pp 106–120.

Kim, H. K., Mirjalili, S. A., and Fernandez, J. (2018). Gait kinetics, kinematics, spatiotemporal and foot plantar pressure alteration in response to long-distance running: Systematic review. *Human Movement Science*, 57, pp 342–356.

Kim, M. J., Neta, M., Davis, F. C., Ruberry, E. J., Dinescu, D., Heatherton, T. F., et al. (2014). Botulinum toxin-induced facial muscle paralysis affects amygdala responses to the perception of emotional expressions: Preliminary findings from an ABA design. *Biology of Mood and Anxiety Disorders*, 4(1), p 11.

King, M. J. (1966). Interpersonal relations in preschool children and average approach distance. *Journal of Genetic Psychology*, 109, pp 109–116.

Kinley, T., Strübel, J., and Amlani, A. (2019). Impression formation of male and female millennial students wearing eye glasses or hearing aids. *Journal of Nonverbal Behaviour*, 43, pp 357–379.

Kleinke, C. L. (1986). Gaze and eye contact: A research review. *Psychological Bulletin*, 100, pp 78–100.

Kleinke, C. L., Bustos, A. A., Meeker, F. B., and Staneski, R. A. (1973). Effects of self-attributed gaze in interpersonal evaluations between males and females. *Journal of Experimental Social Psychology*, 9, pp 154–163.

Klin, A., Saulnier, C. A., Sparrow, S. S., Cicchetti, D. V., Volkmar, F. R., and Lord, C. (2006). Social and communication abilities and disabilities in higher functioning individuals with autism spectrum disorders: The Vineland and the ADOS. *Journal of Autism and Developmental Disorders*, 37(4), pp 748–759.

Klinzing, H., and Aloisio, B. (2004). *Intensity, Variety and Accuracy in Nonverbal Cues and Decoding: Two Experimental Investigations* (Paper presented at the annual meeting of the American Educational Research Association, San Diego, CA).

Knapp, M. L. (1972). *Nonverbal Communication in Human Interaction*. New York: Holt, Rinehart and Winston.

Knapp, M. L., and Hall, J. (1997). *Nonverbal Communication in Human Interaction*, 4th ed. Fort Worth, TX: Harcourt Brave College Publishers.

Knapp, M. L., and Hall, J. (2002). *Nonverbal Communication in Human Interaction*, 5th ed. Wadsworth: Thompson Learning Inc.

Knapp, M. L., and Hall, J. (2006). *Nonverbal Communication in Human Interaction*, 6th ed. Wadsworth: Thompson Learning Inc.

Knapp, M. L., Hall, J. A., and Horgan, T. G. (2014). *Nonverbal Communication in Human Interaction*. Boston: Wadsworth.

Kohn, D., and Eitan, Z. (2016). Moving music: Correspondences of musical parameters and movement dimensions in children's motion and verbal responses. *Music Perception*, 34, pp 40–55.

Konosu, S., Yamaguchi, K., and Hyashi, T. (1987). Role of extractive components of boiled crab. In Kawamura, Y., and Kare, M. R. (Eds.), *Umami: A Basic Taste*. New York: Dekker, pp 235–253.

Koster, E. H., Crombez, G., Verschuere, B., and De Houwer, J. (2004). Selective attention to threat in the dot probe paradigm: Differentiating vigilance and difficulty to disengage. *Behavioural Research and Therapy*, 42(10), pp 1183–1192.

Koumoutsakis, T., Church, R., Alibali, M., Singer, M., and Ayman-Nolley, S. (2016). Gesture in instruction: Evidence from live and video lessons. *Journal of Nonverbal Behaviour* (40) pp 301–315.

Kowner, R. (2001). Psychological perspective on human developmental stability and fluctuating asymmetry: Sources, applications and implications. *British Journal of Psychology*, 92(3), pp 447–469.

Kozlowski, L. T., and Cutting, J. E. (1977). Recognizing the sex of a walker from a dynamic point-light display. *Perception and Psychophysics*, 21, pp 575–580.

Krauss, L. M. (2017). *The Greatest Story Ever Told, So Far.* New York: Atria Books.

Krauss, R., Dushay, R., Chen, Y., and Rauscher, F. (1995). The communicative value of conversational hand gestures. *Journal of Experimental Social Psychology*, 31, pp 533–552.

Kreta, M. E., Jaasmab, L., Biondac, T., and Wijnend, J. G. (2016). Bonobos (Pan paniscus) show an attentional bias toward conspecifics' emotions. *Proceedings of the National Academy of Sciences of the United States of America*, 113(14), pp 3761–3766.

Krumhuber, E., and Kappas, A. (2005). Moving smiles: The role of dynamic components for the perception of the genuineness of smiles. *Journal of Nonverbal Behavior*, 29, pp 3–24.

Krumhuber, E., and Manstead, A. S. R. (2009). Can Duchenne smiles be feigned? New evidence on felt and false smiles. *Emotion*, 9, pp 807–820.

Krumhuber, E., Manstead, A. S. R., and Kappas, A. (2007). Temporal aspects of facial displays in person and expression perception: The effects of smile dynamics, head-tilt, and gender. *Journal of Nonverbal Behavior*, 31, pp 39–56.

Kuehne, S. H., and Creekmore, A. M. (1971). Relationships among social class, school position and clothing of adolescents. *Journal of Home Economics*, 63, pp 555–556.

Kurtz, L. E., and Algoe, S. B. (2015). Putting laughter in context: Shared laughter as behavioural indicator of relationship well-being. *Personal Relationships*, 22(4), pp 573–590.

Kurtz, L. E., and Algoe, S. B. (2017). When sharing a laugh means sharing more: Testing the role of shared laughter on short-term interpersonal consequences. *Journal of Nonverbal Behavior*, 41(1), pp 45–65.

Kuster, D., Krumhuber, E., and Hess, U. (2019). You are what you wear: Unless you moved – effects of attire and posture on person perception. *Journal of Nonverbal Behavior*, 43, pp 23–38.

LaFrance, M. (1985). Postural mirroring and intergroup relations. *Personality and Social Psychology Bulletin*, 11, pp 207–217.

LaFrance, M., Hecht, M., and Paluck, E. (2003). The contingent smile: A meta-analysis of sex differences in smiling. *Psychological Bulletin*, 129, pp 305–334.

LaFrance, M., and Mayo, C. (1979). A review of nonverbal behaviors of women and men. *Western Journal of Speech Communication*, 43, pp 96–107.

Lagerlöf, I., and Djerf, M. (2000). Communicating emotions: Expressiveness in modern dance. *International Journal of Psychology*, 35, pp 225–226.

Lakin, J. L., and Chartrand, T. L. (2003). Using nonconscious behavioral mimicry to create affiliation and rapport. *Psychological Science*, 14(4), pp 334–339.

Lambert, D., and The Diagram Group. (1987). *The Field Guide to Early Man.* New York: Facts on File Publications.

Langlois, J. H., Kalakanis, L., Rubenstein, A. J., Larson, A., Hallam, M., and Smoot, M. (2000). Maxims or myths of beauty? A meta-analytic and theoretical review. *Psychological Bulletin*, 126, pp 390–423.

LaPlante, D., and Ambady, N. (2003). On how things are said: Voice tone, voice intensity, verbal content and perceptions of politeness. *Journal of Language and Social Psychology*, 22, pp 434–441.

Larose, H., and Standing, L. G. (1998). Does the halo effect occur in the elderly? *Social Behavior and Personality: An International Journal*, 26(2), pp 147–150.

Larsen, K. M., and Smith, C. K. (1981). Assessment of nonverbal communication in the patient-physician interview. *Journal of Family Practice*, 2, pp 481–488.

Lawrence, S. G., and Watson, M. (1991). Getting others to help: The effectiveness of professional uniforms in charitable fund-raising. *Journal of Applied Communication Research*, 19, pp 170–185.

Leathers, D. G. (1992). *Successful Nonverbal Communication*. New York: Macmillan.

Leder, H., Forster, M., and Gerger, G. (2011). The glasses stereotype revisited. *Swiss Journal of Psychology*, 70(4), 211–222.

LeDoux, J. E. (1995). Emotion: Clues from the brain. *Annual Review Psychology*, 46, pp 209–235.

LeDoux, J. (1996). *The Emotional Brain: The Mysterious Underpinnings of Emotional Life*. New York: Simon and Schuster.

Lemke, M. R., Wendorff, T., Mieth, B., et al. (2000). Spatiotemporal gait patterns during over ground locomotion in major depression compared with healthy controls. *Journal of Psychiatric Research*, 34(4–5), pp 277–283.

Lennon, S. J., and Miller, F. G. (1984). Salience of physical appearance in impression formation. *Home Economics Research Journal*, 13, pp 95–104.

Levenson, R. W. (1992). Autonomic nervous system differences among emotions. *Psychological Bulletin*, 126, pp 390–423.

Levenson, R. W., Carstensen, L. L., Friesen, W. V., and Ekman, P. (1991). Emotion, physiology, and expression in old age. *Psychology and Aging*, 6, pp 28–35.

Levenson, R. W., and Ekman, P. (2002). Difficulty does not account for emotion-specific heart rate changes in the directed facial action task. *Psychophysiology*, 39, pp 397–405.

Levenson, R. W., Ekman, P., Heider, K., and Friesen, W. V. (1992). Emotion and autonomic nervous system activity in Minangkabau of West Sumatra. *Journal of Personality and Social Psychology*, 62, pp 972–988.

Lewis, M. B. (2012). Exploring the positive and negative implications of facial feedback. *Emotion*, 12(4), pp 852–859.

Lieberman, P. (1991). *Uniquely Human: The Evolution of Speech, Thought, and Selfless Behavior*. Cambridge: Harvard University Press.

Lingle, S., Wyman, M. T., Kotrba, R., Teichroeb, L. J., and Romanow, C. A. (2012). What makes a cry a cry? A review of infant distress vocalizations. *Current Zoology*, 58(5), pp 698–726.

Livshits, G., Davidi, L., Kobyliansky, E., Ben-Amitai, D., Levi, Y., Meriob, P., et al. (1998). Decreased developmental stability as assessed by fluctuating asymmetry of morphometric traits in preterm infants. *American Journal of Medical Genetics*, 29(4), pp 793–805.

Logan-Clarke, V., and Appleby, J. (2009). *What Is Color Therapy?* (Color Therapy Healing Workshops, Bognor Regis).

Lorenz, K. (1939a): Über Ausfallserscheinungen im Instinktverhalten von Huastieren und ihre sozialpsychologische Bedeutung. In Klemm, O. (Ed.), *Charakter und Erziehung. Bericht üner den XV. Kongress der Deutschen Gesellschaft für Psychologie*. Teubner, Leipzig: pp 139-147.

Lorenz, K. (1939b). Vergleichende Verhaltensforschung. *Verhandlungen der Deutschen Zoologischen Gesellschaft Zoologischer Anzeiger*, Supplementband 12, pp 69–102.

Lundberg, J. K., and Sheehan, E. P. (1994). The effects of glasses and weight on perceptions of attractiveness and intelligence. *Journal of Social Behaviour and Personality*, 9(4), 753.

MacLean, P. D. (1973). *A Triune Concept of the Brain and Behaviour*. Toronto: University of Toronto Press.

MacLean, P. D. (1975). Sensory and perceptive factors in emotional functions of the triune brain. In Levi, L. (Ed.), *Emotions: Their Parameters and Measurement*. New York: Raven Publishers, pp 71–92.

MacLean, P. D. (1990). *The Triune Brain in Evolution*. New York: Plenum Press.

Maestripieri, D. (2011). Emotions, stress, and maternal motivation in primates. *American Journal of Primatology*, 73, pp 516–529.

Mahnke, K. (1996). *Color, Environment and Human Responses*. New York: John Wiley and Sons.

Main, J. C., Jones, B. C., DeBruine, L. M., and Little, A. (2009). Integrating gaze direction and sexual dimorphism of face shape when perceiving the dominance of others. *Perception*, 38, pp 1275–1283.

Major, B., Carrington, P. I., and Carnevale, P. J. D. (1984). Physical attractiveness and self-esteem: Attributes for praise from an other-sex evaluator. *Personality and Social Psychology Bulletin*, 10, pp 43–50.

Mancini, G., Ferrari, P., and Palagi, E. (2013). Rapid facial mimicry in Geladas. *Scientific Reports*, 3, p 1527.

Maricchiolo, F. A., Bonaiuto, G. M., and Ficca, G. (2009). Effects of different types of hand gestures in persuasive speech on receivers' evaluations. *Language and Cognitive Processes*, 24, pp 239–266.

Marshack, A. (1971). *The Roots of Civilization: The Cognitive Beginnings of Man's First Art, Symbol, and Notation*. San Francisco: McGraw-Hill.

Martin, D., and Macrae, C. N. (2007). A face with a cue: Exploring the inevitability of person categorization. *European Journal of Social Psychology*, 37, pp 806–816.

Martin, R. A., and Kuiper, N. A. (1999). Daily occurrence of laughter: Relationships with age, gender and type a personality. *Humor: International Journal of Humor Research* (12), pp 355–384.

Masip, J. (2017). Deception detection: State of the art and future prospects. *Psicothema*, 29, pp 149–159.

Masip, J., Garrido, E., and Herrero, C. (2004). Facial appearance and impressions of "credibility": The effects of facial babyishness and age on person perception. *International Journal of Psychology*, 39, pp 276–289.

Masip, J., and Sánchez, N. (2019). How people *really* suspect lies: A re-examination of Novotny et al.'s (2018) data. *Journal of Nonverbal Behaviour*, 43, pp 481–492.

Mathes, E. W., and Kahn, A. (1975). Physical attractiveness, neuroticism, and self-esteem, *Journal of Personality*, 90, pp 27–30.

Matsumoto, C. (1987). Dance research: Problem situation and learning of problem solving II: Qualities of movements and feeling values. *Bulletin of Japan Association of Physical Education for Women*, 87(1), pp 53–89.

Matsumoto, D. (1991). Cultural influences on facial expressions of emotion. *Southern Communication Journal*, 56, pp 128–137.

Matsumoto, D. (2006). Culture and nonverbal behaviour. In Manusov, V., and Patterson, M. L. (Eds.), *The Sage Handbook of Nonverbal Communication*. London: Sage, pp 219–235.

Matsumoto, D., and Hwang, H. S. (2011). Evidence for training the ability to read micro-expressions of emotion. *Motivation and Emotion*, *35*, pp 181–191.

Matsumoto, D., and Hwang, H. C. (2017). Methodological issues regarding cross-cultural studies of judgments of facial expressions. *Emotion Review*, 9(4), pp 375–382.

Matsumoto, D., LeRoux, J., Wilson-Cohn, C., Raroque, J., Kooken, K., Ekman, P., Yrizarry, N., Loewinger, S., Uchida, H., Yee, A., Amo, L., and Goh, A. (2000). A new test to measure emotion recognition ability: Matsumoto and Ekman's Japanese and Caucasian brief affect recognition test (JACBART). *Journal of Nonverbal Behavior*, 24, pp 179–209.

Matsumoto, D., Takeuchi, S., Andayani, S., Kouznetsova, N., and Krupp, D. (1998). The contribution of individualism-collectivism to cross-national differences in display rules. *Asian Journal of Social Psychology*, 1, pp 147–165.

Matsumoto, D., Yoo, S. H., Hirayama, S., and Petrova, G. (2005). Development and validation of a measure of display rule knowledge: The display rule assessment inventory. *Emotion*, 5(1), pp 23–40.

McAdams, D. P., Jackson, R. J., and Kirshnit, C. (1984). Looking, laughing, and smiling in dyads as a function of intimacy motivation and reciprocity. *Journal of Personality*, 52, pp 261–273.

McBride, G., King, M. G., and James, J. W. (1965). Social proximity effects on GSR in adult humans. *Journal of Psychology*, 61, pp 153–157.

McCaul, K. D., Holmes, D. S., and Solomon, S. (1982). Voluntary expressive changes and emotion. *Journal of Personality and Social Psychology*, 42, pp 145–152.

McCormick, N. B., and Jones, A. J. (1989). Gender differences in nonverbal flirtation. *Journal of Sex Education and Therapy*, 15, pp 271–282.

McCroskey, J. C., Fayer, J. M., Richmond, V. P., Sallinen, A., and Barraclough, R. A. (1996). A multi-cultural examination of the relationship between non-verbal immediacy and affective learning. *Communication Quarterly*, 44(3), pp 297–230.

McCroskey, J. C., Richmond, V., and McCroskey, L. (2006). Nonverbal communication in instructional contexts. In Manusov, V., and Patterson, M. (Eds.), *The Sage Handbook of Nonverbal Communication*. London: Sage, pp 421–436.

McGrew, W. C. (1972). Aspects of social development in nursery school children with emphasis on introduction to the group. In Blurton Jones, N. G. (Eds.), *Ethological Studies of Child Behaviour*. Cambridge: Cambridge University Press, pp 129–156.

McIntosh, D. N. (1996). Facial feedback hypotheses: Evidence, implications, and directions. *Motivation and Emotion*, 20(2), pp 121–147.

McNeill, D. (1992). *Hand and Mind. What Gestures Reveal About Thought*. Chicago: University of Chicago Press.

McDonald, J. (1999). Seeds of a Green China. *Spokesman-Review* (AP article, August 15), p A4.

McGee, H. (1990). *The Curious Cook*. San Francisco: North Point Press.

McGraw, M. B. (1943). *The Neuromuscular Maturation of the Human Infant*. New York: Columbia University Press.

McKeown, S. (2010). Introduction. In McKeown, S. (Ed.), *The International Emblem*. Newcastle upon Tyne: Cambridge Scholars Publishing.

McKinley, C. E. (2011). *Indigo: In Search of the Colour That Seduced the World*. London: Bloomsbury.

Mealey, L., Bridgstock, R., and Townsend, G. C. (1999). Symmetry and perceived facial attractiveness: A monozygotic co-twin comparison. *Journal of Personality and Social Psychology*, 76(1), pp 151–158.

Me´hu, M., and Dunbar, R. (2008). Naturalistic observations of smiling and laughter in human group interactions. *Behaviour*, 145, pp 1747–1780.

Mehrabian, A. (1971). *Silent Messages*. Belmont, CA: Wadsworth.

Mehrabian, A. (1972). *Nonverbal Communication*. Chicago: Aldine-Atherton.

Mehrabian, A. (1974). Communication without words. In Civikly, J. (Eds.), *Messages: A Reader in Human Communication*. New York: Random House, pp 87–93.

Mehrabian, A., and Blum, J. (1997). Physical appearance, attraction and the mediating role of emotions. *Current Psychology: Developmental, Learning, Personality, Social*, 16, pp 20–42.

Mehrabian, A., and Williams, M. (1969). Nonverbal concomitants of perceived and intended persuasiveness. *Journal of Personality and Social Psychology*, 13, pp 37–58.

Mehta, P. H., and Josephs, R. A. (2010). Testosterone and cortisol jointly regulate dominance: Evidence for a dual-hormone hypothesis. *Hormones and Behavior*, 58, pp 898–906.

Meltzoff, A. (2012). *From His Abstract for the 2012 Conference on "Mirror Neurons: New Frontiers 20 Years After Their Discovery"*.

Meltzoff, A., and Prinz, W. (Eds.). (2002). *The Imitative Mind: Development, Evolution and Brain Bases* (Cambridge Studies in Cognitive and Perceptual Development). Cambridge: Cambridge University Press.

Merom, D., Ding, D., and Stamatakis, E. (2016). Dancing participation and cardiovascular disease mortality: A pooled analysis of 11 population-based British cohorts. *American Journal of Preventive Medicine*, 50, pp 756–760.

Mesulam, M. M. (1992). Brief speculations on frontoparietal interactions and motor autonomy. In Joseph, A. B., and Young, R. R. (Eds.), *Movement Disorders in Neurology and Neuropsychiatry*. Cambridge, MA: Blackwell Scientific Publications, Inc., pp 696–698.

Meyer, J. (2008). Typology and acoustic strategies of whistled languages: Phonetic comparison and perceptual cues of whistled vowels. *Journal of the International Phonetic Association*, 38(1), pp 69–94.

Mignault, A., and Chaudhuri, A. (2003). The many faces of a neutral face: Head tilt and perception of dominance and emotion. *Journal of Nonverbal Behaviour*, 27(2), pp 111–132.

Miller, F. G., and Rowold, K. I. (1980). Attire, sex-roles and responses to requests for directions. *Psychological Reports*, 47, pp 661–662.

Milne, B. J., Belsky, J., Poulton, R., Thomson, W. M., Caspi, A., and Kieser, J. (2003). Fluctuating asymmetry and physical health among young adults. *Evolution and Human Behavior*, 24(1), pp 53–63.

Mitchell, R. L. C., and Ross, E. D. (2013). Attitudinal prosody: What we know and directions for future study. *Neuroscience and Biobehavioral Reviews*, 37, pp 471–479.

Mithen, S. (2005). *The Singing Neanderthals: The Origins of Music, Language, Mind and Body*. London: Weidenfeld and Nicolson.

Molenberghs, P., Cunnington, R., and Mattingley, J. B. (2012). Brain regions with mirror properties: A meta-analysis of 125 human fMRI studies. *Neuroscience and Biobehavioral Reviews*, 36, 341–349.

Moller, A. P., and Pomiankowski, A. (1993). Fluctuating asymmetry and sexual selection. *Genetica*, 89, pp 267–279.

Molloy, J. T. (1988). *John T. Molloy's New Dress for Success*. New York: Warner Books.

Montagu, A. (1971). *Touching: The human significance of the skin*. New York, Columbia University Press.

Montepare, J. M. (2014). Nonverbal behavior in the digital age: Explorations in internet social communication. *Journal of Nonverbal Behaviour*, 38, pp 409–411.

Montepare, J. M., Goldstein, S. B., and Clausen, A. (1987). The identification of emotions from gait information. *Journal of Nonverbal Behavior*, 11, pp 33–42.

Montepare, J. M., and Zebrowitz-McArthur, L. (1987). Perceptions of adults and children with child-like voices in two cultures. *Journal of Experimental Social Psychology*, 54, pp 829–839.

Montepare, J. M., and Zebrowitz-McArthur, L. (1988). Impressions of people created by age-related qualities of their gaits. *Journal of Personality and Social Psychology*, 55, pp 547 556.

Morris, D. (1971). *Intimate Behaviour*. New York: Random House.

Morris, D. (1977). *Manwatching: A Field Guide to Human Behavior*. New York: Harry N.

Morris, D. (1985). *Bodywatching*. New York: Crown Publishing.

Morris, D. (1994). *Bodytalk: The Meaning of Human Gestures*. New York: Crown Publishing.

Morris, D. (2002). *Peoplewatching*. New York: Vintage Books.

Morris, D., Collett, P., Marsh, P., and O'Shaughnessy, M. (1979). *Gestures*. New York: Stein and Day.

Morris, J. (1974). *Conundrum: From James to Jan – An Extraordinary Personal Narrative of Transsexualism*. New York: Harcourt Brace Jovanovich, Inc.

Moyer, C. A., Rounds, J., and Hannum, J. W. (2004). A meta-analysis of massage therapy research. *Psychological Bulletin*, 130, pp 3–18.

Muchnik, S., Finkielman, S., Semeniuk, G., and de Aguirre, M. I. (2003). Yawning. *Medicina*, 63(3), pp 229–232.

Mukherjee, S., and Ramos-Salazar, L. (2014). 'Excuse us, your manners are missing!' The role of business etiquette in today's era of cross-cultural communication. *TSM Business Review*, 2(1), pp 18–28.

Mundy, L. (1992). Gorilla groupies. *Washington City Paper* (September 11). washingtoncitypaper.com.

Murray, I. R., and Arnott, J. L. (1993). Toward the simulation of emotion in synthetic speech: A review of the literature on human vocal emotion. *Journal of the Acoustical Society of America*, 93, pp 1097–1108.

Murray, M. P., Kory, R. C., and Clarkson, B. H. (1969). Walking patterns in healthy old men. *Journal of Gerontology*, 24, pp 169–178.

Namba, S., Kagamihara, T., Miyatani, M., and Nakao, T. (2017). Spontaneous facial expressions reveal new action units for the sad experiences. *Journal of Nonverbal Behaviour*, 41(3), pp 203–220.

Napier, J. (1962). The evolution of the hand. In *Vertebrate Structures and Functions. Readings from Scientific American*. San Francisco: W. H. Freeman and Co., pp 59–65, 1974.

Neill, S., and Caswell, C. (1993). *Body Language for Competent Teachers*. London: Routledge and Keegan Paul.

Nelson, C. A., and Dolgin, K. G. (1985). The generalized discrimination of facial expressions by seven-month-old infants. *Child Development*, 56, pp 58–61.

Nelson, N. L., and Russell, J. A. (2013). Universality revisited. *Emotion Review*, 5(1), pp 8–15.

Neurath, O. (1936). Isotype: International system of typographic picture education. In Neurath, M., and Cohen, R. S. (Eds.), *Otto Neurath: Empiricism and Sociology*. Boston: D. Reidel Publishing Co., pp 224–248, 1973.

Niedenthal, P., Mermillod, M., Maringer, M., and Hess, U. (2010). The simulation of smiles (SIMS) model: Embodied simulation and the meaning of facial expression. *Behavioral and Brain Sciences*, 33, pp 417–433.

Huazhong Ning, Tony X. Han, Yuxiao Hu, Zhenqiu Zhang, Yun Fu, and Thomas S. Huang. (2006). *A Realtime Shrug Detector* (Automatic Face and Gesture Recognition, p XX).

Nishitani, N., Schürmann, M., Amunts, K., and Hari, R. (2005). Broca's region: From action to language. *Physiology*, 20(1), pp 60–69.

Novotny, E., Carr, Z., Frank, M. G., Dietrich, S. B., Shaddock, T., Cardwell, M., et al. (2018). How people really suspect and discover lies. *Journal of Nonverbal Behavior*, 42, pp 41–52.

Nowicki, S., and Duke, M. (1994). Individual differences in the nonverbal communication of affect: The diagnostic analysis of nonverbal accuracy scale. *Journal of Nonverbal Behavior*, 18, pp 9–34.

Nowicki, S., and Duke, M. (2001). Nonverbal receptivity: The Diagnostic Analysis of Nonverbal Accuracy (DANVA). In Hall, J. A., and Berneiri, F. J. (Eds.), *Interpersonal Sensitivity: Theory and Measurement*. Mahwah, NJ: Lawrence Erlbaum Associates, pp 183–198.

Omark, D. R. (1980). The group: A factor or an epiphenomenon in evolution. In Omark, D. R., Strayer, F. F., and Freedman, D. G. (Eds.)., *Dominance Relations: An Ethological View of Human Conflict and Social Interaction*. New York: Garland STPM Press, pp 21–67.

Omata, K. (1996). Territoriality in the house and its relationship to the use of rooms and the psychological well-being of Japanese married women. *Journal of Environmental Psychology*, 15, pp 147–154.

Oosterhof, N. N., and Todorov, A. (2008). The functional basis of face evaluation. *Proceedings of the National Academy of Sciences*, 105, pp 11087–11092.

Orgs, G., Hagura, N., and Haggard, P. (2013). Learning to like it: Aesthetic perception of bodies, movements and choreographic structure. *Conscious Cognition*, 22, pp 603–612.

Otta, E., Lira, B., Delevati, N., Cesar, O., and Pires, C. (1994). The effect of smiling and of head tilting on person perception. *Journal of Psychology: Interdisciplinary and Applied*, 128, pp 323–331.

Ottati, V., Terkildsen, N., and Hubbard, C. (1997). Happy faces elicit heuristic processing in a televised impression formation task: A cognitive tuning account. *Personality and Social Psychology Bulletin*, 23(11), pp 1144–1156.

Otterson, J., and Otterson, C. (1980). Effects of teacher gaze on children's story recall. *Perceptual and Motor Skills*, 50, pp 35–42.

Paek, S. J. (1986). Effects of garment style on the perception of personal traits. *Clothing and Textiles Research Journal*, 5(1), pp 10–16.

Palmer, M. T., and Simmons, K. B. (1995). Communicating intentions through nonverbal behaviors: Conscious and nonconscious encoding of liking. *Human Communication Research*, 22, pp 128–160.

Parkinson, B. (2005). Do facial movements express emotions or communicate motives? *Personality and Social Psychology Review*, 9, 278–311.

Patel, S., and Scherer, K. (2013). Vocal behaviour. In Hall, J., and Knapp, M. (Eds.), *Nonverbal Communication*. Boston: De Gruyter, Inc., ProQuest, pp 167–205.

Patterson, M. L. (1968). Spatial factors in social interaction. *Human Relations*, 21, pp 351–361.

Patterson, M. L. (1976). An arousal model of interpersonal intimacy. *Psychological Review*, 83, pp 235–245.

Patterson, M. L. (1982). A sequential functional model of nonverbal exchange. *Psychological Review*, 89, pp 231–249.

Patterson, M. L. (1983). *Nonverbal Behavior: A Functional Perspective*. New York: Springer.

Patterson, M. L. (1991). A functional approach to nonverbal exchange. In Feldman, R. S., and Rime, B. (Eds.), *Fundamentals of Nonverbal Behaviour*. Cambridge, UK: Cambridge University Press, pp 458–495.

Patterson, M. L. (1995). A parallel process model of nonverbal communication. *Journal of Nonverbal Behaviour*, 19, pp 3–29.

Patterson, M. L. (2019). A systems model of dyadic nonverbal interaction. *Journal of Nonverbal Behaviour*, 43, pp 111–132.

Patterson, M. L., and Sechrest, L. B. (1970). Interpersonal distance and impression formation. *Journal of Personality*, 38, pp 161–166.

Pease, A., and Pease, B. (2004). *The Definitive Book of Body Language*. London: Orion Books.

Peck, H. (1898). Demosthenes. In *Harper's Dictionary of Classical Antiquities*. New York: Trustees of Tufts University. http://perseus.uchicago.edu/cgi-bin/philologic/getobject. pl?c.0:1:331.harpers (accessed September 29, 2020).

Peck, S. (1982). *Atlas of Human Anatomy for the Artist*. Oxford: Oxford University Press.

Peiper, A. (1963). *Cerebral Function in Infancy and Childhood*. New York: Consultant's Bureau.

Pell, M. D. (2005). Nonverbal emotion priming: Evidence from the facial affect decision task. *Journal of Nonverbal Behavior*, 29(1) (Spring).

Pell, M. D., and Skorup, V. (2008). Implicit processing of emotional prosody in a foreign versus native language. *Speech Communication*, 50, pp 519–530.

Pelligrini, R., and Schauss, A. (1980). Muscle strength as a function of exposure to hue differences in visual stimuli: An experiential test of kinesoid theory. *Journal of Orthomolecular Psychiatry*, 2, pp 144–147.

Penton-Voak, I. S., Jones, B. C., Little, A. C., Baker, S., Tiddeman, B., Burt, D. M., et al. (2001). Symmetry, sexual dimorphism in facial proportions and male facial attractiveness. *Proceedings of the Royal Society of London B: Biological Sciences*, 268(1476), pp 1617–1623.

Penton-Voak, I. S., Perrett, D. I., Castles, D. L., Kobayashi, T., Burt, D. M., and Murray, L. K. (1999). Menstrual cycle alters face preferences. *Nature*, 300, pp 741–742.

Perani, D., Schnur, T., et al. (1999). Word and picture matching: A PET study of semantic category effects. *Neuropsychologia*, 37(3), pp 293–306.

Perrett, D. I., Burt, D. M., Penton-Voak, I. S., Lee, K. J., Rowland, D. A., and Edwards, R. (1999). Symmetry and human facial attractiveness. *Evolution and Human Behavior*, 20(5), pp 295–307.

Perrett, D. I., May, K. A., and Yoshikawa, S. (1994). Facial shape and judgments of female attractiveness. *Nature*, 368, pp 239–242.

Perry, B. D. (2002). Childhood experience and the expression of genetic potential: What childhood neglect tells us about nature and nurture. *Brain and Mind*, 3, pp 79–100.

Perry, M., Berch, D., and Singleton, J. (1995). Constructing shared understanding: The role of nonverbal input in learning contexts. *Journal of Contemporary Legal Issues*, 6, pp 213–235.

Petel, T. (2011). Mirror neurons: Recognition, interaction, understanding. *Berkeley Scientific Journal*, 14(2), pp 1–4.

Peterson, W. W., Birdsall, T. G., and Fox, W. C. (1954). The theory of signal detectability. *Proceedings of the IRE Professional Group on Information Theory*, 4, pp 171–212.

Petroski, H. (1992). *The Evolution of Useful Things*. New York: Alfred A. Knopf.

Pine, K., Bird, H., and Kirk, E. (2007). The effects of prohibiting gestures on children's lexical retrieval ability. *Developmental Science*, 10, pp 747–754.

Ping, R., and Goldin-Meadow, S. (2010). Gesturing saves cognitive resources when talking about non-present objects. *Cognitive Science*, 34, pp 602–619.

Ping, R., Goldin-Meadow, S., and Beilock, S. L. (2014). Understanding gesture: Is the listener's motor system involved? *Journal of Experimental Psychology: General*, 143(1), pp 195–204.

Pisano, M. D., Wall, S. M., and Foster, A. (1986). Perceptions of nonreciprocal touch in romantic relationships. *Journal of Nonverbal Behavior*, 10, pp 29–40.

Pitterman, H., and Nowicki, S., Jr. (2004). A test of the ability to identify emotion in human standing and sitting postures: The Diagnostic Analysis of Nonverbal Accuracy-2 Posture test (DANVA2-POS). *Genetic, Social, and General Psychology Monographs*, 130, pp 146–162.

Platek, S. M., Mohamed, F. B., and Gallup, G. G. (2005). Contagious yawning and the brain. *Cognitive Brain Research* (23), pp 448–452.

Plazewski, J. G., and Allen, V. L. (1985). The effects of verbal content on children's encoding of paralinguistic effect. *Journal of Nonverbal Behaviour*, 19(3), pp 147–159.

Porges, S. W. (1995). Orienting in a defensive world: Mammalian modifications of our evolutionary heritage. A polyvagal theory. *Psychophysiology*, 32(4), pp 301–318.

Porter, G. (1967). *The World of the Frog and Toad*. New York: Lippincott.

Porter, S., Campbell, M. A., Stapleton, J., and Birt, A. R. (2002). The influence of judge, target, and stimulus characteristics on the accuracy of detecting deceit. *Canadian Journal of Behavioural Science/Revue canadienne des sciences du comportement*, 34, pp 172–185.

Provine, R. R. (1986). Yawning as a stereotyped action pattern and releasing stimulus. *Ethology*, 72, pp 109–122.

Provine, R. R. (1992). Contagious laughter: Laughter is a sufficient stimulus for laughs and smiles. *Bulletin of the Psychonomic Society*, 30(1), pp 1–4.

Provine, R. R. (1993). Laughter punctuates speech: Linguistic, social and gender contexts of laughter. *Ethology*, 95(4), pp 291–298.

Provine, R. R. (1996). Laughter. *American Scientist* (Web document, January–February).

Provine, R. R. (2001). *Laughter: A Scientific Investigation*. New York: Penguin books.

Provine, R. R. (2010). Yawns, laughs, smiles, tickles, and talking: Naturalistic and laboratory studies of facial action and social communication. In Russell, J. A., and Fernández-Dols, J. M. (Eds.), *The Psychology of Facial Expression*. Cambridge: Cambridge University Press.

Provine, R. R. (2012a). *Curious Behavior*, 1st ed. Cambridge: The Belknap Press.

Provine, R. R. (2012b). *Curious Behaviour: Yawning, Laughing, Hiccupping, and Beyond*. Cambridge: Harvard University Press.

Provine, R. R. (2017). Beyond the smile. In Fernández-Dols, J., and Russell, J. (Ed.), *The Science of Facial Expression*, 1st ed. New York: Oxford University Press, pp 197–216.

Provine, R. R., and Fischer, K. R. (1989). Laughing, smiling, and talking: Relation to sleeping and social context in humans. *Ethology*, 83(4), pp 295–305.

Provine, R. R., Krosnowski, K. A., and Brocato, N. W. (2009). Tearing: Breakthrough in human emotional signaling. *Evolutionary Psychology*, 7(1), pp 52–56.

Pullin, G., et al. (2009). Fashion meets discretion. In *Design Meets Disability*. Cambridge: MIT Press.

Raloff, J. (1995). Languishing languages: Cultures at risk. *Science News* (February 25), p 117.

Rees, D. W., Williams, L., and Giles, H. (1974). Dress style and symbolic meaning. *International Journal of Symbology*, 5, pp 1–8.

Reid, A., Lancuba, V., and Morrow, B. (1997). Clothing style and formation of first impressions. *Perceptual and Motor Skills*, 84, pp 237–238.

Reiling, J. (1999). Localization of musical centers. *Journal of the American Medical Association*, 282 (July 21), p 218.

Reis, H. T., Wilson, I. M., Monestere, C., Bernstein, S., Clark, K., Seidl, E., and Radoane, K. (1990). What is smiling is beautiful and good. *European Journal of Social Psychology*, 20, pp 259–267.

Remland, M., Jones, T. S., and Brinkman, H. (1995). Interpersonal distance, body orientation, and touch: Effects of culture, gender, and age. *Journal of Social Psychology*, 135(3), pp 281–297.

Restak, R. (1994). *Receptors*. New York: Bantam.

Restak, R. (1995). *Brainscapes*. New York: Hyperion.

Reynolds, A., and Paivio, A. (1968). Cognitive and emotional determinants of speech. *Canadian Journal of Psychology*, 22, pp 164–175.

Richmond, V. P., Gorham, J. S., and McCroskey, J. C. (1987). The relationship between selected immediacy behaviors and cognitive learning. In McLaughlin, M. A. (Ed.), *Communication Yearbook*, vol. 10. Newbury Park, CA: Sage, pp 574–590.

Richmond, V. P., and McCroskey, J. C. (2000a). *Nonverbal Behavior in Human Relations*, 4th ed. Needham Heights, MA: Allyn and Bacon.

Richmond, V. P., and McCroskey, J. C. (2000b). The impact of supervisor and subordinate immediacy on relational and organizational outcomes. *Communication Monographs*, 67, pp 85–95.

Richmond, V. P., McCroskey, J. C., and Johnson, A. D. (2003). Development of the nonverbal immediacy scale (NIS): Measures of self- and other-perceived nonverbal immediacy. *Communication Quarterly*, 51(4), pp 504–517.

Richmond, V. P., McCroskey, J. C., and Payne, S. K. (1991). *Nonverbal Behavior in Interpersonal Relations*, 2nd ed. Englewood Cliffs, NJ: Prentice Hall.

Richmond, V. P., McCroskey, J. C., and Payne, S. K. (2000). *Nonverbal Behavior in Interpersonal Relations*, 4th ed. Englewood Cliffs, NJ: Prentice-Hall.

Riggio, R. E. (2006). Nonverbal skills and abilities. In Manusov, V., and Patterson, M. (Eds.), *The Sage Handbook of Nonverbal Communication*. London: Sage, pp 79–95.

Riggio, R. E., Tucker, J., and Coffaro, D. (1989). Social skills and empathy. *Personality and Individual Differences*, 10, pp 93–99.

Riseborough, M. (1981). Physiographic gestures as decoding facilitators: Three experiments exploring a neglected facet of communication. *Journal of Nonverbal Behavior*, 5, pp 172–183.

Roach, K. D. (1997). Effects of graduate teaching assistant attire on student learning, misbehaviours and ratings of instruction. *Communication Quarterly*, 45, pp 125–141.

Roberts, J. V., and Herman, C. P. (1986). The psychology of height: An empirical review. In Herman, C. P., Zanna, M., and Higgins, E. T. (Eds.), *Physical Appearance, Stigma, and Social Behaviour*. Hillsdale, NJ: Lawrence Erlbaum Associates, pp 113–140.

Robinson, J. D. (2008). Nonverbal communication in doctor-patient relationships. In Guerrero, L. K., and Hecht, M. L. (Eds.), *The Nonverbal Communication Reader: Classic and Contemporary Readings*, 3rd ed. Long Grove, IL: Waveland Press, pp 384–394.

Rohner, J. (2002). The time-course of visual threat processing: High trait anxious individuals eventually avert their gaze from angry faces. *Cognition and Emotion*, 16, pp 837–844.

Ronquillo, J., Denison, T. F., Lickel, B., Lu, Zhong-Lin, and Maddox, K. B. (2007). The effects of skin tone on race-related amygdala activity: An fMRI investigation. *Social Cognition and Affect Neuroscience*, 2, pp 39–44.

Rosenshine, B. (1970). Enthusiastic teaching: A research review. *School Review*, 78, pp 499–514.

Rosenthal, R., and DePaulo, B. M. (1979). Sex differences in accommodation in nonverbal communication. In Rosenthal, R. (Eds.), *Skill in Nonverbal Communication*. Cambridge, MA: Gunn and Hain, pp 68–103.

Rosenthal, R., Hall, J. A., DiMatteo, M. R., Rogers, P. L., and Archer, D. (1979). *Sensitivity to Nonverbal Communication: The PONS Test*. Baltimore: The Johns Hopkins University Press.

Rosip, J. C., and Hall, J. A. (2004). Knowledge of nonverbal cues, gender and nonverbal decoding accuracy. *Journal of Nonverbal Behavior*, 28(4), pp 267–286.

Ross, L. (1977). The intuitive psychologist and his shortcomings: Distortions in the attribution process. In Berkowitz, L. (Ed.), *Advances in Experimental Social Psychology*, vol. 10. New York: Academic Press. pp 173–220.

Ross, M. D., Owren, M. J., and Zimmermann, E. (2010). The evolution of laughter in great apes and humans. *Communicative and Integrative Biology*, 3(2), pp 191–194.

Rowland-Warne, L. (1992). *Costume*. New York: Alfred A. Knopf.

Ruch, W. (1993). Exhilaration and humor. Ch. 42. In Lewis M., and Haviland, J. M. (Eds.), *The Handbook of Emotion*. New York: Guilford Publications, pp 605–616.

Runeson, S., and Frykholm, G. (1983). Kinematic specification of dynamics as an informational basis for person-and-action perception: Expectation, gender, recognition, and deceptive intention. *Journal of Experimental Psychology*, 112, pp 585–615.

Russell, J. A. (1994). Is there universal recognition of emotion from facial expressions? A review of the cross-cultural studies. *Psychological Bulletin*, 115(1), pp 102–141.

Russell, J. A. (1995). Facial expressions of emotion: What lies beyond minimal universality? *Psychological Bulletin*, 118, pp 379–391.

Russell, J. A., and Fernandez-Dols, J. M. (1997). What does a facial expression mean? In Russell, J. A., and Fernandez-Dols, J. M. (Eds.), *The Psychology of Facial Expression*. Cambridge: Cambridge University Press, pp 3–30, 435–446.

Saarni, C. (1993). Socialization of emotion. In Lewis M., and Haviland, J. M. (Eds.), *Handbook of emotion*. New York: Guilford Press.

Sachs, F. (1988). The intimate sense. *Sciences*, 28(1), pp 28–34.

Safdar, S., Friedlmeier, W., Matsumoto, D., Yoo, S. H., Kwantes, C. T., Kakai, H., and Shigemasu, E. (2009). Variations of emotional display rules within and across cultures: A comparison between Canada, USA, and Japan. *Canadian Journal of Behavioural Science/Revue canadienne des sciences du comportement*, 41(1), pp 1–10.

Salemink, E., van den Hout, M. A., and Kindt, M. (2007). Selective attention and threat: Quick orienting versus slow disengagement and two versions of the dot probe task. *Behavioural Research and Therapy*, 45(3), pp 607–615.

Salzen, E. A. (1979). The ontogeny of fear in animals. In Sluckin, W. (Eds.), *Fear in Animals and Man*. New York: Van Nostrand Reinhold, pp 125–163.

Sapir, E. (1927). The unconscious patterning of behavior in society. In Mandelbaum, D. (Ed.), *Selected Writings of Edward Sapir*. Los Angeles: University of California Press, pp 544–559, 1958.

Sapir, E. (1931). Communication. In Mandelbaum, D. (Ed.), *Selected Writings of Edward Sapir*. Los Angeles: University of California Press, pp 104–109, 1958.

Satchell, L., Morris, P., Akehurst, L., and Morrison, E. (2018). Can judgments of threat reflect an approaching person's trait aggression? *Current Psychology*, 37, pp 661–667.

Satchell, L., Morris, P., Mills, C., O'Reilly, L., Marshman, P., and Akehurst, L. (2017). Evidence of Big Five and aggressive personalities in gait biomechanics. *Journal of Nonverbal Behavior*, 41(1), pp 35–44.

Sato, W., and Yoshikawa, S. (2007). Enhanced experience of emotional arousal in response to dynamic facial expressions. *Journal of Nonverbal Behaviour*, 31, pp 119–135.

Sawada, M., Suda, K., and Ishii, M. (2003). Expression of emotions in dance: Relation between arm movement characteristics and emotion. *Perceptual and Motor Skills*, 97(3), pp 697–708.

Schachter, S., Christenfeld, N. J. S., Ravina, B., and Bilous, R. (1991). Speech disfluency and the structure of knowledge. *Journal of Personality and Social Psychology*, 20, pp 362–367.

Schauss, A. (1985). The physiological effect of colour on the suppression of human aggression: Research on Baker-Miller pink. *International Journal of Biosocial Research*, 7, pp 55–64.

Scheflen, A. E. (1965). Quasi-courtship behavior in psychotherapy. *Psychiatry*, 28, pp 245–257.

Scheflen, A. E. (1972). *Body Language and the Social Order*. Englewood Cliffs, NJ: Prentice Hall.

Scheiner, E., Hammerschmidt, K., Jürgens, U., and Zwirner, P. (2006). Vocal expression of emotions in normally hearing and hearing-impaired infants. *Journal of Voice*, 20, pp 585–604.

Scherer, K. R. (1986). Vocal affect expression: A review and a model for future research. *Psychological Bulletin*, 99, pp 143–165.

Scherer, K. R. (1994). Affect bursts. In van Goozen, S., van de Poll, N. E., and Sergeant, J. A. (Eds.), *Emotions: Essays on Emotion Theory*. Hillsdale, NJ: Lawrence Erlbaum Associates, pp 161–196.

Scherer, K. R., and Wallbott, H. G. (1994). Evidence for universality and cultural variation of differential emotion response patterning. *Journal of Personality and Social Psychology*, 66, pp 310–328.

Scherer, S. E. (1974). Proxemic behaviour of primary school children as a function of their socioeconomic class and subculture. *Journal of Personality and Social Psychology*, 29, pp 800–805.

Schmidt, K. L., Ambadar, Z., Cohn, J. F., and Reed, L. I. (2006). Movement differences between deliberate and spontaneous facial expressions: Zygomaticus major action in smiling. *Journal of Nonverbal Behavior*, 30, pp 37–52.

Schmidt, K. L., Cohn, J., and Tian, Y. (2003). Signal characteristics of spontaneous facial expressions: Automatic movement in solitary and social smiles. *Biological Psychology*, 65(1), pp 49–66.

Schneider, K., and Josephs, I. (1991). The expressive and communicative functions of pre-school children's smiles in an achievement situation. *Journal of Nonverbal Behavior*, 15, pp 185–198.

Schroeder, J., Risen, J., Gino, F., and Norton, M. I. (2014). *Handshaking Promotes Cooperative Deal Making* (Harvard Business School NOM Unit Working Paper No. 14–117, Harvard Business School Marketing Unit Working Paper No. 14, p 117).

Sedgewick, J. R., Holtslander, A., and Elias, L. J. (2019). Kissing right? Absence of rightward directional turning bias during first kiss encounters among strangers. *Journal of Nonverbal Behaviour*, 43, pp 271–282.

Semin, G. R., and Smith, E. R. (2008). Introducing embodied grounding. In Semin, G. R., and Smith, E. R. (Eds.), *Embodied Grounding: Social, Cognitive, Affective, and Neuroscientific Approaches*. Cambridge: Cambridge University Press, pp 43–70.

Serrano, J. M., Iglesias, J., and Loeches, A. (1992). Visual discrimination and recognition of facial expressions of anger, fear, and surprise in 4- to 6-month old infants. *Developmental Psychobiology*, 25, pp 411–425.

Sharpe, D. (1975). *The Psychology of Colour and Design*. Totowa, NJ: Littlefield, Adams.

Shavelson, R., Webb, N., Stasz, C., and McArthur, D. (1988). Teaching mathematical problem solving: Insights from teachers and tutors. In Charles, R., and Silver, E. (Eds.), *The Teaching and Assessing of Mathematical Problem Solving*. Reston, VA: NCTM.

Sherman, L. (1885). *A Handbook of Pronunciation*. London.

Shotland, R. L., and Craig, J. M. (1988). Can men and women differentiate between friendly and sexually interested behavior? *Social Psychology Quarterly*, 51, pp 66–73.

Singer, M. A., and Goldin-Meadow, S. (2005). Children learn when their teacher's gestures and speech differ. *Psychological Science*, 16(2), pp 85–89.

Singh, D., and Young, R. K. (1995). Body weight, waist-to-hip ratio, breasts, and hips: Role in judgments of female attractiveness and desirability for relationships. *Ethology and Sociobiology*, 16, pp 483–507.

Singh, N. N., McKay, J. D., and Singh, A. N. (1998). Culture and mental health: Nonverbal communication. *Journal of Child and Family Studies*, 7(4), pp 403–409.

Sinha, S., Alka, R., and Parul, V. (1999). Selective attention under conditions of varied demands, personal space and social density. *Journal of the Indian Academy of Applied Psychology*, 24, pp 105–108.

Sinha, S., and Mukherjee, N. (1996). The effect of perceived cooperation on personal space requirements. *Journal of Social Psychology*, 136, pp 108–111.

Sirigu, A., Duhamel, J. R., Cohen, L., Pillon, B., Dubois, B., and Agid, Y. (1996). The mental representation of hand movements after parietal cortex damage. *Science*, 273, pp 1564–1568.

Sluckin, W. (Ed.). (1979). *Fear in Animals and Man*. New York: Van Nostrand Reinhold.

Smith, J., Chase, J., and Lieblich, A. (1974). Tongue showing. *Semiotica*, 11(3), pp 201–246.

Smoski, M., and Bachorowski, J. A. (2003). Antiphonal laughter between friends and strangers. *Cognition and Emotion*, 17(2), pp 327–340.

Soderkvist, S., Ohlen, K., and Dimberg, U. (2018). How the experience of emotion is modulated by facial feedback. *Journal of Nonverbal Behaviour*, 42, pp 129–151.

Solomon, M. R., and Schopler, J. (1982). Self-consciousness and clothing. *Personality and Social Psychology Bulletin*, 8, pp 508–514.

Sommer, R. (1969). *Personal Space: The Behavioral Basis of Design*. Englewood Cliffs, NJ: Prentice-Hall, Inc.

Soukhanov, A. H. (Eds.). (1992). *The American Heritage Dictionary of the English Language*, 3rd ed. New York: Houghton Mifflin Co.

Soukhanov, A. H. (1993). Word watch. *The Atlantic Monthly* (October), p 135.

Soussignan, R. (2004). Regulatory function of facial actions in emotion processes. In Shohov, S. P. (Eds.), *Advances in Psychology Research*, vol. 31. Hauppauge, NY: Nova Science Publishers, Inc., pp 173–198.

Spinney, L. (2000). Bodytalk. *New Scientist* (April 8).

Stadel, M., Daniels, J. K., Warrens, M. J., and Jeronimus, B. F. (2019). The gender-specifc impact of emotional tears. *Motivation and Emotion*, 43, pp 696–704.

Stern, D. N. (2007). Applying developmental and neuroscience findings on other-centered participation to the process of change in psychotherapy. In Braten, S. (Ed.), *On Being Moved: From Mirror Neurons to Empathy*, Amsterdam: John Benjamins, pp 35–47.

Stern, D. N., and Bender, E. (1974). An ethological study of children approaching a strange adult. In Friedman, R., et al. (Eds.), *Sex Differences in Behavior*. New York: John Wiley and Sons, pp 233–258.

Stevanoni, E., and Salmon, K. (2005). Giving memory a hand: Instructing children to gesture enhances their event recall. *Journal of Nonverbal Behaviour*, 29(4), pp 217–233.

Stevenage, S. V., Nixon, M. S., and Vince, K. (1999). Visual analysis of gait as a cue to identity. *Applied Cognitive Psychology*, 13, pp 513–526.

Stevens, D. J. (1994). Predatory rapists and victim selection techniques. *The Social Science Journal*, 31(4), pp 421–433.

Stewart, G. L., Dustin, S. L., Barrick, M. R., and Darnold, T. C. (2008). Exploring the handshake in employment interviews. *Journal of Applied Psychology*, 93(5), 1139–1146.

Stoddart, D. M. (1990). *The Scented Ape: The Biology and Culture of Human Odour*. Sydney: Cambridge University Press.

Stoddart, M. (2020). *ABC News* (February 7).

Strack, F., Martin, L. L., and Strepper, S. (1988). Inhibiting and facilitating conditions of the human smile. A nonobtrusive test of the facial feedback hypothesis. *Journal of Personality and Social Psychology*, 54, pp 768–777.

Strayer, F. F., and Strayer, J. (1980). Preschool conflict and the assessment of social dominance. In Omark, D. R., Strayer, F. F., and Freedman, D. G. (Eds.), *Dominance Relations: An Ethological View of Human Conflict and Social Interaction*. New York: Garland STPM Press, pp 137–157.

Sundberg, J. (1998). Expressivity in singing: A review of some recent investigations. *Logopedics Phoniatrics Vocology*, 23, pp 121–127.

Suplee, C. (1994). A brief history of time-keeping: How the mechanical clock set a new tempo for society. *Washington Post* (November 16), pp H1, H5.

Suppes, A., Tzeng, C. Y., and Galgueram, L. (2015). Using and seeing co-speech gesture in a spatial task. *Journal of Nonverbal Behaviour*, 39, pp 241–257.

Suslow, T., Ohrmann, P., Bauer, J., Rauch, A. V., Schwindt, W., Arolt, V., Heindel, W., and Kugel, H. (2006). Amygdala activation during masked presentation of emotional faces predicts conscious detection of threat-related faces. *Brain and Cognition*, 61, pp 243–248.

Sutherland, C. A., Young, A. W., and Rhodes, G. (2017). Facial first impressions from another angle: How social judgements are influenced by changeable and invariant facial properties. *British Journal of Psychology*, 108, pp 397–415.

Sutton, C. (1984). *How Did They Do That? Wonders of the Far and Recent Past Explained*. New York: William Morrow and Co.

Terry, R. L. (1993). How wearing eyeglasses affects facial recognition. *Current Psychology* (12) pp 151–162.

Terry, R. L., and Krantz, J. H. (1993). Dimensions of trait attributions associated with eyeglasses, men's facial hair, and women's hair length. *Journal of Applied Social Psychology*, 23(21), 1757–1769.

Tharin, L. (1981). *Dress Codes, Observed Attire and Behaviour in Recreational Settings* (Unpublished manuscript, University of California, Davis).

Tharwat, A. (2000). Common ground. *Golf Journal* (October), p 52.

Thayer, S., and Schiff, W. (1977). Gazing patterns and attributions of sexual involvement. *Journal of Social Psychology*, 101, pp 235–246.

Thorndike, E. L. (1940). *Human Nature and the Social Order*. Cambridge: MIT Press, 1969.

Thornhill, R., and Gangested, S. W. (1994). Fluctuating asymmetry and human sexual behaviour. *Psychological Bulletin*, 5, pp 297–302.

Thornton, G. R. (1943). The effect upon judgements of personality traits of varying a single factor in a photograph. *Journal of Social Psychology*, 18, pp 127–148.

Tinbergen, N. (1964). The evolution of signaling devices. In Etkin, W. (Ed.), *Social Behavior and Organization Among Vertebrates*. Chicago: University of Chicago Press, pp 206–230.

Tomkins, S. S. (1980). Affect as amplification: Some modifications in theory. In Plutchik, R., and Kellerman, H. (Eds.), *Emotion: Theory, Research and Experience*. New York: Academic Press.

Torrence, R. D., Wylie, E., and Carlson, J. M. (2017). The time-course for the capture and hold of visuospatial attention by fearful and happy faces. *Journal of Nonverbal Behaviour*, 41, pp 139–153.

Toscano, H., Schubert, T. W., and Giessner, S. R. (2018). Eye gaze and head posture jointly influence judgments of dominance, physical strength, and anger. *Journal of Nonverbal Behaviour*, 42, pp 285–309.

Tracy, J. C., and Matsumoto, D. (2008). The spontaneous expression of pride and shame: Evidence for biologically innate nonverbal displays. *Proceedings of the National Academy of Sciences*, 105, pp 11655–11660.

Tran, C. (2000). Life in a redwood tree: Julia 'Butterfly' Hill speaks. *Web Document* (October 26). www.studentadvantage.com.

Trevarthen, C. (1997). Music and infant communication. *Nordic Journal of Music Therapy*, 9, pp 3–17.

Trevisan, D. A., Bowering, M., and Birmingham, E. (2016). Alexithymia, but not autism spectrum disorder, may be related to the production of emotional facial expressions. *Molecular Autism*, 7, pp 2–12.

Troeng, J. (1993). *Worldwide Chronology of Fifty-Three Prehistoric Innovations*. Stockholm: Almqvist and Wiksell International.

Troiano, G., and Nante, N. (2018). Emoji: What does the scientific literature say about them? A new way to communicate in the 21th century. *Journal of Human Behavior in the Social Environment*, 28(4), pp 528–533.

Trotter, P. D., McGlone, F., Reniers, R. L. E. P., and Deakin, J. F. W. (2018). Construction and validation of the touch experiences and attitudes questionnaire (TEAQ): A self-report measure to determine attitudes toward and experiences of positive touch. *Journal of Nonverbal Behaviour*, 42, pp 379–416.

Trout, D. L., and Rosenfeld, H. (1980). The effect of postural lean and body congruence on the judgement of psychotherapeutic rapport. *Journal of Nonverbal Behaviour*, 4, pp 176–190.

Twardosz, S., Botkin, D., Cunningham, J. K., Weddle, K., Sollie, D., and Schreve, C. (1987). Expression of affection in day care. *Child Study Journal*, 17, 133–151.

Ulloa, E. R. and Pineda J. A. (2007) Research report Recognition of point-light biological motion: Mu rhythms and mirror neuron activity, *Behavioural Brain Research*, 183, pp 188–194.

U.S. Department of Justice. (2014). *The Fingerprint Sourcebook*. Washington: Office of Justice Programmes, National Institute of Justice.

Usmani, T. (2005). Doing business with other Asian countries. *Asia Pacific Business Review*, 1(1), pp 76–83.

Uvnäs-Moberg, K., Handlin, L., and Petersson, M. (2015). Self-soothing behaviors with particular reference to oxytocin release induced by non-noxious sensory stimulation. *Frontiers in Psychology*, 5, pp 1529.

Valdesolo, F. (2016). How David Bowie changed the way we look at beauty. *Glamour* (January 12). www.glamour.com (accessed January 1, 2020).

Valenzo, L., Alibali, M., and Klatzky, R. (2003). Teachers' gestures facilitate students' learning: A lesson in symmetry. *Contemporary Educational Psychology*, 28, pp 187–204.

Van Dyck, E., Maes, P. J., Hargreaves, J., Lesaffre, M., and Leman, M. (2013). Expressing induced emotions through free dance movement. *Journal of Nonverbal Behaviour*, 37, pp 175–190.

Van Hooff, J. (1967). The facial displays of the catarrhine monkeys and apes. In Morris, D. (Ed.), *Primate Ethology*. Chicago: Aldine, pp 7–68.

Van Kleef, G. A., van den Berg, H., and Heerdink, M. W. (2015). The persuasive power of emotions: Effects of emotional expressions on attitude formation and change. *Journal of Applied Psychology*, 100(4), pp 1124–1142.

Van Lawick-Goodall, J. (1968). The behaviour of free-living chimpanzees in the Gombe stream reserve. *Behavioural Monographs*, I, pp 161–311.

Van Valen, L. (1962). A study of fluctuating asymmetry. *Evolution*, 16, pp 125–142.

Vanderbilt, A. (1957). *Amy Vanderbilt's Complete Book of Etiquette.* Garden City, NY: Doubleday.

Vargas, M. F. (1986). *Louder Than Words: An Introduction to Nonverbal Communication.* Ames: Iowa State University Press.

Vasconcelos, M., Dias, M., Soares, A. P., and Pinheiro, A. P. (2017). What is the melody of that voice? Probing unbiased recognition accuracy with the Montreal affective voices. *Journal of Nonverbal Behaviour,* 41(3) pp 239–267.

Vingerhoets, A. J. J. M., and Bylsma, L. M. (2016). The riddle of human emotional crying: A challenge for emotion researchers. *Emotion Review,* 8, pp 207–217.

Vrij, A. (2004). Why professionals fail to catch liars and how they can improve. *Legal and Criminal Psychology,* 9, pp 159–181.

Vrij, A., Akehurst, L., and Morris, P. (1997). Individual differences in hand movements during deception. *Journal of Nonverbal Behavior,* 21, pp 87–102.

Vrij, A., Fisher, R., Mann, S., and Leal, S. (2008). A cognitive load approach to lie detection. *Journal of Investigative Psychology and Offender Profiling,* 5(1–2), pp 39–43.

Vrij, A., Glin, R. S., and Bull, R. (1996). Insight into behavior displayed during deception. *Human Communication Research,* 22(4), pp 544–562.

Wagner, S. M., Lourenco, S. F., Ellois, V., and Parisi, D. (2003). *Hands on Learning: How Do Children Attend to Teachers' Gestures?* (Poster session at the annual meeting of the Society for Research in Child Development, Tampa, FL).

Wagner, S. M., Nusbaum, H., and Goldin-Meadow, S. (2004). Probing the mental representation of gesture: Is handwaving spatial? *Journal of Memory and Language,* 50, pp 395–407.

Walker, M. B., and Trimboli, C. (1985). The expressive function of the eye flash. *Journal of Nonverbal Behaviour,* 8(1), pp 3–13.

Wallace, I., Wallechinsky, D., and Wallace, A. (1983). *Significa.* New York: E. P. Dutton, Inc.

Walusinski, O. (2004). Yawning comparative study of knowledge and beliefs. *British Medical Journal,* 328(7445), pp 328, 963.

Ware, J., and Williams, R. (1977). An extended visit with Dr. Fox. Validity of student satisfaction with instruction ratings after repeated exposures to a lecture. *American Educational Research Journal,* 14(4), pp 449–457.

Watson, N. M., Wells, T. J., and Cox, C. (1998). Rocking chair for dementia patients: Its effect on psychosocial well-being and balance. *American Journal of Alzheimer Disease and Other Dementias* (November), pp 296–308.

Watson, O. M. (1970). *Proxemic Behaviours: A Cross-Cultural Study.* The Hague: Mouton.

Watson, O. M., and Graves, T. D. (1966). Quantitative research in proxemic behaviours. *American Anthropologist,* 68, pp 971–985.

Watson, P. W., and Thornhill, R. (1994). Fluctuating asymmetry and sexual selection. *Trends in Ecology and Evolution,* 9, pp 21–25.

Webster, P. (1984). *An Ethnographic Study of Handshaking* (Unpublished doctoral dissertation, Boston University, Boston).

Wee, C. J. W.-L. (Ed.). (2002). *Local Cultures and the 'New Asia': The State, Culture and Capitalism in Southeast Asia.* Singapore: Institute of Southeast Asian Studies.

Weisfeld, G. E., and Beresford, J. M. (1982). Erectness of posture as an indicator of dominance or success in humans. *Motivation and Emotion,* 6, pp 113–131.

Weisz, J., and Adam, G. (1993). Hemispheric preference and lateral eye movements evoked by bilateral visual stimuli. *Neuropsychologia,* 31, pp 1299–1306.

Wenke, R. J. (1990). *Patterns in Prehistory: Humankind's First Three Million Years,* 3rd ed. New York: Oxford University Press.

Whalen, P. J., Shin, L. M., McInerney, S. C., Fischer, H., Wright, C. I., and Rauch, S. L. (2001). A functional MRI study of human amygdala responses to facial expressions of fear vs. anger. *Emotion*, 1, pp 70–83.

Wheeler, S., Book, A., and Costello, K. (2009). Psychopathic traits and perceptions of victim vulnerability. *Criminal Justice and Behavior*, 36(6), pp 635–648.

White, J., and Gardner, J. (2011). *The Classroom X-Factor: The Power of Body Language and Nonverbal Communication in Teaching*. London: Routledge.

Wiener, N. (1950). *The Human Use of Human Beings: Cybernetics and Society*. New York: Avon Books.

Wildmann, J., Kruger, A., Schmole, M., et al. (1986). Increase of circulating beta-endorphin-like immunoreactivity correlates with the change in feeling of pleasantness after running. *Life Science*, 38, pp 997–1003.

Wilford, J. N. (1983). Site in turkey yields oldest cloth ever found. *The New York Times* (July 2013, "Science Times"), pp C1, C8.

Wilford, J. N. (1993). Site in Turkey yields oldest cloth ever found. *New York Times* (July 13, "Science Times"), pp C1, C8.

Willis, F. N., and Dodds, R. A. (1998). Age, relationship, and touch initiation. *Journal of Social Psychology*, 138, pp 115–123.

Willis, W. D. (1998a). Motor control by the cerebral cortex, cerebellum, and basal ganglia. In Berne, R. M., and Levy, M. N. (Eds.), *Physiology*. New York: Mosby, pp 214–232.

Willis, W. D. (1998b). The somatosensory system. In Berne, R. M. B., and Levy, M. N. (Eds.), *Physiology*. New York: Mosby, pp 109–128.

Wilson, E. O. (1975). *Sociobiology: The New Synthesis*. Cambridge, MA: Belknap Press of Harvard University Press.

Woo, E. (2001). Designer of 'smiley face' dies at age 79. *Spokesman-Review. Los Angeles Times Story* (Sunday, April 15), p. A6.

Woodworth, M., Hancock, J., and Goorha, S. (2005). *The Motivational Enhancement Effect: Implications for Our Chosen Modes of Communication in the 21st Century* (Proceedings of the 38th Annual Hawaii International Conference on System Sciences, Institute of Electrical and Electronics Engineers (IEEE). doi: 10.1109/HICSS.2005.607).

Worcel, S. D., Shields, S., and Paterson, C. A. (1999). "She looked at me crazy": Escalation of conflict through telegraphed emotions. *Adolescence*, 34, p 689.

Wörmann, V., Holodynski, M., Kärtner, J., and Keller, H. (2014). The emergence of social smiling: The interplay of maternal and infant imitation during the first three months in cross cultural comparison. *Journal of Cross-Cultural Psychology*, 45, pp 339–361.

Wundt, W. (1921/1973). *The Language of Gestures*. The Hague: Mouton.

Wurman, R. S. (1989). *Information Anxiety: What to Do When the Information Doesn't Tell You What You Need to Know*. New York: Bantam Books.

Yaeger, L. (2018). How Jill Wine-Banks uses witty pins to express her progressive politics. *Vogue* (August 8, 2018). vogue.com (accessed December 24, 2019).

Young, J. Z. (1978). *Programs of the Brain*. Oxford: Oxford University Press.

Young, M. P., and Yamane, S. (1992). Sparse population coding of faces in the inferotemporal Cortex. *Science*, 256, pp 1327–1331.

Zaidel, D. W., and Choi, D. (2007). Attractiveness of natural faces compared to computer generated perfectly symmetrical faces. *International Journal of Neuroscience*, 117, pp 423–431.

Zajonc, R. B. (1965). Social facilitation. *Science*, 149, pp 269–274.

Zajonc, R. B. (1980). Compresence. In Paulus, P. B. (Ed.), *Psychology of Group Influence*. Hillsdale, NJ: Lawrence Erlbaum Associates, pp 35–60.

Zajonc, R. B. (2001). Mere exposure: A gateway to the subliminal. *Current Directions in Psychological Science*, 10(6), pp 224–228.

Zajonc, R. B., Murphy, S. T., and Inglehart, M. (1989). Feeling and facial efference: Implications of the vascular theory of emotion. *Psychological Review*, 96(3), pp 395–416.

Zandonella, C. (2016). Electron-photon small-talk could have big impact on quantum computing. *Princeton University News*. princeton.edu (accessed September 27, 2020).

Zeki, S. (1999). *Inner Vision: An Exploration of Art and the Brain*. Oxford: Oxford University Press.

Zickfeld, J. H., van de Ven, N., Schubert, T. W., and Vingerhoets, A. J. J. M. (2018). Are tearful individuals perceived as less competent? Probably not. *Comprehensive Results in Social Psychology, (3) pp 1-21*.

Zilli, I., Giganti, F., and Uga, V. (2008). Yawning and subjective sleepiness in the elderly. *Journal of Sleep Research*, 17, pp 303–308.

Zimbardo, P. G. (1971). *The Power and Pathology of Imprisonment. Congressional Record (Serial No. 15, October 25, 1971). Hearings Before Subcommittee No. 3, of the Committee on the Judiciary, House of Representatives, Ninety-Second Congress, First Session on Corrections, Part II, Prisons, Prison Reform and Prisoner's Rights: California*. Washington, DC: U.S. Government Printing Office.

Zimbardo, P. G. (1974). *The Detention and Jailing of Juveniles (Hearings Before U. S. Senate Committee on the Judiciary Subcommittee to Investigate Juvenile Delinquency, 10, 11, 17, September 1973)*. Washington, DC: U.S. Government Printing Office, pp 141–161.

Zuckerman, M., and Hodgins, H. S. (1993). Developmental changes in the effects of the physical and vocal attractiveness stereotypes. *Journal of Research in Personality*, 27, pp 349–369.

Zupan, B. (2015). Recognition of high and low intensity facial and vocal expressions of emotion by children and adults. *Journal of Social Sciences and Humanities*, 1, pp 332–344.